A Time for Peace

A Time for

The Legacy of the

Vietnam War

ROBERT D. SCHULZINGER

OXFORD

UNIVERSITY PRESS

2006

OXFORD
UNIVERSITY PRESS

Oxford University Press, Inc., publishes works that
further Oxford University's objective of excellence
in research, scholarship, and education.

Oxford   New York
Auckland   Cape Town   Dar es Salaam   Hong Kong   Karachi
Kuala Lumpur   Madrid   Melbourne   Mexico City   Nairobi
New Delhi   Shanghai   Taipei   Toronto

With offices in
Argentina Austria Brazil Chile Czech Republic France Greece
Guatemala Hungary Italy Japan Poland Portugal Singapore
South Korea Switzerland Thailand Turkey Ukraine Vietnam

Published by Oxford University Press, Inc.
198 Madison Avenue, New York, NY 10016
www.oup.com

Library of Congress Cataloging-in-Publication Data
Schulzinger, Robert D., 1945–
A time for peace : the legacy of the Vietnam War / Robert D. Schulzinger.
p. cm. Includes bibliographical references and index.
ISBN-13: 978-0-19-507190-0
ISBN-10: 0-19-507190-5
1. United States—Foreign relations—Vietnam.
2. Vietnam—Foreign relations—United States.
3. Vietnamese Conflict, 1961–1975—Influence.
4. Vietnamese Conflict, 1961–1975—Veterans.
5. Vietnamese Americans—Social conditions.
6. Vietnamese Conflict, 1961–1975—Social aspects—United States.
7. Popular culture—United States.
I. Title.
E183.8.V5S36 2006
303.48'27230597009045—dc22 2006040124

9 8 7 6 5 4 3 2 1
Printed in the United States
on acid-free paper

*To my students, from whom I have learned so much
about the living legacy of the Vietnam War*

Contents

Preface

A *Time for Peace: The Legacy of the Vietnam War* tells the story
of how the American War in Vietnam has been remembered and the effects
different memories have had on current events. Americans and Vietnamese who
lived through the decades'-long fighting remembered the war as an experience
that shaped their lives, their outlooks, their beliefs, and their feelings. More than
a generation in both countries viewed some aspects of contemporary war, politics,
foreign affairs, and culture through the prism of their memories of the Vietnam-
American War. These memories have not been fixed, and they have altered over
time. Nor did the world stop when the Vietnam War ended with the Communist
victory in April 1975. International affairs went forward, and the United States
and Vietnam adjusted to changing circumstances over the next twenty-five years.
Some of these changes were among the most dramatic in modern history as the
Cold War ended and the Soviet Union collapsed.

This book is divided into four parts. Part I, "International Affairs," tells how
the United States and Vietnam went from enmity to reconciliation from 1975 to
2000. Along the way, international alliances shifted and ideologies changed and
sometimes dissolved. Eventually, the United States and Vietnam found they had
great incentives to reach common ground. Part II, "Veterans and Vietnamese
Americans," recounts the ways in which American veterans of the Vietnam War
and Vietnamese who fled their country for the United States in the years after
1975 assimilated their experiences in the present. The veterans' and Vietnamese
experiences helped shape postwar beliefs and memories about the war. Part III,
"Cultural Legacies," analyzes the most popular of the hundreds of movies, TV
shows, novels, and memoirs of the Vietnam era. These representations of the
war helped determine the meaning of the war in the minds of Americans in
the postwar era. Part IV, "Conclusion: Political Echoes of a War," consists of
one chapter, "The Living Legacy of the Vietnam War," which explicitly explains the ways in which American policymakers and ordinary citizens learned
a variety of different lessons from the Vietnam War and how they applied those
lessons in the conduct of their current affairs.

Like my earlier book, *A Time for War: The United States and Vietnam, 1941–1975* (Oxford University Press, 1997), *A Time for Peace* tries to consolidate the findings of much of the existing literature on the legacy of the Vietnam War. My own interpretation of the legacy of the Vietnam War, like that of many of writers who have dealt with the subject, is that it represented a national trauma for the United States. Yet Americans and Vietnamese adjusted to that trauma, even if the scars of the war remained.

Many historians and literary and film critics have written compelling narratives and analyses of many aspects of the legacy of the Vietnam War. Good studies abound on postwar international relations, veterans, the Vietnamese experience in the United States, film, fiction, and memoirs. I have cited these works throughout *A Time for Peace*. Among the most useful of them have been the essays collected by Charles Neu in *After Vietnam: Legacies of a Lost War* and the ones collected by John Carlos Rowe and Rick Berg in *The Vietnam War and American Culture;* several articles and books by Robert McMahon on political leaders' memories of the Vietnam War; Patrick Hagopian's dissertation, "The Social Memory of the Vietnam War"; Arnold Isaacs's *Vietnam Shadows*; Fred Turner's *Echoes of Combat*; Richard T. Childress's and Stephen J. Solarz's "Vietnam: The Road to Normalization"; Stephen Hurst's *The Carter Administration and Vietnam*; Gerald Nicosia's *Home to War: A History of the Vietnam Veterans' Movement*; and Philip D. Beidler's *American Literature and the Experience of Vietnam* and his *Re-Writing America: Vietnam Authors in Their Generation*.

This book is also grounded as much as possible in the archival record, although since the book covers more recent events than did *A Time for War,* many more records remain closed. I have sought to supplement records from the archives by referring to the extensive body of Congressional and other U.S. government publications.

I have been fortunate to try out many of the ideas and conclusions in the book in lectures I have delivered at the University of California, Santa Barbara; the University of Colorado, Boulder; Davidson University; the Oakland Museum of California; the Ohio State University; the Pacific Coast Branch of the American Historical Association; the Society for Historians of American Foreign Relations; and Texas Christian University. I gratefully acknowledge fellowship and grant support from the Council on Research and Creative Work and the Graduate Committee on the Arts and Humanities of the University of Colorado. The Alumni Association at the University of Colorado at Boulder sponsored me on two trips to Vietnam in 1999 and 2001. The International Affairs Program and the History Department of the University of Colorado, Boulder, have been my intellectual homes, and they provided enormous support for me and my scholarship. Sheila Grotzky, the program assistant for International Affairs, has helped in every aspect of completion of this book. I thank two graduate student assistants, Anne Lefever and Kassi Klinefelter, who did research and helped prepare the notes and the bibliography.

Several friends and colleagues have read all or parts of the book. They are Leonard Dinnerstein, Michael Schaller, and Thomas Zeiler. I have also received useful suggestions for sources and topics to include from Steve Chan, Frank Costigliola, Michael Hogan, Christopher Jespersen, Diane Kunz, Lou Ortmayer, Peter Steinhauer, Sr., Leo Ribuffo, Jeff Robers, David Schmitz, Claudine Triolo, and Tommy Le Van. Susan Ferber, my editor at Oxford University Press, gave the entire manuscript a very close reading, and her many suggestions have made it a better book.

As always, my wife, Marie, and my daughter, Elizabeth, have been my greatest strength. They have lived with *A Time for Peace* for years. They accompanied me on a CU Alumni Association trip to Vietnam and Cambodia in 2001, and these two weeks in Southeast Asia were among the highlights of Elizabeth's young life. The enthusiasm she and Marie display every day makes so many of my journeys worthwhile.

Robert D. Schulzinger
Boulder, Colorado
January 2006

Introduction:
Memories of the Vietnam War

When the last Americans left Saigon in April 1975 during the tumultuous final days of the war, many of their countrymen and women at home hoped to close the book on their long, divisive, expensive, and ultimately failed war in Vietnam. In the months that followed, the war took a backseat in the public's consciousness as many unsettling issues preoccupied Americans. The economy was stalled, prices were rising, and it was hard for many to find or keep a job. Bitter memories of the Watergate scandal continued to roil American politics. Watergate and Vietnam had shaken Americans' assumptions that their public institutions were sound and their leaders were honest and competent.

After President Gerald R. Ford pardoned his predecessor Richard Nixon in September 1974, he no longer had the widespread public support he had enjoyed in his first month in office. Democrats swept the Congressional elections of 1974, and their enlarged majorities came to Washington in 1975 vowing to enact laws that would reenergize Lyndon Johnson's Great Society program. At the same time, Congress was deeply skeptical of the powers of the president in foreign affairs. If the debacle of the Vietnam War had proven anything, it was that presidents and their foreign policy advisers needed careful oversight.[1]

Secretary of State Henry Kissinger drew different lessons from the public collapse of the peace agreement he had signed with North Vietnam's chief negotiator Le Duc Tho in 1973. For Kissinger the bitter end in Vietnam meant that the United States had been shamefully disloyal to its longtime ally in the Republic of Vietnam. He warned that the United States would "pay a price for what happened in Southeast Asia," when an emboldened Soviet Union supported revolutionaries elsewhere.[2] Kissinger also encouraged Americans to put the war behind them and not engage in recriminations over who had been responsible for the mistakes of the previous twenty-five years. In May he told the American Society of Newspaper editors that "we do not seek to open wounds" about the Vietnam War.[3] Better to put it in the past and move on.

The Vietnamese too had many reasons to put the American War in the past in 1975 and turn inward in the years immediately following the end of combat. Reconstruction and the integration of North and South took precedence. The country was devastated by thirty-five years of war with first the Japanese, then the French, and then the Americans. For almost all of that period, a civil war had also raged between the nationalist revolutionaries and Vietnamese who had allied themselves to a greater or lesser degree with the outsiders. More than three million Vietnamese had died in the combined wars. By the end of the American War, the North and South differed in many ways. The South was far more individualistic and more urban than the North. Peasants owned their land, but the countryside had been ravaged by relentless bombings during the war. One third of South Vietnamese had been made refugees at one time or another during the war. From 1970 to 1975 the population of the cities had grown to 45 percent from 30 percent of the total population. The largest city, Saigon, was renamed Ho Chi Minh City on May 1, 1975, the day after the Communist triumph. Many of the newcomers to Ho Chi Minh City had worked for the Americans or the government of the Republic of Vietnam. They had no jobs when the National Liberation Front took over, and their previous loyalties made them deeply suspect in the eyes of the victorious Communists. The new rulers undertook a massive resettlement program, moving six hundred thousand residents against their will from Ho Chi Minh City, to what were called "new economic zones," in malaria-infested jungles. Life was hard in these zones, and evacuees sought to escape or bribe their way back to the capital.[4]

While the Communists did not execute officials of the old regime, as had been feared by the South Vietnamese and the Americans, the new government did send tens of thousands to "reeducation camps." There they worked at hard labor and were taught the virtues of Ho Chi Minh's nationalism and the errors of collaboration with the Americans.[5] The new rulers of the South did not fully trust the thousands of Southerners who joined the Communist Party in the immediate aftermath of the war, considering many of them to be opportunists. In June 1976 Pham Van Dong, the prime minister of the Democratic Republic of (North) Vietnam announced the official reunification of both halves of the country under the direct rule of the government in Hanoi. Henceforth it would be named the Socialist Republic of Vietnam.[6]

Memories of the anger and bitterness of the Vietnam War reverberated for decades, and this book tells the story of the ways in which Americans and Vietnamese came to terms with their mutual experiences. All wars leave their marks on memory, and these memories of war have had, in turn, a disproportionate affect on later ideas, beliefs, and emotions. The historian Kurt Piehler has noted, "American national identity remains inexorably intertwined with the commemoration and memory of past wars."[7] The Vietnam War represented a national trauma for the United States, a psychological shock like the Civil War, the Great Depression, and World War II. Vietnam shook some of the basic shared assumptions Americans held about the honesty and competence of their leaders and the wisdom and morality of their actions in foreign affairs. But they disagreed about the memory, the lessons of the war, the integrity of public institutions, and their country's role in the world.

This book explains how these troubled and conflicted recollections colored numerous aspects of public life and culture in the United States. In the decades after 1975 discussions of politics, foreign and military policy, the obligations to and the role of veterans of the war, education, and culture all took place against the backdrop of the Vietnam War. Recollections of the war became focal points of many divisions over how Americans should conduct their affairs in the present. As they recalled their emotional turbulence over the war, Americans created numerous reminders of it—memorials, films, TV shows, novels—to shape their recollections and guide them in the present.

In Vietnam, where the physical reminders of the war were everywhere, the Vietnamese had less trouble than did Americans in resolving memories of the American War. American-built trucks, buildings, and roads, bombed and defoliated terrain, land mines, wounded soldiers and civilians, and thousands of children fathered by American servicemen provided constant reminders of the war. The Vietnamese revolutionaries won the war, so, they could present to their countrymen and women a heroic narrative of resistance and victory. They forced the Americans to leave, they defeated the Republic of Vietnam, and they unified the country. Inside the Socialist Republic of Vietnam the winners determined the acceptable expressions of the memory of the conflict. Most Vietnamese were proud of the success of a nationalist war against outsiders. And those who had supported the Republic either left the unified country or remained quiet about their misgivings. Vietnamese also saw the American War through the lens of a longer sweep of history than did the Americans. For Vietnamese, the war with the United States was only part of a century-long, or even a millennium-long, conflict with outsiders for control over Vietnam. The Americans were only the last outsiders to incur the wrath of Vietnamese nationalists. The approved memory of the war among Vietnamese was a successful nationalist struggle. The war brought destruction. The postwar brought poverty, but the pride at independence from foreign rule was genuine. It enabled Vietnamese to put aside bitterness that might have lingered against the Americans.

While Americans struggled to make sense of the memory of the Vietnam War and apply it to their present circumstances in the decades after the war's end, unresolved issues remained between the governments of the United States and the Socialist Republic of Vietnam (SRV). This book explains the long, bitter, and twisting road to reconciliation between the United States and Vietnam after 1975. Twenty years elapsed after the revolutionaries' victory in

Saigon before the United States and Vietnam restored diplomatic relations. Immediately after the war the United States was angry and vindictive toward Vietnam, imposing an economic boycott, vetoing its membership in the United Nations, and refusing to extend diplomatic recognition. The impoverished Vietnamese pressed for American aid to restore their battered land, but the United States steadfastly refused. The governments of both the United States and the SRV explored normalization of relations in the 1970s, but conflicting memories of the war often blocked the way. Nothing made the restoration of diplomatic relations more difficult than the issue of American servicemen listed as missing in action after the war.

The idea that authorities in Vietnam, Laos, and Cambodia held Americans prisoner after the war froze relations for years. Although it was almost certainly false that Americans were held captive in Southeast Asia after the war, this conviction provided a screen onto which Americans projected their feelings regarding the war, public institutions, and authorities. At various times in the years after the war, government officials, political candidates, private citizens, novelists, and film producers made emotional appeals to the American public to demand the release of POWs in Southeast Asia. As the likelihood of Americans remaining alive against their will in the war zone diminished and the partisans of the POW/MIA cause appeared to be more extreme, the issue changed. Instead of making demands on the Vietnamese to return live POWs, American officials after 1987 increasingly pressed for information about what happened to men when they went missing and for the return of their remains. Domestic politics in both Vietnam and the United States slowed progress toward diplomatic relations. Vietnamese officials had an exaggerated perception of the power of the antiwar movement in the United States. They erroneously believed antiwar protesters had convinced other Americans that the United States owed a moral and monetary debt to the Vietnamese for the suffering they had endured.

The Cold War competition between the United States and the Soviet Union, so instrumental in creating the war in the first place, also interfered with the restoration of diplomatic relations. Once the Cold War ended with the demise of the Soviet Union in 1991, the United States and Vietnam came for the first time to engage one another directly. These personal and political encounters led eventually to normalization. Economics played a major role in the restoration of diplomatic relations. In 1986 Vietnam embarked on a new economic policy of *doi moi*, or state managed capitalism, in which the need for foreign investment grew and with it the desire for commerce with the United States. Americans, too, felt the heat of international economic competition in the post–Cold War years, increasing the incentive to renew ties to Vietnam.

In the United States the years following the Vietnam War coincided with an explosion of interest in the complex relations between past and present. *A Time for Peace* joins a growing list of works that deal with the complexities of memory and history. The historians Jay Winter and Emily Rosenberg and others have labeled the phenomenon of remembering and memorializing the past a "memory boom."[8] Much of this intensified interest originated in American discomfort with the troublesome emotions engendered in the present by the Vietnam War.[9] The historian Michael Kammen has identified a heightened American interest in recalling, memorializing, and recreating more satisfying memories of the past as a "response to postwar anxiety and the sharp sense of discontinuity" that arose in the 1960s and 1970s, partly as a result of the Vietnam War.[10] The Vietnam War left many Americans feeling angry, frustrated, and unhappy with their public institutions. While some took solace in nostalgia, others returned again and again to the trauma and unhappy memories of the Vietnam War. Sometimes they relived it; sometimes they repressed it; often they did both in various combinations.

When Americans reflected on their experience in Vietnam, they often compared them to their vastly different memories of World War II. At it simplest, the "good war" against Germany, Italy, and Japan, which Americans united in the noblest of causes, stood in sharp contrast and rebuke to the sordid divisions of the Vietnam War. For most of the half century since the end of World War II veterans have been lauded as heroes who saved civilization. But the public attitudes toward World War II also underwent subtle shifts throughout the postwar period, most notably in the turmoil of the Vietnam War. As Americans looked back on World War II, they applied the lessons of Vietnam. They were now skeptical of the motives and conduct of the leaders of World War II. And as awareness grew of the difficulties encountered by American men fighting in Vietnam, writers began rewriting the history of World War II to expose the deceit, incompetence, and general hardship experienced by those earlier combatants.

The Chicago journalist Studs Terkel researched *The "Good War,"* a collection of oral histories of World War II written during the Vietnam War era. He put quotation marks around the "Good War," because, after experiencing the wrenching anger and disillusionment of the Vietnam era, he doubted whether any war could be considered "good." When the literary critic Paul Fussell wrote *Wartime* in 1989, the entire book was an assault on what he believed to be the phoniness, the cloying optimism, the lying, and the propaganda of American and British authorities during World War II. The Vietnam War experience suffused every chapter of Fussell's *Wartime*. He noted that in the 1970s a higher skepticism, "fueled by the assassinations of the Kennedys and Martin Luther King . . . and by the Vietnam War" kept the public from believing much, if anything, officials said about the war.[11]

This book explains how Vietnam veterans expressed their memories of the war. Veterans and their relatives played prominent roles in shaping how Americans thought about military service generally, and service in Vietnam particularly. Their experiences had elements in common with those who had fought in earlier conflicts such as World War II, but veterans of the Vietnam War also faced special difficulties in readjusting to life in the United States. Their struggles with their memories of the Vietnam War and the reception they received when they returned home helped determine how Americans remembered the Vietnam War. The position of veterans in American society became emblematic of the divided memories of the war. The men and women who had been to Vietnam carried the burden of the war years. Many veterans returned alienated, unhappy, and unappreciated. Others were little bothered by their Vietnam War experiences, and they readjusted easily to civilian life at home. Non-veterans expressed complicated feelings of guilt, anger, pity, and admiration for those who served in Vietnam.

The serious difficulties some veterans experienced in readjustment to civilian life led to the official identification of a psychiatric condition called Post Traumatic Stress Disorder (PTSD)—the unwanted repetition in the present of suppressed memories of horrifying events. The symptoms of PTSD included intrusive memories of the horrifying event, nightmares, feelings of estrangement and detachment from others, psychic numbing, and difficulties concentrating.[12] Aspects of PTSD extended far beyond the personal psychological stresses encountered by Vietnam veterans to many other areas of American life. Americans who remembered Vietnam in many ways expressed social, collective, and national forms of PTSD.

A Time for Peace explores the construction and reception of the Vietnam Veterans Memorial, often simply called the wall, which was dedicated on the Washington, D.C., Mall in 1982. The wall became an almost sacred site of pilgrimage where millions of visitors poured out their complex feelings about the war. While visitors to the wall remained divided over whether the United States intervened properly in Vietnam and in subsequent wars, they embraced a consensus to honor the service and sacrifice of veterans. *A Time for Peace* tells how veterans' memories of the war developed in the generation after 1975. Some veterans maintained a constant view of their time in the military, while others changed their minds, either growing more disillusioned with their military service or discovering as the years passed that military life had been more valuable than they had earlier believed.

This book tells the remarkable story of more than a million Vietnamese and their descendants who came to the United States after the war. Their exodus from their homeland was harrowing, and they endured difficult times in the United States. Vietnamese Americans helped frame the public recollection of the Vietnam War. Their own memories and their continuing contact with family and friends in Vietnam helped determine the ways in which official relations developed between the governments of the United States and the SRV.

Memories of the war in Vietnam also helped define a generation of literature and film. Most representations of the war in fiction and on the screen had little to do with Vietnam and much to do with the United States. Authors, directors, and actors imbued their work with a sense that the Vietnam War had opened divisions among Americans that might never be bridged. The works reflected widespread beliefs that public institutions were deeply flawed. Much of the film and literature of the Vietnam era was expressly antiauthoritarian. The works depicted a grim world in which leaders lied, evaded responsibility, and only looked out for themselves. At the same time, ordinary people carried the burden of the suffering from a war that left them disillusioned and pessimistic.

This book explains how Americans learned and applied what they thought were the appropriate lessons from the Vietnam War. The war became one of the most written about events in American history. Authors disagreed why and how the United States fought the war, and how the war ended. A majority of authors thought that the United States had mistakenly entered the war, but a significant minority argued that the United States had been right to fight in Vietnam. Disagreements also arose over the importance of antiwar sentiment in changing the course of the war. Some said that the antiwar movement hastened the end of American participation in the war; others claimed that opposition to the war actually prolonged it.

Just as the war itself opened deep divisions about the proper role of the United States in the world, Americans divided over the proper lessons of the war. This book explains how Americans applied these lessons to contemporary international affairs. Some people who had supported the American war effort in Vietnam came to believe that American assertiveness internationally in the postwar era would erase the sense of failure in Vietnam. Others learned precisely the opposite lesson from Vietnam. Policymakers who had been chastened by what they believed had been an arrogant overextension of American power during the Vietnam War sought to limit the use of American military force abroad. Some people, both in positions of power and among the articulate public, changed their opinions about what the United States had done in Vietnam. Their views evolved through a combination of learning more about the war itself and reflection on current events in the years since 1975. People changed views on the Vietnam War in all directions. Some became more "hawkish," for example, becoming more supportive of military action than they had been in the Vietnam era, while others who had once advocated the American role in Vietnam became highly skeptical of the use of American military power after 1975. Whatever their views had been during the Vietnam era, many Americans expressed their concerns about contemporary foreign policies through language, images, and memories of the mistakes and disappointments of Vietnam. Whenever current foreign policies seemed to go wrong, Americans raised the Vietnam analogy and encouraged their leaders to change course based upon what they believed to be unmistakable conclusions from Vietnam. When foreign policies after Vietnam seemed to be successful, Americans also explained how current accomplishments contrasted with the mistakes of Vietnam.

PART

I

* * * * * * * * * * * *

International Affairs

Chapter **1**

* * * * * * * * * * *

Bitterness Between the United States and Vietnam, 1975–1980

When the American-Vietnamese War ended, Americans wanted to move beyond the domestic and international divisions caused by the war, but their efforts to put the war safely in the past failed. Efforts by the Ford and Carter administrations to offer clemency or pardons to men who had violated the draft laws achieved only mixed results. Disappointed and angry American officials tried for years to economically and diplomatically isolate the government of the Socialist Republic of Vietnam (SRV). American anger and frustration with the new rulers of Vietnam ran so deep that it took longer than anyone expected for the United States and Vietnam to restore diplomatic relations.[1] Even during the early years of bitter estrangement, some American and Vietnamese government officials made efforts toward reconciliation. Although these initial approaches failed, they laid the groundwork for later normalization.

As the fighting went on in Vietnam, the U.S. government took tentative steps toward domestic reconciliation over the war. In August 1974, President Gerald R. Ford told the Veterans of Foreign Wars of his plan to allow thousands of draft and military offenders from the Vietnam War to apply for clemency. He favored "throwing the weight of my presidency on the side of mercy."[2] Then, on September 16, a week after he pardoned Richard Nixon, Ford issued an executive order creating a clemency program for draft and military law offenders from the Vietnam War. The program immediately provoked opposition across the political spectrum instead of assuaging bitter feelings about the war. Advocates of amnesty for draft offenders complained that the program was punitive and offered too little, and that Ford announced it to divert attention from his unpopular pardon of Nixon. Supporters of the military considered it to be an insult to servicemen. Moderates waited to see how many offenders would enlist in the program.[3]

The program offered clemency for men who had committed draft offenses, were fugitive military absence offenders, or were former service personnel with bad discharges for unauthorized absence. About 113,000 individuals were known to be eligible to seek clemency under the program, but only 21,800 applied for relief before the program ended in March 1975. Of these over 80 percent received presidential pardons without having to do alternative service, and most of the rest were granted pardons by President Ford after they completed three to six months of alternative service. The program was plagued from the start by inconsistencies in the way different government agencies granted clemency. Department of Defense officials had little interest in the reconciliation promised by the program, preferring instead to use it to clear its files of deserters. As a result, the Defense Department created a confusing and sometimes arbitrary mechanism for resolving cases. Under the program over five thousand men received undesirable military discharges, while some deserters who avoided the clemency procedure and instead went through normal military channels received honorable discharges. The Justice Department and a nine-member civilian clemency board, chaired by former New York Senator Charles Goodell, handled other offenders' cases, but neither of these agencies made a significant dent in the 113,000 cases up for review. The Justice Department received few applications from fugitive draft offenders, since many of these cases were never listed for prosecution. The clemency board reviewed the bulk of the draft cases, but its work was hindered by inconsistent requirements for community service and the fact that poor, uneducated men, who made up the bulk of the offenders, lacked the resources to present articulate cases for clemency before the board. In the end, the Ford program did not deliver reconciliation, because, in the words of Lawrence Baskir and William Strauss, two staff members of the clemency board, "its tone was too punitive, its conditions too unrealistic," and "the clemency it offered was no better, and in some ways worse, than the relief that was available through normal government channels."[4] The question of providing relief for the remaining thousands of draft and military offenders remained unresolved when the war ended with the Communist victory in April 1975.

In the eighteen months following the end of the war both the United States and the SRV adopted hard positions. As soon as the war ended the United States established an embargo on commerce and travel to the new Vietnam.

President Gerald R. Ford and Secretary of State Henry Kissinger said that North Vietnam and the National Liberation Front (NLF) had violated the Paris cease-fire agreement of 1973 with their military offensive against the Republic of (South) Vietnam in the spring of 1975.[5] The victors in North Vietnam demanded that the United States lift the embargo and make good on promises to provide reconstruction assistance.

Washington perceived the North's triumph in April 1975 as a humiliation. American officials' anger boiled over when more than two hundred thousand terrified refugees, mostly former government officials, members of South Vietnam's armed forces, contract employees of the United States government, and their families, began to flee Vietnam, mostly in small, unseaworthy boats beginning in May. This exodus was not a bloodbath of supporters of the South Vietnamese government, as had been predicted for years by advocates of U.S. involvement in the war, but it still crystallized Washington's animosity toward the new government in Vietnam. The Ford administration requested one hundred million dollars from Congress to resettle sixty thousand Vietnamese refugees in the United States. Congress was skeptical, as Senator Robert Byrd, the Democratic whip, explained, "there is no political support for it in the country."[6] Many members adopted new positions in light of the Communist victory. During the combat years congressional doves, opposing U.S. military action in Vietnam, had often supported aid for the millions of internal refugees. While congressional hawks, supporters of the American military effort usually opposed providing humanitarian aid for the South Vietnamese internal refugees. They saw the aid as a diversion from more important military aspects of the war.[7]

Despite American bitterness toward Vietnam, some contacts continued between the U.S. and Vietnamese governments. The United States and the SRV conducted negotiations regarding the opening of diplomatic relations in the six months after the war. Hanoi wanted the United States to acknowledge the Communist's legitimate control over all of Vietnam. On a more practical level, the SRV hoped that by improving diplomatic relations with Washington President Ford would make good on Nixon's promise to provide over three billion dollars in reconstruction aid to Vietnam. But the United States had no desire to provide economic aid and little interest in validating Hanoi's claim to sovereignty over all of Vietnam. However, one issue did bring American officials to the bargaining table: The fate of the twenty-five hundred Americans listed as missing in action remained unresolved in mid-1975. At the end of the war more than twenty-five hundred U.S. servicemen were listed as missing in action (MIA). The Defense Department believed them to be dead, but their remains had not been recovered. The United States wanted an accounting from Vietnam about these MIAs.

Talks between Vietnam and the United States opened in Paris in June 1975 and continued until the end of the year, but the two sides reached no agreement.

The Ford administration tried to frustrate the new government of the SRV by refusing to help it consolidate its rule by ending the embargo, open trade relations, or offer reconstruction aid. Every time the SRV brought up earlier American promises of economic assistance, the Americans took it as extortion. The Vietnamese expressed willingness to address the MIA issue, but the way they approached the subject only angered the Americans further. The Vietnamese negotiators hinted that they would provide information regarding the fate of MIAs, if the United States came up with the promised aid. Kissinger summarily rejected this approach, telling President Ford "Hanoi is obligated under both the Paris Agreement and the Geneva Convention to account for the missing. Linkage [of U.S. aid to information on the MIAs] is unacceptable."[8]

For their part, the Vietnamese badly miscalculated the dynamics of American politics in the wake of the Vietnam War. Since opposition to U.S. involvement in the Vietnam War had grown after 1967, Vietnamese negotiators believed that a majority of Americans opposed the tough stance of the Ford administration. While a small fraction of the U.S. antiwar movement did identify with the revolutionaries' cause, the vast majority of American war opponents simply wanted the United States out of Vietnam and cared little about the future of the country. Negotiations between the United States and Vietnam broke down completely at the end of 1975. As the *Washington Post* concluded in November 1975, American public opinion was no longer divided over the war in Vietnam, because most Americans simply wanted to forget their unhappy memories of it. As a result of this urge to put the war safely in the past, "Vietnam would be foolish to expect a nickel's worth of American aid."[9]

Only the MIA issue aroused public concern. In September 1975 the House of Representatives created a special committee to investigate the fate of American MIAs. Members of the committee disagreed over how generous the United States should be toward the SRV. Some favored lifting the economic embargo to encourage the SRV to account for MIAs. Others took a harder line, demanding that the SRV provide information on MIAs before the United States would consider economic ties. Some members of Congress thought that the MIA issue was a sideshow, and they argued for extending diplomatic relations to Vietnam to generate "commercial opportunities for American businesses." But the Ford administration opposed all American inducements to Vietnam and asserted that the Vietnamese had "a clear, unequivocal and unilateral responsibility to account" for MIAs. Only after the SRV was forthcoming on the MIA issue would the United States even consider extending diplomatic relations to Hanoi. Otherwise, Ford said, the United States would be "dignify[ing] and reward[ing] their posture of linking an accounting for our men to our providing them money."[10]

The memory of the Vietnam War was an issue used by several candidates during the presidential campaign of 1976. President Ford faced a strong challenge for the Republican nomination from a conservative, former California

Governor Ronald Reagan. Reagan condemned the Ford administration's handling of foreign policy across a broad front. According to Reagan, Kissinger's and Ford's efforts to foster détente with the Soviet Union had weakened American standing in the world. Similarly, Reagan denounced Ford's negotiations with the SRV, however tentative they may have been, as another sign of American weakness. The former California governor demanded a full accounting of the fate of American MIAs in Southeast Asia. He promised the National League of Families that he would obtain a full account of MIAs the first week he was president. Reagan's challenge forced Ford to state that he had "never said we would open diplomatic relations" with Vietnam under any circumstances. Even if Ford had wanted to proceed along a path toward normalization, which was very unlikely, Reagan's close ties to the League made it difficult for him to progress with it. Ford maintained this tough stance after he secured the Republican nomination in the summer. In September the United States vetoed the SRV's application for membership in the United Nations.[11]

Jimmy Carter, Ford's Democratic opponent in the fall election, also made Vietnam an issue. He criticized decisions made by a generation of American leaders in Vietnam, and he pledged not to intervene in other nations' internal affairs the way the United States had done in Vietnam's civil war. He praised the good judgment of the American public for having "learned the folly of our trying to inject our power into the internal affairs of other nations. It is time that our government learned that lesson too."[12] He promised to avoid the lies and deceptions that had characterized presidential statements about Vietnam. Carter observed that war had exposed the limits of American power, and he implied that the United States would use its military much more sparingly in his administration. Most of all Carter promised to put the memory of Vietnam behind the country by healing the deep divisions over military service. He criticized the Ford administration's clemency program for draft offenders for benefiting only the more highly educated and prosperous young men who had the resources to fashion a convincing plea for clemency. He promised a broad pardon to men who had been convicted of draft evasion. He chose the term "pardon" carefully as a political quid pro quo for Ford's 1973 pardon of President Nixon.

Carter narrowly defeated Ford in November 1976. Although Vietnam played a relatively minor role in voters' choice, the challenger gained some support because he seemed untainted by the mistakes of Vietnam. Nevertheless, the new administration became embroiled in controversy over the memory of the domestic divisions over the Vietnam War. On his first full day in office, January 21, 1977, Carter promised to pardon any draft offender who asked, and he expected support for this magnanimous gesture at reconciliation. Instead the pardon provoked anger from across the political spectrum. Tip Marlow of the Veterans of Foreign Wars expressed the misgivings of many supporters of the war when he told the *MacNeil-Lehrer Newshour*, "We were very displeased with the pardon. We feel that there is a better way for people who have broken laws to come back into the country, and that's through one of the pillars of the formation of our nation and that is our present system of justice." From the other side, amnesty advocates complained that a pardon, rather than full amnesty, put draft offenders in the same category as the disgraced Richard Nixon. Louise Ransom, affiliate director of Americans for Amnesty, said, "There seems to be a myth that because you once went into the army, there's some kind of esprit that you have accepted or believed in. Well the truth of the matter is that so many of the draft-eligible young men legally avoided the draft that . . . all the services took their people predominantly from poor and minority people in this country—took them right out of high school before they had the opportunity to even examine whether they were conscientious objectors."[13] Carter, like Ford, said that anyone who accepted a pardon acknowledged that he had committed a crime. Conservative supporters of the American involvement in the war attacked the pardon from yet another side. The American Legion, the largest veterans' organization, denounced Carter's pardon for dishonoring the more than two million American service personnel who did go to Vietnam. The Legion complained that men who accepted the pardon would pay no penalty for their refusal to serve.[14]

Carter could not satisfy either side in the intense debates over either the pardon or the larger subject of the wisdom of American participation in the Vietnam War, and his administration never completely recovered from this. Complaints about the pardon also placed him at a disadvantage when he embarked upon an even more ambitious effort to restore diplomatic relations with Vietnam. As had been the case during the Ford administration, the issues of finding MIAs and providing financial aid to Vietnam made the quest for normal relations extremely difficult. Yet Carter administration officials hoped that the fresh start of a new presidency would overcome the roadblocks that had barred the way to normalization in 1975 and 1976. Carter and Secretary of State Cyrus Vance wanted to diminish the range of issues on which the United States and the Soviet Union disagreed, and they advocated reconciliation with Vietnam as a way of taking Southeast Asia out of the arena of superpower conflict. They believed that diplomatic relations with the SRV would help stabilize the entire region. Vance thought that "the Vietnamese [were] trying to find a balance between over dependence on either the Chinese or the Soviet Union." He predicted that normal diplomatic relations with Vietnam would "give the United States the opportunity to have more influence with a nation which obviously plays an important part in the future development of Southeast Asia." Assistant Secretary of State for Far Eastern Affairs Richard Holbrooke became the most ardent advocate within the Carter administration for normalizing relations. According to Holbrooke, the establishment of relations with Vietnam would encourage the SRV to "work in a cooperative and responsible manner as a member of the region."[15]

In its efforts to dampen emotions over the issue of MIAs, the administration received some much needed help from the House Select Committee on MIAs. On January 31, 1977, Mississippi Democratic Representative Sonny Montgomery, the chairman of the committee, and six other members met with Carter at the White House. Montgomery told the president, "the committee does not believe any Americans are still being held alive as prisoners in Indochina," a conclusion Carter affirmed "strengthened my hand" in dealing with MIA advocates. Most members of the select committee favored normalization of relations with the SRV if only Hanoi would drop its insistence on receiving reconstruction aide. Iowa Democratic Representative Tom Harkin, a Vietnam War–era Navy veteran (during the war Harkin flew navy transport planes to and from Japan) and one of the members of Congress most sympathetic to the Vietnamese, encouraged Carter to lift the embargo as a goodwill gesture. He believed such an overture might encourage the Vietnamese to "shove aside the promise of $3.25 billion in funds by President Nixon to rebuild North Vietnam and heal the wounds of war." Harkin, a realist, knew that "Congress would certainly not appropriate that kind of money."[16]

In March 1977 Carter charged Leonard Woodcock, the retired president of the United Auto Workers Union, and a five-member commission with resolving the MIA issue. The commission traveled to Vietnam and Laos in mid-March. The hard-line government of Cambodia refused to receive the visitors, denouncing the U.S. government for "their acts of aggression, subversion and coup d'etat."[17] The Vietnamese, though, were happy to receive Woodcock. They provided the Americans with the remains of eleven missing servicemen. The two sides agreed on a mechanism for exchanging technical information on MIAs, but they did not resolve the dispute over American aid. The SRV adopted an unambiguous position toward economic aid from the United States. Deputy Foreign Minister Phan Hien explained that the United States government bore a legal responsibility for a war that "caused untold human and material losses to the Vietnamese people, destroyed Vietnam's economic bases, cultural establishment and natural resources." The Vietnamese reminded Woodcock that the United States had promised "to contribute to the healing of the wounds of war and postwar reconstruction" of Vietnam in the Paris Agreement of 1973. He also produced a letter from President Nixon to Prime Minister Pham Van Dong promising "$3.25 billion of aid for a period of five years."[18]

Woodcock emphasized that the United States would not consider linking the provision of aid to the restoration of relations. He rejected any American obligation to provide aid, and denounced the characterization of aid as reparations. He told Phan Hien "you are saying in a sense that you will sell us the remains of our MIAs in return for economic aid. No American President or Congress could approve such a deal. If you are truly interested in better relations with the United States you must drop that demand or the day of normalized relations will be put off for years."[19] Woodcock's sharp rejoinder caused the Vietnamese to slightly modify their demands. They appeared to drop the linkage between normalization and aid and spoke instead of humanitarian aid, something to be offered freely by the United States and not as legal obligation. A State Department analysis of the SRV's position noted that Pham Hien "placed the U.S. aid 'obligation' in the somewhat broader context of 'normalization,' so it is still not clear whether Hanoi links aid as a condition to the establishment of relations *per se*."[20] They also proposed that the two sides meet again without preconditions to discuss normalization.

The United States agreed, and on May 3, 1977, Richard Holbrooke and Phan Hien met in Paris to explore normalization of relations between the two adversaries. The Carter administration dropped the linkage between diplomatic recognition and information about MIAs. Instead, Carter adopted the more flexible standard of assurance that "they are acting in good faith and trying to help us account for our MIAs." Holbrooke told Phan Hien that the United States would not provide aid. He did offer to lift the trade embargo once the United States and Vietnam restored diplomatic relations. Even so, he wanted something back from the SRV. Other nations that had agreed to diplomatic relations with Vietnam found that the SRV demanded payments before they could open embassies in Hanoi. The United States would never do this. Holbrooke turned to Phan Hien and said, "May we go out this afternoon and announce normalization? The United States has no preconditions. After our embassies are established we'll lift the trade embargo."[21]

Phan Hien did not rise to Holbrooke's bait. The Vietnamese deputy foreign minister resented the Americans' dismissal of reconstruction aid. He was willing to drop the characterization of reparations, but he believed that both the Paris Accords and Nixon's letter committed the United States to rebuild Vietnam. Phan Hien took further offense at Holbrooke's refusal to agree that the Paris accords still governed relations between the two countries. The meeting broke up without an agreement. Holbrooke stated publicly that the talks had been "constructive" and "useful," diplomatic shorthand for ongoing, but not intractable, disagreement. Phan Hien was much more direct in his meeting with press. For the first time he revealed Nixon's letter to Pham Van Dong promising $3.25 billion to reconstruct Vietnam. While he did not use the word reparations, he said the United States was obliged to rebuild Vietnam. He did not care whether the money came directly or through international aid agencies. "A dollar sent," he said, "regardless of how, is still a dollar."[22] Holbrooke found even this formulation too demanding. He knew Congress would never approve aid for the SRV, no matter how that aid was packaged.

Nevertheless, negotiations continued for the remainder of 1977. Holbrooke met with SRV representatives again in October at the United Nations. Vietnam's Vice Foreign Minister Nguyen Co Thach indicated that his country wanted some promise of aid in return for the opening of diplomatic relation. In response, the State Department raised the prospect of taking an intermediate step before opening diplomatic relations. Under Holbrooke's plan, the United States and Vietnam would open interest sections (offices staffed by diplomats of each in a third country's embassy) in each other's capital and gradually explore raising their status to embassies. But the State Department faced resistance to normalization from within the administration. National Security Adviser Zbigniew Brzezinski was far more skeptical of the advantages of diplomatic relations with the SRV than Holbrooke or Vance, and he thought that opening interest sections "gains us nothing internationally, while conceivably costing us domestically." Initially, President Carter agreed with the State Department's willingness to open interest sections as an intermediate step before opening embassies, but Brzezinski continued to insist that U.S. negotiators press the Vietnamese hard in the next round of talks scheduled for December 1977. Brzezinski wanted Holbrooke to rebuke the Vietnamese whenever they alleged American misdeeds during the war. At the urging of the national security adviser, the State Department's final instructions to Holbrooke said, "We should not table the interest section proposal if the Vietnamese abuse the United States." The United States "should clearly leave the ball in Vietnam's court." Brzezinski told Vance "the burden should not always be ours to make the proposals."[23]

No progress was made at the December meeting. The Vietnamese repeated their linkage of normalization and aid. Holbrooke responded that Congress would not approve any sort of aid to Vietnam. A few weeks after the meeting broke up, relations deteriorated more. The United States demanded that the SRV's UN ambassador leave U.S. soil when the FBI discovered a spy ring in the Vietnamese mission to the United Nations. Michel Oksenberg, a staff member on the National Security Council (NSC), told Brzezinski that the arrest of the U.S. spies and the expulsion of Vietnam's UN ambassador would undermine President Carter's "admirable effort to put the war behind us."[24]

Despite Oksenberg's support for Carter's policy of improving relations with Vietnam, Brzezinski was content to see the president's enthusiasm diminish throughout 1978. He preferred formalizing diplomatic relations with China, the Soviet Union's main rival, to reconciliation with Vietnam, a far less important power. While Brzezinski spent the year seeking closer ties between the United States and the People's Republic of China (PRC), relations soured between China and Vietnam. In January, Vietnamese forces crossed the border into Cambodia seeking to oust the murderous Khmer Rouge regime of Pol Pot. Brzezinski's initial response to the border war seemed to characterize it as a proxy war between China (backing Cambodia) and the Soviet Union (backing Vietnam.) He tilted slightly toward Cambodia. Oksenberg, the China expert on the NSC staff, chided his boss for taking a public stance that might indicate any sort of American acquiescence in the genocide taking place in Cambodia. "We want this conflict to fester," he wrote, since it would weaken both Cambodia and Vietnam. The best way to do so was to establish "a position of equidistance between the disputants." Oksenberg also believed that "our talks with the Vietnamese . . . now take on a different meaning."[25]

By this time, the United States was far less interested in a rapprochement with the SRV than it was in expanding its relations with China. National Security Adviser Brzezinski took the lead in forging closer ties with the PRC, and he expressed even greater skepticism toward normalization with the SRV. In the spring of 1978 he convinced President Carter that the United States could apply pressure on the Soviet Union by growing closer to the PRC. Carter authorized Brzezinski to visit China in May. Before he went he told the president that he feared that "the combination of the increasing Soviet military power and shortsightedness, fed by big-power ambitions, might tempt the Soviet Union to exploit local turbulence (especially in the Third World) and to intimidate our friends" in Southeast Asia. Brzezinski saw "some Soviet designs pointing towards . . . the encirclement of China through Vietnam."[26]

In the month before Brzezinski's visit some fifty thousand ethnic Chinese, or Hoa, had fled Vietnam for refuge in China. The PRC complained that the SRV was systematically discriminating against ethnic Chinese. China also explicitly blamed Vietnam for the war raging between the SRV and Cambodia. In February 1978 a pro-PRC newspaper in Hong Kong, expressing the official government position, wrote that Vietnam had been the aggressor in the war. It sought to conquer Cambodia, and the war would end "only if the attempt [by Vietnam] to expand is given up and the invading army is withdrawn."[27] When Brzezinski arrived in Beijing in May, Chinese leader Deng Xiaoping heaped abuse on the Vietnamese and the Soviets. Deng characterized Vietnam's plans for an Indochina Federation as a thinly veiled attempt to establish Soviet control over the region. Brzezinski agreed. He told the Chinese that he thought the "Vietnamese were fighting a surrogate war for the Soviets and the ultimate target was the United States." The Chinese went so far as to tell the visiting Americans not to complete normalization of diplomatic relations with Hanoi. Michel Oksenberg recalled that earlier the Chinese had let the Americans know that they did not care if the United States and Vietnam established diplomatic relations. "This time," Oksenberg said, "they were vehemently against the Vietnamese and normalization."[28]

Still Vance and Holbrooke at the State Department continued to press for normalization of relations with Vietnam throughout the summer of 1978 despite opposition from the National Security Council. In June Holbrooke denied that the border conflict between Vietnam and Cambodia was a "proxy war" between the Soviet Union and the PRC. Instead, he believed that the conflict was rooted "deep in the historical and geopolitical realties of Asia." He asserted that it was "clearly in our interests" to maintain a power balance in Southeast Asia, and diplomatic relations with Vietnam would help.[29]

Momentum for normalization increased in August when another congressional delegation visited Hanoi and returned with the remains of fifteen American MIAs. The American emissaries came home convinced that Hanoi now wanted relations with the United States. Pennsylvania Democratic Representative John Murtha reported upon his return that the "Vietnamese are anxious to resume negotiations," because "they are afraid of the Chinese."[30] President Carter also wanted to proceed with diplomatic relations. He wrote Brzezinski, "We should evaluate the pros and cons of diplomatic relations with Vietnam, perhaps aiming at simultaneous recognition of China and Vietnam."[31]

The United States and the SRV agreed to meet at the United Nations in September 1978. Facing a new threat from the PRC, Hanoi became more eager for normal relations with the United States. The economy of the SRV went into a deep slump in 1978, and the ruling Lao Dong (Workers) Party concluded that trade with the West was more important than aid. Vietnamese Deputy Foreign Minister Nguyen Co Thach opened the talks with a reiteration of the linkage between normalization, the search for MIAs, and aid. "You won't believe it, Cy," Holbrooke told Vance, "the Vietnamese are still asking for money."[32]

As the discussion proceeded, the Vietnamese acknowledged that the United States rejected linkage among the three issues. They asked Holbrooke a series of questions about economic relations. If the United States would not provide aid, what about credits or loans? Would the United States at least lift the embargo? Holbrooke made it clear that aid was impossible and that once the Vietnamese understood that, other economic relations might be possible. The Vietnamese replied that they knew the "ball was in their court, presumably implying that they would have to drop their demand for aid." A week later they did just that. Thach told Holbrooke that Vietnam favored immediate normalization without any American economic assistance. Oksenberg described the Vietnamese as "panting to lock up the deal."[33] "Okay," Thach told Holbrooke, "I'll tell you what you want to hear. We will defer all problems until later. Let's normalize our relations without preconditions."[34] Holbrooke thought the Vietnamese had thrown in the towel. Oksenberg, on the other hand, believed the Vietnamese were not serious, and they would return to the demand for economic aid before a normalization deal was struck. Immediately after Thach offered to normalize relations without preconditions, Oksenberg turned to Holbrooke and said, "Dick, the Vietnamese are teasing you; they are mocking you."[35]

Despite the appearance of progress, the United States decided against taking the next step to open relations.[36] The NSC, opposed to early normalization, bested State Department officials who favored it. Brzezinski immediately told the president that "the rapid establishment of diplomatic relations with Vietnam . . . could prejudice our relations with China." Washington Democratic Senator Henry Jackson, who advocated better relations with the PRC as a counter to the Soviet Union, wrote Carter that the Chinese "view a move by the US to normalize with

Vietnam as essentially legitimating the Soviets' burden in supporting Vietnam ... while doing nothing to erode Soviet influence there and in Southeast Asia."[37] Carter agreed. Opening relations with China "was of paramount importance," he wrote in his memoirs. In October he "decided to postpone the Vietnam effort until after we had completed an agreement in Peking." Carter also wanted to postpone normalization with Vietnam until after the mid-term congressional elections of 1978. An aide to Holbrooke recalled that "our instructions from the White House after September 27 [the date of the last meeting between Holbrooke and Thach in Paris] were very clear: Do not agree [to normalization] until after the elections."[38]

The elections came and went in November, but still the Carter administration did not move on normalization. Opening relations with China took precedence. On December 15, the United States and China announced that they would open formal diplomatic relations on January 1, 1979.[39] Franklin B. Weinstein, an academic Asian specialist who advocated restoration of diplomatic relations between the United States and Vietnam, thought the Carter administration had lost its nerve. He decried the "political expediency," which, he said, caused the Carter administration to "retreat from its earlier enthusiasm for normalization."[40]

Indeed, the temporary postponement of normalization became permanent, especially given events in Indochina. First, on November 2, 1978, Vietnam and the Soviet Union signed a treaty of friendship and cooperation in which each nation committed to "socialist solidarity." They promised to advance "the struggle waged by the non-aligned countries and the peoples of Asia, Africa, and Latin America against imperialism, colonialism, and neo-colonialism."[41] Second, Vietnam provoked a refugee crisis. Throughout the fall the Vietnamese pushed another one hundred thousand Vietnamese of Chinese origins out of the country. They boarded thousands of small, leaky boats and sought refuge in Malaysia and throughout Southeast Asia. The plight of these boat people brought international condemnation of the SRV. Finally, the border skirmishes between Vietnam and Cambodia erupted into full-scale war as the Vietnamese People's Liberation Armed Force (PLAF) invaded Cambodia on December 25, 1978.

The horrifying genocide in neighboring Cambodia heightened the estrangement between the United States and the SRV. Between 1975 and 1978 the victorious Khmer Rouge systematically depopulated the cities of Cambodia. Pol Pot, the leader of the Khmer Rouge, sought to create a primitive, rural-based Communism. He believed that urban dwellers had been irretrievably corrupted by contact with Europeans and Americans. One and a half million Cambodians died of starvation, while several hundred thousand more were executed. The Khmer Rouge sealed off the country. Neither Western governments nor relief agencies had access to Cambodia in the three years after 1975. Reports of the slaughter in what came to be known as the "killing fields" of Cambodia came from a few audacious journalists and refugees who managed to leave via Thailand and broadcast news of the worst genocide since World War II.

The United States, however, muted its criticism of Pol Pot's murderous attacks on the Cambodians and resisted a United Nations Security Council condemnation of the Khmer Rouge. Vietnam ended up taking the lead in stopping the killing. In November 1978 the Vietnamese PLAF crossed the border into Cambodia. The Vietnamese army quickly captured Cambodia's capital of Phnom Penh. They did not capture Pol Pot, but they did expel him and his army from the capital. The Khmer Rouge fled to the remote border of Thailand and Cambodia. The Vietnamese installed a new government under the leadership of Hun Sen in Cambodia. Not surprisingly, given his new patron, Hun Sen broke from the Khmer Rouge and supported Vietnam.

Any new government in Cambodia would have been an improvement over the Khmer Rouge. Yet the United States drew a different conclusion from the installation of Hun Sen. The Carter administration concluded that the Vietnamese invaded Cambodia, because they wanted to dominate Southeast Asia. The North's victory in 1975 had not validated the domino theory, on which earlier U.S. administrations had based American participation in Vietnam. Only Laos and Cambodia, Vietnam's neighbors, had seen their governments taken over by Communist forces, and all the other states in the region remained non-Communist. Washington's fears of falling dominoes never fully abated, and the Vietnamese invasion of Cambodia convinced U.S. policymakers that Vietnam intended to dominate the region. Vietnam's friendship with the Soviet Union alarmed National Security Adviser Brzezinski. At the same time Vietnam sent its forces into Cambodia, Brzezinski orchestrated the consummation of the diplomatic opening to the People's Republic of China begun by the Nixon administration in 1971, and he traveled to Beijing in November to finalize plans. The United States agreed to transfer its diplomatic recognition from the Republic of China on Taiwan to the PRC. Brzezinski perceived the closer relationship between the United States and the PRC as a way to counter the influence of the Soviet Union.

China had complicated reasons of its own to oppose Vietnam's move into Cambodia. China supported the Khmer Rouge, and it had also granted asylum to Norodom Sihanouk, the traditional head of state of Cambodia deposed by Pol Pot in 1975. Sihanouk surprised most outside observers by supporting Pol Pot and opposing Hun Sen, because he perceived Vietnam as the power behind Hun Sen. If Hun Sen's government became the legitimate authority in Cambodia, Sihanouk would never return to power. The United States aligned its policy with China's in support of Sihanouk. At the United Nations, the United States and the PRC opposed replacing the Khmer Rouge representatives with a delegation representing the new Vietnamese-backed government.

The Vietnamese invasion of Cambodia altered the landscape of Indochina. At midnight on December 24, 1978, General Chu Huy Man, the director of the General Political Department of the Vietnam People's Army, fired a pistol shot into the cold, clear night at the town of Ban Me Thuot in the central highlands of Vietnam, signaling Vietnam's invasion of Cambodia. Within five days, columns of Vietnamese T-54 tanks and trucks carrying thousands of soldiers routed the Cambodian garrison at the provincial capital of Kratie. On January 1, 1979, another Vietnamese force advancing along the Mekong River from Laos seized a second Cambodian provincial capital. At the same time, Vietnam sent the full force of its Seventh and Ninth Military Regions up the Mekong River. Vietnamese bombers, tanks, and artillery pounded thirty thousand Khmer Rouge fighters. China quickly evacuated its military advisers. On January 4, Vietnamese troops had full control of the east bank of the Mekong. Two days later the Vietnamese crossed the Mekong River on Soviet-built pontoon bridges. U.S.-made ferryboats also carried nine Vietnamese divisions across the river to close in on Phnom Penh. Pol Pot and the other leaders of the Khmer Rouge fled in panic on the evening of January 6. The Vietnamese forces entered Phnom Penh on January 8. Hanoi Radio announced that "the revolutionary armed forces and the people of Cambodia" had liberated the capital from the murderous embrace of the Khmer Rouge. A new eight-member revolutionary council, led by Heng Semrin, a former Khmer Rouge commander who had defected to the Vietnamese in September 1978, now governed Cambodia.[42]

Vietnam's attack on Cambodia ignited a firestorm in the region. China was furious. Deng Xiaoping considered Vietnam's attack an effort to dominate the region in concert with the Soviet Union. When Deng visited Washington in late January, he told Carter that the "United States and China had a common enemy," the Soviet Union, "and therefore should collaborate closely."[43] He sought favor with his hosts by characterizing the Vietnamese as "the Cubans of the Orient."[44] The Chinese delegation held a secret Oval Office visit with Carter and his principal foreign policy advisers on January 30. Deng said that Vietnam was doing the Soviet Union's dirty work in Indochina. He said that China intended to "put a restraint on the wild ambitions of the Vietnamese and to give them an appropriate limited lesson." Carter listened and matter-of-factly responded that a Chinese move against Vietnam would be highly destabilizing. Deng appreciated the American concerns, but he repeated, "China must still teach Vietnam a lesson." National Security Adviser Brzezinski personally saw Deng off at a helipad near the Washington Monument and with a wink and a nod, he encouraged the Chinese "to concentrate on a swift and decisive move and not undertake a prolonged engagement" against Vietnam.[45]

Two and a half weeks later China struck hard against Vietnam. In the predawn hours of Saturday, February 17, 1979, the People's Liberation Army launched a ferocious artillery assault against Vietnamese positions. Observers thought that the artillery barrages sounded louder than the bombs dropped by American B-52s during the American War. As the skies lightened, eighty-five thousand Chinese troops supported by tanks and artillery poured across the border at twenty-six different places. The Chinese then funneled their attack into five columns leading to five provincial capitals. The Vietnamese had expected just such an assault. The PLAF had constructed hundreds of tunnels and bunkers along the border. Their machine guns, mines, and booby traps killed thousands of Chinese in the first three days of the fighting. China then put a new commander, General Yang Dezhi, in charge. Abandoning the human-wave tactics of the first attack, Yang had his armor and artillery lead the infantry toward the provincial capitals of the north, and in ten days, the Chinese captured four of these cities, Lai Chau, Lao Cai, Ha Giang, and Cao Bang. The PLA then turned on the last remaining capital, the largest, Lang Son. On February 27 Chinese artillery rained shell after shell on the French-built town. PLA infantry went house-to-house and bunker-to-bunker to rout their erstwhile allies, the Vietnamese. When China finally proclaimed Lang Song theirs on March 5, 1979, the town lay in ruins. Having sufficiently taught the Vietnamese a lesson, the Chinese immediately began their withdrawal from the border region of Vietnam. By March 16 all PLA forces had pulled out of Vietnam, leaving massive devastation behind. American bombers had avoided the northern border region during the war in order not to provoke China. Now the PRC had destroyed a part of Vietnam deliberately spared by the Americans.[46]

Despite the Chinese withdrawal, China and the SRV remained bitter enemies. China clearly aligned with the United States, and the SRV moved closer to the Soviet Bloc. The Soviet Union was careful to avoid provoking China during the war. Moscow did, however, send military equipment to Vietnam and offered moral support. Hanoi expressed gratitude for the Soviets' "firm statement, practical actions, and broad mass movement" during the nineteen-day war. In fact, the SRV probably expected the Soviet Union to have done more under the terms of the treaty the two nations had signed in November 1978.[47]

In 1979 U.S. policy remained committed to strengthening relations with the PRC. Despairing of Brzezinski's tilt toward the PRC, Secretary of State Vance kept trying to maintain contacts with Vietnam. "I believe strongly," he wrote the president in May, "that we are on the wrong course and that we are driving the Vietnamese further into the arms of the Soviets." Vance accepted that normalization was not in the cards, but "the failure to have any dialogue," he asserted, "is forgoing an important opportunity." The secretary of state believed that "we are coming increasingly under attack from both the right and the left." Vance's pleas infuriated Michel Oksenberg. He scrawled, "other than Jane Fonda, who?" next to Vance's assertion that both the right and the left objected to the American isolation of Vietnam. He told Brzezinski that Vance's memo "appalls me." He complained, "for eight years Holbrooke, [Anthony] Lake [head of the State Department's policy planning staff] and their ilk claimed Indochina was in chaos because we were there. Now they tell us there is chaos because we aren't there." Most of all, he thought that the SRV was desperate for American recognition. "Why chase Hanoi?" he grumbled. "They need us more than we need them."[48]

The Vietnamese drew exactly the opposite conclusion from the failure of the efforts to open diplomatic relations with the Americans. They rejected Carter's repeated insistence that the United States and Vietnam put their differences behind them. The Vietnamese believed that the Carter administration continued the animosity expressed by every administration for the previous two decades. Just when it seemed as if relations between the United States and Vietnam could not get any worse, they did. Hanoi suspected that the United States had given the PRC a green light for their invasion of Vietnam. The United States had not objected to China's attack on Vietnam and now proposed that the only way Vietnam could see the end of the Chinese occupation of the northern twenty kilometers of their country was to remove their own forces from Cambodia. For the Vietnamese, Washington's attitude represented the collusion of two long-time outside aggressors. On the ground the Vietnamese fought the Chinese with unexpected ferocity. Instead of China forcing Vietnam to leave Cambodia, Vietnam made the Chinese troops retreat from Vietnam. In neighboring Cambodia, however, the Vietnamese PLAF remained in place to support the new government of Hun Sen. Pol Pot's Khmer Rouge still waged a guerrilla war against the Vietnamese-backed Cambodian government from its bases near the Thai border. China supplied Pol Pot, much to the anger of Vietnam.[49]

With Vietnam embroiled in wars with its neighbors, the subject of reopening diplomatic relations faded in importance from U.S. foreign policy deliberations for the remaining eighteen months of the Carter administration. Also, the United States faced a crisis in Iran and deteriorating relations with the Soviet Union which meant attention was drawn away from potential reconciliation with Vietnam. In the summer of 1979, there was a frightening sense that war might break out between the United States and the Soviet Union in the region of the Persian Gulf. The Iranian Revolution led to a doubling of oil prices. Americans fought one another for fuel in long lines at filling stations. The Strategic Arms Limitation Treaty (SALT) II arms control that President Carter and Leonid Brezhnev, General Secretary of the Communist Party of the Soviet Union, signed in Vienna in June encountered harsh criticism in the Senate. Many opponents of SALT II believed that it placed the United States at a military disadvantage to the Soviet Union. War between the two superpowers seemed more likely than at any time since the Cuban missile crisis. Some observers likened the sense of desperation of 1979 to the situation in Europe in years before the outbreak of the Great War in 1914. Both the Americans and the Soviets feared the encirclement of enemies. Leaders in both capitals worried that their nations were as strong as they ever would be and that the future would be bleaker than the present.

Even as relations with Vietnam took a back seat in discussions among U.S. policymakers, public debate over the appropriate memory of the war revived.[50] As the Carter administration concentrated more on the military threat from the Soviet Union, officials no longer argued that the Vietnam War had proven that the United States should rarely use military force. Critics claimed that the administration did not go far enough in restating the lessons learned from the Vietnam War. Neo-conservatives, mostly former Cold War liberal supporters of U.S. involvement in Vietnam, asserted that the current tension with the Soviet Union originated in the loss of American will to fight in Vietnam and warned of the negative impact of what they called the "Vietnam syndrome." This condition represented a paralyzing fear of military involvement. Former supporters of U.S. involvement in Vietnam believed that the Carter administration had jeopardized the physical security and the prestige of the country by its clear reluctance to use the military. Opponents of the Carter administration asserted that the United States bore a major responsibility for the success of the anti-American Islamic revolution in Iran. These critics complained that the United States had treated the Shah of Iran, its old ally, with the same disloyalty it had displayed toward South Vietnam's president Nguyen Van Thieu in 1975. In a violent world, it seemed to be more dangerous to be a friend than an adversary of the United States. Americans who had looked forward to improving relations with Vietnam, as a way of putting the bad memory of the war to rest, remained largely silent in the midst of this rising tide of fear.

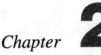

Chapter **2**

* * * * * * * * * * *

Estrangement and Détente,
1980–1988

During the campaign leading to the election of 1980, Ronald Reagan, the Republican Party's challenger to President Jimmy Carter, referred regularly to the lessons of the Vietnam War. In August 1980 Reagan told the annual meeting of the Veterans of Foreign Wars that "for too long we have lived with the 'Vietnam syndrome.'" He insisted instead that the Vietnam War had been "a noble cause" in which Americans had fought and died selflessly. "We dishonor the memory of 50,000 young Americans who died in that cause when we give way to feelings of guilt."[1] Reagan accused the Carter administration of learning the wrong lessons from the American military debacle in Vietnam. Instead of refraining from the use of military power in the wake of the disaster of Vietnam, Reagan recommended that the United States commit more resources to the armed forces. His criticism resonated with voters angry and dispirited by the capture of the U.S. embassy in Tehran. Reagan easily defeated Carter, and for the first time in a generation the Republican Party had a majority in the Senate.

Former Vietnam hawks held several key positions in the new Reagan administration. At his confirmation hearing for secretary of state, General Alexander Haig informed the Senate Committee on Foreign Relations that the time had come "to shed the sackcloth and ashes" worn since the Vietnam War. Caspar Weinberger, the new Secretary of Defense, announced that rebuilding the nation's armed forces would meet an immediate and dangerous threat posed by the Soviet Union and help erase some bad memories of the Vietnam War.[2]

At first the Reagan administration acted on these beliefs far away from Southeast Asia as Central America became a focus of U.S. military action. Just as the United States entered the Vietnam War to demonstrate its credibility against the Soviet Union and China in Europe, Latin America, and East Asia, the Reagan administration entered the fray in Central America to gain advantages in the competition with the Soviet Union in other areas of the world. In February 1981 the Defense Department sent fifty-five military advisers to El Salvador. Public reaction, however, was far different from what officials expected. Many feared that the United States would become sucked into a quagmire in Central America. Congress responded to the public anxiety by barring the administration from sending more than the original fifty-five advisers to El Salvador.

Director of Central Intelligence William Casey, surprised and frustrated by the level of anxiety and opposition to open U.S. support for conservative forces in Central America, preferred that the United States act secretly. From late 1981 until late 1986 the CIA armed the contra rebels in Nicaragua. In 1983 Congress forbade the use of funds for covert actions aimed at overthrowing the leftist government of Nicaragua. In 1984 Casey and Lieutenant Colonel Oliver North of the National Security Council (NSC) staff developed a complex scheme to divert profits from the sale of weapons to Iran to buy weapons for the contras.[3] North and Casey went to great lengths to keep this operation secret, but the United States was clearly on record as supporting the contras. North's and Casey's invocation of the memory of Vietnam caused consternation among other NSC staff members, one of whom warned that a public effort to "flag the lessons learned about U.S. power [in Vietnam] and link it to Central America" would turn into a public relations "disaster."[4] Such fears proved prophetic when the Iran-Contra connection became public in 1986.

While the Reagan administration's attention was focused directly on the global competition with the Soviet Union in its first three years, it reaffirmed its support of the economic embargo against Vietnam. The administration adopted the position that the United States would not consider normalization of diplomatic relations "as long as the Vietnamese occupation of its neighbor [Cambodia] continues."[5] The Vietnamese understood that the presence of their troops in Cambodia hindered relations with the United States, and in 1982 Hanoi offered a partial withdrawal of their forces from Cambodia. Vietnam sent out signals that they had no territorial designs on Cambodia. The U.S. ambassador in Thailand, who favored a thaw between the United States and the SRV, reported to Washington that the presence of Vietnamese troops in

Cambodia "is aimed at dealing with the threat from China" and was not designed to occupy Cambodia permanently.[6]

The continuing flow of refugees from Vietnam also interfered with improvement in relations between the United States and the SRV. Reagan regularly criticized the SRV for forcing several hundred thousand Vietnamese to
flee the country in 1981. In the last days of the Carter administration, the
United States and Vietnam developed an Orderly Departure Program under
which the Vietnamese government agreed to let thousands of refugees leave
legally. In return, the United States, the Philippines, Malaysia, Indonesia, and
the British authorities in Hong Kong agreed not to accept Vietnamese without
exit permits. However, these movements toward dealing with the refugee issue fell apart in early 1981. Hanoi, furious at the Reagan administration's
intensification of the embargo, abandoned the Orderly Departure Program
(ODP) as soon as Reagan took office. Over the summer of 1981 the United
States and the SRV resumed negotiations over the ODP. In October, the two
sides agreed that the United States would accept refugees joining family members, but that all other boat people would be turned away.[7]

The United States hectored Vietnam for dragging its feet on accounting for
service personnel listed as missing in action. Reagan raised the MIA issue to
the highest prominence it had seen since the months preceding the signing of
the Paris Agreement in 1973. In 1983 Reagan told the National League of
Families, the principal organization of relatives of MIAs, that receiving an
accounting for the twenty-two hundred MIAs had his highest priority. The
Reagan administration enhanced the status of the POW/MIA Inter-Agency
Group (IAG) created by the Carter administration. Deputy Assistant Secretary of State for East Asian and Pacific Affairs Daniel A. O' Donohue, chair of
the IAG, and Deputy Assistant Secretary of Defense Richard Armitage met
with the SRV's UN ambassador in November 1981 to reiterate their demands
for a full accounting of those missing in action. For over two months the SRV
did not reply. Some members of the IAG wanted to make a public issue of the
SRV's reluctance to respond, but O'Donohue favored a more nuanced approach. He told the IAG that the "Vietnamese should not be 'forced' into an-
swering 'no' by approaching them at this time."[8]

Instead the IAG pursued a dual strategy. In public, it embarked on an offensive to raise the visibility of the POW/MIA issue, but behind the scenes it
sought a diplomatic solution with the SRV. Ann Mills Griffith, the executive
director of the National League of Families, spearheaded the IAG's efforts to
publicize the fate of MIAs. Through a newly established speakers' bureau, the
IAG offered local civics clubs presentations on the "2,500 POW/MIAs who
remain missing in Vietnam, Laos and Cambodia," sending a clear message
that "recent reports by Indochinese refugees and other intelligence sources
indicate the very real probability that some of these men remain captives."[9]

That was Griffith's and the NLF's public position. Behind the scenes, however, Reagan administration officials worried that the NLF's inflammatory rhetoric about live Americans remaining captive in Southeast Asia would make real progress with Vietnam impossible.

Despite these concerns, the United States continued to send emissaries to the SRV. Armitage returned to Hanoi in February 1982. He alternately badgered the Vietnamese and expressed understanding for their sensitivities. He came with a team of military investigators "who had expertise to impress [the Vietnamese] with Reagan's" and the "American people's commitment" to receiving a full accounting of the missing men. He reported to the IAG, "If we push too hard, the Vietnamese will pull back and not give us anything." He stated that the NLF "cannot implement its program" of public information. Another representative of the Defense Department objected to the United States government embracing the NLF too warmly, noting that the "Vietnamese canceled a meeting to be held last fall because of a strong League letter."[10]

In December 1982 the United States and the SRV commenced what seemed to be regular quarterly technical meetings on the fate of U.S. MIAs. These sessions had an uneven history: the United States pressed for an accounting of the missing, the Vietnamese occasionally turned over remains, and each side accused the other of making unreasonable demands on the other. They met in December 1982, March 1983, and June 1983. At the June meeting the SRV turned over the remains of nine missing U.S. servicemen. A month later, however, the SRV suspended further meetings, citing "hostile statements" from Reagan administration officials who had accused the SRV of dragging their feet. In the fall, Lieutenant Colonel Richard Childress, a Vietnam veteran on the NSC staff in charge of MIA/POW issues, and Ann Mills Griffith met twice with the SRV's Foreign Minister Nguyen Thach. The Vietnamese seemed to offer a major concession when he promised that the SRV would no longer link progress on finding the remains of missing Americans to other issues such as lifting the embargo.

Contacts persisted over the next few months. In November the SRV agreed to receive a high-level U.S. delegation. When Assistant Secretary of Defense Richard Armitage returned to Hanoi in February 1984 the SRV seemed more accommodating than at any time in the past year. Hanoi promised to resume regular quarterly meetings of the technical experts, and over the next few months, the Vietnamese turned over eight remains to the United States, six of which were later identified as the bodies of U.S. servicemen. When President Reagan spoke at the White House ceremony for National POW/MIA Recognition Day in July 1984, he commended the Vietnamese for showing greater cooperation with the United States. Regular technical meetings between officials of Hanoi and the United States became a reality in late 1984. In August 1985 SRV Acting Foreign Minister Vo Dong Giang informed Griffith and Childress that the SRV wanted to resolve the MIA issue "within two years."

That fall teams from the United States and Vietnam for the first time investigated a crash site of a downed U.S. plane in Vietnam.[11]

Despite its initial hostility toward Vietnam, the Reagan administration eventually moved toward improved relations. Childress of the National Security Council staff had principal responsibility for Vietnam. His duties included political and economic relations with the government of the SRV and maintaining the high profile of the MIA issue. An ardent hawk, he thought the American involvement in Vietnam had been "flawed in various ways," principally by the refusal of the Johnson administration to use more force. He continued to believe that the United States should have won in Vietnam, and failed to do so because ignorant opponents of the war had sapped the will of the American public to stay the course. Childress had trouble forgiving opponents of the war for comments they had made years earlier. For example, in 1985, on the tenth anniversary of the Communist victory, and more than thirteen years after the publication of Frances FitzGerald's *Fire in the Lake*, a Pulitzer Prize–winning history of the American experience in Vietnam, he seethed that works such as hers had "demoralized western intellectuals over the Vietnam experience." He grumbled that "she did not know Vietnamese culture from the hamlet up," despite the public acclaim for the book.[12]

Notwithstanding Childress's disdain for liberal critics of American participation in the Vietnam War, he advocated the beginning of engagement between the United States and the SRV. He believed that the SRV's desperate need for an end to the U.S. economic embargo would make its leaders more amenable than they had been to cooperation on the MIA issue. He thought that Americans were open to the idea of improved relations with Vietnam if it would bring closure on MIAs. Yet Childress was almost alone in this view that Americans wanted a breakthrough in relations with Vietnam. Frederick Z. Brown, a former foreign service officer with a deep interest in improving relations between the United States and Vietnam after the war, noted, "the strongest feeling about Vietnam in Congress may well be indifference. . . . [T]he United States, apart from a vague hostility, does not really think *at all* about Vietnam."[13]

Relations with Vietnam improved slowly. Reagan administration officials expressed even greater hostility than Childress did toward liberal critics of the American involvement in the war. On the tenth anniversary of the Communist victory, Patrick Buchanan of the White House communications office recommended that Reagan make a surprise, unannounced address in which he "discards his expected text and devotes an entire speech to the lessons of Vietnam." Buchanan urged the president to counteract what he was certain would be television network harping on what they would characterize as "a stupid, tragic, unwinnable war." Instead, Buchanan urged the president to emphasize how the Communist victory had led to "1) Tyranny. 2) 'Reeducation' camps still holding thousands. 3) Half a million boat people. . . . 4) The new Vietnam is a militarist, aggressor nation, invading Cambodia."

Buchanan's white-hot rhetoric was too much for Childress and National Security Adviser Robert McFarlane, both of whom believed it was time to move beyond sterile discussions of responsibility for the war. They thought there was no need for the Reagan administration to defend the war in the mid-1980s. Childress observed that, contrary to Buchanan's worries about the press, "the media are carrying the ball for us as expected, and there is little to no coverage from those who either opposed our involvement or made apologies for the [North] Vietnamese."[14]

As relations deepened between the League of Families and the U.S. government, extremists, rogues, and confidence men pushed their own ideas about finding MIAs. Some groups found the heightened interest in MIAs to be an irresistible way to fleece desperate and credulous friends and relatives of missing servicemen. Using direct-mail techniques, con men sent letters suggesting that organizations were close to rescuing men still held as prisoners. If friends and relatives sent money, their loved ones would be freed from horrible jungle captivity; otherwise, they might die. One letter from a purported rescuer read, "I'm exhausted. I'm broke. And, I'm reaching the end of my rope. But, I believe we are very, very close to getting our first POW out." He added a phrase that should have set off alarm bells, "I can't give you any more details." Another solicitation promised, "we're close to making contact with an American POW. . . . That effort could fail for lack of funds." These letters raised hundreds of thousands of dollars.

The exploitation of the desperate hopes of family members backfired. New York Democratic Representative Stephen Solarz, chair of the House Subcommittee on Asian and Pacific Affairs, asked the Defense Intelligence Agency (DIA) to investigate the claims made in these solicitation letters. In its scathing denunciation of the scam, the DIA characterized the fund-raising letters as "rambling discourses filled with inflammatory rhetoric." The DIA wrote, "For all their 'proof' and the untold millions of dollars raised, none of these groups or individuals have yet to furnish even the slightest shred of evidence of POWs, much less secure the return of a living American captive."[15]

Some relatives of MIAs also fell prey to would-be swindlers who combined fantasies of heroic rescues with the love of a fast buck by offering to mount paramilitary rescue raids into supposed prison camps in remote areas of Laos, Cambodia, and Vietnam. Critics soon labeled these adventurers "Rambos," after the popular series of movies starring Sylvester Stallone as a comic book-like American veteran who single-handedly rescues American POWs. Richard Childress and Stephen Solarz noted, "Rambo-oriented non-family groups peddled POW-MIA conspiracy and coverup theories, manufactured false POW-MIA 'evidence,' raised millions of dollars based on fraudulent information and photos, and smeared those who did not agree with them."[16] Like the John Rambo character, the would-be rescuers played upon widespread public suspicions about the trustworthiness of government officials. In a paradoxical repetition of the complaints against official duplicity voiced by opponents of the war in Vietnam, the adventurers accused government officials of knowingly leaving POWs behind after 1975 and then covering up their existence. James "Bo" Gritz, formerly with the U.S. Army Special Forces, became one of the most prominent would-be rescuers. "I'm afraid that only God, the mothers, the wives who remained true and the Special Forces want the prisoners back," he told vulnerable families.[17]

Gritz loved publicity. He invited a reporter to visit a private group of commandos training in the Florida Everglades for a foray into Laos. In November 1982 he led a small group across the Mekong River from Thailand into Laos, where they were almost immediately set upon by a rival group of anticommunist commandos. They fled in panic across the border back into Thailand, leaving one man behind. Gritz paid a $17,500 ransom to the captors to release their hostage. This was the only prisoner Gritz ever rescued. Thai authorities arrested Gritz. Upon his release, he held a press conference in which he declared that he had found the skeletal remains of American servicemen. They later turned out to be monkey bones mixed with those of Asian men. Admiral A. G. Paulsen of the DIA told a congressional committee that Gritz's "efforts have seemed like a parody, a caricature of the clandestine operation, the 'surgical penetration' he purports to be capable of mounting."[18]

None of this seemed to deter Gritz. He returned several times to Thailand in 1986 and 1987 where he negotiated with a cast of shady characters who promised information on live Americans in Laos. One of them was Khun Sa, an ethnic Chinese who headed the Shan United Army (SUA), a ragtag group of anticommunist guerrillas committed to the overthrow of the government of Laos, which funded its operations through the sale of heroin. Gritz did not mention the source of the SUA's funds when he went to sympathetic members of Congress for support. Gritz told congressional critics of the White House's actions on POWs that he had the tacit support of the National Security Council. In fact, Gritz had only arranged a meeting with Major Tom Henney, a former congressional staffer working temporarily on the NSC staff, who found Gritz to be an intriguing character.

Richard Childress, the NSC staff member who knew the most about serious efforts to determine the fate of MIAs, exploded in anger when he learned that Henney had met with Gritz. Childress had Henney relay to Gritz that the White House did not support his activities and warned Henney to keep his distance from the ex-soldier, but Gritz pressed on. He asked Henney for a letter on White House stationery testifying to the administration's knowledge and approval of his freelance activities to find MIAs. Once again, Childress told Henney to inform Gritz that the White House did not endorse him. Gritz then had his wife and a mutual friend get in touch with Henney, who by this time understood the kind of person with whom he was dealing. From then on, whenever Henney met with Gritz, he made it clear that the White House did not approve of his activities.[19]

Other unsavory people were also taking advantage of the vulnerabilities of MIA families. Crooks manufactured elaborate reports of MIAs living in Laos. In September 1985 a Laotian anticommunist showed American officials a picture of a tall, well-dressed, neatly shaved Western man standing next to a shorter, well-dressed, smiling Asian man. The Lao informant assured the Americans that this was a recent photo showing an American POW standing with the commander of a prison camp in Laos. The skeptical Americans began asking questions, and within months an American Peace Corps volunteer acknowledged that he had been photographed with a Lao friend, and a member of the Lao resistance had taken the negative. The results were predictable. Soon copies of the picture showed up across Thailand. In one episode a Thai businessman and two representatives from the Lao resistance met an American official in a Bangkok hotel room. If the Americans would pay $1.25 million (10 percent up front), the Lao resistance would rescue Americans held captive in Laos. The Laotians showed the photo, this time with the face of the Asian man cut out. The meeting broke up in embarrassment when one of the Americans pulled from his briefcase the same picture—with the Asian "guard's" face fully visible. When the Americans explained the story behind the photograph, the Thai businessman and the representatives of the Lao resistance fled the room.[20]

The Reagan administration's continuing efforts to pursue a dialogue with the SRV opened a rift with many ardent conservatives. Some of them insisted that the United States pressure the SRV further. In mid-1985 some Vietnam veterans and their supporters in Congress sought the creation of a special presidential commission on POWs/MIAs. Taking the lead were retired U.S. Air Force General Eugene Tighe and North Carolina Republican Representative Bill Hendon. Both of them thought that the Reagan administration paid only lip service to the idea that live American POWs remained in Southeast Asia. Tighe, who directed the DIA at the end of the Carter years and the beginning of Reagan's term, told the House Subcommittee on Asian and Pacific Affairs in June 1981 that he personally believed "American servicemen are being held against their will in Indochina," despite the official view of the DIA that it could verify none of the reports of live sightings of Americans captives in Vietnam, Cambodia, or Laos. Tighe later resigned from the government and began campaigning publicly for a presidential commission on MIAs. Representative Hendon adopted the POW issue as soon as he came to Washington in 1981. He accused the Reagan administration of suppressing evidence of live Americans remaining in Southeast Asia.[21] Tighe and Hendon promoted H. Ross Perot, the Dallas billionaire who had helped the Nixon administration publicize the POW issue, as chairman of a presidential commission on MIAs.

The Reagan administration expressed ever-greater irritation with what it considered to be the relentless self-promotion of advocates of a presidential

MIA commission and it enlisted Democratic as well as Republican officials to oppose the commission's creation. Chapman Cox, general counsel of the Defense Department, wrote Florida Democratic Representative Dante Fascell, chair of the House Committee on Foreign Affairs, that such a commission "would interject a group of people much less experienced in and knowledgeable of the issue" than the government officials currently working on the project. The State Department agreed. Assistant Secretary of State for Legislative and Intergovernmental Affairs William L. Ball III told Fascell that the creation of a commission might backfire, since Hanoi might interpret it as the United States was changing the direction of its MIA policy. "Such a signal," Ball wrote, "could provide the Vietnamese with an opportunity to stall under the mistaken belief that they may be able to obtain leverage over the issue."

Despite their political differences, Childress joined forces with Democratic Representative Stephen Solarz to counteract the unscrupulous pirates who had hijacked the POW/MIA issue. Solarz held a public hearing at which the administration denounced reports that live Americans had been seen in Southeast Asia. He appointed a task force, headed by Republican Representatives Gerald Solomon and Benjamin Gilman, to investigate charges that Americans had been left behind, which delayed action on the creation of the presidential commission for a year. In January 1986 a group of Hendon's supporters chained themselves to the furniture in Solarz's office and spread bones over the carpets, shouting that he had covered up evidence of live Americans in Laos. This was too much for the White House, which decided to collaborate openly with Solarz. National Security Adviser John Poindexter thought that Solarz, Solomon, and Gilman had "been the mainstays of our bipartisan support in the House." Poindexter thought that the creation of the POW/MIA Commission "would damage our strategy by sending the wrong signals to the Vietnamese of divisiveness in this country."[22] In January 1986 President Reagan himself met with Congressmen Hendon and Robert Smith, a New Hampshire Republican who also supported the idea of a commission. The president told the visitors that their commission would interfere with the work of the American team visiting Vietnam to arrange joint searches for MIAs.[23]

Reagan also tried to keep Perot from joining the commission. Reagan said that the American approach toward men listed as missing was "to act as if some prisoners remain alive, even though no evidence is available to verify that approach."[24] He told Perot that the commission would be useless and "would create another umbrella oversight organization where one already exists." Yet Reagan faced pressure from within his own administration to accommodate Perot. Vice President George H. W. Bush wanted the administration to pay more attention to Perot who had adopted the POW issue as his own in 1970.

Perot continued to press for information regarding MIAs after the release of over four hundred American POWs in 1973. He charged that when Bush had served as Director of Central Intelligence in 1975 and 1976, he had suppressed reports that American POWs had been seen alive. Bush spoke with Mississippi Democratic Representative Sonny Montgomery, chair of the House Veterans Affairs Committee, who reluctantly endorsed the idea of Perot heading a commission. Montgomery personally did not believe that Americans remained against their will in Vietnam. His skepticism had earned him the scorn of militant advocates of the POW cause. According to Bush, "Montgomery feels that [the popular movie] 'Rambo,' former New York Republican Representative John LeBoutillier, and others have convinced the American people that MIAs are still being held. . . . He thinks a small commission, headed by Perot, might 'close this thing out.'" The White House remained unconvinced that a commission could satisfy the militant "Rambo" faction and wanted Montgomery to get on board and back the administration's efforts to resolve the MIA issue by sending delegations to Vietnam. "Rather than a commission which runs counter to our strategy," the White House told Montgomery, "what we need at this point is some serious help on the Hill to publicly back the President's efforts and control Mr. Hendon who is still charging DIA with cover-up."[25]

Advocates of a commission continued to press their case even after Reagan refused to create one. Some of the militants demanded that Reagan appoint former Representative LeBoutillier as a special presidential assistant or ambassador in charge of POW issues. A list of Republican notables, including, among others, Richard Nixon, Donald Rumsfeld, Nevada Senator Paul Laxalt, Reagan's former Secretary of State Alexander Haig, speechwriter Patrick Buchanan, General William Westmoreland, and even socialite celebrity Gloria Vanderbilt, urged Reagan to name LeBoutillier.[26] But the NSC demurred, and Reagan did not appoint LeBoutillier to a position likely to detract from the ongoing efforts of the Defense Department to find remains. LeBoutillier then joined forces with Billy Hendon, who had been defeated for reelection in 1986, to offer a one-million-dollar reward to anyone who could provide verifiable information about American servicemen still imprisoned in Vietnam. Hendon tried to release a helium-filled balloon along the Thai border with Laos that carried notices of the reward. The Thai and Lao governments objected. Ann Mills Griffith denounced Hendon's and LeBoutillier's actions as "theatrics" that constituted "a grave danger to . . . efforts" to resolve the MIA issue.[27]

Yet such extreme views had less traction in Reagan's second term. Politically, relations between the United States and Vietnam remained as frosty as ever in the mid-1980s. But the Reagan administration's assertive foreign policy opened the door a crack to engagement with the SRV. Secretary of State George P. Shultz used the occasion of the tenth anniversary of the Communist victory in Vietnam to reflect on the lessons of the war. He berated the SRV for abusing human rights. He pointed out the striking contrast between Vietnam's poverty and the roaring economies of other members of the Association of Southeast

Asian States. He reaffirmed Reagan's characterization of the war as a noble cause. "Whatever mistakes in how war was fought, whatever one's views of the strategic rationale for our intervention the *morality* of our effort must now be clear," he told a crowd of State Department officials. He praised the "healthy rethinking" about the Vietnam War that had taken place over the past decade. Opponents and supporters of the war had come to appreciate the views of one another, leading, he thought, to an emerging consensus about the prudent extension of American commitments to other governments.[28]

The ups and downs of U.S.–Soviet relations also reverberated in U.S.–Vietnam relations. As hostility between the United States and the Soviet Union hit rock bottom in 1983 and 1984, Washington regarded Hanoi, the Soviets' ally, with the greatest distrust. The Reagan administration sought better relations with the People's Republic of China (PRC) in the ongoing competition with the Soviet Union, and the president visited Beijing in May 1984. At about the same time, China threatened another invasion of Vietnam. According to the U.S. intelligence reports, China displayed greater belligerence toward Vietnam to show that "China cannot be intimidated by Soviet-Vietnamese military ties." China bared its military muscle toward Vietnam shortly after Reagan visited Beijing "to leave the impression that Chinese actions have U.S. approval."[29] Naturally, the SRV felt threatened by China's military moves. Surprisingly, however, the Soviet Union urged the SRV to improve their relations with the PRC. When Vietnam's Foreign Minister Thach visited Moscow in October 1984, Soviet Foreign Minister Andrei Gromyko urged Vietnam to normalize relations with China. Gromyko wanted "a Vietnamese pledge not to resume Thai/Kampuchean border fighting (and thereby set off a Chinese response)."[30]

Within months of Mikhail Gorbachev becoming general secretary of the Soviet Communist Party in March 1985 he began a series of reforms that shook the foundations of Communist authority in the Soviet Union and Eastern Europe. Among other things, he encouraged a reduction in the Cold War competition with the United States. He also fostered economic reforms throughout Eastern Europe. Hungary, Czechoslovakia, Poland, and the German Democratic Republic began experimenting with varieties of market reforms. Aftershocks of these changes soon hit Vietnam, where the government faced reduced subsidies from the Soviet Union and explored state-managed capitalist-style economic reforms called *doi moi*.[31]

Under *doi moi* the government and the Communist Party relaxed controls on land ownership, encouraged small private businesses, and began inviting foreign investors and international bankers back to Vietnam. Reformers favored tax breaks for Vietnamese and international investors. They welcomed the advice of outsiders on how to reduce state provided benefits like free education or medical care.[32]

The State Department's Bureau of Intelligence and Research reported on the differences over economics within the Vietnam Communist Party. In 1985 the reform faction of the Communist Party led by Vo Van Kiet, a Southerner, relaxed controls over the economy. Kiet hoped to unleash the entrepreneurial spirit of the Vietnamese and raise living standards in Vietnam as had happened in Eastern Europe. Conservative members of the party leadership opposed Kiet's reforms and they pushed through a new currency in September 1985 that resulted in a surge in prices and widespread public dissatisfaction with the leadership of the Communist Party. After Communist Party Chairman Le Duan died in mid-1986, a succession struggle ensued between conservatives committed to greater control over the economy and liberal economic reformers. The latter, led by Kiet, had a slight advantage, but until the succession to Le Duan was sorted out there would likely be a period of "indecision and inaction." In November a U.S. National Intelligence Estimate (NIE) determined that "public confidence in Hanoi's ability to run the economy has virtually vanished."

The Vietnamese leaders hoped that improving ties with the West would provide economic benefits, and they recognized that their country's continued occupation of Cambodia harmed relations with the West. When the Communist Party Congress met in December, it elected Kiet chairman, and it also stated that it wanted a resolution to the political issues facing Cambodia. It would permit the Khmer Rouge to participate in negotiations. But the NIE warned, "Hanoi's overriding security interest in preserving a dominant position in Cambodia rules out any early compromise." The Congress endorsed further cooperation with the United States on POW/MIA and emigration issues, hoping that this, along with a resolution of the Cambodian question, "will eventually ease the process of normalization." Whatever hopes the new Vietnamese leadership had for normalization, "strong backing for and dependence on the USSR will remain the foundation of Hanoi's foreign policy," wrote the analysts who prepared the NIE.[33]

The opportunities for better relations presented by the new Vietnamese leaders reinforced the desire of Reagan administration officials to put the irritating activities of the outsiders, the Rambos, and the angry members of Congress behind them. Talks between U.S. and Vietnamese representatives continued in 1986. Childress met Vietnam's Deputy Foreign Minister Hoang Bich Son in May. The Vietnamese requested a formal, public U.S. commitment to support Hanoi's plan to resolve the remaining questions of unaccounted-for Americans. Assistant Secretary of Defense Richard Armitage would not go that far, but he wrote Foreign Minister Nguyen Co Thach that progress on MIA searches had "improved the atmosphere between our two peoples." Armitage promised that the United States would help the Vietnamese look for remains and provide technical training of Vietnamese who would join with Americans in inspecting crash sites and grave sites, as well as hard cash. Armitage pledged that "the United States will, for any joint operations, reimburse fully in U.S. dollars. . . . expenses incurred by the Vietnamese side." For these excavations the United States would provide modern U.S. equipment and would reimburse the Vietnamese for the use of their own equipment, so long as at least one American technical person was present at the excavation.[34]

When the Vietnamese sent back the remains of just four U.S. servicemen in the second half of 1986, the Americans accused them of stalling. The Vietnamese resented the constant badgering, countering that there were still over three hundred thousand Vietnamese soldiers listed as missing. One Vietnamese negotiator insisted that it was time for the United States to "have a really cooperative attitude" and for it to "create a favorable atmosphere so that the search for information about Americans missing in action would be fruitful." The Americans heard disturbing echoes of Vietnam's earlier linkage of the MIA issue with Washington's willingness to end the embargo and resume diplomatic relations.[35]

But times were changing. Bombastic rhetoric from Hanoi earlier in the Reagan administration would have hardened Washington's opposition to the SRV as a Soviet client. In 1987 the Reagan administration's foreign policy underwent a pronounced shift toward détente with the Soviet Union. Given closer personal relations between Reagan and Soviet President Mikhail Gorbachev, the United States could try to reduce friction with the SRV. In February Reagan appointed General John Vessey, former chairman of the Joint Chiefs of Staff, as a personal emissary to Vietnam. The Vietnamese agreed to receive Vessey and to discuss the fate of MIAs as "a humanitarian issue not tied to the other political issues" dividing the United States and Vietnam. At the same time the Vietnamese pointed out that they too had humanitarian concerns including their own 300,000 MIAs, 1.4 million people disabled from the war, 500,000 orphans.[36] When Vessey landed in Hanoi in August, he became the highest-ranking U.S. official to visit the Vietnamese capital in ten years. Ann Mills Griffith of the National League of Families and Richard Childress of the NSC staff traveled with Vessey. Like Leonard Woodcock, who went to Hanoi on behalf of President Carter in 1977, Vessey sought a permanent agreement on the MIA issue. He carried a letter from Reagan asking for SRV cooperation for a resolution of the status of American servicemen and civilians who might still be living in Vietnam. The president held out the hope that Vietnamese cooperation on the status of MIAs would "finally put the war behind us by resolving issues which are clearly humanitarian in nature."[37]

Vessey stressed from the start of the meeting with Vietnam's foreign minister Nguyen Co Thach that he had a narrower view of humanitarian issues than did the Vietnamese. For the United States, humanitarian meant agreement on ways to look for MIAs, reunification of families under the Orderly Departure Program, and improvement of the conditions for Amerasian children living in Vietnam. The Vietnamese reminded him of their own bitter legacy from the war—the orphans, the missing, the bombed-out schools and hospitals. Vessey expressed little sympathy, towing the line that the United States "could not and would not attempt to solve Vietnam's problems stemming from the war." He had not come to Hanoi, he said, to start the process of resuming diplomatic relations. The political sticking point between the United States and Vietnam remained the continuing Vietnamese military occupation of eastern Cambodia. "Absent a Vietnamese withdrawal from Cambodia," Vessey told Thach, "there can be no progress toward normalization of diplomatic and trade relations, nor any economic aid." He left it unclear whether the United States would open diplomatic relations under any circumstances, but the Vietnamese understood him to mean that *with* a resolution of the Cambodian impasse, the United States was willing to move forward on trade, diplomatic relations, and even, most astonishingly, economic assistance.[38]

As a result, Thach and Vessey signed an agreement calling for resumption of U.S.-Vietnamese cooperation on searching for MIAs. The Vietnamese agreed to respond quickly and fully to American questions about "discrepancy cases"—the dozens of men who were seen alive after their capture, but did not return with the other POWs in March 1973. For its part, the United States agreed to train Vietnamese participants in joint search and excavation teams and provide more trucks and heavy earth-moving equipment to help with the excavation. It also made some limited gestures toward Vietnam's humanitarian needs, allowing non-governmental humanitarian organizations to provide medical devices—such as prosthetics, crutches, and canes—to war-wounded Vietnamese.[39]

In the aftermath of the Vessey mission the State Department sent a three-member team to Vietnam to survey the needs of the disabled. The American delegation—a Georgia orthopedic surgeon, a wounded Vietnam veteran working for the Veterans Administration (VA), and a representative of non-governmental organizations—met with Vietnamese representatives from the ministries of foreign affairs, health and labor, invalid, and social affairs. The Vietnamese estimated that approximately three hundred thousand had permanent disabilities, leaving them unable to work and dependent upon the government. Of these, approximately sixty thousand were amputees who needed some sort of prosthetic devices and rehabilitation. Also among the amputees were fifteen thousand children between the ages of seven and fifteen years. Many of these had lost limbs by stepping on land mines after the war ended. About thirty thousand Vietnamese needed wheelchairs. Many of these people had cerebral palsy, polio, or spinal-cord injuries. The American investigators also looked into the state of rehabilitative medicine in Vietnam.

The Vietnamese told the Americans that they operated two national prosthetic and rehabilitation centers, one in the North at Son Tay and one in the South at Ho Chi Minh City. The Vietnamese judged the Northern center at Son Tay better, but the Americans did not note much difference between the two, only that the equipment at both locations was about fifteen years old. The team concluded that the Vietnamese prosthetic industry was "outdated in equipment and materials and incomplete in technical skills." Technicians from the German Democratic Republic provided up-to-date help in fitting prosthetics, but everything else about the Vietnamese rehabilitation program needed improvement. Overall, the Americans found "low productivity, uneven quality and a general inability to meet the needs of the Vietnamese amputee."

Transportation problems within Vietnam severely limited the availability of devices for amputees. Patients had to get themselves to the rehabilitation centers. The Son Tay center was approximately two hours by car over very rough roads from the major population center of Hanoi. The Vietnamese government had set aside land near Hanoi where the rehabilitation center could be relocated, and the Americans thought that relocation assistance would be a good use of limited non-governmental organization (NGO) funds. The American team pointed out the short supplies of plastic, aluminum, steel, wood, and leather, the various raw materials the Vietnamese used to manufacture prosthetics, leg braces, and wheelchairs. The Americans thought that NGOs could provide X-ray film, antibiotics, and polio vaccines as well as sponsor the visits of short-term medical specialists—orthopedic surgeons, physical therapists, and prosthetists. Funds could also bring Vietnamese professionals for training in the United States, Canada, Europe, or Australia and be used to educate them at home through courses, videos, library materials, and other training aids.[40]

The Vessey mission marked a major turning point in U.S. relations with Vietnam, since it dealt with concrete practicalities. In its second term, the Reagan administration wanted a resolution of outstanding issues, not new ways to confront Vietnam. As the United States and Vietnam grew closer, Congressional conservatives became more vociferous in their opposition to better relations, and Vessey and the State Department walked a careful line between reconciliation with Vietnam and hostile members of Congress. Vessey told Congress that he did not know if Americans were being held in Vietnam against their will. He said that strong evidence existed that some had been alive at the end of the war. He repeated the statements from high Vietnamese officials that they held no Americans. Robert Lagomarsino, a conservative Republican Representative from California, seemed incredulous. "Why are Vietnamese assurances any more credible or trustworthy today," he demanded of Vessey, "than they were two years ago?" Vessey replied that the Vietnamese now wanted better relations with the United States. The embargo had taken its toll, and Vietnamese government officials finally understood that the United States would not provide economic aid. The Vietnamese leaders, Vessey said, "can see that their previous course of action has gotten them nothing. Their country is very poor; the economy is in bad shape; it doesn't look like it is going to get any better; they have tied themselves to the Soviets."

According to Vessey, the Vietnamese government realized that "their presence in Cambodia has brought them into disrepute with all their neighbors and the General Assembly of the United Nations."[41] David Lambertson, the deputy assistant secretary of state for East Asian and Pacific Affairs, asserted that the embargo on trade with Vietnam would remain in place as long as Vietnamese troops remained in Cambodia. There also was a subtle shift in U.S. policy regarding normalization of relations with Vietnam. Lambertson said "we *will* move toward normalization only in the context of a settlement of the Cambodian problem" (emphasis added). Lambertson gleefully observed that the Association of Southeast Asian Nations (ASEAN) nations had introduced a resolution in the UN General Assembly calling for the Cambodian people to "choose their own government without outside coercion."[42]

Some Congressional critics suspected a plot to open diplomatic relations and be excessively conciliatory toward Vietnam. Representative Chester Atkins, a Massachusetts Democrat, challenged Vessey, "as a result of your mission, we have made good progress . . . on the carrot side. It seems, though, that increasingly there is less and less of a stick of international isolation of Vietnam." Atkins objected that no U.S. ally had officially endorsed the trade embargo of Vietnam. Japan had extended $195 million in credits at very favorable terms to Vietnam. Atkins believed that "if the Japanese continue to increase their levels of trade with Vietnam . . . it will diminish any particular pressures that the Vietnamese feel to be forthcoming on the POW/MIA issue."[43] Peter Kostmayer, a Pennsylvania Republican, objected that the United States no longer could maintain the diplomatic and economic isolation of Vietnam. He noted that several ASEAN nations had broken with the United States. Singapore traded with Vietnam. Singapore, Thailand, and the Philippines had diplomatic relations with the SRV. Kostmayer lectured Lambertson that he had "trouble with your telling the committee here that the nations there believe in isolating Vietnam in terms of diplomacy and trade when three have diplomatic relations and one has substantial trade."[44]

Another congressman, Florida Republican Michael Bilirakis, stated the obvious: "Aren't we ultimately going to renew relations with the Vietnamese? We do with everybody." Bilirakis scoffed, "we have done it with enemies a lot worse in terms of some of the things that they have done to mankind and we are not going to do it with Vietnamese ultimately? Of course we are." Vessey conceded the point and said it was time for both sides to move beyond angry recriminations of who had done what to whom during the war. "Neither we nor the Vietnamese can relive history," he said. Both the Americans and the Vietnamese acknowledged the present reality: Vietnam was poor and wanted an end to the embargo. American businesses worried about competitors from allied countries jumping into a market barred to the United States. The U.S. government was not going to provide economic assistance at this point to Vietnam, but it would support relief efforts by NGOs. The Vietnamese understood that normalization would not come before Vietnamese forces withdrew from Cambodia and told Vessey "[we] will be out of Cambodia in 1990." For Bilirakis and several other angry congressional MIA advocates the administration's emphasis on a Vietnamese withdrawal from Cambodia diminished the importance of the fate of American MIAs. "Aren't our men . . . —some of whom are still there—as important to us as Cambodia? I should think so," Bilirakis said.[45]

In 1987 the National League of Families became a full-fledged partner of the Reagan administration. Its director, Ann Mills Griffith, had become one of the fiercest critics of what NSC staff member Childress derisively referred to as "the Rambo faction in Congress."[46] She reported to Congress on her visit to Vietnam with Vessey and denounced New Hampshire Republican Representative Bob Smith's efforts to force the administration to release intelligence information about sightings of live Americans in Vietnam. She concluded that Smith's call for information "appears aimed at generating domestic pressure against our own government, rather than gaining the release of Americans live or dead." In her view, the one-million-dollar reward offered by former Representative Billy Hendon "only sets us back." The offer of rewards generates "false reporting, encourages extortion schemes, and causes potential sources to withhold information from the U.S. government in the hope of obtaining private compensation."[47] Frank McCloskey, an Indiana Republican, interrupted Griffith to accuse her of slandering former Congressman Hendon. Solarz rushed to her defense and pointedly asked the Department of Justice to investigate whether former Congressman Hendon had engaged in a scam or mail fraud. Although John Rowland, a Connecticut Republican, demanded that Solarz retract his comments about mail fraud or possible scams, the chairman repeated that Hendon might indeed have conducted a fraud.[48]

No one expressed more fury at the possible restoration of diplomatic relations with Vietnam than California Republican Representative Robert K. Dornan, a decorated Korean War veteran who represented Orange County, the epicenter of the Reagan revolution. Dornan promised that a live American POW would come home from Vietnam. His face would be on the cover of *Time, Life, Newsweek, People, The National Review, The New Republic, U.S. News,* and "every other magazine in the world." When that man came home he was "going to shake Billy Hendon's hand. I swear to God he will, and he's going to say, 'Thanks, Billy.'" Dornan went on like this for twenty minutes before Solarz's subcommittee, accusing administrations from 1973 to 1987 of concealing knowledge of Americans left behind in Vietnam and Laos. He recounted the history of the months before the signing of the Paris Accords in January 1973. Talking faster and faster, he shouted that the United States had won the war in January 1973. "We had established total air supremacy, not superiority, supremacy, not a damn MiG was in the air." And then "[u]nder Nixon's orders, Kissinger, Bud McFarlane . . . Philip Habib . . . signed away

our men." Dornan said that Solarz held the key to exposing this terrible conspiracy. "I am begging you, Steve, subpoena Richard Nixon, subpoena Henry
Kissinger, get Bud McFarlane in here to whine like he has done before other
committees and flap his eyes at us." Solarz had never heard anything like this,
even from Dornan. He dryly observed, "This is really the first time in all the
years we have worked on this issue, that you have put this particular proposal
before me."[49]

The "Rambo faction" continued to make life difficult for the Reagan administration. In March 1988 Dornan called Childress to demand a meeting
with National Security Adviser Colin L. Powell. Childress told Powell that
Dornan had spoken "in apocalyptic terms" about an "unnamed" NSC staffer
whom Dornan was certain was discouraging the Vietnamese from accepting
congressional visits. The congressman was so furious that he was "going to
take this 'all the way,'" and publicly denounce the White House for turning its
back on MIAs. Dornan introduced a congressional resolution condemning
Vietnam for continuing to imprison officials of the defunct South Vietnamese
government. Childress, concerned that Dornan could damage opportunities
for obtaining more information from Vietnam about MIAs, wanted the White
House to distance itself from the flamboyant congressman. Childress reminded
Powell that Dornan had made the seemingly absurd suggestion that Solarz
subpoena Nixon, Kissinger, and McFarlane to confess to having left Americans behind in Vietnam. Powell should know, Childress said, that Dornan had
"made outrageous statements about our efforts." In addition, Childress alerted
Powell that Congressmen Frank McClosky, Robert Smith, and John Rowland
acted as spokesmen for the thoroughly discredited Billy Hendon.

In February 1988 Smith called Childress "to bad mouth the League [of
Families]." He also met the Cambodian ambassador in Hanoi to obtain MIA
information, setting off "alarm bells in ASEAN." Childress wanted Powell to
work with Congressman Solarz to block Dornan's resolution denouncing Vietnam for keeping former officials of the South Vietnamese government in reeducation camps. Childress commented that the introduction of the resolution
"could not come at a worse time, since the Vietnamese have recently released
another . . . contingent into society." For years Childress had encouraged the
Vietnamese to release reeducation camp detainees. In 1985 he had delivered a
list of people the United States wanted freed to Hanoi. Finally, in 1988 the
Vietnamese released some of the people on that list.[50]

When Powell met with Dornan he told him that congressional delegations
to Hanoi from the Rambo faction actually set back the cause of gaining information about the fate of men listed as MIA. Despite Dornan's, Smith's, and
the other militants' hostility to the Communist authorities in Vietnam, Powell
insisted that Hanoi actually gained advantages by hosting any sort of critic of
the U.S. government. "The Vietnamese have different messages for different
people," Powell said, explaining how they promised cooperation to official

representatives like Vessey and then hinted to Smith and McCloskey that Vessey, the State Department, and the NSC really had no interest in finding MIAs; they just wanted to end the controversy. Dornan countered that according to the Vietnamese, Childress had attempted to block visas for the visiting congressional delegation. "In that regard," Powell said, "nothing has changed about their attempts to divide Americans." The Rambo faction ran the danger of being used by the Vietnamese.[51]

Powell told Dornan that visits by McCloskey and Smith to Hanoi encouraged Vietnam "to attempt the same domestic strategies they used during the war" when they had welcomed visitors like antiwar activist Jane Fonda as a way of criticizing the actions of the American government. Likening Bob Dornan and his friends to Jane Fonda and other antiwar activists was guaranteed to make the mercurial congressman explode. Dornan did explode, denouncing the NSC and the State Department as dupes of Hanoi. Powell stressed to Dornan that the process set in motion by Vessey's mission had borne fruit. In the wake of Vessey's mission the United States and Vietnam reached a new agreement in 1987 over the fate of Amerasian children. Since 1982 forty-five hundred of them and seven thousand members of their families had left Vietnam for the United States. Approximately seventy-five hundred Amerasian children remained in Vietnam. The Vessey mission put the Orderly Departure Program back on track. In September 1987 the Vietnamese agreed to a U.S. proposal that American consular officials in Saigon would interview prospective Amerasian applicants for admission to the United States. The following month officials taken from the American embassy in Bangkok began to administer the program. The Amerasians approved for departure from Vietnam were admitted to the United States as immigrants but were eligible for benefits as refugees. Once the consular officials approved their applications, the Vietnamese and their families left for Thailand where they spent about twelve days in final processing, and then moved to the Refugee Processing Center in the Philippines, where they spent six months learning English and receiving instruction in American culture.[52]

Between Vessey's visit to Vietnam in August 1987 and February 1988, the Vietnamese had released more remains of U.S. service personnel than in the previous year. The most sensitive issue for the Vietnamese was the American insistence that Vietnam release more people interned in reeducation camps. There too the first progress in years had occurred. In effect, Powell told Dornan to be quiet, back off, and let the White House handle the issue. He told the Congressman that "we are dealing with one of the most difficult regimes in the world and those that face them regularly need backing" not constant sniping from the backbenches.[53]

Dornan and the other members of the Congressional Rambo faction appeared to be relics of a bygone era as the Cold War faded in the last six months of the Reagan administration. In June 1988 thousands of young Russians gave the American president an enthusiastic welcome in Moscow. Reagan and Soviet President Mikhail Gorbachev formed a fast friendship. When reporters asked Reagan why he was now so enthusiastic about the Soviet leadership after years of denouncing them as "the focus of evil in the modern world," he replied, "they've changed." If the Soviet Union was no longer the nemesis it had been earlier in the Reagan administration, then the United States could become friendlier with Vietnam, Moscow's ally. In its last months in office, the Reagan administration sought to normalize relations with Vietnam. Given that Vietnamese forces remained in Cambodia, the United States would not restore diplomatic relations. But now that there was some resolution of MIA cases, the Reagan administration could ratchet down the rhetoric over Vietnam.

Still, the issue of MIAs remained a stumbling block. The National League of Families held its annual meeting in Washington in July, and White House officials debated whether Reagan should give a formal address. Some staff members wanted Reagan to stay away from the League's gathering, because there was nothing new to report. They feared that a high-profile speech by Reagan would only set off alarms from the Rambo faction. On the other hand, Childress identified the League as "our staunchest supporter." He wanted Reagan to appear and receive the League's enthusiastic endorsement. Vice President George Bush supported the idea of a formal address before the League. National Security Adviser Powell also advised Reagan to address the League and speak of progress toward reconciliation with Vietnam. Even if Massachusetts Governor Michael Dukakis, the Democratic presidential candidate, prevailed in the fall election, Powell believed it would be a good idea to identify a bipartisan consensus over U.S. policy toward Vietnam.[54]

Following Childress's and Bush's recommendation, Reagan in his speech at the NLF meeting on July 29 stressed how far the administration had come since 1981. The United States had more than doubled the number of people working on MIA issues at the Defense Intelligence Agency in Washington, the Joint Casualty Resolution Center, and the Central Identification Laboratory in Hawaii. Improvements had occurred on the ground in Vietnam and Laos. More remains of U.S. servicemen had come back than in the five years after the war. For the first time the Vietnamese government had worked to resolve "discrepancy" and "died in captivity cases." High-level meetings between U.S. and Vietnamese officials now occurred routinely. Over one hundred people in the Defense and State Departments and the intelligence agencies now worked full time on MIA issues. He cited the progress made by the Vessey mission.

Reagan's speech to the League signaled to Vietnam that the United States would go as far toward normalization as Hanoi wanted. "The ultimate burden for resolution" of the outstanding issues between the United States and Vietnam rested with the Vietnamese authorities, Reagan said. He reiterated the remarks he had made about the Vietnam War when he ran against Jimmy Carter in 1980. "Who can still question that America's youth fought a noble battle for freedom?" in Vietnam, he asked. He repeated that the United States would normalize relations with Vietnam "only in the context of a political settlement in Cambodia." But normalization would come. If the United States and Vietnam resolved their remaining MIA issues, the two countries could once more exchange ambassadors.[55] Reagan's Vietnam policy now rested squarely in the center of American politics. Most Democrats supported it, and only a small conservative fringe denounced the Reagan administration as betraying the cause of MIAs. The path to normalization was clear, but reconciliation still lay years ahead.

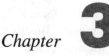

Chapter **3**

* * * * * * * * * * *

Normalization, 1989–2000

　　The United States and Vietnam remained wary rivals as the new administration of George Bush took office and pledged to move beyond the rancor that had divided Americans over Vietnam. During his inaugural address the president noted that the war in Vietnam had begun twenty-five years before, and the time had come to set aside the divisions of the war years. "My friends," he said, "the final lesson of Vietnam is this: no great nation can long be sundered by a memory."[1] During Bush's presidency, the international environment underwent one of the most profound changes in the twentieth century as both the Cold War and the Soviet Union ended. In the 1990s the estrangement between the United States and Vietnam was increasingly seen as an anomalous relic of a bygone era, and the two countries finally reestablished diplomatic relations.

　　Bush tried to put the angry bitterness of the Vietnam War behind his fellow citizens by developing a new consensus on America's role in the world. The tumultuous revolutions throughout the Communist world preoccupied the United States in 1989 and 1990. The Bush administration eventually worked to improve relations between the United States and Vietnam, but it did not reach an agreement normalizing relations. It seemed poised to open diplomatic relations in a second term, but voters turned against Bush in 1992.

Bush's background as the American representative to China, ambassador to the United Nations, and director of Central Intelligence placed him squarely in the center of the foreign policy establishment.[2] He remembered in his Inaugural Address the anger over Vietnam that had frustrated the foreign policy initiatives of presidents from Lyndon Johnson through Ronald Reagan. Still, despite Reagan's advances at reconciliation with Vietnam, the new Bush administration moved more slowly to improve relations with the SRV than might have been expected. Keith Richburg, a *Washington Post* journalist specializing in Asian affairs, characterized the administration as "inching slowly, if reluctantly, toward the formulation of a new U.S. policy toward Vietnam."[3]

Several factors inhibited the Bush administration from quickly engaging with the SRV. Bush employed a more formal, less personal, and less freewheeling style than had Reagan, and Bush was reluctant to move anywhere in the world before his administration had developed a full strategic agenda. In 1989 and 1990 revolutions swept aside Communist regimes, and the Bush administration was preoccupied with managing the transition from Communism to capitalism in Eastern Europe.[4] Asian issues generally, and Southeast Asia in particular, receded. Insofar as the Bush administration paid attention to Asia in its first two years, it focused on China. In the spring of 1989, the same revolutionary, anticommunist enthusiasm that swept across Eastern Europe emerged in China. Thousands of students rallied for democracy in Tiananmen Square. It appeared as if the Chinese, like Eastern Europeans, would overturn its Communist party. Instead, the People's Liberation Army fired on the tent city on the night of June 3-4, killing hundreds and wounding thousands of the protesters. The shock waves from the attack reverberated around the world, but the Bush administration reacted with extreme caution. Bush sent national security adviser Brent Scowcroft on a secret mission to Beijing to reassure China's leaders that the United States remained committed to cooperation. For the time being, the United States chose not to alarm the Chinese by improving relations with Vietnam.[5]

Instead, the United States continued the incremental steps of the Vessey mission.[6] After Bush reappointed him Special Emissary to Vietnam, General John Vessey traveled to Hanoi in October 1989 to negotiate Vietnam's agreement to U.S. access to the SRV's archives. American experts on the MIA issues believed that documents existed telling the story of what happened when U.S. aircraft crashed over North Vietnamese territory during the war. They were less certain that archival material could shed light on the fate of men who were captured alive but were not repatriated at the end of the war. Access to the archives might resolve serious lingering doubts about the fate of Americans in Vietnam. The SRV also agreed to additional U.S. interviews with eyewitnesses of crash sites. Within a few weeks, though, the United States complained that Hanoi had not implemented its promises of greater cooperation. In December Deputy Assistant Secretary of State David Lambertson met in New York with Vietnam's U.N. ambassador Trinh Van Linh. The U.S. representative rehearsed a familiar list of grievances against Vietnam for delaying its cooperation. Linh kept to his script too, repeating Vietnam's own needs for humanitarian assistance and his nation's promise to cooperate with the United States in looking for remains.[7]

Still, Vietnam was not a high priority for the Bush administration, which was preoccupied in 1990 and 1991 with other pressing foreign policy issues. In the first half of 1990 the United States concentrated on bolstering the authority of Soviet President Mikhail Gorbachev. From August 1990 through February 1991 Bush created and nurtured an international coalition to expel Iraq from Kuwait. In the aftermath of the Gulf War, the United States helped organize an international conference in Madrid to address the long-running conflict between Israel, its Arab neighbors, and the Palestinians.

As Soviet power waned in Eastern Europe, the American public considered foreign affairs to be less important than they had been at the height of the Cold War. As Frederick Z. Brown, a former Foreign Service officer and prominent advocate of normalization of relations with Vietnam, observed, "Inevitably, foreign affairs crises of the moment preempt long-term policy, and Indochina is not a crisis but a humiliation better forgotten." Brown argued for engagement with Vietnam despite the public's desire to forget about the war. He wrote that "with a relatively small investment of political and economic resources and through imaginative diplomacy, U.S. strategic interests in the region can be promoted."[8]

In this changed environment, efforts to improve relations with Vietnam proceeded slowly. In September 1990 Vessey and Assistant Secretary of State Richard Solomon met with Vietnam's Vice Foreign Minister Le Mai and pressed for greater cooperation. The Americans held out the carrot of diplomatic recognition once the final Vietnamese forces left Cambodia, a process that was well underway. They also demanded implementation of Vietnam's promises to open its archives. Secretary of State James A. Baker III followed up a few weeks later with a meeting in New York with Foreign Minister Nguyen Co Thach. Baker was well aware that relations improved between the United States and the Soviet Union after Moscow pulled its troops from Eastern Europe and the GDR, and the secretary of state informed Thach that the MIA issues was the only remaining obstacle before the United States and Vietnam opened relations. Thach, the leading proponent within the Vietnamese government of improved relations with the United States, felt a surge of optimism when he heard Baker's hint of normalization.[9]

In October Thach became the first Vietnamese foreign minister to visit Washington since 1975. In talks there Vessey raised the most detailed questions about American access to archival information. Thach agreed to the creation of a joint research "information-seeking" team to locate and make available Vietnamese historical documents about American MIAs. Vessey also repeated a proposal he had made in 1988 for the opening of an American office in Hanoi dedicated to resolving MIA cases. Thach had long favored the creation of such an office, anticipating that it would eventually become the U.S. embassy in Hanoi. Thach told Vessey and several members of Congress that he personally favored the opening of a U.S. MIA office in Hanoi as soon as possible. Vessey sensed some desperation for normalization on Thach's part. The general insisted that the office could open only if there was enough work in the archives to keep the American team busy. Although Thach was willing, the rest of the Vietnamese government was not. They balked at giving officials of their old adversary free access to their military archives. In late 1990 the Vietnamese government told the United States that free American access to the Vietnamese archives would compromise Vietnam's national security. Instead, they would allow Vietnamese researchers to share their research notes with Americans, an offer Vessey rejected as not providing firsthand access. Nevertheless, Vietnam did return seventeen sets of remains identified as Americans in 1990.[10]

The United States and the SRV stepped up the pace of their contacts during 1991. In April Arizona Republican Senator John McCain, a former POW, visited Hanoi for the first time since his release in 1973. McCain came with a new offer from the Bush administration for bilateral cooperation leading in the near future to diplomatic relations. The American proposal soon became known as a Road Map to normalization. The United States proposed a four-phase plan for restoration of diplomatic relations. Washington renewed its demands that Vietnam leave Cambodia, and the Vietnamese completed the withdrawal in late 1991. The Road Map also insisted on Vietnam opening its archives to full American investigation. Following these steps the United States would open an office in Hanoi, lift the ban on its citizens' travel to Vietnam, and ultimately, end the U.S. trade embargo on Vietnam. Once trade relations resumed, the United States planned to take another look at Vietnamese efforts at accounting for the missing in action. If the United States was satisfied with Vietnam's cooperation in accounting, the United States and the SRV would once again exchange ambassadors.[11]

Hanoi both welcomed and resented the Road Map. On the one hand, it represented the first formal promise of opening diplomatic relations from the United States. Vietnam's economic and political position deteriorated with the end of the Cold War. The collapse of the Soviet Union removed Vietnam's major source of foreign economic assistance. Noncommunist states of Southeast Asia such as Thailand, Malaysia, Indonesia, and Singapore boomed while Vietnam stagnated. Politically too, the demise of the Soviet Union left Vietnam exposed. In the 1980s the Soviet Navy leased the former U.S. base at Cam Rahn Bay, and Soviet engineers built bridges, roads, and governments buildings throughout Vietnam. In the fifteen years after the end of the war the East German health ministry operated the major rehabilitation facilities in

Vietnam. The GDR also welcomed tens of thousands of Vietnamese guest workers. Now this assistance was gone, as the death of the Soviet Union and the incorporation of the GDR into the Federal Republic of Germany dried up millions of dollars worth of economic assistance to Vietnam. Moscow had supported Vietnam's positions against China and Cambodia. Now, with the Soviet Union defunct, Vietnam's leaders worried about facing China alone. Yet Vietnam considered the tone of the Road Map insulting. It put the onus of better relations on Hanoi's cooperation in finding MIAs. Under Washington's plan, the United States would decide if Hanoi had met the standards set by Washington. Hanoi continued to press its own needs for humanitarian assistance.[12]

Whatever affronts Vietnam's leadership took at the American conditions for normalization, Foreign Minister Thach believed that further cooperation with the Americans was vital. When Vessey returned to Hanoi in April 1991, he and Thach agreed on the creation of a U.S. POW/MIA office in Hanoi. The American military officers who staffed the Joint Task Force–Full Accounting Office soon called it the Ranch. The Americans hoped to explore the archives looking for reports of missing servicemen. Vietnam did not, however, permit the unrestricted access to the archives the United States long had sought. Thach himself lost a power struggle. In July he was dropped from the Politburo and lost his post as foreign minister to Nguyen Manh Cam. At the same time Vo Van Kiet became prime minister. Both Cam and Kiet wanted better relations with the United States. For its part, the Bush administration recognized the divisions within the Vietnamese Workers Party. To bolster the position of those like Prime Minister Kiet and Foreign Minister Cam who sought improved relations with Washington, the United States announced a grant of $1.3 million for rehabilitation services for war disabled. In October Secretary of State Baker took another historic step, praising Vietnam for supporting the United Nations' peace plan for Cambodia. In return the United States lifted its ban on travel by U.S. citizens to Vietnam. Assistant Secretary of State Richard H. Solomon met Vice Foreign Minister Le Mai in November 1991. Solomon repeated that the United States was committed to normalization with Vietnam once Hanoi completed its withdrawal from Cambodia and resolved remaining POW/MIA issues.[13]

The time seemed ripe for addressing Vietnam as an economic as well as a political issue. Members of Congress pressed the administration to lift the embargo, but as *Congressional Quarterly* observed in April 1991, "the administration is far from ready to treat Vietnam as just another nation," and it moved very slowly.[14] When Vessey returned to Vietnam in January 1992, the Vietnamese were exasperated with his repeated demands to open their archives. His delegation met with a variety of Vietnamese officials, all of whom seemed to refer to the same set of talking points. They considered the American insistence on unlimited access to the archives to be an invasion of Vietnam's sovereignty.

Yet Vietnamese attitudes softened noticeably two months later when Assistant Secretary of State for Far Eastern Affairs Richard Solomon led another high-level U.S. delegation to Vietnam. This time Vietnam accepted U.S. proposals for joint teams to investigate reports of live sightings of Americans in Vietnam. Hanoi also granted more access to their military archives.

Congress emerged as an important participant in setting policy toward Vietnam in 1992. The Senate Select Committee on POW/MIA Affairs chaired by Massachusetts Democratic Senator John Kerry, a Vietnam veteran, sent its own delegation to Vietnam in April. Kerry led a team of five senators, including the committee's vice chair, New Hampshire Republican Bob Smith, who next to California's Robert Dornan was the most outspoken member of the congressional Rambo faction; Iowa Republican Charles Grassley; and Virginia Democrat Charles Robb and Republican Hank Brown of Colorado, both Vietnam War veterans. The group met with the former number two Soviet diplomat in Hanoi. He reported that in 1985 Mikhail Gorbachev had ordered the ninety-five hundred Soviet advisers in Vietnam to look for signs of living Americans then in Vietnam. They did not find any.

The high point of the visit to Hanoi was the delegation's meeting with Communist Party General Secretary Do Muoi, another Vietnamese official committed to opening diplomatic relations with the United States. On three separate occasions Muoi asked the visiting senators exactly what the SRV needed to do in order to open diplomatic relations. The U.S. group repeated the demand for full physical access throughout Vietnam to sites where MIA remains might be found. Muoi made the significant concession of allowing the U.S. investigative teams to travel to Vietnamese territory bordering Laos. Many of the reports of Americans remaining in Southeast Asia after the war had come from Laos. Muoi repeated that no American prisoners had remained in his country after the war. For years those critical of Vietnam's cooperation with the search for the missing had claimed that Vietnamese authorities had cruelly kept the bodies of Americans and returned them only intermittently. In response, Muoi denied that his government had ever "warehoused" the remains of Americans after the war. He balked at the American demand to travel freely about the Vietnamese countryside in U.S.-built helicopters, worried that the sights and sounds of American military helicopters flying over the countryside would induce flashbacks among traumatized Vietnamese peasants.

After the senators met with officials in Hanoi, they investigated sites across Vietnam. They visited Thanh Liet prison, about twenty kilometers south of Hanoi, where the camp commander showed them the areas of the camp in which Americans had been held during the war, but refused them free access to the entire prison. The senators complained to their Vietnamese handlers, who telephoned higher officials at the foreign and interior ministries. Understanding what was at stake with the congressional delegation, officials in Hanoi ordered the camp commander to let the senators look at whatever they wanted at the prison. They found nothing suggesting that any American POWs had been at Thanh Liet since 1973. The senators left with the impression that their visit to Thanh Liet set a precedent for subsequent short-notice inspections at other sites.

The delegation then split up and fanned out across the countryside. Senators Kerry and Smith, two men who barely spoke to one another because Smith claimed that Vietnam held MIAs and Kerry did not believe it, flew by Russian-made helicopter to three separate sensitive areas in the South. They made short-notice visits to an active Vietnamese naval base at Phu Quoc; Dong Tam, the former headquarters of the U.S. 9th Infantry Division; and the former U.S. Cobra helicopter base at Can Tho. The surprise visits irritated the Vietnamese officers at these facilities, but they quickly received word from Hanoi how important it was to accommodate the Americans visitors, and they showed them what they wanted to see. At none of the installations did Kerry or Smith see anything indicating that Americans had been there after 1975. Senator Brown flew from Hanoi to Da Nang where he met with the former Soviet KGB station chief at the Russian consulate. The chief had been in Vietnam since 1972 and said he had from time to time heard reports of Americans living in Vietnam after 1975, but he was certain that none of them had ever been prisoners. All of the reports referred to people with European features living freely in Vietnam.[15]

Even while the Kerry delegation traveled throughout Vietnam in April 1991, the Bush administration took the next step along the Road Map to normalization. Among its concessions, it allowed the sale to Vietnam of more American products for health, safety, and nutritional needs. It permitted non-governmental and non-profit relief organizations to work freely in Vietnam and allowed direct phone contacts between the United States and Vietnam. Most significantly of all, the U.S. government permitted Vietnamese Americans to wire money directly to relatives in Vietnam.

Vietnamese on both sides of the Pacific rejoiced at the arrival of wire transfers. For more than a decade Vietnamese Americans had mailed cash—mostly fifty and hundred dollar bills—to their loved ones in Vietnam. Vietnamese authorities opened the mail, and very little of the money attached to letters ever reached its intended recipients. Vietnamese Americans learned quickly to hide their gifts home, concealing bills in books, dolls, jars, food, or anything else that might elude inspection. None of it worked. Before the United States government lifted restrictions on direct transfer of funds to Vietnam, the only way Vietnamese Americans could be sure that their money would reach their relatives was to personally deliver it.[16]

Progress in U.S. relations with Vietnam was entangled in the presidential election campaign in 1992. The Bush administration planned to proceed with normalization after it was safely reelected. However, securing a majority of the votes turned out to be far more difficult than the Bush team expected. The entry of Texas billionaire Ross Perot in the presidential race sharply cut in to Bush's support. At one point in late June 1992 Perot actually led in public opinion polls. Perot particularly attacked Bush on opening relations with Vietnam. He claimed that Bush as CIA director had suppressed valid evidence that Americans had been left behind in Vietnam. He also charged that the Bush administration had blithely accepted Vietnamese assurances that it held no living Americans. Perot implied that the Bush administration simply did not care. "Can't we all agree," he asked veterans groups, "that we'll never leave Americans behind again?" The audiences roared their approval of his suggestions that the United States had done just that after Vietnam.[17]

Meanwhile, in July Frances Zwenig, the staff director of the Senate Select Committee on POWs/MIAs, met Vietnamese and Laotian government officials in Southeast Asia. In her meeting with Vietnamese Vice Foreign Minister Le Mai, he agreed to speed up access to archives and scenes of live sightings. For the first time an American civilian employee of the Defense Department had unfettered access to the Vietnamese archives. The availability of thousands of pages of Vietnamese military records prompted Acting Secretary of State Lawrence Eagleburger to invite a Vietnamese delegation to Washington in October. Eagleburger and Secretary of Defense Dick Cheney hosted Vietnam's Foreign Minister Nguyen Manh Cam and Le Bang, the director of the Foreign Ministry's America's Department, on October 8. At the meeting the United States requested a formal agreement permitting continuing access to Vietnam's archives. The Vietnamese representatives made no commitment on archival access, but they invited Vessey to return to Vietnam. When the general, accompanied by Senator McCain, did so on October 17, the Vietnamese quickly agreed to the American terms. Vessey and McCain hailed the agreement as a breakthrough. President Bush praised the agreement at a Rose Garden ceremony. "Today, finally," he said, "I am convinced that we can begin writing the last chapter of the Vietnam War."[18]

Despite the appearance of progress toward normalization of relations with Vietnam, the Bush administration had another reason to adopt a tough stance toward Vietnam during the 1992 election campaign. Bush used the memory of Vietnam to attack the record of his Democratic opponent, Arkansas Governor Bill Clinton, contrasting his heroic record as a Navy aviator during World War II with Clinton's avoidance of military service during the Vietnam War. Clinton's own Democratic Party rivals first referred to his efforts to avoid induction into the armed forces during the Vietnam War. Nebraska Senator Bob Kerrey, who won a Congressional Medal of Honor for his wartime service, said that Clinton would "open up like a boiled peanut" when the facts were known about his draft record.

In 1969 Clinton was studying at Oxford University as a Rhodes Scholar. He applied for membership in the Arkansas National Guard to continue his studies. There was nothing unusual about Clinton's effort; many other young men sought to avoid service in Vietnam by enlisting in other branches of the armed services. But Clinton made matters difficult for himself by writing a long, revealing letter to the commander of the Arkansas National Guard, telling him, "I loathe the military, and all it stands for." He wanted a guard commission so he could stay at Oxford and "maintain my political viability." Clinton was admitted to the guard, with a plan to take basic training in the summer of 1970. When the draft lottery took place in December 1969, Clinton had a high draft number and his likelihood of being drafted was low. He then resigned from the guard. When questioned about his draft record, Clinton said he could not recall what he had done in 1969. Thinking that the letter would never see the light of day, Clinton denied having sent it. Days before the March 1992 New Hampshire primary, the *Manchester Union Leader* published the letter.[19]

Clinton faced furious criticism for his evasive responses to questions about his draft record. But he focused doggedly on the poor state of New Hampshire's economy and recovered sufficiently to come in second in the primary. He then went on to win the Democratic Party nomination for president. His success suggested that many voters no longer cared that much about what young men had done during the Vietnam era. Moreover, Clinton's experience with the draft had been similar to many other men. Yet the Bush reelection campaign hammered away that Clinton's resignation from the Arkansas National Guard and his damning comments about the military rendered him unfit to serve as commander in chief. And to keep alive the memory of the emotional battles of the 1960s, the Bush administration froze movement toward ending the embargo against Vietnam or opening diplomatic relations with the SRV.[20]

Much to Bush's surprise, most of the public showed little interest in foreign affairs in general and in Clinton's lack of Vietnam service in particular. Bush lamented a week before the election, "I haven't heard anything about foreign affairs" in the public question-and-answer forums at which Clinton excelled. After Clinton won the election, he declared, "in foreign affairs, we're going to focus like a laser on the economy." It did not appear as if restoration of diplomatic relations with Vietnam would be among his priorities, since he pledged that "there will be no normalization of relations with any nation that is at all suspected of withholding any information on POWs-MIAs."[21]

After the election but before Clinton's inauguration, more senators returned to Vietnam. In mid-November South Dakota Democratic Senator Tom Daschle, another Vietnam veteran, joined committee members Kerry and Brown in meetings with Vietnam's President Le Duc Anh, Foreign Minister Nguyen Manh Cam, and other officials of the defense and foreign ministries. Kerry carried a letter from outgoing President Bush praising Vietnam for the progress it had made in resolving MIA cases and saying that continued cooperation would result in full normalization. The Vietnamese insisted that they had held no Americans against their will after 1973 and that the government held no American remains. They did not deny that individual Vietnamese might have remains of American servicemen and, in the spirit of negotiation, encouraged private citizens to come forward. Ted Schweitzer, the American investigator who had gained access to the Vietnamese archives, believed that a lot of information about missing Americans remained in the hands of individual Vietnamese, and he thought they would be more forthcoming in providing information if they believed that the United States was likely to act more favorably toward Vietnam.[22]

The Vietnamese told the visiting senators that they would continue to grant Schweitzer and other Defense Department researchers access to their archives in Hanoi. They also promised to open two new archival research offices in Da Nang and Ho Chi Minh City. In response to the senators' repeated demands, the Vietnamese also promised to make Vietnamese war veterans available for oral histories to American researchers. In December Vessey testified once more before the Kerry committee. He gleefully reported that the "agreement to get at the war-time archival material puts in place . . . the last bit of procedural machinery" leading to full normalization of relations.[23] Many observers expected that Bush would announce the formal lifting of the embargo before he left office, but he declined to do so. He did take one additional step, though, announcing that American firms could open offices in Vietnam and sign contracts with the Vietnamese pending the formal lifting of the embargo.

Kerry and Smith returned to Hanoi on December 17 and 18. The Vietnamese promised to make available to U.S. investigators "all POW/MIA-related documents, files and other information," including debriefings of U.S. POWs. The Vietnamese government promised amnesty for private Vietnamese citizens who turned in the remains of Americans. Up to this point it had been illegal for private Vietnamese citizens to keep the remains of downed or captured American servicemen, and fear of prosecution may have kept many Vietnamese citizens from cooperating. The Vietnamese government also put the word out that it would permit the families of Americans listed as missing to visit their country and search freely for their relatives' bodies.[24]

The new Clinton administration took additional steps toward economic relations with Vietnam. In early July 1993 the United States dropped its previous objections to other countries' proposals allowing the International Monetary Fund (IMF) to refinance some $140 million in loans owed by Vietnam. The way was now cleared for public and private multilateral lending institutions to help Vietnam build roads, bridges, ports, rail lines, telecommunications links, and other basic infrastructure. Yet the embargo remained in place, shutting out American businesses from making bids. Senator Charles Robb expressed some of the frustrations of American businesses when he complained that "the rationale for purposely not giving United Technologies, Caterpillar, Fluor, Halliburton and others a piece of the action is simply a mystery to me." Alaska Republican Frank Murkowski also believed that commercial interests now should take precedence over continuing to punish Vietnam for any perceived lack of cooperation on MIA issues.

Murkowski believed that more trade and more openness would lead to greater cooperation from the Vietnamese side on MIAs. He told a story about a U.S. businessman who had opened an office in Hanoi in early 1992. At least five different Vietnamese saw the American flag on the door and brought dog tags and other articles they said had come from Americans. They did so because they remembered the United States fondly. Murkowski encouraged the Clinton administration to "give the go-ahead to U.S. businesses to bid on at least those Vietnamese projects that will be funded by loans from the international lending agencies." He thought that maintaining strict restrictions on U.S. businesses "results in the ironic situation of having tax dollars fund our competitors' business ventures in Vietnam." Commercial competition played a key role in the new administration's foreign policy. "If we truly want to compete globally," Murkowski taunted the new Democratic administration, "then the current situation with regard to Vietnam, could prove to be counterproductive."[25]

Vietnam veterans in Congress took the lead in calling for dropping economic restrictions and normalizing relations with the SRV. South Dakota Republican Senator Larry Pressler linked diplomatic and economic issues. He thought improving relations with Vietnam could provide a counterweight to China's influence in Southeast Asia. He complained that "China has her paws on Vietnam and expressed his belief that a close relationship between the United States and Vietnam and other nations bordering China might limit Chinese hegemony in the region. He also thought that Vietnam "will emerge as another of the Asian tigers," states like Thailand, Singapore, Malaysia, Indonesia, and Taiwan whose economies had boomed in the last decade. Give Vietnam five years, Pressler predicted, and it "will be among them." The United States faced stiff competition in the Vietnamese market from France, Japan, and China.[26]

Senator Kerry agreed that the future of U.S. political and economic interests lay in the Pacific Rim. He said that the United States had recently focused too much on problems in the former Soviet Union and Eastern Europe whose difficulties were so intractable that decades might pass before they could be resolved. China, on the other hand, was "of far greater concern to the United States than any other area in the world today." China's fast rate of economic growth combined with its "aspirations which could undermine the security of the ASEAN nations," notably its military presence on the Spratley Islands off the coast of Vietnam, threatened the stability of the region. Kerry argued that the economic ties created by opening relations with Vietnam would benefit the United States, and at the same time would "close the book on the pain and anguish of the war and heal the wounds of the nation and help us to put it behind us once and for all."[27]

Advocates of improved relations with Vietnam argued that U.S. failure to press forward along the Road Map of normalization would make matters worse. Kerry thought that every time the United States held back "we strengthen the hand" of "those in Vietnam who do not want to cooperate with the United States." Vietnamese politics was sharply divided between reformers and hard liners. The former favored opening the Vietnamese economy to market forces and looked to improved relations with the United States. The latter, Kerry said, "would rather stay with China [and] still believe in the original goals of the revolution." Kerry argued that progress on POW issues was threatened more by the continuation of the embargo than it would be by the possibility that the United States would open trade relations with Vietnam. When he went to Vietnam with Senator McCain and Florida Democratic Congressman Douglas "Pete" Peterson, another former POW, Kerry found growing impatience among Vietnamese authorities with the continuation of the embargo. In the Vietnamese view, the Americans had become intransigent over the POW issue, but would become more accommodating soon. The Vietnamese thought that the Americans needed them for commercial reasons. Economics now held the key to the future of Southeast Asia. Vietnam's economy had grown at a 7 percent annual rate in the past several years, far exceeding the nearly flat United States economy in the recession-plagued early 1990s. Vietnam's rate of economic expansion came close to the explosive growth of the five Asian tigers. Japanese, French, Singaporeans, Chinese, and Taiwanese investors had poured $2.6 billion into Vietnam in 1992.

These investments made a noticeable difference in the country, which Kerry reflected on. When he first arrived in April 1991 Vietnam was a poor place with few shops and little to buy. He saw nothing but bicycles or cyclos on the streets. By 1993, in Hanoi he said, "there are mostly motorbikes, motorcycles, cars." He even had seen a Porsche outside the old French-colonial Metropole Hotel. This grand old structure had fallen on hard times in the previous twenty years, but French investors were restoring it to its former colonial-era opulence. He found it intolerable that U.S. businesses could not participate in similar sorts of foreign ventures.[28]

The Vietnamese seemed to have moved beyond what they had called the American War. Kerry thought it now was time for the United States to stop thinking of Vietnam as a war and start thinking of it as a country. He argued that restoration of normal relations with Vietnam would be the best way to honor the Americans who had fought there. Millions of Vietnamese in the South of that country who had supported the Americans also looked forward to seeing the return of the United States, he said. It was not even far-fetched to believe that American forces might again sail in to Cam Ranh Bay, the naval facility the Soviets had taken over after the war. "One oil rig with an American oil company's name on it would have more impact than the entire Seventh Fleet with the respect to China and others in that region." Kerry pleaded for engagement with Vietnam "on behalf of those who gave their lives in Vietnam."[29]

The Clinton administration sent its own delegation to Hanoi in July 1993. Assistant Secretary of State for East Asian Affairs Winston Lord and Herschel Gober, the deputy secretary of Veterans Affairs and a long-time advocate for MIAs, led a team of diplomats, military officers, and representatives of veterans groups. Significantly, the delegation did not include representatives from the National League of Families. The exclusion outraged the group given its warm relations with the previous Republican administrations.[30] The delegation met with Do Muoi, the general secretary of the Communist Party, and several officials of the foreign and defense ministry. For the first time an American delegation met formally with Vietnam's Interior Minister Bui Thien Ngo who was responsible for domestic security. His ministry was in charge of the country's prison system, and he was in the best position to determine if any Americans had ever been held in Vietnamese prisons after 1973.

Lord impressed upon the Vietnamese four areas in which the United States expected progress before full normal relations could be opened. The United States wanted 1) the recovery and repatriation of the remains of U.S. personnel; 2) continued resolution of some ninety-two cases in which there were discrepancies between Americans listed as living after they were shot down and those who returned in 1987; 3) further cooperation in implementing trilateral investigations along the Vietnamese-Lao border; and 4) more access to archives and documents explaining the fate of POWs/MIAs. Lord found it encouraging that the Vietnamese leaders believed all four areas were appropriate. That said, Lord's team reported, "[we] do not expect to make any breakthroughs in discovering large numbers of new remains or documents." The Vietnamese leaders thanked Clinton for lifting the block on Vietnam's access to international lending institutions. "President Clinton has demonstrated goodwill," said General Secretary Do Muoi, "and so will Vietnam." The more reserved Lord replied, "although the assurances from Vietnam's leaders are positive signs, they are merely words." Lord did not simply go to the Vietnamese with more demands. He brought with him the first installment of some three million pages of documents American troops had captured from the Viet Cong and from North Vietnamese forces during the war. He also promised that the State Department would send three consular-level officials to Hanoi to assist American families in obtaining the appropriate travel documents to go to Vietnam to search for their relatives. Their work would free up time for the American members of the joint U.S.-Vietnamese task force to concentrate exclusively on accounting for POWs and MIAs.[31]

Acutely sensitive to any potential criticism from the administration's opponents that the United States was opening relations via the back door, Lord stressed to Congress that "this temporary arrangement does not represent any change in U.S.-Vietnamese relations." He insisted that "we are *not* opening a diplomatic mission in Hanoi. We are *not* establishing a U.S. interest section there. What we *are* doing is strengthening our efforts to try to find the answers for the families of our missing men."[32]

Lord's team also tried to do something for the relatives of veterans of the South Vietnamese Armed Forces. Since 1973 the government of the SRV had provided no pension benefits and no access to rehabilitation hospitals for South Vietnamese veterans. Fighting for the losing side in the Vietnamese civil war had left veterans of the Army of the Republic of Vietnam (ARVN) in a terrible predicament. Ordinary soldiers had not been singled out for special hardship or abuse, but officers had endured weeks, months, and, in a few cases, years in squalid reeducation camps. The 80 percent of the population of the South who worked on the land returned quickly to their daily routines, but urban veterans had found it difficult to find jobs, especially in schools, hospitals, or government offices. Until the *doi moi* economic reforms went into effect in 1986, ARVN veterans had trouble finding work but thereafter, they had opened numerous retail stalls and restaurants and began working in the offices set up by the foreign investors. ARVN veterans who had been wounded during the war suffered the most. The Lord mission visited a rehabilitation center in the South that for the first time treated ARVN veterans needing artificial arms or legs. The Vietnamese government promised that an American-Vietnamese foundation could supply funds to outfit prostheses on approximately one thousand disabled ARVN veterans. Lord's mission also visited an Amerasian Transit Center that processed the travel documents of thousands of offspring of American fathers and Vietnamese mothers seeking entry into the United States.[33]

The Clinton administration faced a Catch-22 in opening relations with Vietnam. It had to satisfy the demands of MIA advocates, but everything it did on behalf of MIAs delayed the opening of diplomatic relations. Anything slowing the process of normalization irritated businesses wishing to partake in the bounty of commerce with Vietnam.[34] Lord noted that "if you back off and have no contact at all [with Vietnam], which is essentially what we did up until two years ago, you make very little, if any, progress. But we also feel if you make great leaps forward that you give up your leverage."[35] The Clinton administration felt the complaints all the more acutely because of the president's own strained relations with the U.S. military.

Advocates of normalization finally got Assistant Secretary Lord to admit that a full accounting for MIAs in Vietnam could take as much as twenty years. Lord noted that even with the best of efforts, many discrepancies and unresolved cases would remain. Trying to put this in perspective, he noted, "We still have something like 75 to 80,000 MIAs from World War II and about 8,000 from the Korean War." Both Lord and Edward Ross of the Defense Department strongly denied any sort of government cover-up about MIAs. Ross likened the persistent belief that the government had covered up reports of live Americans in Vietnam to "the various assassination theories of President Kennedy." It strained belief that "everyone in the government had to have participated in the cover-up and was keeping it a secret." In the case of suspected MIAs in Vietnam it was all the more unlikely. "We do not have any secrets," Ross insisted, "because we have worked very hard to try to declassify and put all this information out into the public record."[36]

Senators in favor of opening relations with Vietnam worked hard to debunk the views of Senator Bob Smith, who passionately continued to argue that the U.S. government had not done enough to recover remains. Senator Frank Murkowski, who desperately wanted commercial relations with Vietnam, tried to reason. "You are not going to have full accountability because some were lost. There will never be a recovery of remains. They were either lost at sea or to [enemy] fire."[37]

The Clinton administration faced a congressionally imposed September 14, 1993 deadline on deciding on a full lifting of the trade embargo with Vietnam. Senator Murkowski introduced legislation lifting most aspects of the embargo, effectively linking Vietnam's trade status to that of China's. U.S. firms could export goods to Vietnam, but they would be barred from sending "dual-use" materials that could be used for either military or civilian purposes. The administration would not go as far as Murkowski wanted. Lord believed that the incremental steps taken by the Bush and Clinton administrations were the most likely to resolve the MIA issue. He believed that until the Bush administration started to engage Vietnam in 1991, Vietnam's "record was duplicitous and was very unhelpful and played upon the emotions of the families." After Clinton allowed the international financial organizations to meet Vietnam's debts, the Vietnamese told the Americans "tell us what you want, and we'll do it." Even though Murkowski found their words reassuring, he said, "They still might not produce dramatic breakthroughs." He therefore believed it made more sense for the United States to reappraise the Vietnamese efforts at regular intervals.

Some senators thought Lord was too cautious. Harlan Matthews, a Tennessee Democrat filling the term of Vice-President Al Gore, believed it would help more if the United States simply opened relations with Vietnam. "Once we begin to interact with the people of Vietnam, the people on the street, the [Vietnamese] officials know that we stand to get greater cooperation as they know us and we know them, as we expand the economic opportunities for them and they in turn interact in the trade area."[38] Virginia's Charles Robb also encouraged the administration to allow U.S. banks to participate in the refinancing of Vietnam's debts, which Lord flatly refused. The Clinton administration had only withdrawn its objection to international financial organizations that used U.S. funds to finance Vietnamese projects. This did not satisfy Robb. He noted the incongruity of using U.S. government funds to support infrastructure projects in Vietnam but then barring U.S. firms from competing for the business. Lord acknowledged that Clinton was "extremely interested in the American economy and reviving it, and helping American business and exports."[39] Vietnam was in a different category, however, from trade expansion with other countries. Lord insisted that the Clinton administration's overriding preoccupation was with the "the families and pursuing the MIA question." That was why the administration had not linked the embargo question and the decision to allow international financial institutions to reschedule Vietnam's debt.[40]

The Clinton administration faced pressure for improved relations with former opponents of the war in Vietnam and the business community. The president of the Vietnam Veterans of America Foundation, John Terzano, characterized U.S. policy toward Vietnam as vindictive and spiteful, and told Congress it had to accelerate the progress it had made in the past two years. He thought that the United States "can only play a positive role in the economic, political and social development shaping the future of Vietnam by normalizing our diplomatic and economic relations."[41]

Business leaders outspokenly advocated normalization. William Beddow, an official of Caterpillar, noted, "there is no longer a U.S.-*led* embargo—there is only a U.S. embargo."[42] The total market for overseas investment in Vietnam stood at about five billion dollars in 1993. While other nations raced to seize business opportunities, representatives of about 160 U.S. companies waited impatiently for the end of the embargo. Japan's government, with its long post–World War II tradition of directly aiding Japanese exporters, stood ready to invest $1.5 billion in Vietnam over the next three years. Mitsubishi Motors expected to become the principal automobile seller in Vietnam.[43]

Al Baker, CEO and chairman of the board of Halliburton, an energy services company, represented the National Foreign Trade Council (NFTC) before Congress. He explained that about five hundred American businesses belonging to the NFTC wanted a part of the burgeoning Vietnamese market and resented the disadvantages of the American embargo. Private firms in Japan, Thailand, Taiwan, and Europe had moved quickly into an emerging market. Baker was dismayed that in February 1993 representatives of more than three hundred non–U.S. companies met with French President François Mitterrand when he visited Hanoi. Baker noted that Vietnam's economy had grown at an 8 percent annual rate in the previous several years. In 1991 Vietnam had received more foreign investment, $1.2 billion, than India or South Korea. It now exported food and energy and could easily import $40 million each year from the United States if the embargo was lifted.

As an oilman, Baker paid particularly close attention to Vietnam's growing petroleum industry. He observed that Vietnam now had the third-most-active petroleum-exploration industry in the region. The Southern part of the country had no refining or petrochemical industry, so it imported oil. Vietnam had invited bids for a joint refinery and had received seventeen proposals from European and Pacific Rim countries. U.S. firms like Halliburton had been shut out, despite their being the world's technological leaders. Baker feared that the United States could not keep that leadership for long. "The danger we presently confront is that as more time passes our competitors will become too well established to dislodge." The United States had great advantages derived from its extensive presence in Vietnam before 1975. "But," he warned, "this is a wasting asset which diminishes as foreign competitors, free from the competition of American companies, acquire their own experience and business relationships."[44]

It was not just oil. Vietnam's infrastructure still had vast needs, and American firms could fill many of them. Vietnamese agents had made discreet inquiries about the price of Caterpillar earth-moving equipment. The Vietnamese then took these prices to their Japanese bidders and received better deals. A Swiss company was building a cement plant in Vietnam. The Swiss were ready to purchase about $50 million worth of American cement-plant equipment. The financing would come through Swiss and foreign borrowing. Under the embargo, however, the U.S. cement makers could not submit bids.

Although the existence of the embargo stood as the major stumbling block to American commerce with Vietnam, the way it was administered also hindered U.S. business access to Vietnam's markets. The Office of Foreign Assets Control administered U.S. sanctions against Vietnam. Individual U.S. companies seeking waivers of the embargo could apply to the office, and a few had received them for humanitarian reasons, but the offices decisions then remained secret. The NFTC urged that "so long as the embargo is retained, the private sector needs a clear statement defining permissible activity."[45]

American businesses based in Asia also pressed for the embargo to be lifted. The American Chamber of Commerce in Hong Kong formally called for an immediate halt, lamenting that "other countries, including all of America's closest allies, are rapidly developing commercial ties with Vietnam." The embargo seemed to hurt the United States more than it did Vietnam. By the end of 1992 about 556 foreign business ventures operated in Vietnam, investing $4.6 billion in the country. Vietnam's total foreign trade in 1992 was $4.8 billion. U.S. competitors were consolidating their position in Vietnam in industries in which the United States had traditionally been the strongest. Despite the fact that the United States remained the world's leader in oil and gas exploration, telecommunications, chemicals, construction services and equipment, and international finance, firms from other countries were already in Vietnam serving these needs. For example, Vietnam had granted concessions to the Dai Hung oil field off the coast of Vietnam, originally explored by Mobil, to Sumitomo (Japan), Total (France), Broken Hill Properties (Australia), and Petronas (Malaysia). Three foreign firms—OTC (Australia), Siemens (Germany), and Alcatel (France)—had started telecommunication projects in Vietnam. The representatives from the Hong Kong Chamber of Commerce thought that "if this process is allowed to proceed for much longer, dislodging these competitors in the future will be extremely difficult, if not impossible."[46] International financial institutions also saw opportunities in Vietnam. Six foreign banks had opened branches there: ANZ (Australia), BNP, Credit Lyonnaise, Banque Indosuez, Banque Francais du Commerce Exterieur (all from France), and Bangkok Bank (Thailand). American banks were bigger than these, but they needed the opportunity to compete.

Vietnam had twenty years of pent-up demand for foreign goods and investment. The work force was highly educated, and a large proportion of it in the South had relatives living in developed countries. These overseas Vietnamese let their relatives know the differences in living standards. For American businesses the opportunities to participate in this development were irresistible.

Advocates of dropping the embargo said that closer commercial relations would improve the human-rights situation in Vietnam. The Hong Kong business people thought that lifting the embargo would inevitably give Vietnam a vested interest in stable relationships with the United States. For years Vietnam had hoped for direct payments from the United States government. Since Vessey's 1987 visit to Hanoi, Vietnamese officials understood that the only economic assistance from the United States would come through commercial relations. The American Chamber of Commerce in Hong Kong asserted, "lifting the embargo would give America greater leverage over Vietnamese political and economic policy." These business leaders thought that once economic ties had taken hold in Vietnam, that country's leaders would have no choice but help the United States in resolving remaining MIA cases. Commerce would "foster western ideals of freedom, democracy and free market systems."[47]

American firms seeking entry into the Vietnamese market had a friend in Secretary of Commerce Ronald Brown. Brown became the most outspoken advocate of expanding U.S. trade and investment abroad of any secretary of commerce since Herbert Hoover. He traveled the world with business leaders to China, Japan, and the Asian tigers, but he did not go to Vietnam because of the embargo. Clinton saw the advantages of dropping the embargo but faced complaints about his own Vietnam service and a new controversy over his loosening of restrictions on gay men and lesbians serving in the military.[48]

The president's touchy relations with the military constrained him from making bold moves on Vietnam. He encountered hostile demonstrators when he appeared at the Vietnam Veterans Memorial on Memorial Day 1993. Hundreds of veterans rode motorcycles from Arlington National Cemetery to the wall. They waved signs demanding that the United States government do more to look for POWs and MIAs in Southeast Asia. They booed when Clinton rose to speak and shouted that he had no place at the hallowed memorial site. He mollified them somewhat by calling disagreement "freedom's privilege." He asked, "Can any Commander in Chief be in any other place but here on this day?" The jeering stopped, and he received some mild applause when he sat down.[49]

On February 4, 1994, during the Vietnamese New Year holiday of Tet, the Clinton administration took the final step to ending the embargo on trade and travel to Vietnam. Still wary of the emotional power of the MIA issue, Clinton stressed that the end of the embargo did "not constitute a normalization of our relationship. Before that happens," he went on," we must have more progress, more cooperation, and more answers" on MIAs. Lifting the embargo represented a sea change in U.S. policy. John Terzano of the Vietnam Veterans of America, who stood behind Clinton as the president made his announcement, rejoiced that ending the embargo "ends the war for the nation and for Clinton."[50]

U.S. citizens could now apply directly to the Vietnamese mission to the United Nations in New York for a visa. Previously they had to apply to SRV consulates outside the United States for the right to travel to the SRV. U.S. businesses no longer faced fines for exporting goods to Vietnam and could now set up offices in the SRV. The lifting of the embargo did not mean, however, that the United States government would provide any direct consular help to Americans doing business in Vietnam. There still were no diplomatic relations between the two countries. What lifting the embargo meant was that the United States no longer made it illegal for American citizens or firms to have dealings with the Vietnamese.[51]

The lifting of the embargo proved widely popular. "We waited for this day for a long time," proclaimed a Pepsi Cola executive in Saigon. Bottles of locally produced Pepsi began appearing on the streets of the city just hours after Clinton made his announcement, and billboards featuring Miss Vietnam 1994 soon went up extolling the virtues of the soft drink. Later that same day officials of American Express signed an agreement with the government of Vietnam to permit the use of the company's credit cards there. Although Hanoi had endured the embargo since 1975, millions of Vietnamese remembered American styles, brands, and services fondly. An American property developer who had worked for several years in Vietnam explained, "It's like they're living in a time warp when American products were at their peak." And it was not just consumer goods. Within hours of the embargo being lifted United Airlines announced that it would start service between Los Angeles and Saigon as soon as it could reach an agreement with Hanoi. Boeing expected to sell between sixty and eighty billion dollars worth of aircraft to Vietnamese airlines over the next ten to fifteen years. In fact both plans proved to be highly exaggerated. United's service between the United States and Vietnam was delayed repeatedly until 2004. Boeing sold fewer planes than did its European rival Airbus, and the American airplane manufacturer earned less than $6 billion in sales to Vietnam over the next ten years.

Although American companies were bringing products and services into their country, the Vietnamese considered the terms of lifting the embargo discriminatory. Vietnam was one of only eight countries including China, Iran,

Iraq, and Syria that did not enjoy the benefits of America's most favored nation status, meaning that tariffs on goods produced in Vietnam and imported into the United States were 40 percent higher than from countries designated most favored nations. A Vietnamese economist complained, "A one way street can't be maintained for a long time. Vietnam needs to pay for its imports." [52]

The recent influx of capital from Asia, Australia, and Europe had minimized the embargo's effects, but the SRV's development was still retarded by the difficulty of trading with the United States. U.S. firms now had the possibility of competing for business with other non-Vietnamese businesses, but the playing field was far from level. Without consular relations or a commercial treaty between the two countries, economic relations would not flourish like those of countries that had full diplomatic interchange.

With the end to the embargo, only one issue stood in the way of diplomatic relations between Washington and Hanoi. The Clinton administration inherited its predecessors' commitment to search for POWs and MIAs. The United States and Vietnam conducted negotiations in New York and Washington for seventeen months after the lifting of the embargo. The United States insisted that Vietnam expand the joint patrols searching for remains to which the Vietnamese readily agreed. Although the Clinton administration did not believe that any live Americans remained in Vietnam, it sought protection against charges from domestic critics that it had abandoned servicemen there.

In July 1995 the United States and Vietnam announced an agreement to exchange ambassadors and open embassies and consulates in each other's capitals. President Clinton focused attention on the American benefits of normalization, saying primarily that it would foster progress on finding MIA remains. When he addressed Vietnamese concerns, he preached about the benefits of Western-style political democracy and free economics. He predicted that "normalization and increased contact between Americans and Vietnamese will advance the cause of freedom in Vietnam, just as it did in Eastern Europe and the former Soviet Union." [53] Vietnam appointed Le Van Bang as its first ambassador to the United States. Bang had served as the SRV's representative to the United Nations and had represented the SRV in the talks with the United States. Clinton nominated Florida Congressman and former POW Douglas "Pete" Peterson as the U.S. ambassador.

Secretary of State Warren Christopher traveled to Hanoi a month later where he announced, "A powerful revolution of ideas has swept the world. Indeed, the main story of the late twentieth century is the ascendancy of open societies and open markets in country after country."[54] The United States pressed Vietnam to open both its markets and its political system. The secretary of state advised the Vietnamese that "the key to success in this rapidly changing world is the freedom to own, to buy, to sell: the freedom to participate in the decisions that affect our lives." He told the Vietnamese to be bold. He likened economic reform to a passage over a ravine—"only one giant leap will get you across."[55]

The Vietnamese welcomed the restoration of diplomatic relations after twenty years, but they resented the lectures on political pluralism. General Vo Nguyen Giap, the commander who had outlasted the Americans and defeated the South, warned in retirement that the opening of relations with the United States held as many dangers as opportunities. "We had problems in wartime and now we have to deal with the problems of peacetime," he said.[56] Diplomatic relations with the United States made Vietnam feel less vulnerable to Chinese dominance. It also opened the way for Vietnam to join the Asian Pacific Economic Conference and the World Trade Organization, but participation in these prominent organizations of global economy carried grave dangers of the corrupting influences of American materialism. Thousands of American tourists visited Vietnam each week, bringing with them clothing, video recorders, cameras, computer software, music cassettes, and cigarettes from the developed world. Many visitors were recent emigrants from Vietnam who opened a window onto life in the freer, richer West, as did fax machines, e-mails, cell phones, and direct-satellite TV.

The view from outside deeply distressed the party leadership. President Le Duc Anh used his address on the fiftieth anniversary of Ho Chi Minh's Declaration of Independence to denounce "various hostile forces" that had "repeatedly attacked the party's guidance, seeking to change the nature of the Communist Party and the State of Vietnam and derail our revolution." Party officials ominously noted that a few overseas Vietnamese had been arrested in April for attempting to plant a bomb in Saigon at the celebrations of the twentieth anniversary of the Communist victory. Prime Minister Vo Van Kiet also complained about the "negative and law-violating actions" that were "causing more impact on our ideology and aspirations, and are eroding our traditional morality and customs." *Cong An*, the newspaper of the police department of Ho Chi Minh City, expressed dismay at how the youth of the country's largest city had been led astray by rap music. The pounding rhythms and profane lyrics (regardless of how difficult they were for Vietnamese speakers to understand) made the listeners "crazy and stirs them to disrupt our peaceful social order." An official with the Union of Literature and Arts Association saw threats all around from Western culture. "No small section of our youth," he lamented, "is attracted to foreign 'culture,' and is vulnerable to the 'modern' way of life and are disassociating themselves from the nation's cultural quintessence." He saw a "dark scheme of imperialist forces which are intent on cultural aggression against our nation."[57] Some longtime Western supporters of the Vietnamese revolutionaries also expressed their dismay at the way in which the Communist Party had embraced the new economic orthodoxy of free markets and free trade. The historian Gabriel Kolko wrote that the Communist Party's efforts to create a hybrid "market-oriented socialism" were doomed, and he predicted that the "Party will be destroyed and Vietnam will also go the way of the East bloc nations."[58]

Inside the United States reaction to the restoration of diplomatic relations with Vietnam proved to be surprisingly favorable. Most Americans agreed that twenty years was long enough for the two sides to remain estranged, and only a few dissenters denounced the move. Representative Robert Dornan and Senator Robert Smith, both of whom had crusaded for the POWs and MIAs, vowed to block the opening of diplomatic relations, but few other members of Congress joined them.

When "Pete" Peterson took up his post as U.S. ambassador to Vietnam in May 1997, he proved to be enormously popular with both the Vietnamese and the Americans. He traveled everywhere in the country, visiting schools, university hospitals, government offices, and businesses in the North and the South. Everywhere he supported reconciliation. He never complained about his suffering as a POW and he never apologized for the American War in Vietnam. Everywhere he went, he stressed the need for greater communication, cultural exchanges, and business contacts. At a party at the Israeli embassy in Hanoi in the summer of 1997 Peterson met Vu Li a Vietnamese woman and now an Australian diplomat. Their marriage a year later represented a symbolic step in American-Vietnamese relations.

But the reality of the new relationship between the two countries proved far less glamorous. The Vietnamese government remained committed to exercising overall control of the economy. State enterprises accounted for approximately one quarter of Vietnam's GDP and they created over half of the government's receipts. Government officials remained deeply suspicious of private businesses. One foreign diplomat who had longtime experience in Vietnam before the Americans reopened their embassy observed that Vietnamese officials "think, with some justification," that business men and women "are all tax cheats."[59] Foreign investors and local entrepreneurs faced frustrations at every turn. A French oil company pulled out of a $1.2 billion refinery project after the government added $300 to $600 billion in unrecoverable infrastructure costs. An Australian company became frustrated with the red tape in Saigon. "Despite many attempts at meaningful negotiations" with the Ben Nghe Port Authority an executive with P & O Australia said, "no serious progress has been made for eight months." P & O Australia gave up. Other foreign companies resisted government demands that they increase the percentage of local ownership of joint ventures. Local entrepreneurs usually had no capital of their own, so non-Vietnamese investors valued the land at excessive rates.[60]

Over the next five years Westerners in Vietnam were struck by the apparent contradiction of the enormous energy of the people and the crushing burden of official red tape and corruption. "Vietnam is poor, not wretched," the *Economist* concluded in 1995.[61] People everywhere were busy. Students went to school six days a week, and it was not unusual for them to show up at 7 A.M. on Sunday for extra lessons.[62] Cities hummed with activity, and many people held two jobs.[63]

Not all was rosy for Vietnamese working in foreign-operated firms. South Korean- and Taiwanese-owned factories acquired a particularly bad reputation for abusing their Vietnamese employees. In 1998 a Saigon court convicted Jang Mi Baek, a twenty-nine-year-old Korean forewoman for Sam Yang Vietnam, a Nike footwear subcontractor, of humiliating fifteen Vietnamese workers. Baek flew into a rage at what she considered to be the poor quality of the shoes coming off the assembly line. She lined up fifteen of the young Vietnamese women workers and beat them about their faces with an unfinished shoe. The thousand or so other Vietnamese workers in the plant who saw the appalling scene went on strike immediately. Sam Yang Vietnam fired Baek, but the damage to the reputation of both the Koreans and Nike was enormous. A Saigon newspaper reported that many Vietnamese assembly workers, who had once been so eager to work for foreign firms, now felt that "they are being exploited by their capitalist bosses." About twenty strikes occurred every year in Vietnam, and there were dozens of other lesser job actions.[64]

Much of the excitement over Vietnam's potential to become another Asian tiger ignored the reality of the country's traditional, agricultural way of life. Over 70 percent of Vietnam's workforce in the 1990s was engaged in agriculture. Trade and services, the next largest component of the workforce and the sector most likely to join the global economy, accounted for about 5 percent of the workforce. Finance, science, and transportation made up just another 9 percent. In sum, maybe 15 percent of Vietnam's workforce and economy were likely to join the global economy.[65]

Vietnam faced formidable obstacles as it went forward with an ambitious effort to switch from a centrally planned to a market economy. The government still exerted significant control, and there was little support for the private sector. Transportation lagged badly. Vietnam had one single-track rail line joining the North and the South. Ruts, holes, and washed-out sections marred Highway 9, the old French-built major coastal road. Many Vietnamese continued to transport goods on bicycles and on their backs. Tourists marveled at the energy of the Vietnamese farmers, mostly women, who rose at two or three each morning to cycle to major towns and cities to sell vegetables, fruit, chickens, ducks, and pigs at markets.[66] Their fierce determination recalled the fortitude of the thousands of Vietnamese who had carried supplies down the Ho Chi Minh Trail to the Peoples Liberation Armed Forces and Viet Cong troops fighting in the south, but it did little to foster the growth of a modern economy. As Vietnam prospered in the late nineties, the transportation problems intensified. Motorbikes joined bicycles, and in the major cities thousands of cars put a severe strain on the antiquated roads and streets.

The sale of state enterprises proceeded slowly in the mid-1990s. Officially, the number of state-owned firms dropped from twelve thousand to barely half that number by 1996. But many simply merged. Since private savings were miniscule, it was more difficult for ordinary Vietnamese to create independent businesses, but thousands of families managed to start up retail shops selling hardware or clothing, restaurants, and mini hotels with money sent from relatives living abroad. Vietnam did not make much progress, however, in creating midsize enterprises like the "village-township" businesses (joint ventures between local towns and private investors) that dotted the landscape of rural China.[67]

Larger, highly ambitious enterprises flourished for a while. Vietnam opened a small stock exchange in Saigon in 1995. Western businesses responded with the creation of several mutual funds devoted exclusively to Vietnam. Each collected about one hundred million dollars from eager investors, a relatively small amount by the standards of the overheated stock market of the mid-1990s. But even those relatively small sums proved to be too much for Vietnam to absorb. There simply were too few Vietnamese businesses likely to provide a return for the outside investors. Fewer than twenty stocks traded on the Saigon stock exchange. In 1998 both Merrill Lynch and Fidelity Investments closed their Vietnam country funds and returned the money to disappointed contributors. Vietnam's banking system could not bear the weight of foreign investment either. Saigon's local banks had considerable funds deposited. In fact the ratio of deposits to loans was far higher than anyplace else in developing Asia. And that precisely was the problem. Banks lent money for only six months, making it impossible for businesses to plan. There was no formal structure for banks to trade with one another. Some Vietnamese banks did engage in bilateral swaps and other deals, but lacking a market, these exchanges tended to be cumbersome. The influx of foreign banks did not invest in Vietnam so much as act as clearing houses for business activities.[68] In sum, Vietnam's market became known more for its potential than its reality in the five years after the United States and Vietnam opened diplomatic relations in 1995.

The Clinton administration responded to this enthusiasm for greater commerce with Vietnam by pressing forward with moves for a full trade agreement. Secretary of State Madeleine Albright opened a U.S. consulate in Ho Chi Minh City in June 1997. During Albright's visit the United States opened a Trade and Development Agency for Vietnam. In November 1997 Vietnam opened a consulate in San Francisco. Under the Jackson-Vanik legislation passed in 1974, Vietnam, like the Russian Federation, remained on the list of countries whose exports were taxed at the highest rate until it relaxed its restrictions on free emigration. In March 1998 Clinton signed a waiver of the Jackson-Vanik Amendment restrictions on trade with Vietnam. His move paved the way for the U.S. Export-Import Bank and the Overseas Private Investment Corporation to extend credit to Vietnam.[69]

Yet politics continued to interfere with better economic relations. A trade treaty between the United States and Vietnam remained blocked by the United States' linking most-favored-nation status to Vietnam's policy on emigration. Despite the urgings of various business interests, substantial opposition remained to a trade treaty between the United States and Vietnam. Richard Childress, the point man for the Reagan administration on POW issues, strongly opposed the Clinton administration's efforts to expand the trade relations between the two powers. He complained that the Clinton administration had adopted the Vietnamese interpretation of normalization and that the administration's efforts since 1993 had been built upon "false certifications" to Congress of Vietnam's compliance with American demands for free emigration. He also perceived a paradoxical similarity between the Clinton administration's insistence that greater trade would inevitably lead to democracy and Vietnamese Communist officials "who believe that American business is part of a sinister plot to overthrow their government." Notwithstanding the Clinton administration's having "moved further and faster on all of Vietnam's agenda in less than two years than all of their predecessors combined," the Vietnamese, he charged, had done little to liberalize their economy or permit free emigration.[70]

Nguyen Dinh Thang, a leader of the Vietnamese community in the Washington area, agreed that Vietnam continued to harass would-be emigrants. He deplored the "rampant corruption" that "plagued Vietnam's emigration process." He accused the State Department of turning a blind eye to the common practice of Vietnamese officials charging as much as several thousand dollars under the table for an exit permit. This clearly violated the principles of Jackson-Vanik. He said that Vietnamese government officials constantly intimidated anyone who sought to help Americans. He told of a Vietnamese American who provided information to U.S. military officials in Malaysia about the location of the remains of a downed American flyer. The Vietnamese government retaliated by fining her family in Vietnam the equivalent of five hundred dollars, about two years' wages. Thang also criticized Vietnam's heavy-handed economic policies. "If you go to any bookstore in Vietnam," he charged, "you can find software, CDs, books, videotapes pirated from the U.S. Is that a government that we can trust and that we want to do business with?"[71]

For business leaders the answer was still yes. Frances Zwenig, the vice president of the U.S.-Vietnam trade council, looked on the bright side. She noted that Vietnam had issued 91,500 visas for Americans to visit the country, 66,000 of which had been issued to Vietnamese Americans. She acknowledged that the 1997 Asian financial crisis had taken a serious toll on the Vietnamese economy. Seventy percent of Vietnam's foreign investment still came from Thailand, Taiwan, Hong Kong, Malaysia, Indonesia, and Singapore, the very countries worst hit by the financial panic of August 1997. Vietnam had insulated itself somewhat by its uneven progress toward a market economy, but the delays in embracing the market made it all the harder for Americans to prosper in Vietnam. The promised stock exchange remained a mirage. Vietnam still banned converting its currency, the dong, into dollars or any other foreign currency. Zwenig urged Congress to renew the Jackson-Vanik waiver in order to keep the United States and Vietnam on a path to a full commercial treaty. Zwenig asserted that the Vietnamese accepted the American terms of a draft treaty. They also had agreed to liberalize rules for trade, expatriation of profits, and intellectual property rights. Although Vietnam had lagged behind the former Communist countries of Eastern Europe in economic reform, the American companies that comprised Zwenig's council "are in a strong position to win over $2 billion worth of projects" in the near future.[72] Bradley LaLonde, Citibank's principal executive in Vietnam, explained the need for a new commercial treaty. The potential of a market with more than seventy-five million people, more than half of whom were under the age of twenty-five, had to be tapped by American exporters. But U.S. firms had come late and lagged behind Asian and European competitors. After the restoration of diplomatic relations in 1995 "the lack of a bilateral trade agreement and most-favored-nation status for Vietnam puts U.S. firms at a disadvantage in investing in Vietnam, moving goods in and out of the country, and leaves us without strong protection for intellectual property."[73]

Clinton continued to waive the Jackson-Vanik restrictions in 1999 and 2000. Ambassador Peterson told Congress in 1998 that the waiver of Jackson-Vanik had become an "essential tool in our policy of engagement." Emigration had improved under this policy, he said. Ten thousand Vietnamese left for the United States with visas issued by U.S. consulates in 1998, and he expected an additional thirty thousand in 1999. The bilateral trade treaty between the United States and Vietnam would be one more opportunity for Washington to obtain from Hanoi commitments "to undertake necessary economic reforms and to make changes to their trade and investment regimes that will directly benefit U.S. businesses."[74]

U.S. and Vietnamese negotiators signed the Bilateral Trade Agreement (BTA) on July 13, 2000.[75] The BTA slashed tariffs from 20 percent to 3 percent, and Vietnam agreed to abolish non-tariff restrictions such as quotas and discriminatory licensing arrangements. Vietnam also agreed to abide by the World Trade Organization's standards protecting intellectual property. Within a year of ratification Vietnam promised to apply WTO-level standards for patents and trademarks, and within eighteen months to apply them to copyrights and trade secrets. Charlene Barshevsky, the U.S. special trade representative in charge of the U.S. end of the negotiations, told Congress that the agreement would set Vietnam on "a course for greater openness to the outside world . . . and help Vietnam to integrate itself into the Pacific regional economy and build a foundation for future entry into the World Trade Organization."[76]

The BTA also set the stage for President Clinton's triumphal tour of Vietnam in November 2000. Clinton sought reconciliation—both with the Vietnamese and with the Americans who still bore scars of the war. As he flew on Air Force One to Vietnam Clinton expressed some empathy for President Lyndon Johnson, whose escalation of the war in Vietnam Clinton had opposed as a student. Having led NATO forces in a war against Serbia in 1999, Clinton said, "I believe [Johnson] did what he thought was right under the circumstances. These decisions are hard. And one of the things I have learned, too, is when you decide to employ force, there will always be unintended consequences." Clinton expressed joy that "the American people have been able to look to the future" in their relations with Vietnam, and he stressed the same message of letting go of old animosities in Vietnam.[77] Tens of thousands of Vietnamese lined Clinton's motorcade route from Hanoi's airport to the American embassy. He told a cheering crowd of students at Vietnam National University in Saigon that they should embrace Vietnam's entry into the global market as the best way for prosperity and political freedom in their country. A seventeen-year-old high school student in Saigon summarized the views of many urban, educated Vietnamese, eager to see the benefits of globalization, "America is a very modern country, and we want to be modern too." A seventy-year-old retired Saigon accountant also expressed his appreciation for Clinton, a man who, he said, was "the American who had done the most to heal Vietnamese-American relations."[78]

PART

* * * * * * * * * * * *

Veterans and
Vietnamese Americans

Chapter

* * * * * * * * * * *

Vietnam Veterans'
Readjustment

The Vietnam War ended badly for the United States, and lingering public bitterness made life difficult for many veterans. American soldiers, sailors, marines, and airmen returned from Vietnam to a civilian public that regarded the war as a mistake and the results a failure. A popular image of the Vietnam War veteran arose of a deeply troubled and psychologically wounded man, condemned to recapitulate mentally and emotionally the anguish of fighting, killing, and dying. The stereotypical Vietnam veteran was a man at odds with the larger society, uneasy at home, and an uncomfortable reminder to non-veterans of a troublesome time in their recent past.

Vietnam veterans had much in common with veterans of earlier twentieth-century wars, many of whom also experienced hardships in readjusting to civilian life. The pervasive image of World War II veterans as integrating well into postwar life was often inaccurate. Many World War II veterans carried with them the physical and psychological scars of their war years for decades.

While many of the physical and psychological hardships endured by veterans were similar, the attitudes of veterans and non-veterans changed dramatically between the post–World War II and post–Vietnam War eras. The culture of the post-Vietnam decades, glorifying the expression of emotion, deeply suspicious of public institutions, and, for much of the period, pessimistic, accounted for much of the ambivalence of the larger society toward veterans.

Both veterans and non-veterans were shaken by the Vietnam experience. Their divisions about the war transformed in its aftermath into divided opinions of Vietnam veterans. Americans who did not go to Vietnam perceived veterans as traditional heroes who served honorably; villains who committed inexcusable atrocities; victims of incompetent political or military leaders; suckers who needlessly put themselves in harm's way; or people so physically or psychologically damaged they could not live productive, stable lives in peacetime. Non-veterans sometimes held many of these contradictory ideas at the same time.

A wide gulf separated Vietnam veterans and the majority of their age cohort who stayed home. The experience of Lewis Puller Jr., a marine lieutenant badly wounded in combat in 1968, illustrates the alienation Vietnam veterans felt from their non-veteran peers. The son of Lewis "Chesty" Puller, the most highly decorated marine during World War II, the younger Puller was shocked by the indifference of his countrymen to his service and sacrifice. "Everywhere I looked," he recalled "it seemed that Vietnam veterans were being shunned and reviled, and . . . I could not reconcile my father's generation's triumphal return from World War II with my own experience."[1] Military service during World War II was not absolutely universal, but it was the common experience for young men. During the Vietnam War, on the other hand, only a minority went into the military. The Vietnam War loomed over twenty-six million American men between the ages of eighteen and twenty-six during the fifteen years of U.S. involvement in the war. While most men eligible for military service *thought* about Vietnam, in reality a minority entered the military. About 8 of 26 million eligible males served in the military during the Vietnam years, and of these, approximately 2.2 million went to Vietnam. An even smaller minority of these men, anywhere from 400,000 to 1 million, actually saw combat.[2] A 1973 Nader report on Vietnam veterans conducted as tens of thousands of men returned home concluded that "the Vietnam veteran confronts a people who never really went to war. . . . The conflict has been waged without any privation at home, and the result has been an enormous disproportion of sacrifice."[3]

The experiences of Vietnam veterans at home varied widely. By 1981, the popular image of a Vietnam veteran was that of a maladjusted, troubled man, at war with his country, his family, and himself. Unable to find a job or form satisfying relationship, these men drifted angrily on the margins of society. This stereotype distorted the truth in some ways, since many Vietnam veterans readjusted well to civilian life. Nevertheless, the war did psychologically wreck hundreds of thousands of veterans.

Some veterans faced hardships, torments, and distress. Others found their wartime experiences rewarding, or at least not damaging, and they readjusted easily to civilian life. What a soldier did in the military explained a lot about his or her experience as a veteran. Men who saw heavy combat had more trouble readjusting to civilian life than did those who served mostly in the rear. The degree of support from family, friends, communities, workplaces, and government and non-governmental agencies also played large parts in determining how veterans came to terms with their memories of the war and their positions in contemporary society.

Veterans who were in Vietnam were more likely to have had their lives significantly changed by the war, but they also supported the American war effort more than any other group. Vietnam veterans surveyed in 1981 reported that 43 percent supported U.S. involvement in the war, and 32 percent of Vietnam-era veterans (those who did military service elsewhere during the war years) supported the war effort, while only 18.5 percent of non-veterans thought the war was appropriate.[4]

Many veterans lamented the loss of their early idealism in the transition from the comfortable certainties of life at home to the chaos of combat in Vietnam. One of them was Navy Lieutenant John Kerry, who recalled his disillusionment thirty-five years later while running for president in 2004. He spoke of "a journey of idealism that was challenged, of easy assumptions that were broken, of growing up, of transitioning" from "carefree days to a world of a lot of death and confrontation with our ideals and our hopes."[5] In 1971 Kerry wrote in his journal that "not many people went to Vietnam because they wanted to fight or because they felt in the slightest that they were fighting for a country or a people. . . . It was tour of duty—a one year absence from all that made sense and all that one wanted to do. And so, it was that absurd it struck even harder. One moment there was beauty and the silence and the next moment there was the macabre and the chaos."[6] Later that spring Kerry testified against the war in Vietnam before the Senate Committee on Foreign Relations. He denounced the Johnson administration for blundering into a war and then having "deserted the troops." The Nixon administration, was if anything, worse. It had needlessly prolonged the war out of arrogant pride. "How do you ask a man," he questioned the hushed chamber, "to be the last man to die in Vietnam? How do you ask a man to be the last man to die for a mistake?"[7] Kerry went on to a highly successful political career, but many others were not as fortunate.

Readjustment to civilian life posed a variety of problems for Vietnam veterans, especially those who served in combat. Time and time again veterans lamented the lack of a hero's welcome when they returned home. One told a House Committee in 1981, "There were no bands playing 'Johnny Comes Marching Home Again,' no Victory Day celebrations as there were after World War II."[8] Men often relived and reflected on the horrors of war when they returned home. One remembered that he often sat in the heat of the jungle, with steam rising all around and bugs biting him, wishing that "everybody in the world could be right where I was for at least one week. Because I strongly felt that if people could see the horror that one man could do to another human being, they would do away with war."[9] Others reported the shock of the death or wounding of their combat buddies. A veteran told Congress, "Your mind got messed up" seeing the killing on both sides. If a serviceman's friends were shot, a survivor wished "there was something you could have done for them to help them." Men often hated the Vietnamese enemy in the abstract, but the sight of a dead Viet Cong soldier often left men wondering "if he had a family, a wife, kids."[10] Others reflected on the futility and absurdity of their combat experience. One man said, "What stands out most in my mind is the total waste of the whole thing in terms of certainly human life first, and the dollars that it cost the country to maintain that fiasco."[11]

Yet a sizeable number of Vietnam veterans viewed their war experience differently. Some said it had been positive and had helped them grow up. A typical response was "when I left the service, I was more outgoing than before I went in and much more mature." He acknowledged, however, that "the age difference was more responsible for this than anything that happened in the military, because when I went in I was 17 and when I came out I was 23." These positive experiences were most pronounced for veterans who did not engage the enemy in face-to-face combat. An Air Force pilot reflected, "Our base in Thailand was a very nice base. . . . I really didn't think much about my bombing of Vietnam—it was a job." Other men valued the comradeship of war. "What stands out," reported one Navy vet, "is that I was having a good time with the guys, just the very day working together and knowing we were all in the same boat. . . . I felt detached from the war *per se*, being in the Seabees. We did not have to shoot anybody, I was a plumber. . . . The war was good for me, I needed the discipline."[12]

Some African-American veterans reported that seeing the carnage of Vietnam and the deaths of other minority soldiers encouraged them to strive for something better when they returned home. One man who witnessed racial conflict in his unit lamented that "black veterans are nothing, because a lot of them have never really recovered, they cannot find jobs. . . . When I returned to the United States, I knew that I was going to seek my share of freedom and capital and education and I was going to settle for nothing less. I was prouder and more aware; I wanted to accomplish something that had meaning. And I have realized my goals."[13]

Combat took the heaviest toll. Veterans noted the fighting in Vietnam differed from earlier wars, when there were clearly defined front lines. While Vietnam soldiers may have been exposed to the enemy for shorter periods of time than the troops fighting on the front lines in both world wars and Korea, the dangers of guerrilla attacks weighed on the soldiers. One reported, "Going through the jungle and not knowing where the enemy was, who was armed . . .

emotionally it kind of messed me up." The edginess of combat reverberated for years. "When I got shot at, I was frightened, not knowing what is going to happen next. You couldn't sleep, because if one guy got in there, he would have cut everybody's neck." He believed that the war had permanently changed him for the worse. He listed "shell shock, fears . . . messed up, nervousness . . . confusion, sleep troubles, nightmares, [and] loss of interest in usual activities" as his ongoing symptoms. His marriage broke up after he returned home. Overall, he complained, "Things turned out worse than I expected." He called himself "a struggling man, trying to do the best I can." But he wasn't doing very well. "The war made me a little bitter." He recommended that every combat veteran get psychiatric help when he returned home "because you never come out the same."[14]

In 1980 about two-thirds of Vietnam veterans claimed that they had not delved very deeply into their experience, according to a survey conducted by the House Committee on Veterans Affairs. The veterans' very reluctance to discuss their wartime experiences had a variety of explanations. For some men it simply meant that the war had not affected them emotionally. Some thought that the gap between themselves and those who did not go to Vietnam was so great that it was pointless to speak of their wartime activities. One man recalled that he had little understanding of the war while he was in Vietnam. After he returned home, he was surprised at the depth of antiwar sentiment among his fellow students at a college he attended. "I found it hard to adjust," he reported, "because at that point there was a lot of criticism about the people who had served in Vietnam." Faced with what he considered the hostility of his classmates, he kept quiet. "I did not verbalize my beliefs while in college," he said. "I stayed to myself. I felt like nobody, unwanted."[15]

The wartime experience generally exerted a more powerful impact on combat veterans than on soldiers who did not see fighting. Many combat veterans felt that Vietnam was the most important factor in their lives, but they were deeply divided about what it meant for them. White combat veterans, who made up approximately 75 percent of combat soldiers and marines, were far more likely than black veterans, about 20 percent of combat fighters, to claim that their combat experience was positive. About 62 percent of whites thought that their time fighting in Vietnam had been good for them, mostly as a time of maturation. Far fewer blacks (24.7 percent) said their combat experience had been good for them, particularly lamenting the loss of African-American lives.[16]

One of the most complex aspects of veterans' postwar reflections of Vietnam came from those veterans who denied that the Vietnam War had had much effect on them. For some, the absence of bad memories simply meant that nothing really bad had occurred or the veteran could easily assimilate difficult experiences. On the other hand, a significant number of veterans pushed painful memories of the war deep into their subconscious. In the immediate aftermath of the war several psychologists noted higher levels of stress among veterans than among the civilian population. Even when veterans denied that Vietnam had shaken them, therapists argued that the very reluctance of their patients to dwell on their wartime experiences indicated the depth of the shocks they had suffered. Robert J. Lifton, a psychiatrist at the Yale University School of Medicine and an outspoken critic of the U.S. involvement in the war, likened the postwar experiences of Vietnam veterans to that of the atomic bombing victims of Hiroshima. He noted that people who had experienced devastating losses or seen horrifying events withdrew from emotional involvement. He characterized this as "psychic numbing."[17] An air force psychiatrist noted that Vietnam veterans at (Veterans Affairs) VA hospitals "were denying and channeling the trauma of their anxieties and conflicts."[18]

Sarah Haley, a psychiatric social worker at the Veterans Administration outpatient clinic in Boston, noted that many deeply depressed and guilty veterans had repressed the memories of their service in Vietnam. In 1974 she published her findings as an article entitled, "When the Patient Reports Atrocities." According to Gerald Nicosia, who has written the most extensive study of Vietnam veterans, "Haley established that the Vietnam veteran who had witnessed or taken part in atrocities . . . presented a completely new challenge to psychotherapy."[19]

In the 1970s a growing movement of health workers, veterans' activists, and public officials worked to provide official medical recognition to the special psychological distress of Vietnam veterans. In the latter years of the war, Chaim Shatan, a New York psychoanalyst who had worked closely with troubled Vietnam veterans, noted that some veterans seemed to get worse the longer they were home. He characterized a "post-Vietnam Syndrome" that set in some nine to thirty months after a veteran returned. In this "delayed massive trauma" veterans expressed guilt and rage. They felt alienated from the larger society. Their psychic numbing took the form of inability to resume ties to loved ones or friends, and the incapacity to form new relationships. They could not keep jobs or marriages. They drank and took drugs. They thought the government had failed them in the war, and the VA disdained them in peacetime. Shatan wrote that the post-Vietnam Syndrome represented the "unconsummated grief of soldiers—impacted grief in which an encapsulated, never-ending past deprives the present of meaning."

These survivors seemed to trust no one, said no one understood them, and believed that anyone who expressed a desire to help them lied to them. "Much of what passes for cynicism," Shatan wrote, "is really the veterans' numbed apathy from a surfeit of bereavement and death."[20] When Shatan published a popular version of his account, "The Grief of Soldiers," as an op-ed piece in the *New York Times* in May 1972, his telephone started "jumping off the wall" with calls from veterans, family members, and mental health workers.[21]

Shatan and Lifton soon started working with a coalition of antiwar groups and veterans at odds with the established veterans' organizations to press for better treatment of the mental and emotional needs of Vietnam veterans. The Vietnam Veterans Against the War went from organizing antiwar demonstrations to advocating special programs for Vietnam veterans. The coalition created the National Vietnam Resources Project (NVRP), which supported the work of an informal network of alternative treatment centers for returned soldiers. In large- and medium-sized cities across the country veterans met in "rap groups" of about a dozen men to discuss their experience in Vietnam and at home. Shatan developed many of his ideas about post-Vietnam Syndrome while participating in these groups in New York. (The mental health professionals always referred to themselves as participants in, rather than leaders of, these groups. They offered no special psychological insights, letting the vets reach their own conclusions. Unlike previous group therapies, the rap groups often publicized what went on in the meetings.)[22]

As Arthur Egendorf, a veteran who participated in one of the earliest New York rap groups, explained, "The rap groups became known as a place where you could tell your story." Men who had been silent about their wartime experiences let loose bitter torrents about the sense of betrayal they felt. Egendorf, who went on to direct the VA's major study of Vietnam veterans' postwar adjustment, recalled that "the vets who came to the early rap groups brought with them, as an overwhelming residue from the war, a deep demoralization and loss of trust in their leaders, in the cause, and in the person they were before going in."[23] Two psychiatrists concluded that what worked about these rap groups was their similarity to the tightly knit combat units in Vietnam. "Combat was experienced in a group setting and can best be abreacted [a technical psychological term meaning to recreate an event in order to overcome it] in one." Men who have experienced the tight bonds of combat express "purposelessness and estrangement from those who have not shared the overwhelming emotions of combat. For these men, we deliberately recreate a 'band of brothers.'"[24]

The coalition of mental health workers and veterans' activists lobbied the Veterans Administration, Congress, and the American Psychiatric Association to provide assistance to veterans suffering from post–Vietnam Syndrome. Combat veterans who experienced delayed reactions to their Vietnam experiences initially had trouble getting the VA's attention. The Diagnostic and Statistical Manual II (DSM II), the standard physicians' listing of psychiatric disorders in use in the early 1970s, had no separate category for combat stress. An edition of DSM compiled in the early 1950s when the memory of World War II and the Korean War was still fresh had included combat stress, but it did not include delayed reactions. The VA refused to consider psychiatric disorders that set in more than a year after leaving the service as combat related, but the activists argued many of the men most in need of special help had delayed reactions.

One psychologist who counseled returning veterans explained why some of the worst symptoms of post–Vietnam Syndrome took more than a year to develop. While in Vietnam men could often hold out until they came home. Even though some veterans resented the lack of public welcoming ceremonies, most drew comfort from the warmth of their families' homecoming. "However, after a year or more, the veteran would begin to notice some changes in his outlook." No matter how sympathetically he was treated by loved ones and friends, he came to believe that those who hadn't shared his Vietnam experience could not understand his feelings. "He began to feel depressed, mistrustful, cynical and restless. He experienced problems with sleep and with his temper." Even if he hated his life in Vietnam, "he became somewhat obsessed with his combat experience." He starting asking why he had returned alive and others had died or been maimed. His depressed, cynical, and obsessive outlook became "a chronic lifestyle affecting not only [him] but countless millions of persons" close to him.[25]

A typical veteran explained to a congressional committee in 1981 his lonely alienation since he returned from Vietnam. He drifted across the country, had two failed marriages, and could not keep a job. "There have been periods of deep depression in my life since Vietnam, and I have turned to alcohol during these moments," he admitted. The lack of human connection and meaningful work made him feel "sick of my life, tired of failing at everything I attempt." He had trouble sleeping, as memories of the war intruded at all hours of the day and night. He flew into unpredictable rages and feared that he was capable of violence. He resented what he considered to be the more favorable treatment given to World War II veterans and the hostages returning from Iran. The Vietnamese boat people entering the United States seemed to enjoy a better reception. "When I got home I was asked how many babies I killed or how good was the dope."[26] Other veterans flew into rages at what they saw as better treatment given others. "We watched as those who burned draft cards and fled to Canada received amnesty. We watched as the Iran hostages received a hero's welcome" in 1981. The apparent unfairness of it all burned deeply into some veterans' souls. "All the time, we degenerated further and lost whatever faith we had in self, our country, and society."[27]

Another veteran, who spent time in jail after his homecoming, characterized the terrible conditions of imprisoned returnees from Vietnam. We "fought in an unpopular war, returned home to a hostile society, who had been tagged as out-of-control killers of innocent men, women, and children in the name of democracy." He complained that the Veterans Administration did not know and seemed not to care how to treat veterans who ran afoul of the law. After release from prison, many could not find work and felt "completely discouraged." Careful studies indicated that Vietnam veterans did not go to jail in any greater numbers than did the general population, but, of course, some Vietnam veterans did engage in criminal behavior after the traumas they incurred in Vietnam.[28]

Many members of Congress, the VA, and the established medical organizations—traditional supporters of veterans' causes—expressed skepticism that Vietnam veterans actually had special problems. World War II veterans dominated congressional committees on veterans' affairs. Like the established veterans' organizations—the American Legion, the Veterans of Foreign Wars, and the Disabled American Veterans—many congressional leaders active on veterans' issues had supported the American war effort in Vietnam. They were often skeptical of the motives of the Vietnam veterans' advocates, and some older veterans feared that special programs for Vietnam-related disabilities would dilute their own benefits. The chairman of the House Committee on Veterans Affairs, Texas Democrat Olin "Tiger" Teague, himself a decorated, wounded World War II veteran, had trouble understanding the Vietnam veteran. One congressional staff member characterized Teague's attitude this way: "Well, you know, this is tough, but we [World War II veterans] sucked it up and we didn't need to go into . . . counseling." The old warrior once screamed at a Vietnam veteran lobbying for new health benefits, "How can you little wimps be sick? A tour of duty lasted only twelve months. In World War II, soldiers fought in the war for years. How can you be traumatized?"[29]

The movement to provide new mental health benefits for Vietnam veterans ultimately proved to be overwhelming. Since 1945 members of Congress had often put aside their differences on defense and foreign policy to support veterans' benefits, and advocates for Vietnam veterans also discovered that focusing on the personal needs of returned soldiers could bridge the chasm separating hawks and doves. California Democratic Senator Alan Cranston, a World War II veteran who chaired the Senate Committee on Veterans Affairs, had been an outspoken liberal critic of the Vietnam War, but in 1971 he introduced legislation to provide additional counseling for veterans suffering from alcohol and drug abuse. Alcohol-related disorders made up the largest category of conditions treated in VA hospitals. There had been reports of widespread heroin addiction among troops in Vietnam and drug abuse treatment also fit very well into the existing structure of therapy at the hospitals.

A relentless opponent of the bill, Teague blocked its passage in the House. He complained that the concentration on alcohol and drug problems unfairly stigmatized the vast majority of Vietnam veterans without these problems who held jobs or attended school. Besides, by the mid-1970s the earlier near hysteria over soldiers using heroin in Vietnam subsided. Much to the surprise of specialists in addiction, about 90 percent of the soldiers who smoked or injected heroin in Vietnam never did so again once they returned home. Veterans' advocates helped convince Cranston to shift the focus of his proposal away from concentrating on alcohol and drugs to stress counseling for a variety of psychological problems.

Cranston pressed on throughout the 1970s for special programs to help Vietnam veterans readjust to civilian life. His efforts bore greater fruit after Jimmy Carter was elected president in 1976 and appointed Max Cleland as director of the Veterans Administration. Cleland had lost both legs and an arm in combat in 1968 and spent nearly a year in a VA rehabilitation hospital. He resented being treated as a "claim number." When he was wheeled into a rehab ward, he was stunned at how nearly all the other patients, many of them veterans of World War II or Korea, were more than twenty years older than he. "Some stared at me like I was a man from Mars. . . . It was obvious that these men had not the slightest inkling of what service in Vietnam had been all about."[30] His months of hospitalization convinced him to devote his life to improving the lot of Vietnam veterans. Over the next few years he testified before Congress, went to work on Senator Cranston's staff, and headed the Georgia state commission on veterans' affairs when Jimmy Carter was governor. In this position he made unannounced visits to VA hospitals to get an accurate view of conditions. A staff member recalled that after one such inspection he "wasn't back ten minutes and I got all kinds of phone calls from people in the Veterans Administration. Who is this man Cleland raising hell in this hospital? They wanted to know who this wild man was."[31]

Cleland kept up the pressure in his role as director of the VA. Working with Cranston and the coalition of Vietnam veterans activist groups, he pressed for legislation to recognize the psychological needs of Vietnam veterans. The House resisted including special counseling for Vietnam veterans for two years, but finally relented in 1979. In July of that year, Congress created the Vietnam Veterans Outreach Program to open a nationwide network of Vet Centers to meet the psychological needs of returnees from Vietnam. At the same time, the coalition pressured the American Psychological Association (APA) to include a formal description of combat-related stress in the third edition of the Diagnostic and Statistical Manual (DSM-III). Psychiatrists Chaim Shatan and Robert J. Lifton and activist Jack Smith joined the APA's Committee on Reactive Disorders, which was preparing a portion of the DSM-III. Largely as a result of their initiative the 1980 DSM-III included a new condition called Post-Traumatic Stress Disorder (PTSD), which the APA identified as a traumatic event "outside the range of usual human experience" that would be "markedly distressing to almost anyone." People suffering from PTSD reexperienced the events through memories of them or recurrent dreams of the event, or even by acting or feeling as if the event was happening in the present. People with PTSD showed "reduced responsiveness to the external world" and could experience difficulty in falling or staying asleep; irritability or outbursts of anger; difficulty concentrating; hyper-vigilance; and exaggerated startle responses.[32] The VA acknowledged PTSD as a disorder affecting thousands of Vietnam veterans as well as characterizing it as "a new name for an old condition," something psychiatrists and psychologists "recognized in combat veterans from previous wars."[33]

The creation of the Vet Centers and the accepted definition of PTSD set in motion counseling services specifically tailored for Vietnam veterans. Under Operation Outreach the VA opened 137 centers across the country by 1981.[34] Since the centers had been established in part because of Vietnam veterans' distrust in the care provided by the network of existing VA hospitals, the new centers were physically separate, often located in storefronts in run-down areas of large- and medium-sized cities. Centers consciously recruited veterans suffering from some PTSD symptoms as counselors. Customarily a center had a trained psychologist or social worker as a director and a staff of four to six men who had all served in Vietnam. The centers actively sought out newcomers to participate in the rap groups. In their first two years of operation the centers treated about 52,000 veterans and declared that 10,700 of these cases had been completed successfully.[35] To some veteran advocates, the number treated and the rate of success was far too low. The Disabled American Veterans estimated that five hundred thousand men who served in Southeast Asia required readjustment counseling. The VA gave an even higher estimate of seven hundred thousand.[36]

The most dramatic failure of effective counseling occurred when many took their own lives. The number of veteran suicides was not easy to determine precisely. A figure often cited in the press was that over 150,000 Vietnam veterans committed suicide after the war. Some veteran advocates reported an even more astonishing number, 500,000. While terrible, the actual number of suicides was not as high as these reports indicated. The Centers for Disease Control found that 9,000 Vietnam veterans had committed suicide by the early 1980s. The suicide rate for Vietnam veterans in the first five years after their return home was about 25 percent higher than that of the population in general, and after that time, the rates were the same as for the general population. Regardless of the careful assessment of suicides among Vietnam veterans, stories continued to abound about their astronomical suicide rates.[37]

Despite the inclusion of PTSD in the APA's Diagnostic and Statistical Manual, it remained a controversial categorization for Vietnam veterans. No one could say with certainty how many veterans had PTSD. Advocates for Vietnam veterans offered estimates as high as 1.5 million, nearly 50 percent of the 3.14 million men who served in or around Vietnam. Studies prepared by various health professionals and the VA gave much lower figures, but these too varied widely. One serious study conducted by the Centers for Disease Control put the incidence rate of PTSD at 2 percent. Another psychiatrist estimated that 1 percent of the general population experienced some sort of PTSD, while the rate for Vietnam veterans was 3.5 percent, and for men wounded the rate was 20 percent. Another equally serious study found that 19 percent of Vietnam veterans had PTSD. The National Vietnam Veteran Readjustment Survey found that 15.2 percent of male theater veterans experienced PTSD and another 11.1 percent had a few of the symptoms. The survey concluded that about 30 percent would display symptoms of PTSD over their lifetimes.[38] In short, there was no easy answer to how many veterans needed treatment.

When Ronald Reagan became president in 1981, the VA's Operation Outreach became a target of cost cuts. Reagan proposed terminating the program when its original authorization expired in September 1981, because it seemed to cost too much and its benefits seemed to be modest. The Office of Management and Budget (OMB) argued that the storefront centers had "contacted the majority of veterans who might be helped by this approach," so the centers' work was largely complete. OMB complained that the continued existence of Veterans' Centers would create "another anachronism of the federal government, a permanent program for the solution of a transitory problem."[39]

Public outcry saved the program. Traditional veterans' organizations like the American Legion, the Disabled American Veterans, and the Veterans of Foreign Wars (VFW) joined supporters of Vietnam veterans and members of Congress in calling for continuation of Operation Outreach. A Harris survey found that over two thirds of the public opposed cuts in veterans benefits. Robert Muller of the Vietnam Veterans of America reported that his office received over five thousand letters in the first months of 1981 insisting that the storefront centers be maintained. A *New York Times* editorial faulted the Reagan budget for maintaining twenty-five billion dollars a year for traditional veterans' programs, which aided millions who were not "truly needy," while threatening to cut the Vietnam veterans' programs, which the *Times* asserted "would, at minimal cost, continue important services for people who need them badly." *Washington Post* columnist Philip Geyelin decried what he characterized as "shabby treatment" of Vietnam veterans.[40] Congress responded by continuing the Vet Centers throughout the Reagan administration.

That extension hardly stilled arguments over the psychological well being of Vietnam veterans. As time went on, most of these veterans resumed some degree of normal life. The whole idea of "readjustment" diminished in importance as the veterans grew older. Erwin Parson, a psychiatrist who directed twenty-three Vet Centers in the Northeast in the 1980s, objected to the continuing claim that Vietnam veterans needed to readjust to civilian life. The term readjustment, he told Congress in 1989, " goes beyond a misnomer in terms of its potential damage to veterans' images. . . . This word becomes just another way of keeping the Vietnam veteran young, and politically under-developed and immature." Most Vietnam veterans were around forty years old fifteen years after the war ended, and they could not be expected to resume the same residences, work, schooling, or associations they had had before they entered military service. Parson feared that the concept of readjustment "tells the veteran, 'You will never grow up. You will never mature.'"[41]

Even though the Vet Centers continued to treat thousands of veterans for PTSD in the 1980s, the nature of the disorder proved difficult to pinpoint. While the VA recognized PTSD as a distinctive problem, it remained difficult to specify exactly what PTSD was, who suffered from it, and whether or not their symptoms came from their wartime experiences. Wartime combat certainly was an abnormal condition, but studies of PTSD among fire fighters, paramedics, and people involved in serious industrial accidents also showed heightened levels of PTSD and demonstrated that different people reacted in many different ways to stressful situations. The actual traumatic event had less to do with someone's reactions than his or her psychological makeup. Those with a prior history of depression were about three times more likely to develop symptoms of PTSD. Simply put, the same event produced different levels of PTSD in different people. There were further complications in determining how widespread PTSD was because many men sought treatment at the Vet Centers years after their return home. This made it hard to tell whether their current difficulties came from what had happened in Vietnam or from their post-war experiences.[42]

One aspect of troubled veterans' postwar recollections was that some men invented traumatic wartime experiences. After every war, some men try to capture undeserved glory by claiming to have performed heroic acts. What made the Vietnam situation so different was that a small but significant number of men invented war stories in which they were villains. Men who had never served in the military, had been in uniform but not been to Vietnam, or who had served in desk jobs in the rear told their rap groups harrowing tales of combat, destruction, and random killing of people and animals. One made up a story about "putting a guy on a helicopter after a firefight. We lifted him up, and before we got him in, his body broke in half. When I first got to Vietnam, I spoke out against some of the awful things I saw going on. But then I got wrapped up in the killing scene."[43]

The domestic unpopularity of the war at the time it was fought, and the exposure of American atrocities in Vietnam, provided a context for men to proclaim their own involvement in war crimes. These public confessions occurred at a time when therapists paid ever-greater attention to recovered memories of long-suppressed traumas.[44] Americans clearly did commit atrocities in Vietnam, murdering unarmed non-combatants, committing rapes, burning villages, or desecrating the bodies of dead National Liberation Front or People's Liberation Armed Forces fighters. These atrocities occurred because American troops were poorly led and American commanders measured progress in the war through the body count. American soldiers and marines were often enraged by the absurdity of a war without front lines and limited support at home. For Vietnam combat soldiers dangers were everywhere, yet invisible. Any peasant could be a guerrilla, an ambush could occur at any time. The enemy did not wear uniforms, and American soldiers regularly considered all Vietnamese hostile. An American combat soldier had to be on heightened alert and he could fire his weapon in an instant.

Still, some veterans told stories that were sheer fantasies. Men invented false war records for a variety of reasons. By the 1980s the popular image of the Vietnam veteran had changed from an aggressive, remorseless killer into a victim of a heartless U.S. government and military. The activism on behalf of legitimizing PTSD intensified the public belief that many Vietnam veterans deserved pity and compassion. At the most cynical level, veterans stood to gain financially by inventing wartime horror stories. A year's VA benefits for total disability could be worth as much as eighteen thousand dollars in the 1980s, but a VA health professional had to certify that a veteran was totally disabled in order for him to receive maximum benefits. This requirement put subtle pressure on the veteran to display the appropriate symptoms of PTSD.

Further complicating the situation, therapists sometimes encouraged veterans to display the symptoms of PTSD as a first step toward diminishing the condition's unhealthy manifestations. If someone constantly repeated horrifying narratives of his tour of Vietnam duty, he suffered from PTSD. But the willful forgetting of a trauma also indicated that someone had PTSD. When veterans participated in the rap groups, the psychologists and the other members of the groups told men who did not recall traumatic events that their very lack of memory proved that they had some deeply suppressed recollections. In order for a man to be fully accepted by the other members of a rap group, he had to bring something to the discussion. Group members praised their fellows for "sharing" traumatic events, and they berated men who did not relate tales of hardships for mental and emotional laziness. They were told that they were "not working" and, even worse, by shirking their responsibilities, they shifted a burden onto the shoulders of the other group members. Someone who persistently refrained from narrating traumatic events could even be discharged from a treatment center.[45]

Often other veterans were quicker to spot fraudulent claims than the therapists. Veterans were able to compare a fellow group member's experience to their own. If someone's claims seemed wildly exaggerated, other veterans dismissed them. On the other hand, veterans believed a patient whose narration included rich details characterized an "event" (in contrast to what they called a "war story"). Clinicians, few of whom served in Vietnam, found it harder to distinguish the genuine from the counterfeit. They also asserted that the advantages for a patient of sharing memories, however embellished, far outweighed the psychological costs of keeping quiet.[46]

Psychologists had a vested interest in validating a veteran's claims that he had seen or participated in horrific wartime activities. Even when therapists doubted if veterans actually experienced some of the harrowing events they related, there were strong professional incentives to continue to treat the veteran for PTSD. The elastic definitions of PTSD covered many potential disorders. Therapists worried about how they could explain why they accepted some men for treatment and denied it to others. One therapist told his colleagues "one day we're going to have people coming around here and they're going to ask us to account for the guys we've refused. In a lot of cases, we can't give a coherent explanation about how exactly we came to the conclusions that we came to."[47] To be safe, therapists leaned toward diagnosing PTSD in men who presented memories of wartime atrocities.

Allen Young, a social anthropologist who wrote a skeptical study of treatment of PTSD among Vietnam veterans, observed the subtle way in which therapists suppressed their doubts about a veteran's story. One man claimed to have been a member of an airborne brigade in Vietnam, but his stories lacked specific details of people, places, and events. He once described an ambush in which his closest buddies were killed. As was the custom in the group, another veteran asked him, "What was it like for you? I mean you were there and you were looking at their dead bodies. What went through your mind? How did you feel?" His reply lacked emotion: "There's no use crying over spilled milk," he said. "You win some, you lose some."[48] Some of this veteran's details were absurd. He claimed that a helicopter pilot once refused to lower his craft to the ground to allow his unit safely to climb out onto the battlefield. The pilot told the men to jump out, dropping seventy feet to the ground. An incredulous therapist asked, "You know that's like jumping off the roof of a ten story building. Is that what you're saying?" "Hell, yes," the veteran replied. "We just dusted ourselves off and laughed our heads off."

This man's therapist came to doubt if his experiences were real. The therapist remarked at a debriefing, "You know, you listen to Chris talk about himself and Vietnam, and he makes it sound as if he was watching a cartoon of himself." But *something* was going on with this man. He often flew into fearful rages or collapsed in fits of sobbing. When the other members of the group would comfort him with hugs and kind words, he would erupt in fury at "the politicians" who, he said, "left him hanging in the wind." It was hard to tell what made him so upset, and when the therapists probed for more details he became even angrier. The therapists then broke off their questions, afraid that the man might harm himself or some other members of the group.

After several weeks, the lead psychologist came to question whether or not this man had actually ever been in Vietnam and doubted that the diagnosis of

PTSD was appropriate. Instead, he believed that the man had a severe personality disorder, not PTSD, and should not be treated in group therapy sessions with the other veterans. He recommended that he be discharged from the VA facility and receive more conventional treatment in a psychiatric hospital. The ward's clinical chief upbraided the therapist for suggesting that someone could be misdiagnosed with PTSD. This veteran, like the other residents in the program, had already been given the PTSD label. Therefore, whether he remained silent or spoke, he projected his symptoms. His stories, no matter how unlikely, had to be taken seriously as evidence of the deep psychological wounds left by Vietnam, and he remained in treatment.[49]

Veterans' recollections of having committed or seen atrocities coincided with the development of a confessional culture in the United States in the post–Vietnam War decades. Psychologists welcomed verbal openness about shocking experiences as the best step to recovery from earlier traumas. Some therapists encouraged troubled patients to recall having been sexually molested by close relatives in their childhoods, occasionally pushing patients so hard to recall events that they invented memories of early abuse. Lurid tales of incest naturally found a ready outlet in newspapers and local and national television newscasts, and by the late 1980s hysteria swept across the country. Other stories invented by those with "false memory syndrome," the recollection of past events that did not occur, became even more grotesque. Purported victims of long-forgotten sexual abuse recalled being forced to participate in weird satanic rituals. They sometimes alleged mutilations of domestic animals and even murder. By the mid-1990s, though, a backlash developed against many of the sensational claims of recovered memories. Parents or caregivers who had been accused of having committed some of the most heinous crimes created the False Memory Foundation. Pamela Freyd, executive director of the foundation, noted that "recovering a false memory as a war atrocity is not as unusual as you might think."[50] Some of the accused conducted a media campaign to restore their reputations. They enlisted the help of conventional psychologists who doubted the widespread existence of true recovered memories. Many of them who earlier had validated the claims of recovered memories changed their minds and recovered memory became a rare diagnosis.[51]

At the same time writers turned a skeptical eye to some Vietnam veterans' recollections of shocking events. Jerry Lembcke, who opposed U.S. participation in the war, examined the often-repeated tale of howling mobs of antiwar protesters spitting on veterans at airports when they returned from Vietnam. He could not find a single contemporary account of such an event and concluded that they were urban legends. He concluded that "stories of veterans being abused by antiwar activists only surfaced years after the abuses were alleged to have happened."[52] Writing from the other side of the political spectrum, Bernard Gary Burkett, a supporter of the U.S. involvement in the war, provided numerous examples of veterans falsely confessing to atrocities that never took place.[53]

One of the more sensational, and later discredited, atrocity stories received widespread attention in June 1998 when CNN broadcast "Valley of Death," an hour-long documentary alleging that the United States military used deadly nerve gas during a secret September 1970 mission in Laos. CNN claimed that that the U.S. military and intelligence services had violated numerous international treaties by using sarin nerve gas, one of the world's deadliest poisons, during Operation Tailwind. The report claimed that the object of the raid was to kill about a dozen U.S. servicemen who had supposedly defected to the Communist side.

Charges that the United States had killed its own servicemen and violated international conventions to do so were astonishing and explosive. The day after the report was broadcast, hundreds of servicemen who participated in or knew of Operation Tailwind at the time cried foul. Participants claimed that they had used gas, but it had been nonlethal tear gas of the sort that had been employed throughout the war. They denied that Americans had been the target of the operation or that any Americans had been in the area when the U.S. helicopters landed. The Pentagon began its own investigation of the allegations, as did CNN. The network employed Floyd Abrams, a prominent New York attorney, to investigate whether the report was credible and whether CNN should have broadcast it.

The Defense Department consulted its records and interviewed the participants in Tailwind. The Secretary of Defense unequivocally denied that Tailwind had used poisonous gas or that the operation had killed any American prisoners of war. But was the denial credible? Those who accused the military of using lethal gas claimed that Tailwind had been a "black operation," one that could later be denied by the Pentagon. But Abrams's investigation also found the accusations made in the program to be false. Abrams, an advocate for the First Amendment rights of journalists, concluded that the producers and reporters who broadcast "Valley of Death" believed the story was true. So deep was their conviction that they "discounted contrary information they received." They relied on hypothetical questions posed to the participants and confused tear gas with nerve gas. "I mostly got nerve gas questions and I gave tear gas answers," said one of the pilots afterwards. Abrams concluded that CNN's story that "United States troops used nerve gas during the Vietnamese conflict on a mission in Laos designed to kill American defectors is insupportable. CNN should retract the story and apologize." The network did on July 2, 1998.[54]

The fiasco over "Valley of Death" exposed some enduring fault lines in the memory of Vietnam combatants. For a generation, some Americans remembered Vietnam veterans as one part victim, one part barbarous killer. The "Valley of Death" report made the case for the soldier as a victim of a heartless and deceptive government, willing to kill its own service personnel and then lie about it. It also suggested that the men who conducted the operation were willing to use deadly and illegal weapons, even against their fellow soldiers.

There was an obvious reason for the public's willingness to believe that the U.S. government might have used deadly nerve gas against its own men: The government *had* employed deadly chemicals in Vietnam and then denied the harmful health effects for many years. The U.S. military subjected tens of thousands of U.S. personnel and thousands more Vietnamese to harmful and sometimes deadly defoliants, commonly known as Agent Orange, a mixture of the chemicals 2, 4-D and 2, 4, 5-T. Between 1961 and 1970, the U.S. military sprayed twelve million gallons of Agent Orange over the jungles of Vietnam in an effort to kill the foliage under which the National Liberation Front (NLF) and the People's Liberation Armed Forces (PLAF) took cover. After officials became increasingly aware of the deadly effects of the dioxin contained in the 2, 4, 5-T in the late 1960s, the United States stopped spraying Agent Orange over Vietnam in 1970.[55] Yet both the government and the manufacturers of the defoliants steadfastly denied that they had caused harm or that they bore responsibility for damages.

Soon after the war, veterans complained of numerous ailments that, they said, had been brought on by exposure to Agent Orange, but the government dismissed these claims as fantasies.[56] The problems caused by Agent Orange were widely publicized in March 1978 when Chicago TV station WBBM broadcast a documentary titled "Agent Orange, The Deadly Fog" narrated by popular local TV reporter Bill Kurtis. "Agent Orange, The Deadly Fog" told harrowing tales of men sprayed with chemicals thicker than the Los Angeles smog. Many had cancer, some died. Their female partners had numerous miscarriages or bore children with birth defects like spina bifada, cerebral palsy, or sensory integration dysfunction. Over the next several months, dozens of reports appeared in newspapers, magazines, and on TV of veterans with cancer, severe skin conditions, infertility, and children with birth defects, all resulting from exposure to Agent Orange. Later in 1978 two veterans, Frank McCarthy and Paul Reutersham, organized the Agent Orange Victims International (AOVI). This network of health workers and over one thousand veterans turned the effects of Agent Orange on veterans into a prominent international issue. [57]

In 1979 AOVI and the Vietnam Veterans Against the War (VVAW) brought class-action lawsuits involving over two hundred thousand veterans and their families against Monsanto Corporation, Dow Chemical Company, Hercules Chemicals, and four other manufacturers of Agent Orange. A federal court in Long Island, New York, considered the suit over the next six years. During that time the conservative AOVI and the radical VVAW had a bitter falling out. The AOVI forced the original lead lawyer, Victor Yannacone, a tough and highly successful advocate for the veterans, off the case. The chemical companies denied that Agent Orange caused illnesses, stillbirths, or birth defects. Even if it did, they insisted that they had no liability because they had valid contracts with the government. Eventually, just before the case was to go to trial in May 1985 federal Judge Jack Weinstein crafted a settlement. The chemical companies would pay $180 million into a fund for the veterans and their children. The companies admitted no wrongdoing, and the veterans retained the right to sue the government for injuries resulting from exposure to Agent Orange.[58]

Individual veterans suffering from Agent Orange-caused disorders received little money from the settlement since the court set numerous restrictions on the way the money was paid.[59] Fewer than 5 percent of the plaintiffs received any compensation from the fund. One of the plaintiff's lawyers told the judge that an "overwhelming majority of" the two thousand veterans he represented "are opposed to this settlement." Weinstein refused to amend the settlement, and the Supreme Court later upheld his ruling. With interest the fund grew to $240 million. Veterans who could demonstrate a 100-percent disability due to Agent Orange received compensation of $12,800.[60]

Veterans' advocates continued working for more than a decade to have the federal government compensate the victims, but they encountered strong resistance from the VA, which consistently denied any health risks associated with the defoliants. Even in 1979, when VA Administrator Max Cleland first heard reports of men suffering skin blisters or cancers, he said, "It's hard for me to believe that walking by and touching some jungle foliage, all of a sudden I had a better risk of coming down with cancer."[61] Dr. Alvin Young, an air force major who had advocated the use of herbicides in Vietnam, became the VA's point man in denying that Agent Orange caused harm. He claimed a haphazard agency registry of men exposed to Agent Orange did "not support the thesis that there [are] any unusual long-term health problems" connected to the spraying of defoliants in Vietnam. Another VA official denied that Agent Orange could cause birth defects because "birth defects can only be caused by exposure of the pregnant female. We had very few pregnant females serving in Vietnam."[62] Some members of Congress were incredulous at this point of view. Tennessee Democratic Senator Al Gore replied, "Years ago, people did not believe that the male had anything to do with procreation. It is just as simplistic to believe that genetic damage can be caused only if the mother is the one exposed."[63]

In the late 1980s frustrated lawmakers ordered first the VA and then the Centers for Disease Control (CDC) to study the health consequences of exposure to Agent Orange. After intense pressure the two agencies acknowledged it caused one bad effect, chloracne, a severe skin disorder. Members of Congress were not satisfied that the CDC study had gone far enough. Senators

Daschle and Kerry drafted legislation for more scientific studies of the health effects of exposure to dioxin in Vietnam. The measure passed the Senate but languished in the House. In November 1988 the American Legion, a conservative veterans organization long suspicious of the antiwar views of Vietnam veterans, found a strong correlation between exposure to Agent Orange and benign tumors and skin diseases. They confirmed the higher rate of miscarriages, stillbirths, and birth defects among the female partners of men exposed to Agent Orange.[64]

A new cabinet-level Department of Veterans Affairs began operating in 1989. Its first secretary, Edwin Derwinski, had served for decades as a Republican representative from Illinois. Seeking to resolve the controversy over Agent Orange, Derwinski appointed retired Admiral Elmo R. Zumwalt, Jr., as his special consultant on Agent Orange. Zumwalt led U.S. Navy forces in Vietnam in 1968 and two years later he became chief of Naval Operations. He ordered the use of Agent Orange in Vietnam in order to clear foliage along riverbanks paroled by navy Swift boats. His son, Lieutenant Elmo Zumwalt III, had commanded a Swift boat that had been heavily exposed to the chemical. Lieutenant Zumwalt's son Elmo IV was born developmentally disabled in 1977. In 1983 Elmo Zumwalt III developed non-Hodgkin's lymphoma and Hodgkin's disease, brought on, his doctors believed, by Agent Orange. He died five years later.

Even after his son's death Admiral Zumwalt insisted that he "would order the spraying of Agent Orange again under similar circumstances, because in my judgment it kept thousands of American servicemen from being killed and maimed."[65] Nevertheless, he was determined to uncover the health effects of Agent Orange and provide compensation for those who had become sick. He read thousands of pages of studies, and he became convinced that Agent Orange caused dozens of deadly conditions, among them were deadly non-Hodgkin's lymphoma, soft tissue sarcoma, chloracne, liver disease, Hodgkin's disease, neurological effects, and numerous birth defects. He also learned to his dismay that chemical companies and VA scientists had engaged in "deception and fraud" to hide the harmful effects of Agent Orange. Zumwalt recommended that the VA disband its advisory committee on Agent Orange and replace it with an independent body. Derwinski delayed acting on Zumwalt's finding, but Congress responded with legislation signed by President George H. W. Bush in January 1991 requiring the National Academy of Sciences to conduct its own independent review of the health effects of Agent Orange.

In 1994 the Academy's Institute of Medicine concluded that exposure to Agent Orange was associated with the development of soft-tissue sarcoma, non-Hodgkin's lymphoma, Hodgkin's disease, chloracne, and pophryia cutanea tarda (another severe skin disease). It also found suggestive evidence of an association between Agent Orange and respiratory cancers (including lung and larynx), prostate cancer, and multiple myeloma.[66] The institute updated its findings at two-year intervals after its initial report. By 2002 it had added type 2 diabetes and spina bifada in children of men exposed to Agent Orange to the list of conditions for which there was limited or suggestive evidence of an association.[67] In 1996 the Clinton administration agreed to provide compensation to veterans who had conditions that the Institute of Medicine certified were associated with Agent Orange. The VA estimated it would pay $350-600 million over the next decade.[68]

Chapter

* * * * * * * * * * *

Vietnam Veterans Memorials
and Memories

As Vietnam veterans struggled with a variety of physical, psychological, and social wounds, a public movement grew to honor them. The widespread public belief that veterans had been badly mistreated by the government and ignored by civilians who had not gone to Vietnam paved the way for the construction of the Vietnam Veterans Memorial in Washington, D.C. This memorial and others like it across the country became sacred sites of commemoration where veterans and non-veterans alike came together to heal the wounds of war. In the decades after the war ended, veterans found a variety of venues in which to publicly express their memories and current beliefs about their wartime experiences. These expressions helped shape a new public consensus that honored Vietnam veterans' service, sympathized with their struggles with incompetent and often uncaring government officials, but remained deeply divided about the wisdom of American involvement in the war.

The idea of a memorial to recognize the men and women who lost their lives in Vietnam came to Jan Scruggs, a Vietnam veteran, one night in 1979 after he watched the movie *The Deer Hunter*. Scruggs was overwhelmed by the scenes in the movie of the disillusioned working-class veterans "who had believed in their country, which then abandoned them when the war turned sour." During a night of drinking and crying over the war, Scruggs suffered a flashback to his combat days, in which the "faces [of his dead comrades] continued to pile up in front of him. "The names," he thought. "The names. No one remembers their names." Tormented by the memory of the fallen, whom he believed the larger society had forgotten, he vowed "to build a memorial to all the guys who served in Vietnam. It'll have the names of everyone killed."[1] Scruggs began to raise money for the memorial, telling potential donors that "the whole idea behind [this fund] is a societal acknowledgment of the sacrifice and national reconciliation after the war." He hoped that the creation of a memorial would help ease the "embarrassment" he and other veterans had of "having served in Vietnam." [2] Over the next three years, Scruggs and a core group of committed veterans and their supporters raised money for the Vietnam Veterans Memorial Fund (VVMF), lobbied Congress and federal agencies, obtained official approval for a site adjacent to the Lincoln Memorial, organized a design competition, selected a plan for the memorial, and fought for its construction against opponents who considered the plan to be an inappropriate apology for United States participation in the war.

From the beginning, the creators of the memorial consciously sought to avoid resurrecting the political controversies that had raged during the war. They recruited officeholders who had supported and opposed the war to endorse the idea of a memorial honoring the warriors without commenting on the war. Robert Doubek, a Vietnam veteran who had developed numerous Washington connections as a lawyer, joined the fundraising effort. He told Congress that the "Vietnam Veterans Memorial is conceived as a means to promote the healing and reconciliation of the country after the divisions caused by the war."[3]

In 1980 Congress approved the construction of the memorial. Maryland Republican Senator Charles Matthias, the sponsor of the Senate resolution approving the donation of land for the memorial, emphasized that "for all Americans this memorial will express the spirit of reconciliation and reunion that preserves us as a nation." Today, he declared, "Vietnam is now far enough in the past that we can hopefully look to the reconciliation of the country after the divisions caused by the war."[4] Matthias characterized the memorial as a "visible sign" of the "reconciliation" among Americans deeply divided over the war. Representative Lucien Nadzi, a Michigan Democrat who had cosponsored the resolution in the House of Representatives, called the memorial a "harmonious and unifying" project, developed from a "disharmonious period of our national history."[5]

President Jimmy Carter elaborated on the theme of healing Americans' divisions by honoring the warriors, not the war, when he signed the resolution authorizing the memorial. He regretted that "for too long we tried to put [the] division [over Vietnam] behind by forgetting the Vietnam War . . . we ignored those who bravely answered their nation's call, adding to their pain the additional burden of our nation's inner conflict." On the surface it also appeared as if Carter reinforced the idea that the construction of the memorial took no stand on the war itself. "In honoring those who answered the call of duty," he remarked, "we do not honor the war." But this was a nearly impossible stand to maintain. His next sentence seemed to indeed validate the war effort. "We honor the peace they sought, the freedom they sought to preserve, and the hope that they held out to a world that's still struggling to learn how to settle differences among people and among nations without resorting to violence."[6]

Carter also quoted at length from an elegy to Walter Levy, a fallen soldier to whom Philip Caputo dedicated his bitter war reminiscence, *A Rumor of War*. "So much was lost with you," Carter read. "So much talent, intelligence and decency . . . [Y]ou embodied the best that was in us." The president quoted Caputo's lament that "the country for which you died wishes to forget the war in which you died. Its very name is a curse. . . . it was not altogether sweet and fitting, your death, but I am sure you died believing it was *pro patria* [for your country]. You were faithful." But Carter did not read the next sentence: "Your country was not." Instead, he paraphrased it by saying, "Caputo goes on to say that our country has not matched the faithfulness of that war hero, because our country tried to forget the war." The president said the memorial would reverse that amnesia. "Now, we'll build a memorial to the Walter Levys who died on the other side of the world, sacrificing themselves for others, sacrificing themselves for us and for our children's children." The president believed the memorial would prove "that we care, and that we will always remember." John Wheeler, the chair of the Vietnam Veterans Memorial Fund (VVMF), recalled that when he heard Carter's remarks he smiled and whispered to his wife, "Just you wait, Levy's name will be on the Mall a couple of blocks from here."[7]

Draining political controversy from the construction of the Vietnam Veterans Memorial proved to be easier said than done. In November 1980 the VVMF invited artists to enter a competition for a design for the memorial. The same process had been used to select designs for the Lincoln and Jefferson Memorials earlier in the century. The American Institute of Architects organized a jury of landscape artists, museum curators, and architects to judge the entries. The design criteria promised that the winning proposal would "make no political statement regarding the war or its conduct," allowing that the "creation of the Memorial will begin a healing process, a reconciliation of the grievous divisions wrought by the war." The organizers hoped that "through the memorial both supporters and opponents of the war may find a common ground for recognizing the sacrifice, heroism, and loyalty which were also part of the Vietnam experience." The VVMF also stipulated that the design should be reflective and contemplative, should harmonize with the nearby Lincoln Memorial and Washington Monument, and should list the names of all who had died or were missing in the Vietnam War. This final requirement of inclusion of the names proved to be the centerpiece, as well as one of the most controversial elements, of the winning design.[8]

The jury received about fourteen hundred entries for the competition, yet selecting a winner was easy. After a brief discussion, it unanimously selected the design proposed by Maya Lin, a twenty-one-year-old Yale University undergraduate majoring in art. Her design consisted of a wall cut into the earth in the shape of a shallow V or chevron. Invisible from the street, the wall was seen by visitors who walked down a wide concrete path in front. At its height, at the center, the wall stood ten feet. The memorial gradually tapered to ground level. Lin proposed that the names of the dead and missing be inscribed in the order of the date of their death or when they were declared missing. The list would begin where the two walls intersected, continuing along the right wall to its end and beginning again at the left side. The final names would appear at the intersection of the walls, adjacent to the earliest ones, to enhance the impression of the enduring legacy of the war. The memorial would be built of highly polished black granite so that visitors to the site would alternately see the names and a reflection of themselves and the others who had come to pay homage to the fallen. Lin told the commission when she submitted the design that "it is up to each individual to resolve or come to terms with this loss. For death is in the end a personal and private matter and the area containing this within the memorial is a quiet place, meant for personal reflection and private reckoning."[9]

Controversy erupted as soon as the VVMF named Lin's design the winner in October 1981. Opponents, mostly associated with politically conservative causes, complained that Lin's design pressed the agenda of domestic opponents of the war and dishonored the cause for which the warriors had fought, because it included no American flag, no inscription, and no statue. James Webb and Tom Carhart, a navy and army Vietnam veteran respectively, resigned from the VVMF in protest over the winning entry. Ross Perot, an extremely wealthy Texas businessman who had underwritten the cost of the design competition, organized opposition as soon as he saw the design drawings. He insisted that Interior Secretary James Watt, who exercised authority over the National Parks Service (the agency in charge of Washington memorials) block Lin's design. Tom Wolfe, the novelist and journalist, added that the successful design represented the triumph of elitist, modern art. Wolfe objected that the proposed design mocked the values of traditionally minded Americans who had little use for modern art and preferred art to represent something. The abstraction of the wall was as different as could be imagined from triumphal war memorials like the Iwo Jima statue that stood across the river at Arlington National Cemetery.[10]

Carhart, who had submitted an unsuccessful entry to the competition, bitterly denounced the design at a public meeting of the Commission of Fine

Arts on October 13, 1981. He called the memorial a "black scar . . . a black shaft of shame thrust into the earth." He complained about the color of the stone: "black, the universal color of sorrow and shame in all races, in all societies worldwide." The subterranean character of the memorial infuriated him. He complained that Lin created a memorial "in a hole, hidden as if out of shame. . . . Can America truly mean that we are to be honored by a black pit?" He repeated his denunciation in a widely circulated and reprinted *New York Times* op-ed piece. Lin's wall, he complained, was "pointedly insulting to the sacrifices made for their country by all Vietnam veterans." In public he called the wall nothing but "a black gash of shame and sorrow"; privately he likened the design to an open urinal. His language was too much for General George Price, an African-American veteran supporting the VVMF, who denounced Carhart's pejorative references to the color black.[11]

Political conservatives echoed Carhart's condemnation of the design. Phyllis Schlafly, a conservative political activist, thought the wall was a "tribute to Jane Fonda." Illinois Republican Representative Henry Hyde wrote an open letter to President Ronald Reagan denouncing the wall as a "political statement of shame and dishonor." The conservative magazine *The National Review* also demanded that Reagan step in and change the design. "OK, we lost the Vietnam war," the magazine began. "But American soldiers who died in Vietnam fought for their country and for the freedom of others, and they deserve better than the outrage that has been approved as their memorial." *The National Review* objected to the black granite as opposed to the white marble of the triumphant monuments of the nation's capital and said that the wall's invisibility from ground level symbolized "the 'unmentionability' of the war."

Interior Secretary Watt shared the conservatives' objections. He failed to scrap the wall entirely—too many people admired its contemplative power—but he did insist that another, traditional representational piece of art go up alongside the wall. He threatened to prevent the construction of the wall unless a statue called *Three Soldiers* designed by Frederick Hart went up as well. Lin found this alteration an appalling desecration of her design, and she hired a law firm to oppose sitting the statue at the apex of the V in her design.[12]

The organizers of the VVMF reluctantly agreed to a compromise in which the statue and an American flag would stand about one hundred feet away. A separate walkway connected the statue and the flagpole to the wall. The compromise partially mollified Lin who was able to claim that the flag and statue were not really part of the Memorial. When the *Three Soldiers* was added to the memorial site in 1984, two years after the dedication of the wall itself, the statue included a white soldier flanked by an African-American GI and another of indeterminate, but probably Hispanic, ethnicity. They are huge, muscular, but also deeply tired figures whose weapons hang from their shoulders. They stare at the wall as if transfixed by its power—as indeed were the tens of thousands who visited the wall each day.

In the end, the noisy outcry against Lin's design represented the views of only a small minority. Far more people admired the wall precisely because it reminded the visitor of the intolerable human cost of the fighting. Its attention to the men and women who served in the war, rather than to the leaders who sent them or the reasons for the war, appealed across political divisions. The historian Kurt Piehler has noted the similarity between the Vietnam Veterans Memorial and post–Civil War efforts at battlefield commemorations stressing reconciliation in North and South. "In the late nineteenth century," he writes, "elites in both regions of the country emphasized the need to honor the sacrifice of those who had fought in the Civil War. By focusing on the battlefields, they hoped to gloss over the causes of the conflict."[13] Even conservatives took note of the wall's powerful reminder of the cost of war. James J. Kilpatrick, a conservative syndicated columnist, remarked that this "will be the most moving memorial ever erected . . . each of us may remember what he wishes to remember—the cause, the heroism, the blunders, the waste."[14]

At the memorial's opening on Veteran's Day, November 11, 1982, one Vietnam veteran carried a sign reading:

I am a Vietnam veteran
I like the memorial
And if it makes it difficult to send people to battle again
I like it even more.[15]

His views were typical of the thoughts of the multitudes that visited the site. Almost immediately upon the opening of the memorial, visitors treated it as a shrine or a sacred space.[16] They became hushed and reverent as soon as they began walking down the gentle slope of the walkway in front of the wall. Many stopped at the entry to consult a large directory to the names on the wall. As countless pilgrims to church graveyards had done before them, some visitors laid paper on the wall and rubbed the surface with the crayons to take away visual representations of names on the wall.

People poured out their souls on notes they left at the wall. Some immediately acknowledged the self-reflective power of the polished granite. A man wrote, "the memorial puts you in the Vietnam War. You see the names, but you see yourself, too, and that makes you part of it." A Virginia woman commented, "I think it's one of the most reverential places I've ever been." A veteran offered thanks to "Maya Lin, Jan Scruggs, and the American people who put up the Memorial." Disappointments also came through. A man wrote that he could not "understand why it has taken so long for the government to do something like this for their families." Most of the letters were addressed to loved ones or fallen comrades. A mother wrote: "My son Ralphie: How I miss you . . . I think of you everyday and every hour of the day and night." Another mother mourned her son, "My dearest Ben, I miss you and think of you so much." "Dear Lieutenant," wrote one sergeant, "the memory of you and the loss of you is with me almost every day. I miss you, I love you and I'll never forget you. . . . Rest well, my Lieutenant." A wife wrote, "thank you for your love and this child, I will always love you. Margaret." Another mother told her son, " I miss you and think of you so much. Every day in my prayers, I thank God and Jesus for caring for you . . . I'm bringing 'Teddy bear' and a picture of your beloved racecar. I realize they can't stay there long, but they are yours and I want them to be with you. In time, I hope we can all be together."

Some comments were also political. One mother wrote, "[the war] changed me for life, forever. I don't think it was a fair war. I believe if it had been a declared war a lot of our sons would be home today." Veterans also vented their anger. One said "we should never allow a political leader to plunge us into a political war again. These boys died like it was a real war, but it wasn't."[17]

Visitors left mementos of every sort at the wall. The National Park Service (NPS) had expected people to bring flowers, as they did all the time to national cemeteries. Workers were also prepared to pick up trash—candy wrappers, cigarette butts, or even the stray beer can. For the first few days after the wall opened the NPS threw away what people had left behind, but service staff members realized almost immediately that no one had littered the site. People were too engaged and reverent for that. The NPS concluded that everything left at the wall had sanctity for those who brought it. People often attached heart-rending notes to their offerings. There actually were more objects than written material left at the wall. Many left medals, items related to POWs or MIAs, photographs of the dead, U.S. flags (some partially burned), and military clothing. But there were also random objects that had symbolic significance for remembering the war. A can of Colt 45 had a note attached: "Hey, Bro, Here's the beer I owe you. 24 years late." There were cans of C rations, cigarettes, lighters, dog tags, copies of the U.S. constitution, state flags, bullets, Bibles, prayers, baseball gloves, high-heeled shoes, tennis balls, key chains, and wedding rings. Some of the objects showed a great deal of preparation—embroidery, plaques, and collages of photographs. Some were more spontaneous or improvised. Many of the notes and cards bore the letterheads of local hotels. As time went on, it became expected, even obligatory, to leave *something*. Boy Scout and Girl Scout troops and school groups frequently left offerings at the wall as part of planned trips to nation's capital.

While most of the offerings were intensely personal, sometimes the objects or the messages attached to them contained commentary on war in general, American society, and the Vietnamese. A marine sergeant who left a wedding ring at the wall attached a note: "This wedding ring belonged to a young Viet Cong fighter. He was killed by a Marine unit in the Phu Loc province of South

Vietnam in May 1968. I wish I knew more about this young man. I have carried this ring for 18 years and it's time for me to lay it down. This boy is no longer my enemy." The copies of the U.S. Constitution, the state flags, the burned U.S. flags, the peace posters, the POW items, the signs reading "Learn from History" all made implicit statements about the war. They presented views from across the political spectrum, but all conveyed that something terribly wrong had occurred during the Vietnam War.[18]

The offerings left at the wall found a home in the Vietnam Veterans Memorial Collection. Every evening the NPS workers collected the items left that day in large plastic trash bags and stored them in a warehouse outside Washington. Beginning in 1985 the NPS began cataloging the items—referred to as "icons of a sacred site" by one of the devoted curators. In 1992 the Smithsonian Institution's National Museum of American History displayed a small portion of these relics in an exhibit titled, "Personal Legacy: The Healing of a Nation." The Smithsonian originally intended a short, six-month run for the exhibit, but the throngs of visitors never stopped. The museum kept the show open indefinitely and regularly refreshed it with items from the wall.[19]

Not only did people bring things to the wall; the site itself took on a central place in the recollection of the war. Lin's design achieved its central purpose of having each visitor bring his or her own thoughts and emotions to the wall. The NPS banned public demonstrations at the wall, allowing only approved ceremonies, but sometimes speakers violated the ban. In January 1991 Democratic Senator Paul Wellstone of Minnesota called a news conference in front of the wall on the eve of the Gulf War against Iraq to denounce U.S. participation in the war. The circumstances under which public figures and ordinary citizens chose to visit or avoid the wall suggested their attitudes toward the legacy of the war. Former President Richard Nixon never made a public visit to the wall. President Reagan, aware that his more conservative supporters opposed Lin's design, did not attend the opening ceremony of the wall but did so two years later after most of the controversy surrounding Lin's design dissipated. Then, in 1984 he presided over the dedication of Frederick Hart's statue of *Three Soldiers*. He asked Americans to "forgive themselves for those things which may have been wrong" in the conduct of the war. He turned this spirit of reconciliation into a plea for an activist foreign policy: "It's time we move on, in unity and with resolve, with the resolve to always stand for freedom, as those who fought did, and to always try to protect and preserve the peace."[20]

The wall retained its sanctity for presidents in the post–Cold War era. President George H. W. Bush emphasized that the memory of the Vietnam War would not deflect his administration from using military force abroad. He referred often to Vietnam during the conflict with Iraq in 1990–1991. He also visited the Vietnam Veterans Memorial on Veterans Day 1992, shortly after losing his bid for reelection, when he joined in reading the names of the dead.

All the more surprising, he shared the speaker's platform with George McGovern, the Democratic Party presidential nominee in 1972 who had run as an ardent opponent to American participation in the Vietnam War. McGovern recalled his own combat during World War II and affirmed his commitment to veterans. The audience, made up of many Vietnam veterans, cheered. They also applauded the remarks of a general who claimed that the end of the Cold War cast the American Vietnam experience in a new light. Since the United States was the only remaining superpower, Vietnam should no longer be remembered as a defeat, he said.[21]

Probably, the most emotional presidential visit to the wall occurred on Memorial Day 1993. President Bill Clinton confronted a rowdy crowd when he spoke at the wall four months into his term. Despite boos, whistles, and jeers of "draft dodger," Clinton finished a speech in which he asked for reconciliation among Americans who differed over the Vietnam. He also won over at least some of the crowd when he said there was no place else that a president should be on Memorial Day.[22]

The wall became one of if not the most visited sites in Washington. Despite the ban on public demonstrations at the memorial, the area nearby saw controversial gatherings. Vendors set up stalls selling a variety of Vietnam memorabilia. Many of the T-shirts, books, pins, flags, and posters raised the issue of missing servicemen. The material conveyed the message that the government had abandoned American MIAs in Indochina. In response the NPS limited the number of vendors at all sites on the Washington Mall in 1997.[23]

The success of the wall inspired continuing efforts to remember other aspects of the Vietnam War at the site. The most successful was a campaign to recognize the contributions of American women veterans in the Vietnam War, who supporters called "the invisible veterans." Organizers of the Vietnam Women's Memorial Fund argued that the healing process, which had been helped enormously by the construction of the wall, was still incomplete. They petitioned Congress for a women's memorial "to let the world know that America has not forgotten the American women who contributed and sacrificed during the Vietnam War." The Washington Fine Arts Commission held another design competition. This time, the commissioners did not make a unanimous decision. While the artists and architects on the commission favored an abstract proposal, the veterans' preference for a representational statue like Frederick Hart's prevailed. The commission selected a design by the sculptor Glenna Goodacre that was completed and dedicated on Veterans Day 1993. Located in a grove of trees about one hundred yards away from the wall, it consists of four figures: A female nurse cradles a wounded U.S. soldier. An African-American nurse comforts the white woman holding the soldier. A third woman kneels over the soldier's helmet and some medical equipment.[24] Visitors to the wall often pay their respects at the Vietnam Women's Memorial too, but they do not leave physical relics at either representational statue the way they do at the wall.

The Washington wall inspired the construction of hundreds of other Vietnam memorials across the country. As the organizers of the Vietnam Veterans Memorial Fund had done, the creators of the local memorials tried to separate the politics of the war from honoring the fighters. An organizer of a Kentucky memorial explained the need for recognition for "the guys who went over there and did what the country said needed to be done." The organizers of the New York City memorial used the slogan "It's Time" to generate funds. Some memorials used polished black granite from the same quarry in Indiana that provided the stone for the wall in Washington. Many listed the names of local dead. Many had statues of servicemen similar to *Three Soldiers*. The memorial in Angel Fire, New Mexico, a few miles north of Taos, actually completed in 1972, long before the construction of the wall, received visitors site after the wall went up. Dr. Victor Westphall created the memorial in honor of his son David, a GI killed in Vietnam, and all other war dead. Westphall explained that the memorial did not honor the heroism of the fallen, but promoted peace and reconciliation. He wanted their deaths to "become a symbol that will arouse all mankind and bring a rejection of the principles which defile, debase, and destroy the youth of the world."[25] In 1984 the Disabled American Veterans took over the operation of Angel Fire. Literature for this DAV Vietnam Memorial argued that it represented an even more contemplative, non-didactic way of remembering Vietnam than the wall. Angel Fire held a chapel and a large cross for quiet (obviously Christian) reflection.

But nothing could challenge the dominance of the wall as *the* central place of remembering the American experience in Vietnam.[26] A small replica of the wall traveled to communities in every section of the country. Spokesmen and women from the Vietnam Veterans Memorial Fund addressed veterans groups, students from the elementary to college level, and community organizations on the sacrifices made by Vietnam veterans.

While the ceremonials of healing and reconciliation at memorials brought a sense of psychological acceptance to many, some continued to engender feelings of remorse and bitterness. Divisions remained between veterans and men who avoided military service during the Vietnam War. For example, journalist James Fallows provoked a firestorm with a 1975 *Washington Monthly* article entitled, "What Did You Do in the Class War, Daddy?" in which he recalled his efforts to avoid the draft as a Harvard University undergraduate in 1969. He explained how he and his classmates employed a variety of ruses to fail their pre-induction physicals. (He starved himself for several weeks before his physical exam, so as to fall below the military's minimum weight standards.) Some of his classmates disrupted the pre-induction physicals. A few threw their urine samples into the faces of the military orderlies instructed to collect them. He recalled looking sheepishly at the other young men from working-class Boston who were going to be inducted into the military.

Fallows wrote again about his encounter with the draft board in the mid-1980s. He recalled "a generalized shame at having gotten away" with deception that kept him out of the military. "My fears of getting shot were naïve. If physical safety had been my only concern, I could have aimed for a safe, college-boy berth in the military." Fallows wondered publicly if he and other privileged men had not missed out on something highly valuable by avoiding Vietnam. When Fallows spoke out in the 1980s he claimed to have more empathy as an adult for the less-privileged men who had gone to war. Some readers scoffed that Fallows waited until the war was over and the draft abolished to express remorse over avoiding military service. Instead of healing wounds left over from the Vietnam War, these statements from former opponents of the war saying that they wished they had served came across as self-serving. Stung by such criticism, Fallows admitted to a smug self-righteousness in the years immediately after his article appeared. He regretted having taken on the role "of the publicly repentant performing bear draft dodger."[27]

Other men who avoided the draft during Vietnam and later served in the government faced even sterner criticism as "war wimps" when they advocated a muscular American foreign policy in the 1980s. Notable hawks of the 1980s who had educational, marriage, or medical deferments during the Vietnam War included Texas Republican Representative Dick Armey, Assistant Secretary of State Richard Burt, Wyoming Representative (and later Vice-President) Dick Cheney, Georgia Representative (and later House Speaker) Newt Gingrich, New York Representative Jack Kemp, Mississippi Representative (and later Senator) Trent Lott, Assistant Secretary of Defense Richard Perle, and conservative columnist George Will. They were mocked as "chicken hawks"—"a person who is enthused about one's country entering a war (hence a hawk) but makes sure his or her own butt isn't anywhere near the fighting (hence a chicken)."[28] Wounded Vietnam War veteran Lewis B. Puller, Jr., ran unsuccessfully as a Democratic candidate for Congress in Virginia against Republican Representative Paul Trible, who avoided the draft through a medical deferment. Puller seethed with resentment at what he considered Trible's facile post-Vietnam hawkishness. "When I saw Paul Trible wave the flag and call for increased defense spending," Puller bitterly recalled, "I wondered where the boy wonder had developed his perspective. If he indeed had the remotest idea of the dangerous potential of drum-beating and Red-baiting, I was not able to ascertain it."[29]

Some of these men expressed modest regret at having spent the Vietnam years on college campuses, but they were less anguished than was Fallows. In 1985 Newt Gingrich predicted that his draft deferment was "one of those things that will hang over me for the rest of my life." Still, he acknowledged, "part of the question I have to ask myself [about military service] was what difference

I would have made" in the armed forces. Richard Burt said, "I thought it would be better for me to go on with my education" than to serve as an enlisted man. At the time he felt lucky for having received a student deferment. But in retrospect, he admitted, I'm probably missing something from my background" for not having firsthand military experience like "a number of my countrymen." George Will took graduate student deferments at Oxford and Princeton Universities during the war. He reflected in 1985 that "the country didn't demand my presence in the war." Assistant Secretary of Defense Richard Perle said, "I was never called and I certainly didn't regret that." He thought at the time the war was misguided and in retrospect he considered it unwinnable. He would not have resisted the draft had he been called, but "I wouldn't have been keen to go as a draftee to Vietnam."[30]

While Americans poured out their complex personal emotions and memories of wartime, many high school and college students filled thousands of courses that focused on the human cost of the war both in the United States and in Vietnam. Researcher Marc Jason Gilbert who surveyed the state of teaching the Vietnam War noted "a number of scholars came to the conclusion that America's ignorance of the Vietnamese, its ethnocentric view of the wider world, and its lack of self-knowledge contributed to the failure of American policy." Some instructors sought to remedy this ignorance by devoting more attention to Asian themes. When Asian specialists taught the sources, they emphasized the price paid in Vietnam. Teachers with a background in U.S. subjects tended to stress the price paid at home. Yet a serious imbalance remained in favor of covering American themes and issues. Gilbert observed how educators acknowledged the need to include more Asian material. However, he found that many were reluctant to do so because they had little background in Asian subjects. He also found that their students came to their classes to learn about "America's Vietnam War, not about Vietnam, Southeast Asia, world history or the place of the war in the greater pageant of American hasty."[31]

Academic focus on the Vietnam War coincided with changing ideas about American educational approaches. Hands-on, or experiential, learning was catching on in the classroom. And many of the Vietnam courses made wide use of personal testimony from people who had been touched by the war. Theodore R. Kennedy, a professor of anthropology at the State University of New York at Stony Brook, taught a class called the "Vietnam Involvement Seminar" that enrolled more than eight hundred students in the 1980s. Kennedy invited numerous policymakers and veterans to share their recollections of the way they fought the war. Walter Capps, a professor of religious studies, taught one of the most popular early courses on the Vietnam War at the University of California at Santa Barbara in the 1970s and 1980s. Veterans of the war poured out their personal experiences to the rapt classroom. Capps explained that his class taught "how values are transmitted within contexts of highly volatile social and political change." At its height it enrolled more than one thousand students and was even featured on the CBS TV show *Sixty Minutes*.[32]

The testimonials of veterans were so charged and so personal that some teachers worried about their impact on their students. Veterans were so eager to appear before classes that many teachers had to limit their numbers. The quality of their presentations varied widely, and teachers became skittish at inviting strangers into their classrooms. A North Carolina school district warned teachers: "before having someone speak in your class, do some preliminary screening. This is especially important when someone volunteers his or her services without having been trained or sponsored by an organization you know."[33]

Veterans told their stories of induction, training, combat, and coming home. Antiwar activists recounted how opposition to the war had become often the principal focus of their lives in the late 1960s and early 1970s. The veteran with a slide show became a staple in Vietnam War courses. These presentations often were intensely emotional affairs. Graphic pictures occasionally caused students to cover their eyes or even leave the classroom. Many courses paired a veteran who hated the war with one who had found his experience ennobling. A disillusioned veteran might present slides showing the changes in his appearance during the year he was in combat. At first he appeared thin, clean shaven, with closely cropped hair and a smile on his face. As his tour of duty wore on, he looked shabbier and sadder. The last slide, showing him a year later with hair below his shoulders and a big black beard, never failed to bring a gasp from the students. [34] Veterans scarred emotionally by their wartime experiences reminisced about years of loneliness and depression after the war. They spoke of how few family members or old friends who had not been in the war cared about what they had done. They explained that talking to students helped them heal their wounds from the war. Others, with happier recollections of the war showed slides of men relaxing around the barbecue at a rear base, the Bob Hope show, excited Vietnamese children, or cheerful homecomings.[35]

However gripping the testimony of individual veterans was for the students, the veterans' presentations were essentially highly personal, and it was not easy for students to put them into the larger perspective of what happened in the war. Customarily, the veteran guest speakers had little familiarity with the vast literature and the scholarly controversies surrounding the war, and they preferred to speak only about what they did, how they felt in Vietnam, and how they remembered the war. Everyone's war experience was different, yet the veterans who flooded the classrooms often presented their version of the war as the truth. Memories changed over time. Some teachers of the Vietnam War distrusted veterans' testimonials. Kali Tal, an editor of the popular journal *Vietnam Generation*, warned that the strength of the emotions presented by the veterans made them especially dangerous in the classroom. "The very thing that makes the veterans' testimony so attractive to us," she warned, "the very *authenticity* of it—makes the testimony suspect as history." Tal concluded, "the Vietnam War as depicted by the veterans we invite to our classrooms may not be the same Vietnam War that we have uncovered in our research, or even the same war that the soldier himself survived some twenty years earlier."[36]

Veterans' testimonials and personal memories of people who had lived through the Vietnam era proved both irresistibly attractive and also problematic in teaching the Vietnam War. Most courses employed a textbook and other secondary sources to provide a chronological and interpretive framework for the students. But scholars' accounts were never enough for either teachers or students of the Vietnam War. The use of original documents created during the war to engage the students had a wide appeal. Some experiential-learning devotees were probably too dismissive of secondary works. One advocate of using documents to study the Vietnam War worried about "the emotional baggage" teachers who had lived through the Vietnam era brought to the subject. Some teachers of the Vietnam War were veterans themselves and likened the secondary sources on the war to combat: "long stretches of boredom punctuated by occasional moments of action."[37]

Vietnam veterans also revisited their wartime experiences by returning to Vietnam as tourists. A few hundred veterans went to Vietnam in the 1980s and early 1990s, often flying into Vietnam from Thailand, filled with anxiety about the reception they might face from old foes. The end of the U.S. embargo on Vietnam in 1994 made it easier for Americans to obtain visas, and thousands more veterans went to Vietnam. For the nearly one million people of Vietnamese origin in the United States the end to the embargo meant they could visit their families in the Socialist Republic of Vietnam without having to apply for a visa outside the United States.[38] Some veterans traveled to make amends for their attacks on the land and the people. Others wanted just to visit old sites. Some sought to make contact with children they had fathered. Nearly all came back with reports of the friendliness of the Vietnamese. Rarely did they hear denunciations of U.S. policies or encounter personal hostility. The warm reception they received and the end of the embargo encouraged others to go.

Many of the visitors expressed surprise and relief at the warmth of the greeting they received from Vietnamese, North and South of the old dividing line. They were somewhat more regretful that some of the landmark sites of the war had not been preserved. Khe Sanh, the marine base besieged by the People's Liberation Armed Forces (PLAF) for five months in 1968, had been bulldozed by U.S. forces in the summer of 1968 immediately after the siege and little remained to suggest the fierce fighting that had occurred there. Many of the large American installations in the South had been abandoned, torn down, or taken over by Vietnamese government or private business offices. American veterans who returned to the war zone often noted that the trip brought about the psychological closure they had sought for years.[39] American veteran tourists often stopped at the tunnels of Cu Chi, about twenty-five miles northwest of Saigon. During the war the Viet Cong hid from the relentless American bombing and raids by the U.S. Army in the intricate seventy-five mile network of underground chambers. The tunnels of Cu Chi came to symbolize the enterprising spirit of resistance of the Viet Cong to the advanced technology of the Americans. In the decades after the war, the residents of Cu Chi turned the tunnels into a tourist destination. Local young people, born years after the end of the war, dressed in the black pajamas of the Viet Cong or the uniforms of the People's Liberation Army, lectured about the war, and guided tourists underground. Visitors too could dress up in replicas of the clothing of the time and crawl through some of the tunnels, specially enlarged to accommodate Western bodies.[40]

Veterans' enthusiastic reception of Vietnam memorials, the reconsideration of their Vietnam War–era experiences by both veterans and those who had not gone to Vietnam, the eagerness of veterans to tell their stories in classrooms, and their emotional revisiting of the battlefields all helped foster an emerging consensus about Vietnam veterans and the war they fought. Many had come to terms with their own service, and they appreciated the belated homecoming they received. While the non-veteran American public still hardly considered them heroes deserving of the same adulation as the victors of World War II, by the beginning of the twenty-first century Vietnam veterans were no longer considered villains who had helped create a mistaken, possibly immoral war. More often the non-veteran public and younger generation who had no personal experience with the war saw the men and women who had served in Vietnam as victims of wartime incompetence and public indifference. Veterans were seen as people who needed help to heal. This attitude toward Vietnam veterans did not especially enhance their status as effective, autonomous human beings, but it did help create a more general sense that scars now covered the emotional wounds of the Vietnam War.

Chapter

*   *   *   *   *   *   *   *   *   *   *

The Vietnamese in America

A mass exodus of immigrants from South Vietnam to the United States began on a small scale in the spring of 1975. Over the next decade hundreds of thousands of Vietnamese made their way to the United States where they settled across the country. Eventually they and their descendants numbered over a million, and they prospered and flourished culturally in their new home. Vietnamese Americans also helped shape the memory of the Vietnam War.

As the People's Liberation Armed Forces (PLAF) and National Liberation Front (NLF) fighters tightened their ring around Saigon in April 1975, tens of thousands of Vietnamese who had worked for the government of the Republic of Vietnam, the American government and military, U.S. construction firms, and dozens of U.S.-sponsored relief agencies were terrified. For years the South Vietnamese government had maintained the tenuous allegiance of its citizens with fear of the terrible retribution awaiting them if the revolutionaries won. In the United States, too, government officials explained the continuing support for South Vietnam as a way of heading off a bloodbath should the NLF revolutionaries and the North Vietnamese, who had fought for decades for a unified Vietnam, win.

Opponents of American involvement in the war dismissed the slaughter as a baseless rumor designed to frighten Americans and South Vietnamese into keeping up the fight. After all, they argued, Ho Chi Minh's victorious Viet Minh had committed no wholesale retributions in the Democratic Republic of Vietnam after 1954.[1] Yet more recent events made the possibility of terrible vengeance on the supporters of the South Vietnamese and Americans seem all too real. In February 1968 Viet Cong forces held the old imperial capital of Hué for three weeks. During that time, approximately twenty-one hundred people disappeared, including local officials, supporters of the South Vietnamese government, and ordinary people who for one reason or another had made enemies among the Viet Cong. At first Communist spokespeople made light of the disappearances. They indignantly denied that their forces had harmed any non-combatants. Six months later, however, the missing people's family members discovered hundreds of bodies in mass graves on the outskirts of the city. Communist officials never admitted that their forces had conducted the massacre. The nearest they came was to acknowledge that deaths had occurred after spontaneous outbreaks of anger by the local population against the Saigon government, but they denied that a planned massacre had taken place.[2]

Few South Vietnamese officials or Vietnamese who worked for the Americans found these claims reassuring, and they desperately sought the protection promised to them by the United States. They were betrayed. In Washington, during the last week of April 1975, Secretary of State Henry Kissinger ordered Ambassador Graham C. Martin to send American dependents out of the country. Martin, fearing that the evacuation would deflate the last remaining breath of South Vietnamese resistance, delayed and defied the order for two weeks until Kissinger finally screamed at him to get the families out. U.S. Marines pushed back thousands of frantic Vietnamese who sought refuge from the approaching Communists inside the gates of the American embassy in Saigon before the South Vietnamese government collapsed and NLF fighters raised their flag over the presidential palace on April 30.[3]

Many of these Vietnamese who were unable to crowd their way onto the last few hundred square yards of American property in the capital expected the United States to make good on its promise never to abandon them. Some of these hopes were realized; others cruelly dashed. In the final week of existence of the Republic of Vietnam, the United States evacuated about sixty-five thousand Vietnamese. An equal number left without the aid of the United States. High-ranking officers had access to planes or boats. Air-force pilots took off with their planes full of families, friends, mistresses, and even strangers to whom they charged ten thousand dollars each and flew them to American bases in Thailand. Others fled in boats or overland through Laos or Cambodia to the relative safety of Thailand where they were admitted temporarily only if they promised to leave Thai soil soon.[4]

Over the next several months approximately 200,000 Vietnamese fled the country, and 130,000 eventually made their way to the United States where they received a mixed reception. [5] Some longtime foes of American involvement in the war, who had sympathized with the plight of the many internal Vietnamese refugees during the war, expressed less sympathy for postwar refugees. Senator George McGovern, a prominent critic of U.S. participation in the war, believed the refugees represented some of the most corrupt and even bloodthirsty officials of the discredited South Vietnamese government. Democratic Representatives Jack Brooks, John Conyers, and Barbara Jordan objected to the open-ended admission of Asian refugees who might take work away from the black working class. [6] Critics of earlier U.S. war policies in Vietnam pointed out that a majority of the Vietnamese who entered the United States in 1975, approximately seventy-five thousand people, were low-level soldiers, farmers, fishermen, bar girls, and farmers, people not at high risk of political reprisals back in Vietnam. Others who had not been fortunate enough to leave the country genuinely faced jail, reeducation camps, and other hardships imposed by the victorious revolutionaries. Hawks, who had never before thought refugees merited much American concern, came to view the new refugees as a debt of honor owed by the United States. Conservative Arizona Senator Barry Goldwater, an ardent supporter of U.S. involvement in the war, believed that American support for the newest wave of refugees was the least the United States could do for the Vietnamese it had promised never to abandon. [7]

The Ford administration found itself in the middle. Most Americans wanted nothing so much as to forget the Vietnam War, and Vietnamese refugees were a constant reminder. The presence of Vietnamese in the United States also recalled the frantic last days of the evacuation from Saigon, a disgraceful episode Ford administration officials clearly preferred to bury. For domestic political reasons, support for refugees inside the United States offered few advantages. The Ford administration also expressed concerns about the possibility that Vietnamese refugees would concentrate in small areas like the Cuban Americans who had fled from their homeland after the 1958 revolution and had settled mostly in southern Florida. They had gained such enormous power and influence over local and national politics that state and local officials in south Florida had come to fear the power of Cuban refugees. The Ford administration faced significant pressure not to repeat this experience with Vietnamese refugees. [8]

Accepting Vietnamese refugees soon became a way for the Ford administration to embarrass the Communist authorities in Vietnam by shining a spotlight on their abuse of their own citizens. The flight of tens of thousands of desperate Vietnamese, fearful for their lives, became a constant reminder that the new regime in Vietnam had created many internal opponents. Vietnamese who had worked for the defeated government did not believe their new rulers' insistence that they had nothing to fear in the new Vietnam. The Ford administration justified its economic sanctions against Vietnam based partly on the mistreatment of the thousands forced to flee their homeland in the aftermath of the war. The U.S. government pressed the United Nations to characterize the more than seventy thousand Vietnamese living in the United States as refugees. In 1975 the United States contributed $8.6 million of the $12.4 million the United Nations High Commission for Refugees (UNHCR) requested to assist Thailand in accommodating the fleeing Vietnamese. The United States promised to provide more, if others followed suit. In return the United States insisted that the Vietnamese be classified as refugees facing persecution at home rather than displaced persons who might be expected to return.[9]

The river of refugees became a flood in 1978 when the second wave of boat people left, fleeing Vietnam's war with China. About eight thousand people left Vietnam each month in late 1978. Six months later two thousand Vietnamese refugees a day were coming ashore in countries throughout Southeast Asia. By mid-1979 over three hundred thousand, the majority of whom were ethnic Chinese forced out by nationalist hatred whipped up by the Vietnamese government authorities, had left Vietnam. Chinese Vietnamese recalled that government cadres told them that they had only two unpalatable choices: "We could remain in Vietnam and be relocated to the mountains, or we could leave." Most took to the high seas in makeshift rafts or leaky boats.[10]

These desperate people faced even greater hostility than did the first wave. Governments in Malaysia, Indonesia, the Philippines, and British Hong Kong all resisted taking any more refugees. In 1979 Thailand was pushing back tens of thousands of people who had fled the killing fields of Cambodia. In June Thai troops forced residents of a camp to board buses, ostensibly to Bangkok. Instead they took them to the top of a hill overlooking the Cambodian border, pointed their guns at the terrified refugees, and ordered them to "go forward and down. There is your country."[11] In 1978 Malaysia began denying entry to any "seaworthy" boats. By mid-1979 Malaysia was towing away nearly 80 percent of the vessels approaching its shores. In the first six months of that year, the Malaysians had towed out to sea 267 boats containing more than forty thousand Indochinese.[12] Marauding gangs set upon some refugee boats. One refugee recalled three bands of marauders attacking his beached boat in a single night. "The last one, completing their search [of the boat] drove all the men and youths into a cave and stood guard over it while they took the women away to rape them."[13]

Yet approximately two hundred thousand boat people made it to teeming, unsanitary camps run by the UNHCR. There were seventy-five thousand people in camps in Malaysia, fifty-nine thousand in Hong Kong, ninety-five hundred in Thailand, and five thousand in the Philippines.[14] The best of the camps were those in the British colony of Hong Kong where authorities permitted the residents to come and go more or less freely. In the rest of Southeast Asia the local authorities surrounded the camps with barbed wire fences and posted guards to make sure that no one escaped and sought local asylum. So unwelcoming were these countries to fleeing refugees that Prime Minister Mahatir Mohammed of Malaysia himself threatened to "shoot on sight" any Vietnamese trying to enter his country.[15]

A British TV crew shrank in horror at the sight and smells of the camp at Bidong Island off the coast of Malaysia in 1979. They found that "the beach was full of heaps of rubbish rotting in the heat and humidity. . . . Flies swarmed everywhere and the stench of human excrement was oppressive."[16] A camp resident who later managed to emigrate to New Zealand remembered that the UNHCR provided the refugees with material to build houses and some food. "The worst thing was the water—there was no pure water for drinking and cooking." Camp residents had to buy most of their essentials at exorbitant prices. "Malaysian fishing boats tried to come with very expensive food. . . . We had to waste our money and pay high prices for food. Prices rose at the same time as the number of dead bodies."[17]

Southeast Asian governments, experiencing "compassion fatigue," demanded international relief from the growing refugee crisis in the summer of 1979. The foreign ministers of the Association of Southeast Asian Nations (ASEAN) declared that their countries had "reached the end of their endurance and have decided they would not accept any new arrivals." Hong Kong, straining to accommodate fifty-six thousand Vietnamese, pressured the British government for relief. Prime Minister Margaret Thatcher insisted that the United Nations convene a meeting about refugees and displaced persons in Southeast Asia. The sixty-five-nation conference opened in Geneva on July 21, 1979. U.S. Vice-President Walter Mondale likened the fate of the boat people to that of Jews forced from Germany in the 1930s. He urged the participants to increase the numbers of Vietnamese allowed to settle permanently. The United States agreed to double its annual quota to 168,000. Worldwide, nations agreed to accept 260,000 refugees in 1979 and 1980.[18]

Eventually the UNHCR worked out an Orderly Departure Program (ODP) among Vietnam, its neighbors, and potential final destination countries in the rest of the world. Vietnam would permit a limited number of its citizens to exit legally. The recipient countries agreed to maintain their camps, so long as they could predict how many Vietnamese would arrive on their shores. They also received assurances that their camps would only be for transit, and that within a matter of months, the refugees would leave for permanent residence elsewhere. The key to the success of the ODP were American assurances that the United States would guarantee entry permits for Vietnamese if they fell into one of three categories. The first were close relatives of Vietnamese living in the United States, defined under this family reunification provision as grandparents, parents, children, and unmarried grandchildren. A second category was political. It included former U.S. government employees who had worked for agencies in Vietnam for a least a year at any time after January 1, 1962, and Vietnamese who had worked for U.S. government contractors during the war. Their family members too would be eligible for entry if they fit into the categories outlined in the family reunification program. A third category was broad enough to include former officials of the South Vietnamese government, anybody else who had supported the United States and the Republic of Vietnam during the war, and Vietnamese who had studied abroad under U.S. government sponsorship during the war.

Amerasian children of American servicemen also were eligible to enter the United States under Category 3 of the ODP. Amerasian Vietnamese could present an affidavit signed by an American serviceman certifying that he was the father. In most cases, this was unlikely. But American consular officials in Thailand where the ODP began had instructions to interpret Category 3 broadly. If someone looked like his or her parent or appeared to be white or African American, they usually received the coveted permission to enter the United States. After the United States opened an office in Hanoi in 1986 the ODP operated more smoothly.

The journey from Vietnam to America was dangerous and frightening for both waves of refugees. Desperate to leave Vietnam in 1975, the refugees did not know what lay ahead. Most Vietnamese had little idea where America was, let alone how to get there. Their aim was to leave Vietnam—fast. In the last days of the war, the seventeen thousand Vietnamese with ties to the U.S. military had the best connections to get out. They flew on military transports and were completely dependent upon the Americans who told them little about their final destinations. Other South Vietnamese soldiers received informal help from the Americans. A man who happened to be attached to a joint U.S.-Vietnamese military headquarters received from a friend some U.S. currency in the final days, allowing him to buy passage on a sturdy boat to Hong Kong where an American sponsor awaited his arrival. This refugee knew English and had a group of attentive friends waiting for him in America. "I was very lucky," he recalled.[19]

Most had a much harder time. Whatever the psychological hardships encountered by the Vietnamese military associates of the Americans, they paled in comparison with the terror that awaited Vietnamese who tried to make it out of the country on their own. They had little water and no food. Marauding gangs stole their valuables and even the clothes off their backs. Some fled overland into neighboring Laos and Cambodia. As they made their way into territory controlled by Vietnamese forces they could be shelled as "Southern sympathizers." Worse awaited them in Cambodia where the Khmer Rouge killed thousands of them. Survivors could not get the horrible sights of death and destruction out of their minds. One woman told the sociologist Paul Rutledge her anguish at seeing people "die of hunger and I could not help them. I did not know if I would die also so I save food for my [six year old] daughter." Her family kept going even though "every step made us afraid. . . . If we went back we would die, so we just went forward hearing stories all of the time about others who had made it [out] OK."[20]

Those who left by boat reported especially harrowing memories to Rutledge. Mai, a fourteen-year-old girl whose father had served the South Vietnamese military, joined her family and about eighty others on a small fishing boat that sailed into the South China Sea. They hoped that an American naval vessel would pick them up. After three days at sea with nothing to eat, Thai pirates boarded the ship. One of them grabbed Mai and forced her and several other teenage girls onto the pirate ship. "Four men took me into the boat and raped me over and over again," she remembered. Over the next four days, the young women were raped repeatedly by nine different Thai men. A few days later, the pirates threw Mai and the other young women overboard. She spent hours in the water until another refugee boat rescued her and another girl. She never again saw her family.

Another Vietnamese woman named Soon told of similar degradations. She and six other members of her family walked for fourteen days through Cambodia to a port where they had heard that fishing boats would take Vietnamese to American vessels waiting offshore. The refugees had no money, so they offered food, clothes, religious articles, and anything else they had of value. After hours of pushing, shoving, and screaming, Soon found herself on a remarkably large and seaworthy vessel. She later learned that two of her daughters had slept with the captain and his assistant in order to secure passage for the family. Yet no American ship awaited the refugees, and the fishing boat drifted for days. Pirates attacked twice, stealing the refugees' belongings and money. They raped several women and killed several men. During another attack the pirates kidnapped five girls and three boys who were never seen or heard from again. After this six-day ordeal, the boat approached the Malaysian coastline. The desperate refugees onboard saw the wreckage of other boats broken on the rocky shoreline, and some seventy-five yards from land many jumped overboard and began to swim to shore. As they got closer, they saw a large group of people throwing rocks at them to keep them away. Angry Malaysian civilians armed with knives and clubs set upon a few who made it up the beach. The starving refugees swam back to the boat, which continued to drift down the coastline. Finally, after two more unsuccessful attempts at landing, Malaysian government officials took charge of the boat and escorted Soon and the other survivors to a small camp.[21]

Many refugees told of the cruelties inflicted by the victorious Communist forces. One night Loc, a boy of nine in 1975, left his village with his family, carrying nearly everything they owned. They hid during the day and walked at night. The second night of their journey, Vietnamese soldiers arrested the whole family and took their money and most of their food. The troops separated Loc from his father. After Loc sat alone for about two hours "the soldier in charge came over and asked me if we had any gold with us. When I told him 'no' he hit me with his fist and told me to tell the truth. He hit me three times and then placed his pistol barrel on my stomach and said he was going to shoot me if I didn't tell him where the gold was hidden. I cried and could not talk. The soldier spit on me and walked away." Stripped of all their valuables, Loc and his family escaped through Cambodia to a refugee camp in Thailand where they stayed for two and a half years. As they languished in the camp, one of Loc's sisters died, and his father became very sick. Somehow they transferred to another camp run by American refugee officials who permitted them to immigrate to California.[22]

Both the Ford and Carter administrations sought to disperse the newcomers widely across the United States. Initially, in 1975, the government tried to limit the number of Indochinese in any state to no more than three thousand. Yet by 1980, when the last refugees had left the camps in Southeast Asia, eleven states had more than three thousand Vietnamese, or more than 58 percent of the Indochinese in the United States. Most Vietnamese settled on the West Coast.[23] In 1979 some seventy-one thousand Vietnamese lived in California, mostly in and around Los Angeles and San Diego. Many went to hot, humid areas of the United States, Gulf Coast states like Texas, Louisiana, and Mississippi. Texas was home to twenty-two thousand, Louisiana, eighty-three hundred. A smaller number of Indochinese refugees went to major metropolitan areas across the country. Vietnamese settled in New York, Chicago, Boston, Philadelphia, Washington, D.C., and Detroit. The influx of Vietnamese to cities, which long had been the first point of entry for immigrants to the United States, was not unexpected but less obvious was the migration of Vietnamese to places like Minneapolis, Dallas, Denver, and Phoenix.[24]

Local volunteer organizations helped ease the initial transition of Vietnamese into American life. Religious organizations such as Catholic Charities, the Lutheran Church, the Hebrew Immigrant Aid Society, the Southern Baptist Convention, and the Church World Service Organization collected funds designated specifically for the refugees from Indochina. These charities also trained volunteers to help newcomers navigate through the maze of official government agencies. They found apartments and renovated old houses to accommodate the large, extended families typical among the Vietnamese. Volunteers also provided English-language instruction for adult Vietnamese. Yet helping them find jobs proved to be especially difficult.[25]

Many of the first wave had held white-collar jobs at home, but these were not available in the United States to people with limited or no facility with English. Instead they had to find work that did not require English-language skills, like cleaning buildings, washing dishes, cooking in restaurants, and doing other forms of manual labor. At the beginning of their new lives in America, many Vietnamese were forced to rely on public assistance.[26] Before 1980, these voluntary organizations often worked independently. In 1980, under the terms of the Refugee Act, Congress created the Office of Refugee Re-settlement as part of the Department of Health and Human Services, which provided state and local governments with millions in aid. Over the next decade the office provided state governments with $710 million earmarked for social services to refugees.[27]

Apart from the help of aid organizations, Vietnamese faced significant resentment in the United States. As one former South Vietnamese infantry officer put it, "we can accept" the unfamiliarity of a new country. "The problem for us, almost always, is being accepted."[28] Especially during the economic downturn of the late 1970s and early 1980s, Americans were fearful that Vietnamese would take their jobs and remained resentful of the high cost of the Vietnam War. Unemployment grew to 11 percent in the six years after 1975, and it never fell below 7 percent. Manufacturing industries faced notorious difficulties in the midst of overseas competition, much of it from Japan. Agriculture suffered, as prices for most farm products fell even as inflation raged. Vietnamese found it especially challenging to gain acceptance from their American neighbors under these economic circumstances.

Anti-immigrant sentiment surged during the economic doldrums of the late 1970s and early 1980s. The complaints were typical anti-immigrant bigotry: Vietnamese were said to be too close knit and employ too many of the members of their extended families. Asians became a special target of the wrath of American workers who believed that their jobs were disappearing to Japanese firms. Never mind the fact that Vietnamese, from a poor rural country, had little in common with Japan and its modern industrial economy. Confusing Vietnamese with Japanese was not the only mistake nativists made when they lashed out at Vietnamese immigrants.

Eerie echoes of combat reverberated when Vietnamese immigrants heard charges that they were Communists. Just as some American soldiers and marines considered all Vietnamese, including those whom they were supposedly protecting, to be sympathizers of the Viet Cong, Americans in the United States often accused the anticommunist immigrants of being Communist agents. Antagonism erupted in some cities with many Vietnamese stores and restaurants. Local hoodlums sometimes assaulted Vietnamese shopkeepers or restaurant workers. The assailants turned over display carts, broke glass windows, and beat up workers.[29]

Some of the worst violence occurred on the Gulf Coast where the fiercely anticommunist Vietnamese were, paradoxically, accused of being Communists. A few Vietnamese had arrived on the Gulf Coast with the first wave of refugees in 1975. Ten years later approximately two thousand Vietnamese lived between Corpus Christi and Galveston, Texas. Vietnamese families pooled their resources, bought shrimp boats, and began laying nets in the rich waters off the coast. Often they paid exorbitant prices for boats described by native-born shrimpers as worn out—"nothing but plywood glued together." One white fisherman admitted, "I saw one piece of junk you couldn't give away. And the Vietnamese fisherman paid $7,500 for it."[30]

The Vietnamese worked hard, too hard according to the local shrimpers, who resented the crews of Vietnamese families who didn't collect wages. The Vietnamese shrimped longer hours than did the Americans, and they either did not know or ignored the unwritten rules governing the territories where boats could lay their nets. One white American complained about how the Vietnamese worked their boats together, sweeping long nets through the gulf. The native-born whites shrimped as individuals. Some native-born shrimpers echoed the insults spewed by Americans who fought in Vietnam. "These refugees are practicing communism. They all work together for the group. They are communists in the purest way. I can't compete against that."[31] The Vietnamese anchored their nets to the seabed, which overfished a shrimp bed and drove down prices. Local shrimpers burned several Vietnamese boats in Seabrook, Texas, in 1984. A fight then broke out between mobs of whites and Vietnamese. Two Vietnamese killed an American shrimper, but a jury acquitted them, concluding that they had acted in self-defense.[32]

Violence against the Vietnamese continued all along the Gulf Coast. Hooded Ku Klux Klansmen armed with high-powered rifles rowed small boats into Vietnamese shrimp fleets in the gulf. Klansmen burned crosses and replicas of a shrimp boat named USS *Vietcong* at rallies and in the front yards of Vietnamese. Louis Beam, the grand dragon of the Texas Klan sneered, "There are a number of Vietnam veterans like myself who might want to do some good old search and destroy right here in Texas. They don't have to ship me 12,000 miles to kill Communists. I can do it right here." Other Klansmen admitted that the refugees had fought against the NLF, but damned them for fighting poorly. "We [the Americans] didn't lose the war. The Vietnamese lost the war."

Terrified immigrants obtained a federal injunction to stop the intimidation, but the violence spread eastward. A gunfight over fishing rights broke out in New Orleans between local shrimpers and Vietnamese refugees. Mississippi shrimpers printed up bumper stickers with the message "Save Your Shrimp Industry: Get Rid of Vietnamese, Contact Your Local Congressman."[33] A Vietnamese college student who helped out on his father's boat reflected, "We're scared. . . . I feel as though violence is chasing me from Vietnam to America. Shrimping is a hard job and it's not our first choice." He noted that his father had shrimped all his life. "That's all my family has known, but you ask any of the Vietnamese if they want their children to be shrimpers, I'd guarantee you, they say no."[34]

Vietnamese immigrants encountered abuse in other parts of the country too. At a time of severe antagonism between blacks and local Korean shopkeepers, a mob of young African-American men in New York City roughed up a group of Vietnamese mistaking their victims for Koreans. Elsewhere the issue was a different sort of racial antagonism. The worst violence against

Indochinese refugees took place on January 17, 1989, in Stockton, California, when a man opened fire with an AK-47 on the playground of Cleveland Elementary School. He murdered five children and wounded another twenty-nine and one teacher. Nearly all of the victims were refugees from Cambodia, Laos, and Vietnam.[35]

Gradually the antagonism diminished as the nativists became more accepting of the refugees' presence and the Vietnamese adapted to American ways. The shrimp wars along the Gulf Coast died down. Vietnamese stopped bumping their boats against those of their American counterparts. They also adopted the American standards for net size and quotas on the number of shrimp that could be harvested daily. The Americans began to acknowledge the values of hard work and family solidarity animating the Vietnamese. A Galveston fisherman admitted that the Vietnamese "do work hard. You have to give them that, and now that we have given them the rules I think that it will work out."[36]

Vietnamese families also adapted over time to life in the United States. In Vietnam, two to four generations typically lived in the same household. Often several adult men and their wives and children resided with their parents. In any household, therefore, there could be numerous aunts and uncles, as well as parents and grandparents, caring for children. Men worked outside the home and were traditionally in charge, while wives and mothers remained at home and cared for the children. Formally, women fell under the "three obediences," first to their fathers, then to their husbands, and finally, when widowed, to their eldest sons. But women had considerable autonomy, especially inside the house where the mother was often identified as "the home minister." In Vietnam the house was the center of religious and cultural activities. Shrines of ancestors were located in the house or right outside the door. Leaving the site of their ancestors' bones or ashes was one of the most painful experiences for many Vietnamese refugees. Major religious celebrations took place in the home, as did the annual Lunar New Year Tet festival. Within its walls children learned how to behave toward elders, peers, younger siblings, and people outside the home. The home also served as the place to care for aging parents.[37]

The Vietnamese family in America retained many of these characteristics, but it was also smaller and more nuclear than the ones in Vietnam. One study of Vietnamese Americans in the mid-1980s found that household or family size ranged from one to eighteen people. About 34 percent of Vietnamese-American families had six to eight people; 32.4 percent had nine to eleven; and 12.5 percent contained twelve to fourteen people. The Vietnamese Americans in the mid-1980s were quite young. The median age for all Vietnamese Americans was 21.5; 20.6 for males and 22.7 for females. The higher number for females probably reflected a larger number of elderly mothers and grandmothers brought to the United States among the waves of refugees.[38] The shape of the Vietnamese family in the United States differed from the family in Vietnam. In the mid-1980s 22 percent of Vietnamese households in the United

States had just one generation, whereas in Vietnam only 7 percent of the households were single generation.[39]

The process of Americanization occurred quickly within Vietnamese families. Seventy-five percent of Vietnamese in the United States expected to stay and did not contemplate visiting Vietnam in the near future; 20 percent wanted to visit Vietnam but remain permanently in the United States; while only 5 percent believed they would return permanently to Vietnam. Most of these were older Vietnamese who had great difficulty learning English.[40] Young people became more individualistic and thought less of the needs of the family unit. If young Vietnamese took jobs in family shops or restaurants, they continued to turn their paychecks over to their fathers. But many found work elsewhere or went away to college and abandoned this practice of turning their paycheck over to the male head of the household. Many young Vietnamese also broke the traditional pattern of living with their parents until they got married. One seventeen-year-old Vietnamese described how his McDonald's coworkers laughed at him when he turned his first paycheck over to his family. Initially, he was a dutiful son. "When I get paid I give my paycheck to my father for the family. He gives me food and I am glad to do it." A few months later, he changed his mind. "Now I need my money for my car and for my dating," he said. "I tried to tell my father that this is how we do it in America, but I don't think he understands."[41]

Like countless generations of immigrants before them, Vietnamese admired how their children adapted quickly to American ways. Still, the transition was rough on the oldest Vietnamese. Grandparents found it especially difficult to come to terms with the independence of the new generation of Americanized Vietnamese. "I do not know what is happening," lamented one grandmother. "If I had treated my grandmother with disrespect my parents would have beat me until I learned how to act." This sixty-eight-year-old woman explained how lonely she felt. Other Vietnamese who studied English with her at a church told her that was just the way American children behaved. "But I cannot accept this, it is too hard. If I do not have my family, who do I have?"[42] An elderly Vietnamese man lamented the changes he saw all around him. In public, he noted, Vietnamese parents praised their children's accomplishments, but when they got together privately they bemoaned the collapse of the old Vietnamese family structure, "how children disobeyed and showed no respect, how they told their parents not to interfere in their lives because it's none of their business, how they said they had a higher regard for their spouse than their parents." He knew that physically he and his family were safer in the United States than in Vietnam where "the Communists would put me in a reeducation camp, which would kill me." But he felt terribly isolated in America—"my wife and I will die a lonely death, abandoned by our children," he said.[43]

Many older Vietnamese felt increasingly lonely. They learned English slowly and with difficulty, if at all. The young people took to it easily, and so they had to interpret for their parents and grandparents and help them with everyday tasks. The sense of dependence weighed heavily on older Vietnamese immigrants. Added to that were the other obvious manifestations of a generation gap. A Vietnamese women told of the shock she felt when she heard the teenage daughter of her sponsoring family shout at her mother. "When I heard this I was in total disbelief. You see, obedience is taught to be a virtue in our culture. . . . Believe it or not, a few years later, my oldest daughter shouted at me in the same way."[44] Young Vietnamese wore Western clothes and jewelry, cut their hair in the Western manner, and listened to American music, all of which tended to widen the cultural gap between them and the older generation.[45] When some teenage boys showed up at a Tet celebration sporting baggy pants, earrings, and spiked hair, a man called it "disgusting. Why does his father let him do that?" Another middle-aged man complained, "We are losing control. I cannot imagine what our children will be like in ten years."[46]

Gender roles also changed in America. Vietnamese men lost some of the dominance they exercised in traditional Vietnamese society. Women worked outside the home far more than had been the case in Vietnam. Both husbands and wives found it difficult to adapt to the greater equality in the United States. One man reflected sadly, "Everything has changed here. In Vietnam I would slap my wife and children to discipline them." He said he believed that such violence expressed how much he loved his family. "Here in the United States, if I slap my wife, she may call the police, and I could be arrested." Women found the adjustment equally hard. One wife, a mother of seven who worked outside the home, complained that "most of the time, my husband sits in the big chair and relaxes when he comes home from work." She tried to get him to pitch in with the household chores, but this help came at a steep psychological cost. He wasn't very good at cooking. "This is hard for him. It is also hard for me," she said. "I try to show him that he is still the head of the family and that his helping doesn't change that."[47]

The changes in the United States were probably the greatest for women. Many greeted the opportunity to earn money outside the home as an unalloyed benefit. One reported, "I like helping to pay the family expenses, and I think my husband is starting to accept this." She said that the children liked having more money to pay for clothes. The whole family welcomed the opportunity to move into a bigger house. Another refugee woman happily explained, "I like to work because I get a chance to meet more Americans and to know the city better. If I stay home all day, I would not have anything to do." Other women believed that greater independence weakened the strong bonds that held Vietnamese families together. Divorce, virtually unknown in Vietnam, became more prevalent in the United States, even though it still carried a heavy stigma. "This independence of the family is causing divorce, which we did not have like this in Vietnam. I think this is very bad," lamented one refugee.[48]

Vietnamese-American teenage girls tended to have different expectations about their futures than did their mothers. The younger generation wanted more education, higher-status jobs, and fewer children than their mothers had. The younger generation retained the ferocious work ethic of their forbears. A survey of preferred cultural values among refugee families reported that 99 percent considered "Educational Achievement" highly important. Following closely, with 97 percent agreement, were "A Cooperative and Harmonious Family" and "Responsibility About Carrying Out Obligations."[49]

Vietnamese students often excelled at school. Their parents expressed pride, and also wistful regret, at how far their children had surpassed them at learning the ways of their new country. One father expressed the older generation's ambivalence this way: "My son speaks English better [than I do]. Sometimes I have to get him [to translate for me] and I don't like. It makes him think he is better."[50] Parents and grandparents stressed the value of education. They demanded long hours of homework from the younger generation. They restricted TV watching, hanging out with friends, as well as smoking, drinking, and drug taking. Some parents demanded that their children do homework even when the teachers assigned none. Eager to see their offspring excel in their new country, some Vietnamese parents would try to read ahead in the schoolbooks and ask their children questions. Sometimes it worked, but when the parents did not know English, the results hardly seemed worth the effort. Many young people responded just the way their parents hoped and expected, obediently hitting the books and working in the family businesses. A 1982 study of Indochinese refugee children in California found that they did better on a standard achievement tests than did all students nationally. Sixty-one percent of the refugee students placed in the top 30 percent in mathematics. They were slightly below the national average in reading and language.[51]

Naturally, some teenagers did not meet their parents' high expectations. One teenage boy explained how his father tried to control his every move, threatening to beat him if he failed to live up to expectations. The boy said he would leave home if his father actually hit him. "He cannot make me be like him. My father is very important to me, but lately we do not get along very well. I wish there were some way he could accept me. I am an American. I am not a Vietnamese like he is."[52]

Traditional courtship patterns also came under severe strain in the United States. Arranged marriages were common in Vietnam, especially for the older generation. Even when Vietnamese decided on their own to marry they asked for parental permission. In America these customs fell under attack. Sixty percent of Vietnamese mothers wanted their daughters to marry Vietnamese men, yet only 40 percent of the daughters wanted a Vietnamese husband, and 30 percent of the younger females reported that they did not care about the ethnicity

Defoliants sprayed from American airplanes left vast areas of Vietnam
denuded of vegetation for years. (Courtesy Peter Steinhauer, Sr.)

Ponds left by American bomb craters dot the landscape of postwar Vietnam.
(Courtesy Peter Steinhauer, Sr.)

President Gerald Ford with members of the Clemency Board he appointed in September 1974 to review the cases of men with draft or military offenses during the Vietnam War. (Courtesy Ford Presidential Library)

Facing page   President Gerald Ford and Julia Taft, head of the Interagency Task Force on Indochinese Refugees, greet Vietnamese newcomers at Fort Chaffee, Arkansas, August 1975. (Courtesy Ford Presidential Library)

President Jimmy Carter with Leonard Woodcock, U.S. special representative to Vietnam, February 1977. (Courtesy Carter Presidential Library)

President Jimmy Carter speaking at the bill-signing ceremony authorizing the construction of the Vietnam Veterans Memorial, July 1980. (Courtesy Carter Presidential Library)

President Ronald Reagan with General John Vessey who traveled to Vietnam in 1987 to resolve the MIA issue and begin the process of normalization. Secretary of Defense Caspar Weinberger, who announced a military doctrine designed to avoid future Vietnam-style involvements, looks on. (Courtesy Reagan Presidential Library)

Facing page President Ronald Reagan addresses the National League of Families of Missing in Action in Vietnam, January 1983. Reagan raised the profile of the MIAs, only to find that political opportunists manipulated the issue. (Courtesy Reagan Presidential Library)

Above and facing page   The Vietnam Veterans Memorial Wall on the mall
in Washington, D.C., designed by Maya Lin, has become a sacred site at
which to remember the Vietnam War. Visitors leave mementos and rub the
names of the dead onto paper they carry with them. The polished black
granite wall reflects the visitors. (Photo by Marie Schulzinger)

The bronze sculpture *Three Soldiers* by Frederick Hart was added to the
Vietnam Veterans Memorial site in 1984. (Photo by Marie Schulzinger)

Facing page   The Vietnam War Women's Memorial was placed adjacent to
the wall in 1994. (Photo by Marie Schulzinger)

American medical teams bringing supplies and expertise, here shown at Hanoi's Bach Mai Hospital, were among the first veterans to return to Vietnam in the late 1980s. (Courtesy Peter Steinhauer, Sr.)

The French and later North Vietnamese prison, the Maison Centrale, nicknamed the Hanoi Hilton by its American prisoners of war, became an often-visited site by Western tourists in the 1990s. (Courtesy Peter Steinhauer, Sr.)

Only a few cells remain of the Hanoi Hilton. The rest were torn down and replaced by the large luxury Regency Hotel, which rises above the wall. (Courtesy Peter Steinhauer, Sr.)

A Vietnamese family rows its boat on the Perfumed River in Hué in front of one of the hotels catering to Western tourists. (Photo by Marie Schulzinger)

The tunnels of Cu Chi, twenty miles northwest of Saigon, have become a tourist attraction where local Vietnamese dress in uniforms of North Vietnam's Peoples Liberation Armed Forces and reenact scenes from the war. (Photo by Marie Schulzinger)

President Bill Clinton flanked by Senators John Kerry (left) and John McCain (right), two Vietnam veterans who advocated improved ties between the United States and Vietnam, announces the restoration of diplomatic relations between the two countries, July 1995. (Courtesy Clinton Presidential Library)

Douglas "Pete" Peterson became the first U.S. ambassador to Vietnam since the war, serving from 1997 to 2003. (Courtesy U.S. Department of State)

President Bill Clinton greeted with enthusiasm on a street in Hanoi during his visit to Vietnam, November 2000. (Courtesy Clinton Presidential Library)

of their future husbands. The older generation of Vietnamese women wanted their daughters to have at least four children. The daughters themselves wanted no more than two children.[53] Parents expressed shock when they saw their children holding hands or, even worse, kissing boyfriends or girlfriends. One mother who believed that her seventeen-year-old daughter was too fragile to watch out for herself explained, "I do not allow my daughter to go out with a boy. She can go with a group of girls but not with a boy." Boys presented a similar problem to their parents. A father of a nineteen-year-old knew that his son, a college student, had gone out on dates. "He knows that I do not want him to date, but he is in the university, and so he has a lot of his own time." The father tried "to tell him to make good grades so he can get into medical school. I am afraid that if he has a lot of dating he will not have good grades."[54]

In many ways, however, Vietnamese Americans retained their Vietnamese heritage. Like generations of their forebears who had resisted centuries of Chinese cultural domination, Vietnamese borrowed heavily from American culture while maintaining their own customs. Even after young people learned English, Vietnamese continued to be spoken in the home. The celebration of Tet remained the high point of the year for Vietnamese, and they traveled to spend the three-day holiday with family members. The first day children paid their respects to parents and everyone offered homage to deceased ancestors. The second day was a time for honoring teachers. Vietnamese of all ages presented gifts and letters of appreciation to inspiring teachers. Older Vietnamese customarily presented these well wishes to the moral leaders of the community. The younger Vietnamese who were educated in the United States adapted this custom, often giving thanks to their schoolteachers. Tet ended with a huge community celebration with food, singing, dancing, and speeches. In the United States the final day took on a distinctly political flavor. Vietnamese gathered in community halls to sing the national anthems of the United States and the defunct Republic of Vietnam. They spoke of their longing for an end to Communist rule at home and their gratitude for living in the United States.

Vietnamese families saved all year for the Tet festivities. They repainted, remodeled, and carefully cleaned their homes and decorated them with the flowers and branches of plum trees. People hung banners in their homes, stores, and public streets in Vietnamese neighborhoods expressing hopes for happiness, longevity, and prosperity. They added hopes for a new beginning in the United States. The night before the celebration all Vietnamese bathed thoroughly. "It reminds us that we have a clean beginning in our new country." Occasionally younger American-born Vietnamese found the incense and the prayers unfamiliar, but they liked the spirit of belonging. As one young man put it, "I don't understand what it all means, but Tet is a way of just being Vietnamese. For my folks it is a way of remembering. For me it is a way of saying that that's part of me, but so is America."[55]

One outcome of the close family ties fostered by the annual Tet celebration was a migration by Vietnamese within the United States to be closer to extended families. Originally the U.S. government had purposely dispersed Vietnamese throughout the United States. Once in America, Vietnamese began a secondary migration to be with their country folk. The strongest pull came, of course, from family members who may have been separated in the initial turmoil of migration to the United States, but Vietnamese also sought out people from the same region whom they adopted as "fictive kin." For many Vietnamese in the United States simply being with others from their homeland was an important inducement to relocate.

Vietnamese Americans adapted their own religious and cultural institutions to their new country. For the small minority of Vietnamese Catholics the transition may have been the easiest, since Catholicism was considered to be a "safe" Western-style religion. American-Catholic charities had taken the lead in sponsoring Vietnamese refugees in the United States. Yet even Vietnamese Catholics encountered local resistance to their presence. In 1982 a group of Vietnamese occupied a Catholic church in San Jose to demand a separate Vietnamese parish after the local bishop suspended Vietnamese-language mass.[56] Settling in was a more challenging experience for the Buddhist majority, but they too were able to create thriving temples and cultural centers.[57]

Vietnamese Americans also gradually became involved in politics in their new country. Some of their activities explicitly continued their animosity toward the SRV. In 1985, ten years after the Communist victory in South Vietnam, they created the National Congress of Vietnamese in America, modeled on the highly effective Cuban-American National Association (CANA). Like the Cubans immigrants, the Vietnamese were staunchly anticommunist. In 1987 they protested against a commencement speech given by Tom Hayden, the prominent antiwar activist, at San Jose City College, which had an enrollment of over 40 percent Vietnamese. They also protested East Germany's efforts to recruit some sixty thousand Vietnamese laborers to work in that country's dilapidated industries.

Other Vietnamese immigrants made even more drastic political statements to call attention to repression in Vietnam and discrimination in America. In 1990 Nguyen Kim Bang, a veteran of the Army of the Republic of Vietnam (ARVN) who had come to the United States in the first wave of refugees, entered the grounds of the U.S. Capitol, poured gasoline over himself, and burned himself to death. He left a note proclaiming that "our country is in shambles and our people in abject misery." Everywhere Vietnamese go in the world, he wrote, "we are mistreated, raped, and persecuted."[58] Binh Gia Pham, a Vietnamese refugee who lived in the United States for eleven years, immolated himself in Connecticut to protest repression of his fellow Buddhists in the SRV. Connecticut authorities charged four men, who belonged to the Buddhist youth association Pham had founded, with manslaughter for helping him with the suicide. Thousands of Vietnamese throughout the country signed a petition demanding that the prosecution be dropped. Anticommunist Vietnamese also attacked other Vietnamese Americans who favored reconciliation with the SRV. In Orange County, California, home to more than one hundred thousand Vietnamese, there were more than a dozen arsons, beatings, and even murders in the 1980s. The victims usually were Vietnamese who had visited the SRV, made disparaging remarks about the old regime, and advocated better relations with the new government.[59]

Yet many Vietnamese Americans maintained ties to their homeland. The pull of family was just too great for politics to get in the way. One Vietnamese American explained how many of his generation sought to move beyond the horrors of the Vietnam War. The war, he said, "is an ugly scar we try to forget. If you keep touching a scar, you can't concentrate."[60] In the early 1980s Vietnamese living in the United States sent home eighteen million dollars each month, but corrupt SRV officials skimmed off much of the money. Vietnamese Americans who wanted their relatives to benefit from their hard work in the United States actively advocated ending the economic embargo and establishing diplomatic relations and a trade agreement between the United States and the SRV. In the years after the restoration of diplomatic relations between the United States and the SRV the amount of money sent by overseas Vietnamese to relatives in the country surged to more than two billion dollars per year.[61]

Vietnamese Americans also participated directly in American politics. More supported Republicans than Democrats, although both major political parties sought their backing. Former Vietnamese military officers living in California actively recruited ARVN veterans to the Republican side. A Vietnamese man who worked for a California Republican congressman explained, "the Republicans have a staunch anti-communist position. In essence, we are here because the Democrats drove us out. We know the Republicans will stand up to the communists." About 47 percent of Vietnamese voters in California registered as Republican while the Democratic Party had the support of about 20 percent in the state. But many civic issues of interest to Vietnamese Americans had little to do with the traditional divisions between the two major political parties. They took to the courts to fight discrimination over housing, employment, and language instruction in the schools.[62]

By the 1990s politically active Vietnamese lobbied for public support for the actions of the old Republic of Vietnam. City councils in Virginia and California with large Vietnamese populations demanded that the United States recognize the flag of the old Republic of Vietnam, not the current Socialist Republic, at schools and public gatherings. Vietnamese Americans insisted that their children learn to appreciate the values and sacrifices made by their parents and other ancestors in defense of anticommunist Vietnam. Van Trem, the Vietnamese-American mayor pro tem of Garden Grove, California, a city with a large Vietnamese-American population, said, "the war may have ended for the United States, but for many Vietnamese refugees the war still continues."[63]

In 1996 Westminster, California, home to one of the largest Vietnamese-American communities, adopted plans for a war memorial honoring both Americans and South Vietnamese fighters. Mayor Frank Fry authorized a design competition for an appropriate, representational sculpture. Fundraising was slow, an indication that for some Vietnamese-Americans memories of the war had softened. Eventually Westminster raised $1.75 million. In April 2003 the city dedicated a Vietnam War memorial to the Vietnamese and American soldiers who fought together for the Republic of South Vietnam. Tuan Nguyen, who was born in Vietnam in 1963 and who emigrated to the United States in 1988, designed the sculpture at the center of the park. It showed an American GI carrying an M-16 in one hand and his helmet in the other. The ARVN solider carries an M-16 and wears a flak jacket and a helmet. The sculptor explained that, "I tried to show that for the Americans the war is ending and he's ready to go, but for the Vietnamese the war is still going on. We lost our country."[64]

By the 1990s approximately one million Americans traced their heritage to Vietnam. They were spread across the country, but Vietnamese-American communities thrived in urban areas on the West Coast, especially California. Vietnamese had adapted well to life in the United States. Educational and employment levels were high among Vietnamese Americans born in the United States. Vietnamese Americans continued to support the Republican Party and conservative political causes. They also actively followed events in Vietnam. Most stridently opposed the policies of the government of the SRV, and some actively sought to overthrow it. Yet Vietnamese Americans traveled regularly to Vietnam. Once the United States and the SRV established formal diplomatic relations, more than twenty thousand Vietnamese Americans visited Vietnam each year. By 2000 hundreds of Vietnamese Americans had started joint businesses in Vietnam, and they became the principal bridge between the two old adversaries. The Vietnamese in America helped shape the ways in which people remembered the war and also the ways in which they put those memories behind them.

PART

* * * * * * * * * * * * *

Cultural Legacies

Chapter

* * * * * * * * * * *

The Burden of Memory in
Vietnam Literature

The vast literature of the Vietnam War reflects the many conflicting and unresolved emotions of the era. Memories of the brutality of combat and the furious disagreements at home over the wisdom of American involvement ran deep, but so did the urge to forget and move beyond a painful and traumatic epoch. Over one thousand novels with Vietnam themes have appeared, and they continue to be published.[1] The most compelling of the Vietnam fiction reinforced the troubling paradox that Americans simultaneously wanted to relive the Vietnam years and to put it out of their minds. When novelists addressed Vietnam most successfully, they often played upon this ambivalence. The best fiction about the Vietnam War came to the subject almost indirectly or obliquely through dreams, fantasies, flashbacks, and broken segments. Some of the most arresting Vietnam novels were not set primarily in Vietnam; instead they went back and forth in time and place from present-day America to war-torn Vietnam.

The fiction varied widely in style, scope, and quality. Many novels dealt with combat, but most of the more widely read and critically acclaimed explored memories and emotions engendered by the war. Novels ranged from the complex Graham Greene classic, *The Quiet American* (1955), to contemplative veterans' tales to simple popular literature. Tim O'Brien's *Going After Cacciato* (1978) and Larry Heinemann's *Paco's Story* (1986) both won National Book Awards for their meditations on memory. American readers also responded positively to Vietnamese fiction reflecting on the pain of the physical, psychological, and emotional losses of war. Realistic accounts of battles, pulp fiction, and outright pornography acquired a larger readership. Many of these more popular stories drew upon waves of regret about the way the war had turned into a national trauma for the United States. They expressed longing for victory or vengeance, sometimes over the Communist Vietnamese and sometimes over treacherous or incompetent American officials.

Authors' fascination and revulsion with Vietnam resembled most of the earlier experience of Europeans and Americans grappling with the troublesome legacy of the Great War of 1914–1918. At that time too, novelists carried a burden of loss and disillusionment. As Philip D. Beidler, a literary critic of Vietnam fiction put it, "like their forebears of 1914–1918, the American generation of Vietnam fought a war not of their own making but of the making of politicians and experts, a war of ancient animosities that cost nearly everything for those involved and settled virtually nothing." But Vietnam novels did not simply retell the traditional war story of innocent young men facing the horrors of combat. Thomas Myers, another cultural critic, observed in 1988, Vietnam literature told both the story of fighting and the overwhelming cultural impact of the United States on Vietnam. These novels explored the relationship between the two lands, one of "parent to child, ally to ally, and mistrusted benefactor to recalcitrant client."[2] Whatever format the fiction of the Vietnam War took, the works expressed many common themes and emotions— memory and forgetfulness, grief, anger, loss, regret, rare heroism, and occasional acceptance of the ruins of war.

Some recurring themes of Vietnam War novels emerged before the United States played a major military role in Indochina. These included woeful ignorance of the ancient civilization of the Vietnamese and misplaced idealism that caused more harm than good to both Vietnamese and Americans. Graham Greene's *The Quiet American* (1955), one of the earliest books on Americans in Vietnam, captured many of the moral ambiguities of the U.S. war in Vietnam before the United States sent its troops into the fight. Set in Indochina during the waning days of French rule, *The Quiet American* constructed a frame around American involvement in Vietnam. On one level *The Quiet American* is a love triangle, but it is also an allegory for American blunders in Vietnam. The narrator, Thomas Fowler, a tired, cynical British journalist, loses Phuong, his beautiful Vietnamese mistress, to Alden Pyle, a seemingly naïve American aid worker. But it is no simple love story. In Fowler's own mind, in Greene's, and in the imagination of generations of readers, the competition between an aging Briton and a youthful American also symbolized a declining, imperial Europe displaced by an assertive United States. The Americans who displaced the Europeans may have had wealth and military power, but they lacked a sense of history, understanding of other cultures, and aware-ness of the limits of their power. Fowler is contemptuous of the Americans' ignorance even as he recognizes that has become "a bore on the subject of America. . . . My conversation was full of the poverty of American litera-ture, the scandals of American politics, the beastliness of American chil-dren. It was as though she [Phuong] were being taken away from me by a nation rather than by a man."[3]

Most of all, *The Quiet American* challenged American conceptions of al-truism, innocence, and saving Asians from the dangers of Communism. Pyle is not the innocent young man he appears to be. Even though he looks like a boy, he is actually thirty-two years old, and Greene makes it clear that he should know better than to spout theories about democracy, Communism, free-dom, or the Vietnamese's need for a Third Force of honest nationalists op-posed to both the French colonialists and the Communists. Fowler always capitalizes these abstractions to mock Pyle's ignorance of the everyday de-sires and needs of the Vietnamese. According to Fowler, Pyle "never saw any-thing he hadn't heard in a lecture hall."[4] Fowler is very lonely and he strikes up an unlikely friendship with Pyle who talks to him for hours about serous subjects that alternately intrigue and irritate the older man. Pyle begins to expound a version of the domino theory: "If Indo-China goes . . ." But Fowler cuts him off in mid-sentence, and he completes Pyle's thought with his own version of Vietnamese reality: "I know the record. Siam goes. Malay goes. Indonesia goes. What does 'go' mean? If I believed in your God and another life, I'd bet my harp against your golden crown that in five hundred years there may be no New York or London, but they'll be growing paddy in these fields, they'll be carrying their produce to market on long poles wearing their pointed hats."[5]

Pyle's very name symbolizes how overbearing some Europeans found the Americans during the Cold War. He's literally a pile, a pain in the posterior, to Fowler.[6] Pyle is no unassuming aid worker, either. He's operating under-cover, probably for the CIA, to discredit the Communists and enhance the appeal of General Thé, an unsavory self-promoter whom the Americans have anointed as the leader of their cherished Third Force. At the climactic mo-ments of the novel, Pyle orchestrates a deadly bombing that kills more than a dozen innocent Vietnamese at a café on the Rue Catinat, Saigon's main street. Pyle wants the blame to fall on the Communist Viet Minh. The loss of inno-cent life shocks Fowler, usually a disengaged observer. Fowler betrays Pyle, his sometime friend now rival in love, to a Viet Minh cadre, who then kills Pyle. His death saddens Fowler, who thinks Pyle never should have been in Vietnam in the first place. "I never knew a man who had better motives for all the trouble he caused," is one of the more stringent of the many judgments Fowler makes of Pyle's misadventure in Vietnam.[7] It stood for decades as a damning indictment of the United States's misguided efforts to manipulated Vietnamese politics and society in the Cold War competition with the Soviet Union.

The Quiet American received mixed reviews when it appeared. Some American critics found the book unremittingly hostile and condescending to Americans. It acquired more and more readers in the 1960s when the U.S. involvement in the war deepened. Thomas Myers called *The Quiet American* "the textual loom . . . on which future novelists would test the intricacy, consistency, and overall design of their individual tapestries."[8] It also became the source for two significant Vietnam War movies (see chapter 8).

Few American authors wrote about Vietnam before 1966. Then the war intensified, and novelists began to project local, American themes onto a war half way around the world. The growing popular uneasiness with the war prompted Norman Mailer to try to answer a question troubling many Americans with a novel bluntly titled, *Why Are We in Vietnam?* (1967).[9] Mailer, of course, first gained prominence with his World War II novel *The Naked and the Dead* (1947), based on his own combat experience in the Pacific. In his new book, he wasn't able to draw on his personal experience, so *Why Are We in Vietnam?* was an explicitly didactic novel. Mailer found the answer to the question in his book's title at home, in the frontier, can-do, violent spirit of first Texas (LBJ's home state) and then Alaska (the last frontier). The characters are blustering overbearing men with no sense of the consequences of their actions. The protagonist, D.J. Jellicoe, is the son of Rusty Jellico, a huge, loud, profane Texas oilman. No reader could miss Rusty's resemblance to Johnson, but Mailer goes further and likens the father to "a high-breed crossing between Dwight D. Eisenhower and Henry Cabot Lodge," two other officials intimately involved in the American War effort in Vietnam.[10] Most of the action in *Why Are We in Vietnam?* takes place on a hunt in Alaska's Brooks Range. D.J. flies north to hunt wild game with two obnoxious corporate executives. They slaughter wolves, caribou, and bighorn sheep, taking to the air in helicopters to hunt their prey. Despite their overwhelming firepower, they often miss, and when they do hit the beasts, they open gaping wounds. Occasionally, Rusty and D.J. seek communion with the sheer beauty of nature, but their half-hearted efforts to leave behind a high-tech form of hunting never get very far. Indeed, father and son come to hate the wilderness, which they believe hides a grotesque, immoral secret: D.J. puts it, "God was a beast, not a man, and God said, 'Go out and kill—fulfill my will, go and kill.'"[11] For Mailer, the American War in Vietnam fulfilled this diabolical prophecy. At the end, a crazy D.J., about to be shipped off to fight the war, giggles, "We're off to see the wizard in Vietnam. Vietnam, hot damn."[12] Mailer's *Why Are We in Vietnam?* was not highly successful. Its characters were one-dimensional, it had no sense of place, and it was almost exclusively allegorical in its explanations of the development of the war.

More compelling Vietnam novels and memoirs recounted the experience of American soldiers in Vietnam as a mixture of reality and fantasy. Numerous critics have noted this blend. Philip H. Melling, a prominent critic of Vietnam War literature, has observed that "the brokenness of the Vietnam experience is embodied in [the Vietnam novel's] lack of sequence and structure."[13] Michiko Kakutami, a reviewer for the daily *New York Times*, characterized much of the Vietnam literature as displaying "a fragmented approach to story telling . . . a tendency to see everything in the present tense, as though the past or future were impossible to connect."[14] The literary critic Samuel Hynes has also commented on the lack of narrative continuity and flow in Vietnam literature. The war had no front lines and few major battles. It was, he writes, "a long war fought by short timers." He explains that "because the fighting itself had no meaning, Vietnam war narratives neither begin nor end with the teller's time in combat." Instead, they often shift backwards and forwards in time and in place from the United States to Vietnam.[15]

Tim O'Brien, an army veteran of Vietnam, wrote a series of Vietnam memoirs, novels, and short stories over a period of nearly two decades. In his literary world, men are simultaneously drawn to service in Vietnam and repulsed by it. In his early memoir *If I Die in a Combat Zone* (1973), O'Brien criticized the Vietnam War as "wrongly conceived and poorly justified."[16] Although O'Brien went to Vietnam because of "family, the hometown, friends, history, tradition, fear, confusion, exile: I could not run," he rejects the main premises of American involvement.[17] Five years later in his novel *Going After Cacciato* (1978), O'Brien explained how the horror of war led fighting men to try to escape, if only through fantasy. The story opens with Specialist Fourth Class Paul Berlin all alone in an observation post by the South China Sea. For the remainder of the novel he muses on the nature of the war. "What part was fact and what part was the extension of fact?" he wonders.[18] Many members of his platoon die horrible deaths. One succumbs to fright as he tries to lace his boot onto his blown-off leg. In the midst of this chaos, Private Cacciato decides to leave for Paris. He chooses the City of Light carefully. Its gaiety, devotion to high civilization, and nightlife could not form a sharper contrast to the tedium, horror, and surrealism of the war in Vietnam. In addition, Paris is the site of the negotiations that ended the American War. Berlin leads the rest of the platoon after him—at least they follow him mentally. The name of the pursuer, Berlin, also stands in contrast to Paris. If the City of Light represents joy and release, Berlin, the capital of Bismarck's empire and a major arena of the Cold War, embodies duty.[19]

Berlin and his patrol never capture Cacciato, but they do make it to Paris. There Berlin finds an old 1969 copy of the *International Herald Tribune* in which he reads of the death of President Dwight Eisenhower, the liberator of Paris. He muses that "the world went on. Old facts warmed over. Nixon was President. . . . The war went on. 'In an effort to bring the Peace Talks to a higher level of dialogue, the Secretary of Defense ordered the number of B-52 missions dropped from 1,800 to 1,500 a month;' meanwhile, in the South, it was a quiet week, with sporadic and light action. Only 204 more dead men. And Ike. Ike was dead and an era had ended."[20] *Going After Cacciato* presented Vietnam as a quagmire from which no realistic exit seemed possible. Caught up in the absurdity of the battlefield, men escape in acts of imaginary desertion.

O'Brien continued to explore the burden of the memory of the Vietnam War in his subsequent novels. He set his third book, *The Nuclear Age* (1985), ten years in the future, 1995, when he projected an unremitting fear of nuclear war would be hanging over the United States. The protagonist William Cowling, an antiwar veteran of the turbulent sixties, tries to live down his past in an era that has forgotten about Vietnam. Forty-nine-year-old Cowling lives in rural Montana where he's building a bomb shelter. His wife and young daughter think he's a "nutto" because he cannot let go of the passions of the antiwar era of the 1960s. He wonders, "Where's the passion? Where's Richard Daley? Where's Gene McCarthy in this hour of final trial? No heroes, no heavies. And who cares? That's the stunner. Who among us really cares?"[21] In the end, Cowling destroys everyone closest to him—his wife, his daughter, and finally himself—because he cannot accept that the people he cares about do not understand or are not concerned about the enduring psychological wounds of the Vietnam War.

O'Brien returned once more to the theme of the heavy burden of memories of Vietnam in *The Things They Carried* (1990), a collection of interrelated short stories set in the post-Vietnam era. Like a generation of veterans, O'Brien's characters are at odds with their contemporaries who did not go to Vietnam because they "shared the weight of memory."[22] One narrator reflects that "I feel guilty sometimes [because I'm] forty-three years old and I'm still writing war stories. My daughter, Kathleen tells me it's an obsession. . . . In a way, I guess she's right. But the thing about remembering is that you don't forget." [23] O'Brien's characters consider the possibility of letting go of these painful memories unusually frightening, because doing so might erase their connection to their wartime experiences and the friends they lost.

O'Brien and his fellow combat veterans carried memories of the sheer strangeness of Vietnam as a physical environment and the absurdity of the war. "They carried diseases. They carried lice and ringworm and leeches and paddy algae and various rots and mold. They carried the land itself. . . . The whole atmosphere, they carried it, the humidity, the monsoons, the stink of fungus and decay, all of it, they carried gravity." The exotic nature of the place seemed to strip them of reason and civilization. The incomprehensibility of the war created "a kind of emptiness, a dullness of desire and intellect and conscience and hope and human sensibility." Soldiers lived on instinct. "Their calculations were biological," he recalled. "They had no sense of strategy or mission." The men literally did not know what they were doing or why they did it. "They searched the villages without knowing what to look for, not caring, kicking over jars of rice."[24]

O'Brien lamented how the burden of memory seemed to have crushed some veterans who got in touch with him after his stories first appeared. "The thing is," one wrote him commending his stories, "there's no place to go. Not just in this lousy little town. My life, I mean. It's almost like I got killed over in Nam." This veteran paradoxically seemed to prefer his isolation. He didn't believe in the process of healing. Inconsolable in his grief, he rejected efforts to honor veterans or treat their psychological wounds. "One thing I hate—really hate—is all those whiner vets. Guys sniveling about how they didn't get any parades. Such absolute crap. I mean, who in his right mind wants a *parade?* Or getting his back slapped by a bunch of patriotic idiots who don't know jack about what it feels like to kill people or get shot at or sleep in the rain or watch your buddy go underneath the mud. Who *needs* it?"[25] Three years later, this man hanged himself.

O'Brien revisits the complex relationship between remembering the war and escaping its burdens in his novel *In the Lake of the Woods* (1994). The protagonist's name, John Wade, so similar to John Wayne, the actor noted for his portrayal of heroic and nationalistic figures, is another disdainful comment on a war without heroes. Wade, a Vietnam veteran, hates serving in the war. His combat buddies admiringly call him the Sorcerer, both for his mastery of magic tricks and his apparent ability to make the horrors of war disappear. On a night patrol "somebody would say, 'tonight we're invisible,' and somebody else would say, 'That's affirmative, Sorcerer's got this magic dust, 'gonna make us disappear.'"[26] But, of course, the soldiers aren't invisible, and the war doesn't disappear. In a brilliant touch, adding clinical reality to a story that takes place in dreams and memories, O'Brien includes two psychiatrists' accounts, written after World War II, of the effects of combat. "There is no such thing as 'getting used to combat.' . . . Each moment of combat imposes a strain so great that men will break down in direct relation to the intensity and duration of their exposure. Thus psychiatric casualties are as inevitable as gunshot and shrapnel wounds in warfare."[27]

Wade bears some of the deepest scars, for he was present at, and *maybe* participated in, the ghastly My Lai massacre of March 16, 1968. Wade wandered around My Lai, or Pinkville, and noticed "something was wrong." Amidst the fires, smoke, and hot wind, "he found a young woman laid open without a chest or lungs. He found dead cattle." Disoriented, "Sorcerer didn't know where to shoot. He didn't know what to shoot. So he shot the burning trees and burning hootches . . . If a thing moved, he shot it. If a thing did not move, he shot it. There was no enemy to shoot, nothing he could see, so he shot without aim and without any desire except to make the terrible morning go away." Wade didn't know if he killed any Vietnamese that morning, but he was acutely aware of one death. As he stood "in the slime at the bottom of an irrigation ditch," a friend, Private First Class Weatherby, looked at him. "'Hey, Sorcerer,' Weatherby said. The guy started to smile, but Sorcerer shot him."[28]

Wade shot Weatherby in a fit or a momentary blackout. Weatherby's death reinforced Wade's view that he could magically make past traumas disappear. "Sorcerer thought he could get away with murder. After he shot Weatherby . . . he tricked himself into believing it hadn't happened the way it had happened." His comments on Weatherby's death also stood for many Americans' faulty memories of their country's misadventure in Vietnam. "He pretended he wasn't responsible; he pretended it didn't matter much; he pretended that if the secret stayed inside him, with all the other secrets, he could fool the world and him-self too."[29]

O'Brien's Vietnam fiction resonated with those American readers who felt deceived and betrayed by their government's conduct of the Vietnam War. Officials had misrepresented and lied about the reasons for committing Ameri-can troops. Neither the people in charge nor the men and women who fought the war knew what they were doing. They wandered through the landscape of Vietnam as if in a bad dream. O'Brien's novels and short stories presented a murky world between fantasy and ugly reality. Emerging from this twilight was the harsh glare of moral disapproval of what went wrong in Vietnam.

Robert Stone was another prominent Vietnam novelist whose work was often set far from Vietnam and who depicted the war as a self-inflicted wound. He won the 1975 National Book Award for *Dog Soldiers* (1974), a grim, phan-tasmagorical story of the Vietnam War in which the action takes place almost exclusively in the United States. Like O'Brien's fiction, Stone's Vietnam nov-els explore a mental rather than a physical landscape. *Dog Soldiers* is a thriller that begins in Vietnam but quickly moves to the California desert. John Con-verse, the protagonist, enlists an old Marine Corps buddy, Ray Hicks, to de-liver three kilograms of heroin to Converse's wife. As in so many of the Vietnam novels, the characters' names suggest larger themes. Converse is the opposite of the traditional American values of optimism and perseverance, since he embodies the disillusionment of the original American effort in Vietnam. He cynically acknowledges American atrocities in Vietnam, "the place," he tells Hicks, where "everybody finds out he pretended he couldn't have done it and therefore hadn't." Hicks, who despite his name is no rural ignoramus, replies, "What a bummer for the gooks." Converse comes back with, "You can't blame us too much. We thought we were something else."[30] At the novel's core, the war was absurd. Much of the action in Vietnam involves helicopters shooting NLF fighters. Converse observes, "if the world is going to contain elephants pursued by flying men, people are just naturally going to want to get high."[31]

However surreal the Vietnam landscape had become for the Americans, the country they returned to had become even stranger. Hicks admonishes Con-verse to take care when he goes home. "It's gone funny in the states." Converse can't believe it. "It can't be funnier than here," he replies. "Here everything's simple," Hick warns. *Everything* is absurd in Vietnam, but back in the United States there is an illusory sense of normality. "It's funnier there. I don't know who you've been running with but I bet they've got no sense of irony."[32] The war so traumatizes Converse that he sees nothing wrong with importing heroin into his own country. In a post-Vietnam era in which public officials cannot be trusted, Converse explains how evading the police brings him back to life: "I feel this is the first real thing I ever did in my life. I don't know what the other stuff was about."[33]

Memories of Vietnam haunted Stone's next novel, *A Flag for Sunrise* (1981), set in war-torn Central America. When Stone published this book, the growing conflict between leftists and anticommunists in Central America had generated unwelcome echoes of Vietnam, especially among Americans who had opposed their government's policies in Vietnam. Frank Holliwell, a cultural anthropologist who once was a covert agent in Vietnam, finds himself in the midst of a revolution in the impoverished nation of Tecan. Holliwell, in particular, and the United States, in general, are almost crushed by the "dreadful nostalgia" of Vietnam.[34] Americans had been arrogant and ignorant in Vietnam. "We believed," Holliwell proclaimed in a drunken monologue, "we knew more about great unpeopled spaces than any other European nation. We considered spaces unoccupied by us as unpeopled. At the same time, we believed we knew more about guilt. We believed that no one wished and willed as hard as we, and that no one was so able to make wishes true. We believed we were more."[35] One of the revolutionaries will have none of Holliwell's excuses that the Americans didn't really know what they were doing in Vietnam. Americans, he says, "of all people, should be aware of how it's going in the world." They had experienced defeat in Vietnam, where "a lot of gringo asses got kicked forever."[36]

The fantastical, almost mythical, aspects of Vietnam were conveyed in other popular and well-regarded Vietnam fiction. Gustav Hasford's *The Short Timers* (1979) presented the Vietnam War as a nightmare narrated by Corporal Joker, a reporter for *Stars and Stripes*, the army paper. *The Short Timers* reached its largest audience in Stanley Kubrick's film adaptation *Full Metal Jacket* (1987) (see chapter 8). The novel did more than the film to capture the surrealism of the Vietnam War. *The Short Timers* relates the signal events of 1968—the siege of Khe Sanh, the Tet Offensive, and the relief of the city of Hué from the Communist conquest—all of which combine to drive the characters mad. The war is so preposterous and absurd that the soldiers protect themselves with dark, demented humor. There's Crazy Earl who fires a Red Ryder BB gun at the Viet Cong. Yet he expresses a grudging admiration for "these giants, walking the earth with guns. These enemy grunts are as hard as slant-eyed drill instructors. These people we are wasting here today . . . are the finest human beings we will ever know. After we rotate back to the world, we're gonna miss having anyone around that's worth shooting."[37]

There's Cowboy, who explains, "We're the Lusthog squad. We're lifetakers and heartbreakers. We shoot 'em full of holes and fill 'em full of lead."[38] There's Rafter Man, a combat photographer, who desperately wants to earn the respect of the grunts, the real soldiers. At one point, he grabs part of the body of a dead GI. "Rafter Man puts the flesh into his mouth," Joker reports, "onto his tongue, and we think he's going to vomit. Instead, he grits his teeth. Then, closing his eyes, he swallows."[39] Joker stands somewhat apart because he's a combat reporter. He writes sanitized lies about the war. He calls them "paper bullets fired into the fat black heart of communism."[40] When the grunts denigrate him for standing apart, he tells them: "You know I do my job. I write that 'Nam is an Asian Eldorado populated by a cute, primitive but determined people. War is a noisy breakfast food. War is fun to eat.'" Joker seems to go mad as he tells his fellow soldiers, "I love the little Commie bastards, man, I really do. These are great days we're living in bros! We are jolly green check ups. War cures cancer—permanently. I don't kill. I write 'Grunts kill.' I only watch."[41] The cumulative message of *The Short-Timers* is a war without rules and fighters without boundaries.

While much of the Vietnam literature stressed the absurdity of the war by breaking down chronology, place, time, and the lines between consciousness and dreams, occasionally effective Vietnam literature harkened back to heroic models and realistic narratives. John M. Del Vecchio's 1982 novel *The 13th Valley* was based on the author's experience as a combat correspondent with the 101st Airborne Division in 1970 and 1971, late in the American War. *The 13th Valley* is a proudly naturalistic depiction of men in combat. Del Vecchio created a mythic army unit explicitly representational of mid-twentieth-century American society. *The 13th Valley* is a huge nearly six-hundred-page book, patterned on Herman Melville's *Moby Dick* for its reflections on an endless quest and Norman Mailer's *Naked and the Dead* for its depiction of the conflicts among men in combat. It traces the quest of Alpha company for an elusive North Vietnamese Army headquarters. The narrator characterizes the men as "products of the great American experiment, black brown yellow white and red, children of the Melting Pot. . . . What they had in common was the denominator of American society in the '50's and '60's, a television culture."[42] One character, Lieutenant Rufus Brooks, is a young African American with an M.A. in philosophy from Berkeley. He stands out among fictional officers for his wisdom and compassion. He believes in his mission—winning the hearts and minds of the Vietnamese—and his methods—fighting humanely if possible, caring for the safety of his troops, and dampening racial animosities. He dissents respectfully from foolish or sadistic orders. Brooks has his men's respect and even love. He stays with them, but he also inhabits a deep, reflective inner world in which he meditates on the nature of leadership, combat, race relations, and U.S. society. While the battle goes on Brooks and his men talk endlessly about why the United States fights in Vietnam. He is writing a dissertation he calls "An Inquiry into Personal, Racial, and International Conflict." "We think ourselves into war. The antecedents are in our minds," Brooks says to his men in one of the long evening bull sessions that the platoon engages in during the fighting in the 13th valley.[43]

Sergeant Daniel Egan, an Irish-American warrior, is almost the compete opposite of Brooks. He is hardly ever self-reflective, but he does long for home where his girlfriend Stephanie "was the antithesis of Nam. She was the good, the peaceful, the loving."[44] Egan is a fighter, but he admonishes soldiers against atrocities. When one cuts off the ear of a North Vietnamese soldier, Egan denounces him as a "savage."[45] One main character who descends into barbarism is James V. Chelini. Nicknamed "Cherry" for his innocence at the beginning of his tour of duty, Chelini literally goes mad from the killing. At first he's scared, then he's uncomfortable, and finally he's consumed with blood lust. Vietnam becomes an absurd landscape of death and devastation. "Don't mean nothin'" is his and the other GIs' constant refrain. The book ends when Chelini hears that Brooks and Egan are dead. He growls, "F___ it. Don't mean." The platoon's new commander interrupts and tells him, "Don't say it, soldier."[46] The critic John Hellmann observed that the book's ending showed "a traumatized American . . . lost in the meaninglessness of Vietnam. Gazing at this specter [of dead bodies of comrades and adversaries] the American consciousness can only blaspheme or deny."[47] Thomas Myers, another literary critic, drew slightly different meaning from the phrase "it don't mean nothing." He focused on the double negative. For Myers Vietnam certainly meant something, and the war's memory contained many complex and often contradictory meanings. He found the book for all of its ponderous digressions and unrealistic bull sessions "an acknowledgment that the appraisal of complex human action and thought require effort, patience, and a number of tools."[48]

Echoes of the horror of Vietnam reverberated for years with many combat veterans, and some of the most evocative and moving Vietnam War literature addressed the complexities of memory in the postwar decades. Larry Heinmann's *Paco's Story* (1987) portrayed the loneliness and despair better than almost any account, and it remains the best fictional account of the ravages of Post Traumatic Stress Disorder. "This ain't no war story," begins the story of Paco Sullivan, a crippled, lost soul. Like virtually every sentence in this complicated book, this one is deeply ironic. Whatever else *Paco's Story* is, it is essentially a tale of the impact of the Vietnam War. By denying that the novel is a "war story," Heinemann means it is not a heroic or fairy tale.[49] The narrator also consciously echoes the satiric disdain some veterans undergoing psychological counseling expressed for their fellow veterans who invented heroic or villainous stories about themselves.

Paco Sullivan, haunted by having alone survived a furious firefight and wracked with guilt over participating in a brutal rape of a Viet Cong woman, wanders across the American Southwest seeking something to end the night-mares. Nothing, not booze, not drugs, and certainly not a fantasy sexual rela-tionship with a twenty-year-old college woman can assuage the memories, ease the guilt, or make him forget the ugly scars covering his torso.

Paco's very name is steeped in irony. His first name can mean peace, and the book is, indeed, set in peacetime, or at least post-Vietnam America. But there is no relief for Paco. His last name, Sullivan, directly summons to mind the heroic age of World War II, when the five fighting Sullivan brothers went down together on a warship in the Pacific. Their deaths became a national cause of celebration and mourning. Millions poured in for bonds to fund the expenses of the "good war." The fictional Paco Sullivan survived the fight-ing, but he came home alone, unwelcomed, unnoticed, and eventually scorned.

Paco's Story has an omniscient narrator, never identified, who addresses a particular reader called James. Heinemann plays with the name James. The narrator insists that the imagined reader is not Jim or Jack or Jake, because these nicknames would be too informal. But that's precisely the point. *Paco's Story* derides the formalities of military life and the pieties of post-Vietnam America. The narrator announces that "James" suggests the "tongue in cheek punch line, Home James."[50] And no one is less likely to employ the services of a liveried driver than the impoverished, drunken, scarred Paco Sullivan. He could never afford a chauffeur, nor would he want one. Paco is a practically homeless outsider, living on the margins of a society whose acceptance he longs for but at the same time by which he is repulsed. Heinemann says that James specifically is not James Jones, author of *From Here to Eternity,* a novel set among naval officers and sailors in pre–World War II Honolulu. Despite the denial, Heinemann pays homage to Jones. It is clear that *From Here to Eternity*'s depiction of the hypocrisies of military life sets the framework for Heinemann's work. *Paco's Story* explicitly compares the postwar experience of Vietnam veterans with the fate of World War II veterans. But there's a catch. Heinemann doesn't contrast the "good war"—World War II—with the disas-ter of Vietnam, since both wars leave horrible memories.

Paco's Story compares and contrasts the experiences of World War II and Vietnam War veterans. Ernest is an older man, a Marine Corps veteran of World War II and Paco's boss at Texas Lunch where Paco works as a dish-washer. The gruff, unsentimental old marine is unmoved by Paco's wounds, his scars, and his horrible memories, because Ernest has his own pains. "I was wounded on Guadalcanal *and* Iwo Jima. I guess that makes me a f—-ing pa-triot, but I'll be f—-ed if you'll see me fly the flag. Not Flag Day or the Fourth of July. Not Memorial Day or Veterans Day not any kind of goddamned day. And I don't fly it right side up, upside down, inside out, crosswise, ass back-ward or f—-you otherwise." [51] Contempt for the heroic and prominent members of society is a persistent theme of Heinemann's. In his earlier novel, *Close Quarters* (1977), the battle-hardened combat grunts express limitless scorn for officers and rear echelon "housecats" who don't experience the mud, the cold, and the blood of war.[52]

Everyone is alone and needy in *Paco's Story*, and none of the traditional means of connection successfully heal physical or psychological wounds. Paco fantasizes about having sex with a neighbor, Cathy, a young college student. He crawls into her room and reads her diary. Her ambivalence toward him—attraction mixed with disgust—represents some of the attitudes of the larger society toward Vietnam veterans. She confides to her diary that she briefly finds him "good looking, with nice tight buns."[53] But soon he's repulsive, "a dingy, dreary, smelly, shabby, *shabby* little man."[54] She hears him writhing and moaning in his sleep as he has unbearable nightmares about the death and rape in Vietnam. "He's all pasty. And crippled. And honest to God, ugly."[55] Still, she has a dream of the two of them having sex. She sees them "on the bed everything . . . And I just can't bring myself to touch him . . . and I think I hear *screams*, as if each scar is a scream." Finally she wakes up. "I just shuddered . . . It made my skin crawl."[56]

Jesse, another Vietnam veteran, is just as enraged as Paco at the indifference of the larger society. He can express his rage more articulately, as when he tells Paco that he has "been waiting for one of those snappy-looking little girlies from some rinky-dink college to waltz up and say . . . 'You one of them vet'rans ain'cha? Killed all them mothers and babies. Raped all them women, di'n'cha'—I only got two hands, lady."[57]

An almost unbridgeable chasm separates Vietnam veterans from people who did not go to war. Jesse continues his brutal denunciation of the young college woman. Enraged at what he considers the condescension of more privileged young people who did not personally experience combat, Jesse fantasizes how "I'm gonna grab her up by the collar of her sailor suit . . . slap her around a couple times, flip her a goddamned dime, and say, 'Here, Sweet Chips, give me a ring in a couple of years when you grow up.'"[58]

Public celebrations could do little to help heal the psychological wounds of the war in Heinemann's account. Jesse, verbal and manic, provides a dark prospectus for a memorial to those who served in Vietnam. He claims to have mentally designed a memorial "years before anybody ever thought of one." He offers the antimemorial mocking the real one built on the Washington Mall. It occupies "a couple acres of prime Washington, D.C. property, see, somewhere in line with the Reflecting Pool." Members of Congress can that way admire what their support of the war created: "Thousands and thousands of f—ed-up lives." Jesse's memorial is made of the "whitest stone God makes," a direct contrast to the black granite of the real monument. Like Maya Lin's design, Jesse's design also lists the names of the dead. But the comparisons end there. In the middle of "all that marble" stands a giant granite bowl. An endowment will fund the collection of thousands of hundred-dollar bills. "Then gather every sort of 'egregious' excretion that can be transported across state lines from far and wide—chickenshit, bullshit, fecal goop, radioactive dioxin sludge, kepone paste, tubercular spit, abortions murdered at every stage of fetal development." Someone would mix the hundred-dollar bills with the slop, and then it all would be hosed down until it was "good and soggy; nice and mucky." At that point the National Park Service would advertise: "Any and all comers may fish around in that bowl of shit and keep any and all hundred-dollar bills they come across, barehanded, but first they must take off their shoes, roll up their trousers, slug through all that knee-deep muck, and wind upslopping it all over that marble."[59]

Heinemann's vision of Vietnam veterans rejected by a complacent and uncompehending civilian society is unsparingly bleak. Nothing can offer the psychically scarred veterans relief from the burden of memory. All the customary balms for returning warriors are exposed as useless or false. Not human friendship, sex, work, nor public gratitude seem to be available to Paco. And even if they are available in some attenuated form, they cannot expunge his nightmares, dry his night sweats, or calm him writhing moans. At the end of the book, Paco leaves town in the middle of the night. No one notices that he's gone.

Paco's Story may have been one of the unhappiest accounts of the travails of veterans ever written, but some of its pessimism was matched in Vietnamese literature on the war. *The Sorrow of War,* a novel by Bao Ninh, echoed Heinemann's sense of dislocation, loss, and despair for veterans.[60] Ninh, a North Vietnamese veteran of the American War, served in the Glorious 27th Youth Brigade, and he was one of only ten survivors who went to fight in the South in 1969.[61] Kien, the protagonist, is tormented by nightmares of horrific scenes of combat, wartime rapes, and cold-blooded murders of Peoples Liberation Armed Forces by their own officers. The nameless narrator says that Kien, home at last in Hanoi after fighting for more than a dozen years, "refights all his battles, relives the time when his life was bitter, lonely, surreal, and full of obstacles and horrendous mistakes."[62] North-Vietnamese politicians and public officials appear to be just as corrupt and self-serving as their most venal American counterparts. Kien is appalled at the forced patriotism of postwar Vietnam. Someone tells him that young Vietnamese were eager to fight China in 1979. "But he knew it wasn't true that young Vietnamese loved war. . . . No. The ones who loved war were not the young men but the others like the politicians, middle-aged men with fat bellies and short legs. Not the ordinary people. The recent years of war had brought enough suffering and pain to last them a thousand years."[63]

Similar themes of disillusionment with the human cost of war permeated the fiction of Vietnamese author Thu Hu Duong, another veteran of the wars against the Americans in the 1960s and the Chinese in 1979. She spent seven years in the South and was one of only three members of a forty-member unit to return home. Her bleak stories of revolutionary hopes dashed in a corrupt postwar Vietnam told in *Paradise of the Blind* and *Novel Without a Name* got her into trouble with the Communist Party, which expelled her and put her under house arrest for a while. *Novel Without a Name* recounts the growing bitterness of Quan, an idealistic young officer, who rejects the gap between the cloying propaganda of the home front and the gritty realities of sudden death in combat. Quan voices the anguish of veterans in both America and Vietnam when he recalls how "we were drunk on our youth, marching toward a glorious future." When he was a raw recruit fighting the Americans, he and his comrades believed that the war "was our chance for resurrection. Vietnam had been chosen by History. After the war, our country would become humanity's paradise." Now, in postwar Vietnam he felt it was all a sham.[64]

Writer Robert Olen Butler, who served as a Vietnamese linguist with the U.S. Army in Vietnam, explored the enduring edginess and inability to find peace in a series of novels peopled with American, Vietnamese, and Amerasian characters. In Butler's *The Alleys of Eden*, Clifford Wilkes, an enlisted man, deserts from an intelligence unit at the very end of the war. Along with his Vietnamese lover, he has to make his way through a surreal postwar America. He never finds rest. Dreams intrude of a naked, dead Viet Cong, who suffers a heart attack in the midst of a brutal interrogation. In Butler's *Sun Dogs,* Wilson Hand, who served with Wilkes in Saigon, finds postwar America too alienating and too boring. He's drawn to the excitement and adventure of war, and can find it only in the North Slope oil fields of Alaska. He's a detective exposing industrial espionage in a twisting plot that eventually claims his life. Along the way his mind returns to Vietnam, where he was kidnapped by the Viet Cong while visiting an American-supported orphanage. In Butler's *On Distant Ground,* Captain David Fleming, who also served in the same Saigon interrogation unit, faces wartime court martial for having released a captive Viet Cong. Back home in America Fleming is haunted by memories, and he returns to Vietnam to rescue a son he fathered during the war.[65]

Butler delved into the ways in which Vietnamese and Americans became entwined in the war and its aftermath in *The Deuce*. The narrator is the son of an American GI and a Saigon bar girl. He says, "I wish it were simple just to say who I am. But me, I've got three names. . . . I'm Anthony James Hatcher. Tony. I'm Vo Dinh. Thanh. And I'm the deuce."[66] The name "Deuce" is the key, suggesting the duality and the inability of men who had fought in Vietnam and their offspring to fit in anywhere. Like many Vietnam novels, *The Deuce* is set in the United States. Deuce lives by his wits in an urban combat zone, New York's 42nd Street near the Port Authority bus terminal. "They call Forty-second Street out there the Deuce," a more streetwise young man tells Tony/Thanh/the Deuce, "and you're gonna have to watch out for that street. . . .You watch out for the motherf—ers out there who want to eat you alive.

But that street is still the Mekong, the river that runs right through all of us around here."[67]

Butler acquired a deep love of ordinary Vietnamese during his wartime service, and he included them more than most writers in his stories. He set his Pulitzer Prize–winning collection of short stories, *A Good Scent from a Strange Mountain* (1992), among Vietnamese or Amerasians living in Louisiana after the war. One young woman, the daughter of a Vietnamese mother and an American GI father, remembers that after the war, "I was a child of dust . . . that's what we were called . . . At one look we were Vietnamese and at another look we were American, and after that you couldn't get your eyes to stay still when they turned to us, they kept seeing first one. The young thing, then another."[68] Her father and mother were married in wartime Vietnam, but they lost the marriage license and the girl's birth certificate. Her father went home to America and prepared the way to bring his family with him. Then Saigon fell to the Communists, and her father spent a fortune battling the American bureaucracy to let his daughter enter the United States. "What is the crap that you're trying to give me now?" he explodes in frustration toward uncaring immigration officials in one of the letters that his daughter later finds in an old footlocker. "It has been nine years, seven months and fifteen days since I last saw my daughter, my own flesh and blood daughter."[69] Later he accuses the authorities of a subtle form of racism. He complains, "If this was a goddamn white woman, a Russian ballet dancer and her daughter, you people would have them on a plane in twenty-four hours. This is my wife and my daughter. My daughter is so beautiful you can put her face on your dimes and quarters and no one could ever again make change in your goddamn country without stopping and saying, 'Oh my God, what a beautiful face.'"[70]

Not all Vietnam literature was surrealistic or kept Vietnam set offstage. C.D.B. Bryan surveyed scores of Vietnam novels in 1984 and discerned what he called the "generic Vietnam War narrative" set in Vietnam. These stories chart "the gradual deterioration of order, the disintegration of idealism, the breakdown of character, the alienation from those at home, and, finally, the loss of all sensibility save the will to survive."[71] Philip Caputo's memoir *A Rumor of War* (1977) set the stage for the realistic depiction of growing disillusionment. He describes how when his company marched into rice paddies searching for the elusive Viet Cong "we carried . . . the implicit conviction that the Viet Cong would be quickly beaten and that we were doing something altogether noble and good. We kept the packs and rifles; the convictions we lost." Eventually, Caputo describes in detail the deepening bonds between men in combat, a "communion between men . . . as profound as any between lovers."[72]

Winston Groom, a southern writer deeply influenced by James Jones, the World War II writer, provided good examples of more naturalistic Vietnam fiction in a powerful series of novels. Groom's *Better Times Than These* (1978), a vast battle epic, offers sympathy to ordinary soldiers and battle-hardened officers. At the same time, it reviles rear echelon high officials who do not comprehend the hardships faced by the men they send into danger. Groom describes the noise, fear, chaos, and brutality of jungle warfare where the enemy is everywhere, but nowhere to be seen. He describes the shock of the first encounter of large U.S. and PLAF units in the Ia Drang valley in the fall of 1965. It was just "killing for killing's sake."[73] The relentless demands from the command in Saigon to boost the body count hardened the young American soldiers. GI's spat out the bitter phrase "sorry about that at least six thousand times between Reveille and Taps."[74] Groom broke through to the wider public with the film version of his novel *Forrest Gump* (1986, film 1995). Gump, the idiot savant of the Vietnam War and the 1960s, somehow manages to show up in most of the significant events of that turbulent era. Gump, the idiot, understands the war better than most of the supposedly more informed politicians, soldiers, and antiwar activists he meets in his career. Vietnam "is a bunch of shit," he says.[75] Gump, a sweet character, has good intentions and a large heart. "I may be an idiot," he says at the end, "but most of time, I tried to do the right thing."[76] This very purity of spirit touched audiences by the millions in theaters in the summer of 1995 (see chapter 8).

While most novels of the Vietnam War condemned the U.S. enterprise in Vietnam, some writers supported the war effort. James Webb, a prominent conservative author, placed the onus for the American failure in Vietnam on the antiwar movement. Webb's novel provided a fictional counterpart to the Vietnam revisionism of the immediate postwar years. In *Fields of Fire* (1978), Webb advances the traditional warrior virtues. When someone goes to Vietnam, he possesses an implacable "will to face certain loss, unknown dangers, unpredictable fates" passed down to him by previous generations of warriors.[77] Soldiers, both officers and enlisted personnel, display dignity, courage, honesty, and integrity—in a word honor. These disciplined, patriotic supporters of the war effort willingly follow their leaders.

Yet they know as well as any character in the bitterest antiwar account the sheer horror and brutality of battle. "That's the game out here. That's what we're here for. To kill gooks. Kill gooks and make it home alive."[78] All that mattered was the fate of one's fellow soldiers. A platoon leader remarks that "importance was keeping them alive through another week."[79] Webb describes a chasm between fighters and civilians. "We been abandoned, Lieutenant" by Americans at home, one GI growls. "We been kicked off the edge of the goddamn cliff. They don't know how to fight it, and they don't know how to stop fighting it. They ain't worth dying for."[80]

Webb complains that these fine men's virtues went unrecognized and their sacrifices mocked. "Who are these young men we are asking to go into action against such solid odds? You've met them. They are the best we have." But there's a bitterness alongside this positive assessment, as Webb rages against the avoidance of service by the sons of the elite. These common soldiers "are not McNamara's sons, or Bundy's. I doubt they're yours." (The man addressed is a reporter, another representative of the cultural elite so despised by conservatives.) "And they know that they are at the end of the pipeline. That no one cares. They know." [81]

One wounded survivor returns home to berate thousands of antiwar demonstrators at Harvard University. Offended by their chant, "Ho, Ho, Ho Chi Minh, Viet Cong are gonna win," and their Viet Cong flag, he screams, "LOOK AT YOURSELVES. AND THE FLAG. JESUS CHRIST. HO CHI MINH IS GONNA WIN. HOW MANY OF YOU ARE GONNA GET HURT IN VIETNAM. I SAW DUDES. MAN. DUDES. AND TRUCK DRIVERS. AND COAL MINERS. AND FARMERS. I DIDN'T SEE YOU. WHERE WERE YOU? FLUNKING YOUR DRAFT PHYSICALS. WHAT DO YOU CARE IF IT ENDS? YOU WON'T GET HURT."[82]

Webb became even more defiantly critical of the antiwar movement in *A Country Such as This* (1983). The style of the novel—a straightforward, almost operatic narrative—is as traditional as Webb's nationalist politics. Webb despised the postmodern, experimental novel form favored by such war critics as Tim O'Brien and Larry Heinemann. In this sweeping epic characters declaim political speeches. Red Lesczynski, one of three Naval Academy alumni whose lives make up the core of the novel, says, "The North Vietnamese are clearly trying to take over the South by military force. It's the North Vietnamese who have almost their entire army in the South right now." It's hard to believe anyone speaks that way, but Lesczynski goes on: "We have stated to the world that the South should not be subjugated against its will. If that's worth fighting over, then it should be worth a serious, total effort." He blames the civilian leadership cowardice or ignorance. "I'll tell you the truth, I don't think McNamara has the guts, and I don't think LBJ has the clarity of thought, to fight this war. It's that simple."[83]

Webb sets up a contrast between two caricatures. One, Judd Smith, a patriotic, warm-hearted, earthy, common-sensical, reasonable southern white man, is a decorated marine veteran of the Korean war. Dorothy Dingenfelder, his antagonist and wife of a Naval Academy classmate of Smith's, is portrayed as strident, self-righteous, liberal, and intellectual. A thinly veiled strain of anti-Semitism runs through the description of Dingenfelder who looks like she is preparing "for a costume ball, a thirty-four-year-old Austrian born, New York–raised Jewish law student dressed up like a cowgirl."[84] Webb also derides her as a woman. She rejects dresses, makeup, and scents.[85]

Both Smith and Dingenfelder are elected to Congress, where they debate the very significant social issue of contemporary America. Dingenfelder favors civil rights and affirmative action. Smith rejects them as "social engineering" and "reverse discrimination."[86] She accuses the United States of promoting genocide in Asia, favors the Equal Rights Amendment, and considers Richard Nixon's Watergate abuses of power to have been the gravest constitutional crisis since the Civil War. Smith disagrees on every count. Webb makes Dingenfelder both a clown and a traitor. "The enemy," she says, is "the United States government." She is an antimilitary "general" in "the Women's Strike for Peace, the New York Peace Council, the Chicago Peace Parade Committee, the Southern Christian Leadership Conference, the Ohio Area Peace Action Council, the Students for a Democratic Society, H. Rap Brown's SNCC, various pacifist, socialist, Maoist, communist and Trotskyist fringe groups."[87] *A Country Such as This* reflected many of the revisionist ideas, popular in the 1980s, of blaming the American defeat in Vietnam on supposedly unpatriotic opponents of American participation in the war.

These themes of betrayal from within filled the pulp fiction about the Vietnam War, which also appeared in the decades after the war ended. American participation in the war lasted so long and affected so many that it became a screen onto which writers projected some basic themes and images. These included lone heroes fighting against the odds; heroes who win every engagement, but since they lack the support of higher officials or the public at home, their valor cannot prevail against the enemy. Many of these novels resembled the B movies of the war: fantasies of vengeance, Americans winning the Vietnam War, rescues of imprisoned Americans, or fighting cruel, indifferent, and incompetent American bureaucrats. The critic David A. Willson thought it noteworthy to comment in his survey of 666 Vietnam novels that "a rather unusual character" in one of the potboilers "is a general officer who is not a complete idiot."[88]

Customarily, the higher ranking the officer, the more foolish he was shown to be. For example, in Cat Branigan's *Wings Over Nam, #3: Linebacker War* (one of six adventure novels Branigan wrote about the air war in the Vietnam War), Tech Sergeant Wyeth risks his life to retrieve American flyers downed in North Vietnam. He tries to help Colonel William Lansdale (whose name recalls an earlier figure in the war, Colonel Edward Lansdale) learn how to survive behind enemy lines. Lansdale is so arrogant and proud of his exalted rank that he steadfastly refuses to learn from his more knowledgeable sergeant. Yet Wyeth won't be deterred, and he eventually brings Lansdale safely back to Saigon. Branigan revisits the theme of honorable and skilled servicemen ignored or betrayed by their superiors in *Wings Over Nam, #6: Eagle Eye* (1990). In this adventure, warrant officer David Anderson invents a way of carrying the war to the Viet Cong. He advises his superiors to load squads of grunts onto transport helicopters, support them with helicopter gun ships, and fly them low over the jungle looking for the enemy. After a lot of shuffling and mumbling, the brass agree. Anderson and his men engage the NLF, but at one point he's shot down. He survives only by bravely calling friendly artillery fire near his own position. Despite his heroics, his commanders refuse to recommend him for a medal.

Series of Vietnam books appeared with titles like *The Black Eagles: Hanoi Hellground, Mekong Massacre, Nightmare in Laos, Pungi Patrol,* and *Saigon Slaughter.* John Lansing, the author of the Black Eagles series, employed a formula in which brave American servicemen, adept at using the most sophisticated and deadly weaponry, wreak mayhem on Communist forces. In the first, *The Black Eagles: Hanoi Hellground,* an intrepid band of American commandos sneak into North Vietnam where they liberate a pagoda used by the Communist leadership as a sex palace, steal some top secret Soviet military equipment, shoot down a jet, and hijack a train. In *Nightmare in Laos,* another book in the Black Eagle Series, they secretly enter that neutral kingdom, blow up a Soviet-made nuclear reactor, and return to Vietnam as quietly as they arrived—by glider. In *Pungi Patrol* the commandos take on a gang of East German terrorists, who, disguised as American soldiers, are committing atrocities across South Vietnam.

"Eric Helm," a pseudonym for two Vietnam veterans, wrote at least thirty-five novels playing out the same theme of lone, brave American fighters who would have won the war had it not been for the incompetence of the top brass. In *Vietnam: Ground Zero* (1986) Special Forces Captain Mark Gerber leads his Green Beret unit into Cambodia where they kill a Chinese officer. But his heroics are not recognized, because a careerist American general brings charges against the Green Berets for straying beyond the officially recognized battlefield into neutral Cambodia. Gerber is acquitted of disobeying orders, and he then leads his courageous men back into Cambodia and captures important NLF prisoners.

Most of the Ground Zero novels feature secret commando raids. Captain Gerber and his brave and loyal subordinate Sergeant Fetterman, maybe the only two American leaders in Vietnam who seem to know how to fight the enemy, consistently outsmart the wily North Vietnamese and NLF. In *Vietnam: Ground Zero: Tet* (1988) they notice the infiltration of young men into Saigon and other signs that something big is about to happen in the capital. They're ready when the NLF attack the U.S. embassy on January 30, 1968, and they repel the attack. Unfortunately, their heroics go unreported because the selfish American journalists on the scene conclude that reporting an American defeat will attract more viewers and sell more newspapers at home than would a U.S. victory.

Desperate, dangerous, and secret missions behind enemy lines were a staple of this genre. In *Vietnam: Ground Zero: Red Dust* (1988) Gerber and his Green Berets steal into North Vietnam to plant a seismic device. They attack a North Vietnamese air base to acquire a radio transmitter, having foolishly declined to bring one of their own. While at the airbase they meet an American antiwar activist named, unsurprisingly, Jane. *In Vietnam: Ground Zero: The Raid* (1988), Gerber and some of his fearless troops sneak north of the 17th parallel to break American captives out of a North Vietnamese prisoner of war camp.

Much to their surprise the supposed prison turns out to be a top secret Soviet base where grizzled Soviet Red Army advisers are training North Vietnamese troops. American superior officers hardly know what to do with this shocking news, but eventually they authorize Gerber to attack the base. Making use of their astonishing capacity for improvisation, Gerber and his squad of experienced fighters blow up the camp. Gerber then returns to Saigon to persuade gullible journalists that he had been away on a routine exercise in the nearby jungle of South Vietnam.

Pornographic literature using the Vietnam War as the storyline also emerged after the war. Star Distributors, a small New York publisher of sexually explicit fiction, brought out numerous works that featured plots involving sex, rape, debasement, and torture. In Everett Avery's *Vietcong Terror Compound* (1979) an American naval nurse is captured and repeatedly raped by the Viet Cong. In *Saigon Hell Hole* and *Slave of the Vietcong,* two books published published anonymously by Star in 1980, the daughter of a U.S. senator is also raped by NLF fighters. In *Viet Cong Torture Camp* (1981) a group of female entertainers is captured and suffers the same sort of sexual degradation. This fate awaits "a whole chopper load of radical lesbian types" who are captured by the enemy in *Viet Cong Rape Compound* (1982).[89] Some of the Vietnam pornography offered brutal homosexual sex. Alvin Dummar, the protagonist of *Infantry Stud* (1983), is both victimized by other soldiers in basic training and a rapist and torturer of captured Viet Cong when he arrives in Vietnam. In *Rear Attack* (1982) Sergeant Butch Brannigan leads the Blowtorch Brigade in a rampage of torture and rape of captured prisoners. The men in the unit also take great delight in degrading a new second lieutenant.

Several consistent themes ran through the American novels of the Vietnam war—from the most sophisticated and serious literature, through the potboilers, to the vilest pornography: War is hell, but the Vietnam experience seemed worse than earlier passages of arms. Characters in Vietnam fiction are almost inexpressibly alone, cut off from the rest of American society, from the Vietnamese, from their superior officers, and from each other. Others, fortunate not to have endured the trauma of combat, reject, misunderstand, or betray them. Veterans long to escape the horrors of the war. They use all the traditional modes of solace or release: family, romance, sex, alcohol, drugs, dreams, and nightmares. But try as they might, the war overpowers them. Their thoughts and their emotions in one way or another remain fixed in the alien and unpredictable landscape of Vietnam.

Chapter

* * * * * * * * * * *

Vietnam Memories
Through Film

The Vietnam War became the setting for over four hundred movies, documentaries, and TV series from the 1960s to the first years of the twenty-first century. If World War II was the "good war" in which a generation pulled together for a common goal, Vietnam was the "bad war," dividing the country and leaving a bitter taste. Yet many Vietnam-era films explored themes that had been raised earlier in World War II movies. Death, disillusionment, and the differences between what recruits expected and the grim realities of combat were features they had in common. But the films of the Vietnam era explored many novel themes. Class, race, and gender issues were featured more prominently than had been the case in earlier war movies. The Vietnam films reflected deep divisions at home over the war. Some reflected pro-war sentiments and vilified antiwar protesters. Others took exactly the opposite approach, criticizing official policies and government officials. They portrayed soldiers as victims of an inhumane war machine. Nevertheless, a common thread—withering contempt for civilian government officials—ran through Vietnam films whether they supported or opposed U.S. policies in Vietnam.

This attitude would, of course, be expected in accounts critical of U.S. involvement in Vietnam, but it is more surprising to find it present in films supportive of the American effort. Sylvester Stallone's John Rambo became an archetype of the independent American hero. During the Reagan administration the word "Rambo" became an emblem for an unrestrained cowboy who acted without thinking. Yet the Rambo movies also contained furious denunciations of self-serving American officers more concerned with protecting their own careers than waging a war.

Most Vietnam-era films criticized the war to some degree. The exceptions proved the rule. In 1958 Joseph Mankiewicz produced the first film version of Graham Greene's *The Quiet American*. The screenplay transformed Greene's dark portrayal of the excesses of American innocence into a paean to America's chosen leader of Vietnam, Ngo Dinh Diem, and the movie was even dedicated to Diem. Alden Pyle, the American protagonist played by Audie Murphy, identifies a leader, clearly Diem, of whom he says, "If all goes well, if Vietnam becomes an independent country, this man will be its leader."[1]

As American commitment to Vietnam intensified, Hollywood grappled with how to produce war films. From the very beginning of the American involvement, producers shied away from triumphant portrayals of heroic Americans and brutal Communist Vietnamese. Albert Auster and Leonard Quart, two astute observers of films with Vietnam themes, remarked in 1988 that "most producers, even the most patriotic, were loath to make pro-war films about Vietnam."[2]

A notable exception was *The Green Berets* (1968), directed by and starring John Wayne. By the mid-1960s Wayne had gained a huge international following for his heroic World War II films and Westerns. Many critics thought his work was overblown, bombastic, and lacking subtlety or nuance, in a word, corny. But audiences flocked to see his films. His conservative political views were well known. His biographers, Randy Roberts and James Olson, note that "in an age where patriotism became suspect among liberals, he wrapped himself in the flag." The film historian Michael Anderegg observed that by the time of the Vietnam War his "image had hardened into a cliché-laden icon of the uncomplicated warrior hero." Wayne ardently backed the Vietnam War and expressed his disapproval and scorn for antiwar protesters. He once said, "I can't believe that people in the U.S. don't realize that we're at war with international communism."[3]

In 1965 Wayne bought the rights to produce a movie version of Robin Moore's 1963 novel, *The Green Berets,* about U.S. Army Special Forces in Vietnam. The production and the film played out American rather than Vietnamese themes. He obtained Pentagon support for the filming at Fort Benning, Georgia, where the piney woods bore little if any resemblance to Vietnam. Changes in the script and actors delayed release until June 1968, after the Tet Offensive had convinced a majority of Americans that it had been a mistake to enter a war to which there seemed to be no end in sight. Wayne had no such doubts as he pressed forward with a project he hoped would convince his fellow Americans to support the war effort.

The movie evokes the heroism of John F. Kennedy's Special Forces, who are portrayed as brave and muscular. Viet Cong fighters are faceless, conniving, brutal, and cowardly. As bullets fly around Colonel Mike Kirby, played by Wayne, he strides bravely through rice fields and villages, dispensing fatherly advice to frightened younger soldiers, misguided liberal reporters, and aid workers. They all learn to toughen up, fight harder, and support the war. Wayne fans liked the action and the special effects, and the film made money, though critics savaged *The Green Berets*. Writing in *The New Yorker*, Renata Adler called it "unspeakable, rotten, and false." Michael Korda's review in *Glamour* damned it as "immoral in the deepest sense. It is a simple-minded tract in praise of killing, brutality and American superiority." The movie and industry publications did not like it either. Wayne seemed out of touch with contemporary styles and mores. The reviewer for *Cinema Magazine* derided the film as "so wretched and childishly sleazy that it is embarrassing to criticize its pretentiousness and banality." *The Hollywood Reporter* called *The Green Berets* "a cliché-ridden throw-back to the battlefield pot boilers of World War II, its artifice readily exposed by the nightly actuality of TV news coverage."[4]

Not only was *The Green Berets* unusual in its support for the American war effort, but it also stood out for having been produced at all while the American War went on. For the most part Hollywood avoided Vietnam subjects from 1965 to 1973 for fear of alienating a part of their audience. The militantly antiwar documentary *Hearts and Minds* was one of only a handful of films about Vietnam to break this pattern when it was released in 1974. Director Peter Davis mixed footage from upbeat scenes of happy soldiers going off to World War II and optimistic testimony of Johnson and Nixon administration officials with graphic portrayals of death and destruction in Vietnam. The unmistakable conclusion was that U.S. officials had lied, and Vietnamese had suffered. A scene in a brothel of two GI's grinning as they fondle child-like prostitutes is a pornographic depiction of the United States exercising a sexual dominance over Vietnam.

Hearts and Minds won the Academy Award for Best Documentary of 1974. Pandemonium erupted at the awards ceremony in March 1975 when director Peter Davis read a telegram from North Vietnam thanking the American antiwar movement "for all they have done on the behalf of peace." Bob Hope, the M.C. for the evening who had regularly traveled to Vietnam to entertain American troops, immediately demanded an apology from Howard Koch, the film's producer. Shirley MacLaine shouted, "Don't you dare." Hope then insisted that Frank Sinatra read an apology from the Academy of Motion Picture Arts and Sciences: "We are not responsible for any political references made on the program and we are sorry they had to take place this evening."[5]

But by 1978 the drought ended for dramatic Vietnam films when four Vietnam-related movies came to theaters. That year Columbia Pictures distributed *The Boys in Company C* by Hong Kong–based producer Raymond Chow. On the one hand, the movie was a standard war film in which undisciplined, raw recruits, mostly impoverished, are forged into marines. They sail into Camh Ranh Bay days before the Tet Offensive of 1968. From that point onward the movie changes tone from the heroic World War II genre. High-ranking officers are stupid, oblivious to the safety of their troops, and concerned only for their own advancement. A captain rushes his men into an obvious ambush and the company sustains heavy losses. The soldiers of Company C are told to escort a convoy containing supposedly vital goods to the front lines. Two die before the soldiers discover that they're protecting cartons of Jim Beam bourbon and cigarettes. The Viet Cong enemy is faceless, but they fight hard. The South Vietnamese on the other hand, are cartoon figures—weak, fat, cowardly, and corrupt. The marines grow more disillusioned with every passing scene. The war aims are both incomprehensible and unattainable. A final voiceover summarizes the futility of the American war effort: "We'll just keep on walking into one bloody mess after another until somebody figures out that living has got to be more important than winning."[6]

1978 saw the release of *Go Tell the Spartans*, starring Burt Lancaster. Set in the earliest days of American involvement in 1964, the movie is a dark, brooding tale of ineptitude. An unbridgeable chasm divides the bright young experts from the Pentagon, sent out to Vietnam with flow charts, operations research, and other tools of the social scientists, from the American soldiers in the field. The enemy Viet Cong are elusive, almost unseen, in *Go Tell the Spartans*. The colonel played by Lancaster, a grizzled veteran of World War II, has seen too much war. He tells an idealistic young lieutenant who has just arrived in Vietnam and believes in the cause, "It's too bad we couldn't have shown you a better war, like hitting the beach at Anzio . . . That was a real tour. This one's a sucker tour, going nowhere, just around and around in circles." Lancaster's men, sent to defend an isolated Vietnamese outpost, grow disgusted with what appears to be pointless sacrifice on behalf of ungrateful South Vietnamese. "It's the war," one dispirited, drunken older soldier says.[7]

Neither *The Boys in Company C* nor *Go Tell the Spartans* achieved major financial or critical success when released. For all of their corrosive disdain for the American mission in Vietnam, they were both traditional war films, and audiences were in no mood to watch two hours of combat in the years immediately following the Vietnam War. Two other films in 1978—*The Deer Hunter* and *Coming Home*—were very different in message and garnered critical and commercial praise. *The Deer Hunter* won five Academy Awards, including Best Picture. *Coming Home* collected three, including Best Actress for Jane Fonda and Best Actor for Jon Voight.

The Deer Hunter, like much of the U.S. war effort in Vietnam, had very little to do with events in Southeast Asia and very much to do with Americans' views of themselves. The film's action cuts back and forth between the steel towns of western Pennsylvania and the battlefields, villages, and cities of Vietnam as it traces the lives of five working-class men in combat and back in their hometowns. The film addresses many of the issues that roiled the United States during the war years, among them the changing relations between men and women, the surreal nature of a war in an incomprehensible place, and the deep scars left on the psyches of men who came home. Some of the scenes of the Vietnam combat were familiar: whirring helicopters, flames coming from nowhere, an unseen enemy, animals eating the burning flesh of a wounded soldier.

The movie's pivotal scenes in which the main characters play Russian roulette were its most controversial. At one point Michael (Robert DeNiro) and his old friend Stevie (John Savage) are captured by Viet Cong fighters, who sadistically force the Americans into a cruel game of Russian roulette. Michael, always the leader of the group of Pennsylvania friends, convinces Stevie to pull the trigger: "You can do it," Michael shouts. The revolver has a bullet in it but Stevie is shaking so hard that the bullet only grazes his head. Later, at war's end, Nicky (Christopher Walken), another of the friends, is wounded, spends time in a Saigon hospital, and then goes AWOL through the haunted streets of the capital of the South. He is sickened by the cheap, meaningless sex in a whorehouse catering to GIs. He stumbles into a smoky, noisy bar where a Russian roulette game is underway. Nicky runs up to the players, grabs a revolver, puts it to his head and pulls the trigger. Like Stevie, before him, he's saved; the chamber was empty. Among the dozens of military and civilian onlookers, wearing civilian clothes is Michael who has been searching for Nicky. Michael runs after the crazed Nicky, but his friend is hustled away by an older Frenchman who organizes the deadly games.

Nicky dies of a gunshot in the game, and the movie ends back in Pennsylvania where the old friends gather for his funeral. After the services the gang gets together at the local bar where they join in the singing of "God Bless America." While critics praised the film's sensitive treatment of the characters' growing disillusionment, they hated both the depiction of Russian roulette, which they said never happened in Vietnam, and the patriotic ending. Opponents of the American War complained that *The Deer Hunter* seemed to absolve the United States for the destruction it inflicted on Vietnam. Yet a more complex reading shows the characters desperately clinging to traditional values and a close-knit community while world events had conspired to destroy them. The film critic Roger Ebert praised the film as an "impressive blending of 'box-office' and 'art.'" He wrote that the movie explored "male bonding, mindless patriotism, the dehumanizing effects of the war, [and]

Nixon's silent majority." But it went beyond any of those subjects. "More than anything else," Ebert wrote, "it is a heartbreakingly effective fictional machine that evokes the agony of the Vietnam time. . . . If it is not overtly 'anti-war,' why should it be? What *The Deer Hunter* insists is that we not forget the war."[8]

Coming Home, the other Academy Award–winning film of 1978, was the personal project of Jane Fonda, a prominent Hollywood actor and daughter of Henry Fonda, whose active opposition to the war was notorious. Fonda had partly inherited her own all-American, seemingly innocent persona from her father who had starred in numerous films celebrating the American character. She said she became an antiwar activist because it just made sense to do so: the war went on too long, cost too much in lives and money, and served no good end. She spoke at antiwar rallies in California and she organized a troupe of fellow Hollywood antiwar activists touring military bases, many of them in the Golden State, called FTA (for either Free the Army, or, more colloquially, F— the Army). In the summer of 1972 Fonda brought her antiwar message to Hanoi. During her visit to the capital of the Democratic Republic of Vietnam she made several radio broadcasts to American troops. A film clip showed her clapping and smiling while sitting in the seat of a North Vietnamese anti-aircraft gun ostensibly aimed at U.S. military planes. She also met with American POWs who resented her presence as a propaganda coup for their captors. Supporters of the war called her Hanoi Jane and labeled her a traitor. For years after her visit to North Vietnam Fonda was vilified as someone who had given aid and comfort to the country's enemy in wartime. [9]

Fonda starred in *Coming Home*, a film she also worked for several years to have produced. She deliberately downplayed some of her more outspoken antiwar views in order to reach a mass audience, but the film still drove home the human costs of a pointless war. The drama of *Coming Home* involved a love triangle consisting of Sally Hyde (Fonda), a paraplegic Vietnam veteran, Luke Martin (Voight), and Sally's marine officer husband, Bob Hyde (Bruce Dern). The film explores the feminist theme of a soldier's wife's growing autonomy while her husband is in Vietnam. Sally works at the VA where she meets and falls in love with the embittered Luke, disillusioned with the war, furious at the loss of the use of his legs, and fearful of being dependent. The film traces Sally's growing independence, Luke's gradual ability to give and receive love, and Bob's homecoming.

The movie sets Luke and Bob as polar opposites of the military experience. The former, an enlisted man, was physically broken but spiritually, intellectually, and politically liberated by the war. He becomes an antiwar activist who chains himself to the fence of the local marine base to protest sending men to their deaths. Meanwhile, the officer who believed in the cause returns home to find an unfaithful wife, no longer the submissive young woman he left behind. Bob confronts Luke, who is guilt-ridden for having slept with the wife of another veteran. Bob feels out of place everywhere. "I do not belong in this house," he yells at Sally, "and they're saying I do not belong [in Vietnam]." He grabs his M-16 and threatens to kill his wife and her lover. It's left to Luke, a highly unlikely mediator, to calm things down between Bob and Sally. He tells the enraged Bob, "I'm not the enemy. The enemy is the f—ing war. You don't want to kill anybody here. You have enough ghosts to carry around."[10] Sobered by what he has heard, Bob drops his weapon, sobs, apologizes, and collapses.

Bob can no longer recapture the innocent hopes he had for military glory or domestic contentment. At the film's end he swims into the Pacific to drown. On the other hand, Luke's voice grows stronger as the film reaches its mournful climax. The movie shifts back and forth between shots of Bob taking off his clothes and entering the water to meet death as a release from his unbearable torments and Luke addressing a crowded high school gym. He warns the young men not to believe the words of a marine recruiter who had just urged them to enlist to fight in Vietnam. Vietnam, he warned, "ain't like it is in the movies." He regretted having "killed for my country . . . because there's not enough reason, man." Having killed and seen friends blown to pieces before his eyes, he could barely live with the memories, and he didn't want the boys he addressed to carry the same burden. He denied feeling sorry for himself, "I'm a lot smarter now than when I went, and I'm just telling ya that there's a choice to be made here."[11]

Coming Home captured the conflicted sentiments of a majority of Americans in the years immediately after the Communist victory in Vietnam. Who had been right and who had been wrong had faded as an issue. Instead, Americans focused on the human costs to those who had fought and those who had stayed behind. The film also appealed to the changing views of veterans as victims of the government. All veterans, regardless of their opinions during or following the war, became objects of pity. Some critics of *Coming Home* complained that the film had drained much of the politics out of the war. *Ms. Magazine* objected that it reduced the story to a pious and sentimental love story. Other conservative critics could not forgive Jane Fonda for her 1968 visit to Hanoi.[12]

For the most part, however, the critical reception, like that of the audiences who wept through it, was highly positive. The movie was about America not Vietnam, and with the war over, Americans were ready for some kind of reconciliation. John Wayne, angry with his friend Henry's daughter for having gone to Hanoi, made his peace with her when *Coming Home* drew huge audiences in 1978. He presented the Hollywood Women's Press Club's Golden Apple to her as female star of the year. Ten years later Fonda sought reconciliation with American veterans and former POWs. She apologized for some of the things she said and did in Hanoi, calling her visit to the anti-aircraft artillery piece a "thoughtless and careless thing to have done."[13]

Like *Coming Home*, most Vietnam War films were at heart about the United States. This self-reflexive quality applied to *Apocalypse Now*, Francis Ford Coppola's 1979 epic. The director worked for more than five years on the project. Filmed mostly in the Philippines, the movie was based on Joseph Conrad's *Heart of Darkness*, a novella set in the Belgian Congo at the beginning of the twentieth century. Both Conrad's account and Coppola's movie depict the descent into a mental or moral hell as Europeans (or Americans) became ever more deeply involved in cultures they did not understand and did not like. At the beginning of the project, Coppola tried to obtain the cooperation of the Pentagon. Defense Department officials hoped to cooperate in a realistic depiction of Vietnam, but they backed out in horror at the unremitting chaos, atrocities, dope smoking, and surfing in the midst of battle presented in John Milius's script.

The plot of the film revolves around Captain Willard (Martin Sheen) being sent up the Mekong River to "terminate" Colonel Walter Kurtz (Marlon Brando) who had been driven mad by the war. Kurtz had withdrawn to Cambodia where he commands his own private army for raiding the Viet Cong and selling dope. Captain Willard, a CIA assassin, embarks on his surreal journey upriver to find Kurtz. On this trip Willard encounters a captain in the air cavalry, symbolically named Kilgore (Robert Duvall), a dashing, crazy character, wearing a cowboy hat and sporting a yellow kerchief. He leads his helicopters on a raid on a Viet Cong hamlet with loudspeakers on the choppers blaring out Richard Wagner's "Ride of the Valkyries." Kilgore calls in an air strike to finish the last resistance. As the fire rains down, Kilgore utters one of the most famous lines of all Vietnam-era films: "I love the smell of napalm in the morning . . . It smells like victory."[14] More chaos and hallucinatory killings follow as Willard makes his way to Kurtz. When the assassin finally meets the rogue colonel in his Cambodian hideout, Kurtz is surrounded by tribespeople, guerrillas, American deserters, and an incoherent photographer on speed played by Dennis Hopper.

In their climactic encounter, Kurtz tells Willard "I've seen the horror." He relates a tale of Viet Cong atrocities—hacking off the arms of recently inoculated children. Instead of being repulsed by the atrocity, Kurtz finds the Viet Cong's "strength to do that . . . perfect and pure," explaining that that steely commitment by the enemy is going to overwhelm the Americans, which is why Kurtz has embarked on a campaign of terror of his own. Willard is wounded and nearly drowns, but he rises from the water and plunges a knife into Kurtz who repeats, "the horror, the horror," Kurtz's final death rattle from Conrad's *Heart of Darkness*. Strobe lights shoot through this death scene, which is intercut with tribespeople slaughtering an ox. Willard escapes back to his boat and another air strike drops bombs and napalm on the ruins of Kurtz's camp.

Coppola meant his movie to disturb the sensibilities of its audiences and he succeeded. Like the story itself, the filming, the music, the dialogue, and the narration have a fantastical air about them. Michael Herr, author of the phantasmagorical war reminiscence *Dispatches* (1968), wrote an almost hallucinatory narration delivered by Willard. The movie opens with a drug-addled Willard lying on a bed staring at a ceiling fan whose slow revolutions mimic the swirling blades of an army helicopter. "Saigon, sh—," he says. "I'm still only in Saigon. Every time I think I'm gonna wake up in the jungle." He remembers what happened during a brief return trip to the United States, "when I was here, I wanted to be there, and when I was there, all I could think of was getting back to the jungle."[15] The tranquil, green beauty of Southeast Asia contrasts with the explosions, the fires, and the pounding soundtrack combining the acid rock band "The Doors" with classical Wagner. Combat, killing, and atrocities take place next to scenes of young American men and women relaxing on China Beach, drinking beer, and surfing. Sometimes the film is double exposed to intensify the surrealistic effect. Characters are stoned, and many hallucinate. Characters mouth clichés about good and evil. Nothing is as it seems. Indeed, *Apocalypse Now* challenges ideas of reality, fact, fiction, truth, morality, and purpose. The effect of the film undermines the justification for the American presence in Vietnam. At the same time, the movie is essentially entertainment. Audiences are drawn into the surreal scenes of combat with the music, the color, and the editing. When Kurtz and Coppola speak of the horror of Vietnam, they do it with the fascination of men transfixed by a calamity from which they cannot turn away.

The Vietnam revisionism of the 1980s reverberated throughout the cinematic portrayals of the war during that decade. The portrait of the veteran underwent some changes in the 1980s from the pathetic, misunderstood Dern character in *Coming Home* to a more independent, still lone figure fighting an uncaring system. Just as Ronald Reagan owed his electoral victory to a widespread public sense that the United States required a more muscular foreign policy toward the Soviet Union, many of the Vietnam films of the 1980s presented more assertive and accomplished Vietnam fighters and veterans.

These views coalesced in revisionist films and TV shows about the Vietnam War and its aftermath. *Magnum PI*, a highly popular weekly CBS private-eye show that began in 1982, recast the Vietnam vet as a comfortable, heroic figure. Tom Selleck played Magnum, a Vietnam vet living by his charm and wits in Honolulu. He doesn't have a steady job, but he lives well (remarkably since he rarely earns a fee), and he's anything but bitter. He's reassembled some of his old army buddies to fight crime, find missing persons, and uncover corruption in the Hawaiian sunshine. He does it all with grace and good humor. A succession of beautiful, sometimes witty, and always vulnerable women falls into his arms along the way.

In each investigation Magnum must overcome the negligence, stupidity, hostility, and self-interest of incompetent government bureaucrats. In some ways the *Magnum PI* series fits well into the earlier hard-boiled detective genre of Raymond Chandler. But just as the setting changed from the corruption of interwar Los Angeles or the foggy cold of San Francisco to the endless summer vacation in Hawaii, Magnum too was far cheerier than Philip Marlowe or Sam Spade ever were.[16]

Sylvester Stallone's two *Rambo* movies, Gene Hackman's *Uncommon Valor*, Chuck Norris's *Missing in Action* pictures, and lesser movies such as *Final Mission* or *Angkor: Cambodia Express* depicted lone, heroic American fighting men, unappreciated and even betrayed by unresponsive, self-interested bureaucrats. The cultural critic Susan Jeffords has written that many of these films represented an effort to recapture traditional ideas of American masculinity. In them men live by their wits and brawn, confronting physically, mentally, and morally weak American officials who lost the war for America by succumbing to feminized, soft, bureaucratic modern culture.[17] The liberal journalist Fred Turner analyzed the *Rambo* films and found that they included numerous "guilt-removing devices," allowing Americans to justify that they didn't lose the Vietnam War but were betrayed by incompetent and dishonest officers.[18]

First Blood (1982) introduced the character John Rambo (Sylvester Stallone). Audiences came in the millions to see this fantasy of a misunderstood, lonely veteran making his way back home in the Pacific Northwest. Stallone's character, John Rambo, is a sculpted hulk of scarred masculine muscle (he rarely wears a shirt) and bravery. He arrives in a small town looking for an old army buddy, but is heartbroken to learn that his friend has recently died, unmourned, from a cancer contracted from exposure to Agent Orange. The vicious sheriff's deputies throw Rambo in jail on a trumped-up vagrancy charge, triggering a flashback to his incarceration by the Viet Cong.

Neither the Communists nor the Washington State troopers are a match for Rambo when he's angry. He breaks out of jail and escapes to the mountains, where his special forces training with bows and arrows and pungi sticks enable him to hold off about five hundred pursuing sheriff's deputies, state troopers, and finally, even the National Guard. His former special forces leader, Colonel Trautman, encourages Rambo to surrender to "friendly civilians," but Stallone denies that such people exist. Civilians "would not let us win" in Vietnam, he replies angrily, the same civilians had screamed obscenities at him and his comrades in arms when they returned home. Still, he spares the life of the vindictive sheriff and surrenders. Critics either ignored or excoriated *First Blood* as a cartoonish vengeance fantasy. Audiences, made up mostly, but not exclusively, of teenage boys, loved the action. It may well be that was all they liked about it, and the latent political content carried less impact than critics or political figures thought.

Three years later, in 1985, the sequel appeared. *Rambo, First Blood: Part II* was the film that gave a name to a generation of angry, militant warriors, determined to refight and win the Vietnam War. Action-adventure was at the core of Rambo, which opened with a huge explosion. It is not, as might have been expected, a war scene, but dynamite used in a quarry where John Rambo, imprisoned for his rampages committed during the first movie, works with other convicts. Colonel Trautman arrives to recruit Rambo for a secret mission to discover the whereabouts of American POWs in Vietnam. Much as Rambo hates breaking rocks in prison, he's wary of taking on another mission for the government he distrusts so heartily. He'll go only, he says, if "we get to win this time," and Trautman assures him that the government stands behind him.

Rambo puts these assurances to the test in the rest of the movie. As he feared, cowardly government officials, concerned primarily with their own jobs and afraid of the power of "liberals" do not want him to find any POWs. Undaunted, Rambo sneaks into a POW camp, kills a sentry with a bow and arrow, finds the emaciated, tortured Americans, and escapes with one. Rambo and his grateful, rescued captive wait for helicopters to take them to freedom. But the CIA has other ideas, and a government agent orders the helicopters not to land. Abandoned by his own government, Rambo is now captured by sadistic Communists, including a visiting commissar from the USSR. His captors brutalize him, but like the thickheaded American troopers in the first film they are no match for his brawn. He escapes, using every trick he learned a decade ago from the Viet Cong. He captures the Soviet helicopter and flies it to a CIA base in Thailand. He tracks down one of his tormentors, Murdoch, the CIA official who has engineered the whole charade, and shoots up Murdoch's headquarters, but spares his life. "There are more Americans out there. Find them or I will," he screams at the cowering bureaucrat. Colonel Trautman tries to calm Rambo. He asks him not to "hate" America for having engaged in a misguided war. Rambo replies that he's willing to die for America. "What is it you want," a bewildered Trautman asks. He's metaphorically asking the question Americans civilians want to know from angry veterans. Rambo grunts out: "I want what . . . every other guy who came over here and spilled his guts and gave everything wants . . . for our country to love us as much as we love it."[19]

Rambo soon made its way into the popular imagination and vocabulary. *Time* magazine did a cover story on Rambo and what it meant for the new nationalism sweeping the country. President Ronald Reagan loved the film and wondered aloud whether Rambo could rescue American hostages in Lebanon. Members of his own National Security Council staff had another use for the movie as they derided the efforts of a "Rambo faction" in Congress and among conservatives to promote a fanciful (and sometimes profitable) belief that the U.S. government concealed knowledge that Americans had been left behind after the war.[20]

The theme of American POWs left behind and betrayed by an uncaring, craven government recurred in several other films. *Uncommon Valor*, released in late 1983, was a barely fictionalized account of the mission of retired Colonel James "Bo" Gritz into Thailand and Laos to find Americans held prisoner; H. Ross Perot, the Texas billionaire, financed the mission. Gene Hackman plays Colonel Cal Rhodes, a character based roughly on Gritz, and Robert Stack plays Macgregor, a wealthy Texan who wants to find his son, missing for years after a fierce firefight in Laos. After smug, lazy Pentagon officials rebuff Rhodes, the old Korean War veteran assembles his own team of heroes who set off for Southeast Asia. In Thailand they are frustrated by the long arm of the U.S. government when shadowy figures (probably CIA) confiscate their equipment. They press on with the help of an unsavory Frenchman, who, for a price, will provide the equipment they need. Rhodes's band of misfits, angry vets, surfers, and druggies are miraculously molded into a tough fighting force that sneaks into Laos and finds a camp holding Americans. They use every trick they learned in Vietnam, and although they are greatly outnumbered by the sadistic Communist camp guards, they are able to rescue several American prisoners. The film ends with a press conference in which a jubilant Colonel Rhodes shows off the rescued POWs and explodes the lies and cover-ups of government officials from every U.S. administration from 1973 to 1983.

Chuck Norris, a karate expert, pushed the theme of Americans held captive in Vietnam in three *Missing in Action* films (1984, 1985, 1988). In each, Norris played Braddock, a former POW who returns to Vietnam to rescue men he knows are still held captive. In each film he must use his wits, the skills he honed in service, his muscled, graceful body, and an impressive array of the most modern military gadgetry to fend off sadistic, dishonest Communist officials of the Socialist Republic of Vietnam and lazy, out-of-shape American bureaucrats. Braddock triumphs every time, coming out of Southeast Asia with live, grateful POWs.

Fantasies of vengeance, retribution, or refighting the Vietnam War were not the only cinematic recreations of Vietnam in the 1980s. By the time the last *Missing in Action* film was released in 1988, the Reagan administration was well on the way to reaching an accommodation with the Socialist Republic of Vietnam and the U.S. government had begun joint search patrols with the SRV. As some of the nationalist anger that had propelled Reagan into the White House in 1980 lifted during his second term, a new wave of Hollywood films emerged.

Occasionally movies dealt in somewhat more realistic ways with the POW experience. *Hanoi Hilton* (1987) featured a Navy pilot named Williamson (played by Michael Moriarity) who is shot down during the U.S. bombing raids following the Gulf of Tonkin incident in 1964. The Defense Department and Arizona Representative (later Senator) John McCain, on whom Williamson was roughly based, cooperated in the production. In the film Williamson and other downed American pilots are imprisoned in Hanoi's Hoa Lo Prison, originally a jail in which the French beat and sometimes executed Vietnamese nationalists in the 1930s, '40s, and '50s, but dubbed by the Americans as the Hanoi Hilton. The movie makes an effort to realistically depict the brutalities inflicted on them by their captors. The North Vietnamese are portrayed as brutal and efficient jailers who deny that the Americans have any rights under the Geneva Convention.

As the captors beat the prisoners, keep them in isolation, and deprive them of mail from home, medical care, and visits from the Red Cross, the North Vietnamese tell the Americans that the French had taught them these techniques to break the will of captives. Eventually, the torture and deprivation wear down the pilots, who one by one sign confessions. The film dwells on the interactions among the POWs. It explores their loneliness and boredom, as well as their contempt for an American peace activist, modeled obviously on Jane Fonda, who visits during Christmas 1969. Some try to escape, only to be recaptured. One is mortally wounded, and his dying remarks summarize the dark mood of many Vietnam War films: "I die not so much for love of my country as for love of my countrymen."[21] The director Lionel Chetwynd contrasted his approach to that of Michael Cimino, director of *The Deer Hunter*, claiming that his portrait of the North Vietnamese was realistic, not fantastic. Using information provided by McCain and the other former POWs, *Hanoi Hilton* depicted the North Vietnamese as "smart, sophisticated, worldly wise people with a whole inventory of torture—learned from their colonial masters, the French, who tortured Arabs in Algeria."[22]

The mid-1980s also saw the release of several critically acclaimed films depicting the Vietnam War from the soldier's, or grunt's, point of view. More than ten years had passed since the end of the U.S. combat role in Vietnam, and the last prisoners had returned a decade earlier. American audiences seemed ready to see films about the actual fighting in Vietnam.

Director Oliver Stone's *Platoon* (1986) was based largely on his own combat experiences. He came from a privileged background, dropped out of Yale, and then went to Vietnam, first as a teacher and then as a volunteer infantryman. He came to Southeast Asia as a hawk and a Cold War warrior. "I believed in the John Wayne image of America," he recalled. But quickly he perceived the brutality and randomness of combat, the incompetence of American officers, and the corruption of South Vietnamese officials, as well as the burning commitment of the Communists. He hated the futility of his wartime service and deadened his pain with whiskey and marijuana.

Stone came home in late 1968, angry that most of his countrymen had no interest in Vietnam. His marriage dissolved, he continued drinking, and he smoked more dope, making him a stereotypical alienated vet. Stone was also an enormously talented filmmaker. He enrolled in New York University's film school, where he directed a short film entitled, *Last Year in Vietnam*. After he graduated, he drifted through a series of menial jobs, wrote several commercially successful screenplays (*Midnight Express, Scarface, Conan*, and *Year of the Dragon*), and moved to Los Angeles where he partied hard. All the while he worked on a screenplay for a movie about his own experiences in Vietnam.

Platoon appeared to great critical acclaim in 1986. It tells the story of Chris, based roughly on Stone and played by Charlie Sheen, the nineteen-year-old son of Martin Sheen, the protagonist of *Apocalypse Now*. Two sergeants, Barnes (Tom Berenger) and Elias (Willem Defoe), provide the poles of the moral dilemma Americans faced in Vietnam. The former is a brutal killer, and the latter a tormented man who reports Barnes's atrocities to the higher authorities. The score features sounds from The Doors, country star Merle Haggard, Jefferson Airplane, and Smokey Robinson and the Miracles. The use of popular music was common enough in Vietnam films, but Stone departed from the standard format with Samuel Barber's "Adagio for Strings." The haunting, minor-key melody evoked the loss of innocence, as did the ironic epigraph from Ecclesiastes, "rejoice, o young man, in thy youth."

Platoon follows Chris through his brutal basic training, incomprehensible combat, atrocities, and his injuries and evacuation from Vietnam. He seems in a daze throughout the movie. It's humid and dark; he's afraid and lonely. Men who have been in Vietnam for a while treat newcomers with suspicion and disdain, and rookies have to prove to veterans their survival skills. Sometimes seasoned veterans think the new soldiers are as dangerous as the Viet Cong. Chris hardly knows what to do or who to trust, and he seeks relief from the terror around him with dope and whiskey. The platoon splits into factions. Chris, aligned with the dopers, supports the saintly Sergeant Elias who reports to his commanders that Sergeant Barnes killed a South Vietnamese woman. The higher-ups display little concern except that the investigation will require their time. Chris is still green and he retains some of his original hopes for an American victory. He's shocked when Elias tells him "we're gonna' lose this war . . .We've been kicking people's asses so long, I guess it's time we got our own kicked."[23]

The platoon patrols some ancient ruins in the midst of a torrential monsoon when the Viet Cong ambush them. For the first time, Chris performs bravely as a soldier. Barnes does not. He finds Sergeant Elias alone and shoots him for having reported Barnes's earlier murder of a South Vietnamese woman. Gravely wounded, Elias survives but the American helicopters lift off without him. The remaining platoon members watch in horror as the Viet Cong finishes him off. Before he dies, the sergeant sinks to his knees and spreads him arms, Christ-like.

The platoon's situation continues to deteriorate as they are ordered out to the border to bait the Viet Cong and the North Vietnamese Army into revealing their positions. Chris and his fellow soldiers are so badly outnumbered that their commanders call in an air strike, which misses the enemy but rains bombs on the Americans. In the ensuing confusion Chris encounters a crazed Barnes who smashes Chris's face with a rifle butt. Just as Barnes is about to murder Chris, all goes black. The audience next sees that dawn has broken on a new day. Chris staggers across the battlefield, grabs one of the enemy's discarded AK-47s, and comes after the badly wounded Barnes. The two men stare malevolently at each other until Barnes shouts, "Do it." Chris pulls the trigger and Barnes collapses dead. The movie ends with Chris, distraught at the thought that he too has just killed a man in cold blood, being helicoptered out of the battlefield. Tears stream down his face as he surveys a scene from hell in which American Army bulldozers pile the bodies of dead North Vietnamese and Viet Cong soldiers into mass graves. He reflects in a voiceover on the catastrophe the Vietnam War inflicted on the American soul: "We did not fight the enemy. We fought ourselves, and the enemy was in us."[24]

Audiences loved *Platoon* even as they emerged from the theater emotionally drained at the physical and psychological costs of a morally ambiguous war. The movie won the Academy Award for Best Picture and Stone won for Best Director. *Time* magazine ran a cover story characterizing *Platoon* as "Vietnam as it really was." Veterans also, for the most part, recommended the film to others who hadn't seen combat as a realistic depiction of the war. But some veterans objected that it confirmed old stereotypes of Vietnam combat soldiers as crazed, incompetent, stoned baby killers. A few critics castigated Stone for overheated language and cheap philosophizing. The acerbic film critic John Simon mocked the director as a pretentious sophomore for claiming that Homer had been his muse. Simon called the narration running through the movie "tie dyed prose."[25] The writer Fred Turner faulted the concluding monologue for ignoring the "incompetent, often immoral, and sometimes illegal decisions of political and military leaders" that created the Vietnam War.[26]

The following year, British-American director Stanley Kubrick's long-anticipated *Full Metal Jacket* was released. Kubrick's film bore many resemblances to *Platoon* in its dark view of the war, but it was less didactic and more phantasmagorical. Kubrick hired Michael Herr, who worked on the screenplay of *Apocalypse Now*, to adapt a screenplay from Gustav Hasford's novel *The Short-Timers*. Kubrick selected the title after having seen an ad in a gun catalogue for military-style ammunition with "full metal jacket," an elongated steel casing surrounding a bullet designed to make it fly faster and straighter.

Full Metal Jacket began, like many war movies, with the main marine boot camp on Paris Island, South Carolina, where incompetent, frightened boys are transformed into efficient, killer marines. The drill instructor (DI), played by R. Lee Ermey who actually served as a marine DI during the Vietnam War, gives nicknames to everything from the rifles to the recruits. The M-16s all have female names. The DI calls the protagonist Joker (Mathew Modine) because of his wisecracks. He hazes mercilessly one he calls Gomer Pyle (Vincent D'Onofrio) after the hapless marine on the TV show of the same name. Pyle never turns into a lean, sculpted fighting marine, and he cannot stand the harassment. When he's finally able to use his M-16, he kills the drill instructor in a barracks latrine. Joker watches in amazement and horror as Pyle then blows his own brains out.

The scene then shifts to Vietnam, where the movie becomes more dream-like and fantastic. Saigon is the now-familiar haunt of pimps, prostitutes, corrupt Vietnamese, and pleasure-seeking, cynical Americans. Joker works for an army newspaper, hating the daily responsibility of spreading half-truths and outright falsehoods about a war he has come to believe is pointless and unwinnable. He goes into the field wearing a helmet emblazoned with a peace sign and the slogan "Born to Kill." A furious general demands to know what it means. Joker replies with some cheap pop psychology, intended to mock both official pro- and antiwar pieties: it's a "Jungian thing," he tells the mystified commander.[27]

The action moves to the Northern city of Hué in the midst of the climactic battle of the Tet Offensive. Kubrick shot the scenes in an abandoned gasworks outside London. The set captures the murkiness of the fighting that went on for three weeks in the gloomy late winter, made even darker by the smoke from the fires set off by the fighting. Joker is reunited with his fellow Marine Corps trainees who are fighting to repulse the Viet Cong, which has captured parts of the old imperial capital.

The film highlights some of the traditional absurdities of war. The men fight, kill, and die in the full knowledge that everything they do will be turned into entertainment, or at least a form of voyeurism, at home in what they call, "the world." They discuss who will play various roles in a plot they make up called, "Vietnam: The Movie." They fantasize that John Wayne and Ann-Margaret will join them in a Western with "the gooks," playing the role of the Indians. The action resembles countless World War II combat films, but with a twist, as commanders are seen as fools, mouthing absurdities. One major tells Joker, "All I ever asked of my men is to believe my orders as they would the words of God."[28] As they patrol the rubble-strewn streets of the Hué, a Viet Cong sniper begins to kill the marines one by one, and the men fire machine guns at the building in which the sniper is hiding. Joker and his fellow marines enter the building to search for the source of their tormentor, and they are surprised at how small the Viet Cong sniper is; they are shocked to discover she is a woman. A photographer nicknamed Rafterman shoots and wounds her. In agony, she cries out for somebody to help her or kill her. Joker looks briefly at her before shooting her dead.

In the final scene of the movie the marines march away from Hué, once more in the hands of the U.S. and Army of the Republic of Vietnam forces. It's evening, and the men are shown in silhouette against the fires raging in the background. They start singing the theme from the Mickey Mouse Club, a song of their childhood. Mickey Mouse is also military slang for all of the stupid, pointless, and degrading aspects of life in uniform.

Critical and popular reactions to *Full Metal Jacket* were mixed. The first part of the film showing the brutal training of the marines won high praise for innovation and sucking the viewer into a foreign, horrible world. Critics also noted, mostly approvingly but sometime with distress, the sexual context of the training scenes. Women are constantly degraded. Trainees learn to dominate women and feminize the enemy. Kubrick clearly intended to demystify the military's linking of sex, violence, and male fantasies of dominance and vengeance. For some film critics, however, Kubrick was not undermining these traditional aspects of male dominance so much as he was glorifying them. Almost all critics thought that the longer, second part of the film was less successful. It was both too traditional and too experimental. In some ways it resembled countless combat films, and in others it was surreal. Throughout, Kubrick intended that contrast to highlight the complexities, absurdities, and ironies of the war. Singing the Mickey Mouse Club song at the end was derided by critics and viewers alike. No marine could do that, and the irony seemed to be heavy-handed and obvious. *Full Metal Jacket* won none of the Academy Awards for which it was nominated.

Kubrick sought to avoid the almost inevitable sentimentalization of the combat experience by using heavy-handed irony and veering into the surreal. The very same year, 1987, Bill Couterie directed *Dear America: Letters Home from Vietnam*, an HBO documentary that took exactly the opposite approach. It tugged at the audience's heartstrings with dramatic readings of real letters written by combat soldiers and marines that had been compiled in a book of the same name. The letters were read by prominent actors, including Ellen Burstyn, Tom Berenger, Robert De Niro, Sean Penn, Michael J. Fox, and Martin Sheen, who donated their time. Actual images of TV footage and a 1960s rock score accompany the reading of the letters. The Vietnam Veterans Ensemble Theater project co-produced the film with the proceeds going to the construction of the New York Vietnam Memorial, which opened in 1988 at the foot of Manhattan in Bowery Park.

The documentary begins with NBC-TV anchor David Brinkley reporting on the 1964 Gulf of Tonkin incident. It then proceeds year by year until the last Americans left in 1975. At the end of each year the number of Americans in Vietnam and the number of deaths are displayed on the screen. The men

record their hopes and fears. In the early years they report some political interest in fighting the war in Vietnam to protect their loved ones at home. But their
messages quickly change to caring about their buddies, longing for home,
comments on the beauty of the Vietnamese countryside, affection for some of
the Vietnamese, and mystification about the strangeness of the customs they
encountered. The last tear-jerking letter, read by Ellen Burstyn, was written
by a soldier who never made it back from Vietnam. In it he expresses his love
for his family and assures them of his safety. A final scene shows relatives and
friends laying flowers at the Vietnam Veterans Memorial as Bruce Springsteen
sings "Born in the USA."

The film had only a limited run in theaters, and HBO ran it for only a few
months, but it became a staple in classes on the Vietnam War in which generations of students choked up as they saw themselves in the faces of the young
letter writers or their loved ones. Critics were not kind. They saw the film as
gooey and some thought it portrayed the young servicemen exclusively as
victims. The Vietnamese were almost invisible, never presented as people with
ordinary lives, who suffered at the hands of the Americans. The film concen-
trates so exclusively on the personal that "historical context dissolves in sub-
jectivity," as the critic J. Hoberman wrote in *American Film*.[29] Yet for all of its
sentimentality and limitations in scope, *Dear America* connected directly with
audiences. It was almost an archetype of Vietnam on film with the focus almost exclusively on Americans and the United States.

Exclusion of Vietnam and the Vietnamese was repeated in *Tour of Duty*, a
CBS-TV series that began its two-year run in 1987. Each week a diverse platoon, consisting of a southern redneck, a hipster from Detroit, a Bronx Hispanic gang member, a young, white college-educated lieutenant, and other
standard characters from the cast of working-class warriors who had become
the staple of Vietnam-era films, goes into battle. The men have few political
ideals or ideas. They fight for one another and they long for home. They endure mud, rain, cold, rotting feet, pungi sticks, and the by-now-familiar am-
bushes from friendly-looking Vietnamese. One of the twenty-six episodes was
shot from the perspective of the Viet Cong, but the producers refrained from
filming others showing the humanity of the enemy after a furious barrage of
criticism. As the series went forward the characters became angrier and more
cynical, and the depictions of wounds and injuries turned more graphic.

Later episodes reverted to another convention of Vietnam War cinematog-
raphy when Lee Major joined the cast as a tough old veteran who joins the
failed 1970 raid into the Son Tay prison camp to rescue American POWs.
Unlike the rescue fantasies depicted in *Uncommon Valor* or *Rambo First Blood:
Part I*, the commanders do not come across as lazy, foolish, or incompetent.
Instead, they are shown to be much like the grunts, men trying to do the best
they can in an utterly unfamiliar setting. *Tour of Duty* also reinforced other

stereotypes of Vietnam veterans. In the very last episodes the plot followed the difficulties the men had in readjusting to stateside living. Nightmares, drinking, drug use, and the inability to form lasting relationships haunted some of them. They often found that their friends, classmates, and loved ones had a hard time grasping what they had seen and done in-country. Yet in a few cases they found comfort in understanding families and in work that helped them overcome their traumas. Audiences found the action impressive and the depiction of ordinary men in difficult circumstances comforting. However, the ordinariness of *Tour of Duty* irritated critics looking for an edgier confrontation with the politics of the war. For example, Daniel Miller, an academic film critic, found that *Tour of Duty* borrowed traditional themes and narratives from venerable Westerns, and he thought that the "dramatizations of the war overwhelmingly present traditional heroic texts in the trappings of reality."[30]

Probably the most critically acclaimed TV series dealing with Vietnam War themes was *China Beach*. Sixty episodes of this medical melodrama ran on ABC-TV from April 1988 to July 1991. It chronicled the story of several female nurses, male doctors, wounded soldiers and marines, and a few American civilians working in Vietnam. The two main protagonists were nurse Colleen McMurphy (Dana Delaney) and Karen Charlene "K.C." Koloski (Marge Helgenberger), a manipulative madam. *China Beach* both confirmed and exploded numerous stereotypes about women in the Vietnam War. It concentrated on their emotions, showing them to be more caring about their fellow human beings than the male warriors. It also showed the medical teams as more successful than the combat forces, because the nurses actually patched men up.

McMurphy never wavered in her convictions that she was there to help, and she found solace in the teamwork. She was no cheerleader, however, and she let many of the men know that their martial heroics were foolish. K.C. was no whore with a heart of gold; she knew everyone's weaknesses and profited from them. The series also appealed to a mass audience by draining the war of political content. William Broyles, Jr., the producer of *China Beach* and himself a veteran, explained that what the women did in Vietnam "was purely heroic." By the time *China Beach* appeared, the idea that Americans could applaud the heroism of the countrymen and women who had served in the war, even as they argued over the merits of the war, had become almost an article of faith. Yet some critics still decried such efforts as sentimental. Carolyn Reed Vartaninan wrote that *China Beach* "displaced the entirety of the Vietnam nightmare into the realm of romanticized fantasy . . . in which historical, political and social implications are all but erased."[31]

The show was geared to an audience of women and men in their forties who had their own recollections of the Vietnam era. It fortified these memories with rock, soul, and blues melodies from the late 1960s and early 1970s, most of whose bitter or cynical lyrics were consciously at odds with the officially stated reasons for fighting the war. The music and the flashbacks between present and past sought to frame the show as a nostalgic journey back to the days of the audience's youth. The nostalgia was key. The program managed to create a sense of distance in the minds of viewers who were never wholly in either the present of the 1980s–1990s or the past of the 1960s–1970s. The last season's episodes took place in the 1980s with flashbacks to the Vietnam War. K.C. has disappeared from her old friends and family, and her grown daughter who has enrolled in film school takes her hand-held camera to her mother's friends and acquaintances in an attempt to find her. Along the way, her informants ruminate about the ways the war changed them and the country. *China Beach* sometimes slipped into 1980s' baby-boomer self-indulgence in which their war, Vietnam, became the most important event in recent history. Such self-absorption could be cloying if taken too seriously, but *China Beach* maintained the right, light touch most of the time.[32]

By the late 1980s a few filmmakers began to explore what had happened to the Vietnamese. Their productions enjoyed only limited critical or box-office success. In 1989 Brian DePalma directed *Casualties of War*, starring Michael J. Fox and Sean Penn, based on a report in the *New Yorker* by journalist Daniel Lang about the rape and murder of a Vietnamese girl. Like other Vietnam War films, *Casualties of War* shifts back and forth between Vietnam and the United States. In Vietnam the movie shows familiar scenes of American men swilling Budweiser, smoking dope, and visiting the local whorehouse. They disparage Vietnamese as "gooks," or "slits," as they call the women. Sergeant Meserve (Sean Penn) tells his men to sneak into a Vietnamese hamlet for some "portable R & R," his slang for kidnapping and raping a Vietnamese girl. The men tear a young woman, played by Thuy Thu Le, from her outraged mother and sister. A naïve private played by Michael J. Fox meekly says, "I'm sorry" to the weeping family. He futilely protests as the rest of his squad rapes her. Later the men shoot her to death to prevent her from reporting their crime to the authorities.

After the horrifying scene, Meserve delivers an ironic twist on the old army-training chant. He grabs his genitals and hollers, "This is a weapon." Then he raises his M-16 and shouts, "this is a gun." He points to his crotch and says, "this is for fighting, and this" pointing to his rifle "is for fun." The message was obvious: Americans' sexual violation of Vietnam was at the core of the war. Some Americans had been so brutalized by the war that killing had become their most satisfying form of entertainment.

The film fared only modestly at the box office, perhaps because of the unremittingly negative portrayal of the American soldiers. Maybe the public had lost interest in combat films with a morally ambiguous message. When Columbia Pictures released the film in Europe it changed the name (calling it

Outrages in France and *The Final Settlement* in Sweden) and downplayed the Vietnam angle, promoting it as a movie that explored the psychological frictions among men under stress.[33]

Oliver Stone's 1989 film *Born on the Fourth of July* followed some but broke other conventions of Vietnam films. Like many others it was mostly about the United States. A very long film at 143 minutes, only 17 of them dealt with events in Vietnam. The movie tells of the crippling wounds suffered by the protagonist Ron Kovic (played by Tom Cruise) and was based on his memoir of the same name. It began with his Catholic childhood on Long Island and traced his journey to Vietnam, where he killed a fellow marine, Wilson, in a friendly fire incident. His own injuries, which left him a paraplegic, occurred because he did not stay prone on the battlefield, but instead looked around and refired his M-16 repeatedly at the enemy. Later, Kovic recalled that he exposed himself to enemy fire because he thought he was John Wayne.

The scene shifts abruptly to a dirty, rat-infested VA hospital in the Bronx. For a while Kovic clings to his belief in the justice of the United States fighting the war on behalf of the Vietnamese. He is furious with the antiwar demonstrators at the Democratic National Convention in 1968. He is determined to walk again. Some would call his struggles with physical therapy denial, while others would characterize them as an indomitable will. Unlike the more uplifting conventions of movies depicting earlier wars, Kovic doesn't walk, is sexually impotent, and sinks into drunkenness and near despair. He can barely endure being feted as a hero in a hometown Fourth of July parade. Overwhelmed with a sense of guilt for having killed one of his own men, he travels to Georgia to beg for forgiveness from the man's family. As Ron begins to tell the story of their son's final battle, the family grows restless; they don't want to hear what they know Ron is about to say. But he cannot stop. Weeping, he tells them that he shot their loved one. A silence hangs over the house until the widow tells Ron, "What's done is done. I can't ever forgive you, but maybe the Lord can." The dead marine's mother, perhaps having seen more grief of her own, is more comforting. She tells their distraught visitor "We understand Ron . . . We understand the pain you've been through."[34]

His confession and the mother's forgiveness is enough for Kovic to start over. He accepts that he'll never walk again, and he changes his opinions on the war and U.S. society. He still sees himself as a patriot, but this time he is the scold, the Jeremiah warning his fellow citizens against blindly following corrupt leaders. Kovic joins a march of Vietnam Veterans Against the War at the Republican National Convention renominating Richard Nixon for president in Miami in 1972. The demonstrators push their way into the convention hall and Kovic begins to speak out against the war. Almost immediately, angry Republican delegates shout him down as a traitor and they force him and his band of protesters outside into a parking lot where police fire tear gas at them. One of the veterans turns out to be an undercover FBI agent, and while trying to arrest Kovic, he knocks him out of his wheelchair. Another, more loyal vet carries Kovic away to safety. It is almost as if the wounded marine is back in Vietnam when he shouts at the remaining demonstrators, "Let's take the hall!" Once more, the screen immediately goes black.

The film resumes four years later at the Democratic National Convention in New York. The war has been over for a year, and Jimmy Carter, who is about to be nominated, assures his audience that he would never mislead the American people into war. Kovic is an honored speaker at this convention. He looks radiant, clean, and happy as he is wheeled out to speak before a jubilant crowd, which gives him a standing ovation as the band plays "It's a Grand Old Flag." Kovic and director Oliver Stone suggest that the country has finally accepted this wounded man and his criticism of the war as a more valid expression of patriotism. This time, the screen turns white as the credits roll across it.

Critics loved *Born on the Fourth of July*. *Time* praised its realism. The excruciating ugliness of the VA hospital gripped viewers. They commended director Stone for going beyond some of the clichés of sexual regeneration that had characterized *Coming Home*. In *Born on the Fourth of July*, the wounded Kovic does not find love and acceptance in the arms of an old girlfriend. He does not reconcile with his traditionally patriotic Long Island family. Vincent Canby in the *New York Times* considered it a "stunning film" of "enormous visceral power." He liked the way it "connects the war of arms abroad and the war of conscience at home."[35] This critic, representing the center of the spectrum of newspaper reviewers, found the concentration on events in the United States a comforting way to approach and release the anger and loss of the Vietnam War.

The film received eight Academy Award nominations, including Best Actor, Best Picture, and Best Director, which Stone won. Despite the praise and the awards, *Born on the Fourth of July* fared less well with audiences. It grossed a respectable $70 million, far less than Stone's earlier box-office success, *Platoon*. That film's audiences were free to concentrate on the combat scenes and ignore its overtly political message. *Born on the Fourth of July*, on the other hand, relentlessly concentrated on the human cost of the war. In real life Kovic became an antiwar activist opposing American military activities in Central America in the 1980s, the Persian Gulf in the 1990s, and Afghanistan and Iraq in the early twenty-first century, taking a position at odds with most Americans, so they might have been less inclined to see a movie based on his life.

Although *Platoon* represented the high point of Stone's commercially successful Vietnam filmmaking, he could not get the war out of his mind. He returned to Vietnam themes with his 1993 release of *Heaven and Earth*, a long, ponderous film version of two books by Le Ly Hayslip, *When Heaven and Earth Changed Places* and *Child of War, Woman of Peace.* The books and the film relate thirty years in the life of a Vietnamese woman, Le Ly, as she sees her homeland wracked by war. Her misfortunes included rape, the devastation of her village, family strife, cruel employers, life as a bar girl, and sexually predatory acts by Americans. She meets and marries a seemingly kind GI, Steve Butler, and moves with him to the unfamiliar landscape of San Diego. There her husband, an almost clichéd version of a veteran suffering from Post Traumatic Stress Disorder, beats her. She leaves with her two sons to make a life on her own. Throughout it all she shows uncommon courage and resourcefulness. She expresses bitterness at no one and works for reconciliation between Americans and Vietnamese during her several trips back to her homeland in the decade after the war ended.

Critics savaged the film; audiences simply ignored it. Both found it nearly impossible to sit through. The scenes of victimization pile up until viewers' senses are deadened. Ly Le's indomitable spirit and her forgiving nature seem too good to be true. Stone acknowledged the potential for slipping into sentimentality when he said that he intended to make a Vietnamese version of *Gone with the Wind.* But it would be fair to say that by the 1990s, Americans had tired of depictions of the horrors of the Vietnam War.

Forrest Gump, a feel-good movie with Vietnam War themes, found a wide, enthusiastic audience when it was released in 1994. Based on the novel by the same name by Winston Groom, the film starred Tom Hanks as a slow-witted, fast-running, sweet-tempered naïf named Forrest Gump. Director Robert Zemeckis used up-to-date digital imaging to superimpose Gump into some of the emblematic scenes of the 1960s and 1970s. He stands beside Presidents John F. Kennedy, Lyndon B. Johnson, and Richard M. Nixon. He's in the crowd when George Wallace as the segregationist governor tries to bar an African-American student from entering the University of Alabama in 1962. He's there when would-be murderers take shots at Presidents Kennedy and Ford. Gump wins the Congressional Medal of Honor for saving his buddies in Vietnam. He addresses an antiwar rally, but is mystified about why the crowd is so angry. Gump has no political or social opinions. Instead, he has a few aphorisms learned from his steel magnolia mother played by Sally Field. "Stupid is as stupid does," he repeats when he's taunted. "Life is like a box of chocolates, you never know what you're going to get," he repeats as he enjoys fame and riches, finds love, loses it, and suffers excruciating humiliations. Gump becomes extraordinarily rich in the gulf shrimp trade. He restores some emotional life to his Vietnam War comrade, a bitter amputee who works as his first mate while getting along well with the Vietnamese immigrant shrimpers.

Nothing seems to bother Gump in the turbulent thirty years covered by the book and the movie, which is perhaps why it attracted audiences. It won the

Academy Award for Best Picture in 1994. It was as if all the traumas of the Vietnam era—the assassinations, the civil rights struggles, and the let downs of the 1980s—had just happened. No one is responsible, no one needed to feel any guilt, or, for that matter, any triumph. Some reviewers praised *Forrest Gump* for being "as poignant as it is romantic." But even those who liked it most admitted it was a fairytale whose hero "is too good to be true."[36]

Others were far more critical. Richard Alleva found Gump to be "a completely ahistorical, apolitical, celebrity-blind man living through an epoch that is overwhelmingly political, historically self-conscious, and choked by celebrity worship." Alleva thought that Zemeckis "showed a touch of savvy" in presenting this version of a simple man to a public that had gorged itself nearly to the point of nausea on celebrity. But Alleva also thought it was a "very cynical savvy at that."[37] Hal Hanson took issue with the public who had taken Gump to their hearts in the summer of 1994. "The harder you look at Gump," he complained, "the less there is to see." He repeats the aphorisms he learned at his mother's knee, but beyond that "Gump believes in nothing and stands for nothing." Things just happen to Gump, just as history just seems to happen. Hanson objects that "history doesn't just happen; history is made . . . events do not occur in a vacuum, but as a result of all kinds of forces in a society."[38]

The desire to assimilate the Vietnam War into a satisfying, safe interpretation of the recent past continued with some of the diminishing number of Vietnam War theme films. 2002 saw the release of the movie *We Were Soldiers*, based on the 1996 book *"We Were Soldiers Once . . . and Young"* by Hal Moore and Joe Galloway. It told the story of the 1st Battalion of the 7th Cavalry Regiment, General George Armstrong Custer's old unit, as it fought the North Vietnamese People's Liberation Armed Forces, in the Ia Drang Valley in the fall of 1965. Most of the movie consists of realistic battle scenes foregrounding two combat-hardened soldiers, Sergeant Major Plumley (Sam Elliott) and Lieutenant Colonel Hal Moore (Mel Gibson). Moore, a Harvard graduate, sees the big picture, including similarities between the American and the French wars against the Vietnamese. The movie shifts back and forth from the men fighting in Vietnam and their wives at home on a Florida army base. Julie Moore (Madeleine Stowe) rears her five children while serving as a pillar of strength to the other military wives. The movie extols the military values—courage, dedication to comrades, honesty—of both the Americans and the Vietnamese. It is dedicated to both the Americans and the "members of the Peoples Army of North Vietnam who died in" the battle of the Ia Drang. Like many combat films from World War II to Vietnam, the soldiers care most about their buddies. Policies, the reasons for the war, even victory or defeat mean very little. "It's about the men next to you," one says. "That's all it is."[39]

By 2002 Vietnam was long in the past, and audiences liked *We Were Soldiers'* realistic battle scenes. The dirt, the blood, the death seemed true to life, but this was no pacifist film about the horror of war. Just the opposite, it portrayed combat as a deeply life-enhancing experience. It turned callow young men into mature, wise souls, who were able to love their comrades as their families and also show respect for the toughness of their enemies. The fighting could have taken place on almost any battlefield of the twentieth century. Vietnam had faded into the past.

Australian director Philip Noyce's adaptation of Graham Greene's 1955 novel *The Quiet American* was filmed in 2001, at about the same time as *We Were Soldiers*. It was to be released in the fall of that year, but Miramax pulled it from the market fearing that the surge of patriotism after the terrorist attacks on September 11 would make American audiences unresponsive to a film that showed American naiveté about the rest of the world. The film received rave notices at the Toronto Film Festival in 2002, and this response emboldened Miramax to release *The Quiet American* in a limited run in New York and Los Angeles in November 2002. It received a huge sendoff when it premiered in Saigon in December 2003. There the Communist authorities rolled out a red carpet for the director and cast. One government official explained that "it shows Americans as bad people in the Vietnam War." That was not quite what Noyce intended, and he interrupted to say, "Americans are not bad people. The movie is about an American with good intentions who made bad mistakes."[40]

Noyce's film remained true to Greene's novel. Unlike Joseph Mankiewiez's 1958 movie, which stripped Greene's novel of its dark portrayal of American good intentions causing horrible suffering to the Vietnamese, Noyce's visually beautiful movie reveals how Alden Pyle (Brandon Fraser) harbors far more sinister ambitions than his boyish features and aw-shucks manners suggest. The crushingly tired British journalist Thomas Fowler (Michael Caine) says of him, "God save us always from the innocent and the good." Pyle is no fresh-faced aid worker, as he wants people to think, but a CIA agent trying to foment opposition to the Communists and backing for a Third Force run by a mysterious General Thé. He is not importing plastic for eyeglass frames, but for explosives to be used in a street bombing that Pyle wants Vietnamese to blame on the Communists. After his bomb goes off, killing civilians, Fowler discovers that Pyle speaks Vietnamese and he has been conspiring for months with the shadowy General Thé. Pyle and Fowler have formed an unusual friendship, all the more unlikely because Pyle has stolen Fowler's beautiful Vietnamese mistress Phoung (Do Thi Hai Yen) with promises of life as his wife in America. At any rate, Pyle suggests that he, a younger, richer man than Fowler, who doesn't smoke opium the way the world-weary British journalist does, is a better catch for Phuong.

In the end, Fowler, who says he cares nothing about politics, lets his Vietnamese assistant, a secret Viet Minh operative, know where he can find Pyle, giving him the green light to kill him. Pyle's body is found floating in the Saigon River by the French police. The irrepressible Inspector Vigot asks Fowler to identify the body of his friend, whom he calls "a very quiet American." As is the case in the novel, Pyle is quiet only because he is dead. In life, torrents of words come out of him, and he expresses opinions on love, Communism, freedom, Americans, Vietnamese, the French, and the British. Fowler cannot stand listening to him, although part of the older man admires how Pyle can believe so much about so many important things. Fowler at times is morally dead and the opium induces some of his indifference to the suffering around him. He wants to believe in something better or higher. In the end he does, by letting the Viet Minh killers know where to find Pyle. The filmmaker omits much of Greene's idiosyncratic Catholicism present in the novel, but also invents a coda of dispatches written by Fowler to British papers every year from 1954 to 1968, which underscore the growing American descent into the quagmire of Vietnam.

True to the novel's principal theme of American efforts to save Vietnam actually causing incalculable grief, the film struck a chord with American and international audiences in the early months of 2003. The idea of good intentions paving the road to hell resonated in the darker atmosphere following the atrocities of September 11, 2001, and preceding the war with Iraq. Noy Thrupkaew, a critic for the liberal-opinion journal *The American Prospect*, wrote, it "warns us of the potential dangers of American arrogance and violent international engagement. . . . It shows us how little America—blinded by hubris, power, or sheer good intentions—may understand the world."[41] Neil McDonald, an Australian critic, thought it was a marvelous film, warning that "self-righteousness and naiveté are no substitute for realism and intelligence."[42] Kenneth Turan, film critic for the *Los Angeles Times*, expressed the views of many when he praised Noyce's *The Quiet American* as a "story about the mutability of acting well and acting badly, about how easy it is to cross that line, a story that underlines the impossibility of staying neutral, and the inevitability of tasking sides."[43]

A rare bad notice came from "Mr. Cranky," a film reviewer syndicated in college newspapers. "This film is virtually unwatchable," he complained, "if you don't know anything about Vietnam in 1952." Even if a viewer did, he opined, "Why is a young beautiful Vietnamese girl like Phuong hanging out with old British hag like Thomas Fowler?" Mr. Cranky did ask one question that resonated: "Does anybody even care about the Vietnam War any longer? I think we're over this now. Let's move on."[44]

Film producers, actors, screenwriters, and audiences had been moving on from Vietnam for forty years. Most of the films and TV shows about the war took place far from Vietnam. They explored aspects of the American emotional landscape, ideas of masculinity, femininity, heroism, and, not often but occasionally, politics. Sometimes the audience connected with the message of the filmmakers. Other times, they responded more to the action, the combat, and the special effects. The films and TV shows of the Vietnam era built on and transformed their predecessors of the World War II era. The cinematic views of the Vietnam War, as refracted through filmmakers' eyes, somberly assessed the physical and emotional toll of the fighting and dwelled on the trauma it inflicted.

PART
IV

* * * * * * * * * * * *

Conclusion:

Political Echoes of a War

Chapter

*   *   *   *   *   *   *   *   *   *   *

The Living Legacy of
the Vietnam War

American leaders conducted their foreign and military policies from the 1970s to the early years of the twenty-first century with an eye to their unhappy experiences in the Vietnam War. Ordinary Americans often perceived contemporary policies through their own memories of Vietnam as well. Nearly everyone agreed on the obvious point that the war in Vietnam had gone badly for the United States, but beyond that, however, differences of opinion proliferated. Americans divided over the proper lessons of the Vietnam War in disagreements that roughly followed the contours of the debate that had raged during the war. Advocates of American participation in the war decided that the United States needed to continue to pursue an active, assertive international policy. For them, the use or the threat of force remained an active element of United States foreign policy. Opponents of the war in Vietnam concluded that the Communist victory highlighted the limits of American military power. Many Vietnam War doves sought to limit the United States' use of military force around the globe in the decades following the Vietnam War.

Despite profound differences of opinion regarding the wisdom and even morality of the use of force in the decades after 1975, Americans consistently praised the motives, valor, and sacrifice of soldiers, sailors, and marines who bore the brunt of the fighting. The historian Robert McMahon has identified "the triumph of a particular kind of official memory about the Vietnam War" in which presidents affirmed the "heroic sacrifice" of troops who had fought in Vietnam and advocated "reconciliation and healing" at home.[1]

Presidents often explicitly presented their foreign policies as contrasts to the failures and disappointments in Vietnam. The pattern of seeing current foreign and military affairs through the lens of Vietnam began almost immediately after the war's end. In the second half of 1975, the Ford administration sought to show that the Vietnam War had not paralyzed the United States, while the public and Congress sought to restrict the potential for intervention. The flashpoint of domestic disagreement was over United States involvement in a civil war for independence in Angola, where Portugal had exercised colonial rule for nearly five hundred years. Some officials in the Ford administration perceived Angola to be a new front in the Cold War competition with the Soviet Union. In late 1974 and early 1975 the United States slowly and secretly provided aid to the National Front for the Liberation of Angola (FNLA), one of three armed factions trying to supplant the Portuguese authorities. Although Secretary of State Henry Kissinger had little interest in the future of Angola per se, he favored intervention in the Angolan civil war as a counter to the Soviet Union, which, he believed, had been emboldened by the American defeat in Vietnam to probe for U.S. vulnerabilities in the Third World. The initial United States aid proved inadequate to improve the FNLA's position in the civil war against other factions armed by the Soviet Union, so in the summer of 1975 Kissinger insisted that the CIA increase its support for the FNLA.[2] The historian Jussi Hanhimaki writes, Kissinger "clearly convinced Ford that, in the aftermath of the collapse of Vietnam, Angola was a test case of the Ford administration's foreign policy."[3]

In September newspaper accounts revealed the presence of American operatives supporting the FNLA and drew explicit comparisons between Angola and the early days of American involvement in Vietnam. Congress rejected the Ford administration's request for additional funding for the covert aid to the FNLA. Indiana Democratic Senator Birch Bayh complained that Ford and Kissinger were setting the stage for another Vietnam. "Despite the tragic and bitter lessons we should have learned from our intervention in civil war in Southeast Asia," Bayh said, "the Ford administration persist in deepening our involvement in the civil strife in Angola." He called Angola "the first test of American foreign policy after Vietnam. . . . We are again plunging into a conflict in a far region of the world as if we believed it was still our mission to serve as policeman of the world." As a result of this widespread anxiety that the small covert intervention in Angola could expand into a full Vietnam-style commitment of U.S. ground troops, Congress passed Iowa Democratic Senator Dick Clark's amendment to an appropriations bill that effectively cut off funds for covert American activities in Angola.[4] Angola then receded as an issue in public consciousness as the presidential election campaign of 1976 heated up.

When Jimmy Carter ran for president in 1976 he explained that one of the lessons of Vietnam was that the United States needed to avoid unnecessary foreign interventions. Carter supported the American participation in the war during the Johnson administration, but, like many Americans, had changed his mind about the wisdom of the Vietnam War in the early 1970s and now expressed regret for his earlier hawkish views. He noted sadly, "We stumbled into the quagmires of Cambodia and Vietnam." When he surveyed American foreign policy in the Cold War, he found that "we have often been overextended, and deeply entangled in the internal affairs of distant nations." He praised the good judgment of the American public for having "learned the folly of our trying to inject our power into the internal affairs of other nations. It is time that our government learned that lesson too."[5]

When he took office in 1977 he sought to reverse what he considered to have been the mistakes of the Vietnam War era. Where earlier presidents had acted covertly, he favored openness. Where his predecessors had seen Vietnam as a test of American credibility in the Cold War competition with the Soviet Union, the Carter administration favored dealing with regional questions on their own terms. The historian Robert McMahon has found that a "rhetoric of atonement" pervaded Carter's discussion of Vietnam when he was president.[6] Carter expressed grave reservations about the use of military force. He believed that a principal lesson of the Vietnam War was that the United States had concentrated too heavily on the Cold War competition with the Soviet Union and Communist revolutionaries. In the process, the United States had neglected even more important issues such as the promotion of human rights and the alleviation of poverty around the world. In May 1977, less than four months into his term, he told a receptive audience at Notre Dame University that an "inordinate fear" of Communism had hung over Americans as they set foreign policy since the beginning of the Cold War. "The Vietnamese War produced a profound moral crisis," he said. The war represented the "intellectual and moral poverty" of decades of arrogant American intervention overseas. He hoped that "through failure [in Vietnam] we have found our way back to our principles and values, and we have regained our lost confidence."[7]

Carter and his principal foreign policy advisers sought to turn U.S. foreign policy away from the use of military force. They believed that the end of the Vietnam War actually freed the United States to devote more attention to areas of the world neglected during the Cold War. Secretary of State Cyrus Vance, himself a prominent participant in the Johnson administration's decisions first to fight and then to deescalate in Vietnam, acknowledged having made mistakes. Now he was a man chastened by the human costs of the Vietnam War who wanted to avoid military interventions abroad. His aversion to the use of military force eventually led him to resign in protest when the Carter administration sent a military expedition to free the U.S. hostages in Iran in April 1980.

The failure of Carter's efforts to move the United States away from the Cold War competition with the Soviet Union provoked a backlash. By 1979 neoconservatives, mostly Democrats who had supported the Vietnam War, began commenting that a "Vietnam syndrome" had overtaken the Carter administration, causing American officials to believe that any threat to use force would sink the United States deeply into a conflict from which it could not extricate itself. Several prominent neoconservative Democrats who had supported the 1972 and 1976 presidential aspirations of Washington Senator Henry Jackson, a supporter of U.S. war policies in Vietnam, helped revive the Committee on the Present Danger (first organized in 1950) to promote a more assertive U.S. military policy. Members of the new Committee on the Present Danger included Senator Jackson; Richard Perle, the senator's principal foreign policy adviser; Paul Nitze, adviser to Democratic presidents from Truman through Johnson; Lane Kirkland, president of the ALF-CIO; Norman Podhoretz, the editor of *Commentary* magazine; and Jeane Kirkpatrick, a Georgetown University professor of international affairs. The committee denounced the Carter administration's efforts to conclude a nuclear arms limitation treaty with the Soviet Union and demanded that the president increase spending on the military. Many of committee's members broke with Carter and supported former California Governor Ronald Reagan for president in 1980.[8]

In his election bid Reagan explicitly referred to the lessons of Vietnam. The ones he and his conservative supporters drew were almost mirror opposites of the ones that Carter and his administration had learned. Reagan believed that the United States needed to take from the Vietnam experience the need for a stronger military. He claimed that the Vietnam syndrome had paralyzed the Carter administration, making the United States appear weak, an ominous invitation to the Soviet Union to press its advantage around the globe. When he became president, Reagan implied, the United States would have nothing to apologize for in its use of force.

Reagan referred occasionally to the lessons of the Vietnam War during his presidency, although not as much as might have been expected given the demand for military assertiveness of his presidential campaign. When Reagan did discuss the Vietnam War, he avoided discussing the war's aims while praising the valor of Americans who fought the war. "We continue to talk about losing that war," he announced at a press conference on April 18, 1985, less than two weeks before the tenth anniversary of the revolutionaries' victory. "We didn't lose that war. We won virtually every engagement." Instead, Reagan, said, "When the war was over and when we'd come home, that's when we'd lost the war." He pointed to a variety of people other than the American military whom he deemed responsible for losing the war—the South Vietnamese, domestic American opponents of the war who demanded an American withdrawal, the media who highlighted failures, and members of Congress who would not fund the continuation of American involvement in the war. None of the culprits included American officials who had directed the war.[9]

Even though he spoke relatively infrequently in public about Vietnam, presumed lessons learned from the war directly impacted decision making throughout his eight years in office. Reagan administration officials projected American military power in ways they hoped would release what they believed to be the debilitating shackles of the memory of the Vietnam War. Alexander Haig, Reagan's first secretary of state, testified at his confirmation hearing that "the time has come to shed the sackcloth and ashes of Vietnam." Haig, Secretary of Defense Caspar Weinberger, and Director of Central Intelligence William Casey believed that the United States could erase some of the shame of having been defeated in Vietnam by defeating leftist revolutionaries in Central America. There, they believed, the United States would hold the advantage, since, unlike the Soviet Union and China, it would have geographic proximity to the arena of conflict.[10]

In 1981 the United States expanded its military role in Central America by sending fifty-five uniformed military advisers to train the army of the anticommunist government of El Salvador. The United States provided aid to the counterrevolutionaries, or contras, fighting the leftist government of Nicaragua. The fiercely anticommunist Central American policies of the Reagan administration ignited a backlash in the United States. "El Salvador is Spanish for Vietnam" read a popular bumper sticker among Americans who feared that the Reagan administration would engulf the country in another endless, inconclusive war fighting leftist rebels. Members of Congress reflected this public anxiety. In 1973 Congress passed the War Powers Resolution designed to restore its authority in dispatching U.S. forces to fight abroad by requiring the president to obtain specific Congressional authorization to maintain American forces in foreign combat for more than sixty days. In 1981 Congress made sure that no more than the original fifty-five advisers went to El Salvador, while demanding that the Reagan administration publicly give evidence to lawmakers that El Salvador had improved its poor record on human rights before committing additional military aid.

Congress imposed further restrictions on the Reagan administration's efforts to undermine the leftist government of Nicaragua. From 1982 to 1984 Congress adopted amendments to spending authorizations written by Democratic Representative Edward Boland, chair of the House Committee on Intelligence. The

Boland amendment prohibited the use of funds "for the purpose of overthrowing the government of Nicaragua," a ban the Reagan administration sought secretly to circumvent. When these activities became public in 1986 they exploded into what got dubbed the Iran-Contra scandal. It was exposed that agents of the U.S. government raised money, including the profits from the sale of weapons to Iran, to support the contras. CIA Director Casey, National Security Advisers Robert McFarlane and John Poindexter, and National Security Council staff member Oliver North, the principal architects of the diversion of money from Iran to the contras, attempted to keep aid to the contras secret to avoid the scrutiny of a public worried about another descent into the quagmire of a Vietnam-style guerrilla war.[11]

After congressional hearings and the investigations of a special federal prosecutor, several high-level Reagan administration officials were tried and convicted of various violations. In December 1992 before he left office, President George H. W. Bush pardoned Caspar Weinberger for any crimes he may have committed in connection with the Iran-Contra affair during his term as secretary of defense. Congressional, judicial, and press investigations of Iran-Contra demonstrated the extent and the limits of the heightened public concern about the president's commitment of U.S. forces to overseas wars. A skeptical public prevented the Reagan administration from acting openly to support the contras in Nicaragua. But Congress hardly restored its authority to wage war as envisaged by the creators of the War Powers Act in 1973 through its investigations of the administration's activities. Political scientist Kenneth Sharpe criticized Congress for its timidity in the face of an assertive president who wanted the United States to overthrow the leftist government of Nicaragua: "A foreign policy commitment was established with minimum scrutiny and public debate. Congress by and large acquiesced and failed to act, even when information was brought to it that private funding was circumventing its decisions."[12]

The ambivalence government officials and the public expressed toward the use of military force abroad took place within a larger context of looking back on the Vietnam War in order to derive lessons for the present. During the late 1970s and 1980s numerous writers reexamined the history of the American entry into and conduct of the Vietnam War, and some of them advocated a historical revisionism that challenged the widely held view that the United States had been wrong to fight the Communists in Vietnam. Like President Reagan, revisionists argued that the United States was correct to enter the war in Vietnam and had failed only in its execution of the war. Norman Podhoretz, a prominent neoconservative critic of the Carter administration's foreign policy, defended the war aims of earlier administrations in *Why We Were in Vietnam* (1983). Podhoretz argued that the United States had properly sought to stop the spread of Communism in Southeast Asia. A firm believer in the domino theory, he contended that had the United States not moved to prevent North

Vietnam from taking over the South in 1963–1965, revolutionaries around the globe would have been encouraged to attack conservative governments. Podhoretz, like the American policymakers of the Eisenhower, Kennedy, and Johnson administration who had deepened the American commitment to Vietnam, believed that the principal reason for the United States to have fought was to demonstrate American credibility and resolve in the rest of the world. Vietnam, per se, had little to do with the American War. In the end, however, Podhoretz blamed the antiwar movement for sapping American public will to persevere in Vietnam. Had the public persevered, he argued, the Republic of Vietnam would have prevailed.[13]

Revisionism regarding the rightness of the foreign policy behind the Vietnam War continued into the post–Cold War era, and its arguments appeared in some college courses on Vietnam. Timothy Lomparis taught a popular revisionist political science course on the war at Duke University in the 1980s. His book, *From People's War to People's Rule*, argued that the North prevailed by brutalizing its own citizens into fighting hard. They imposed a tyranny in the South.[14] The Communist brutality made the American intervention justified. Similarly, Michael Lind, a prominent neoconservative journalist, characterized Vietnam as "the necessary war," one that bought time for noncommunist governments to flourish in Southeast Asia. Lind published *The Necessary War* in 1996 in the triumphal days following the Cold War. The end of Communism and the demise of the Soviet Union made the Vietnam War seem less of a defeat for the United States.[15]

Nowhere did the memories of the Vietnam War have greater practical impact than in the U.S. military, where many senior officers believed that the country had let them down. The believed they had fought well, never lost a battle, but had been abandoned by elected officials and spurned by many civilians. The historian George Herring has noted that "history was a growth industry in the military" in the aftermath of the Vietnam War, as senior officers studied past wars, some thousands of years old, to explain the American failure in Vietnam.[16] All three main branches of the armed services introduced courses on strategy into the curricula of their staff colleges for mid- and senior-level officers. In 1979 the army leadership asked Colonel Harry Summers, a Vietnam War veteran and a professor of strategy at the Army War College, to investigate the military lessons learned in Vietnam. The result was Summers's 1982 book *On Strategy: A Critical Analysis of the Vietnam War* in which he summarized the civilian and military mistakes made in the war. *On Strategy* soon became the standard account of the military's views of what had happened during Vietnam, and it was incorporated into the curricula of the military undergraduate and command colleges. Its criticisms of inept civilian leadership also received a warm welcome among some conservative lawmakers. Georgia Republican Representative Newt Gingrich arranged to have copies distributed to all members of Congress.

Summers explained that both the civilian and military leadership during the Vietnam War ignored what German strategist Carl von Clausewitz characterized as the "remarkable trinity" of the people, the government, and the army. Without the three working together, no war could succeed. Summers determined that the Johnson administration failed to rally popular support for the war and had instead prioritized the Great Society, the president's ambitious program of domestic reform. According to his reading of Clausewitz, Summers concluded that North Vietnam held the offensive advantage throughout the war. Fearful of Chinese intervention and worried about diminishing support for its domestic programs, the Johnson administration opted for the strategic defensive. The United States "took the *political* task (nation building/ counter-insurgency) as our primary mission and relegated the *military* task (defeating external aggression) to a secondary consideration."

The book argued that the United States military should have applied overwhelming and decisive force rather than gradually escalating the war. Summers said the United States lacked clear objectives in the war. Was the goal to defeat the North, to end the insurgency in the South, to enhance the popularity of the government of the Republic of Vietnam, or to demonstrate American resolve in the Cold War competition with the Soviet Union? American officials variously offered each of these explanations, but they rarely defined what "victory" would mean in the war, or projected how the war would end. Summers also complained that civilian authorities in Washington never properly made a transition from preparing for war to waging war. During the former period, many options were properly discussed. Once the Johnson administration committed troops to the ground war in 1965, Summers argued, the president should have stepped back and given his military commanders free reign.[17] Summers argued that Johnson and his principal advisers worried too much about a recapitulation of the Korean War. Summers explained that conditions were far different in the 1960s than in the 1950s, as the Chinese Cultural Revolution effectively limited the ability of China to enter the war and posed no threat in the latter conflict.[18]

As a result of what Summers considered to be the president's unwarranted interference with the conduct of daily operations in the war, the military faced an impossible task, unable to "win" the war and unable to leave the battlefield without the perception of loss. In the last years of the Vietnam War, when the Nixon administration began withdrawing American forces, the American military suffered severe stress. As drug use soared among enlisted troops, some men refused to wear their helmets in combat and some even threw grenades at their officers.[19] Young officers felt threatened by their subordinates, unappreciated by their superiors, and ridiculed by civilians, and many who had planned military careers left the service. Those, like Summers, who stayed vowed that the military would never again be required to undertake impossible missions. Several other American officers in Vietnam wrote books in the late 1970s and

1980s disputing orthodox notions of why the Communists won the Vietnam War. The Tet Offensive came under close scrutiny. Philip Davidson and Ulysses S. Grant Sharp, both high-level commanders in the Vietnam War, joined Summers in claiming that Tet represented a major defeat for the National Liberation Front (NLF) and a victory for the United States and the Army of the Republic of Vietnam (ARVN).[20]

The military writers' conclusions about ineptitude of civilian leadership struck a responsive chord within the U.S. military. Many officers became cautious about the use of force in the post-Vietnam era. The military's reputation, the morale of its members, and perhaps even its very existence would be in jeopardy without crystal-clear assurances of victory and continuing public support for the war aims. Civilian leaders drew complex lessons from Summers's work. Reagan's highest foreign policy officials split over the use of military force in the wake of Vietnam. Paradoxically, Secretary of State George Shultz believed diplomacy would be ineffective without a realistic threat of the use of force, while Secretary of Defense Caspar Weinberger resisted overuse of the military. The dispute between the two became public in the aftermath of the withdrawal of U.S. forces from Lebanon in early 1984. Reagan, at Weinberger's urging, removed U.S. troops from that war-torn country after a suicide bomber had killed 241 marines in their barracks in Beirut in October 1983. In October 1984 Shultz expressed his concern that the United States had withdrawn its troops too quickly. The United States "cannot become the Hamlet of nations," Shultz said, "worrying endlessly how and when to respond."[21]

Pentagon officials found Shultz too willing to risk the lives of American service personnel for ambiguous political ends. General Colin L. Powell, himself a Vietnam veteran, told Secretary of Defense Weinberger that the nation's highest military officers thought that Shultz had ignored their experiences in Vietnam. In response to Shultz and at Powell's recommendation Weinberger outlined six principles governing the use of force in the post–Vietnam era: 1) The United States would use force only to defend its vital interests or those of its allies; 2) the United States had to express a clear commitment to victory; 3) the United States had to have clear political and military objectives; 4) the United States needed to deploy enough force to achieve victory; 5) the public and Congress had to approve the use of force before a military operation was undertaken; and 6) the United States would use force only as a last resort.[22] With the Weinberger (or later, Weinberger-Powell) Doctrine, high-ranking military officials believed that the secretary of defense had restored their services' sense of practical mission. In the future, the American military would undertake jobs they could accomplish or they would stay home. In no case would the American military become the scapegoat for unworkable policies, as they felt had been the case during Vietnam.

The Weinberger-Powell Doctrine gained its greatest prominence during the administration of President George H. W. Bush. A foreign policy veteran from the Nixon years, Bush, in his inaugural address, asked Americans to end their divisions over the Vietnam War. "This is a fact," he said, "the final lesson of Vietnam is that no great country can long afford to be sundered by a memory." Bush's rhetoric rarely soared, but his remarks on Vietnam were an exception. Vietnam "cleaves us still," he sadly recalled. "But, friends, that war began in earnest a quarter of a century ago, and surely the statute of limitations has been reached."[23]

The Bush administration most directly applied the military's lessons learned from the Vietnam War to the confrontation with Iraq over its conquest of neighboring Kuwait in August 1990. The United States assembled an international coalition to force Iraq to quit Kuwait. The Bush administration dispatched an American armed force of five hundred thousand to Saudi Arabia, first to protect the oil-rich kingdom from a potential Iraqi invasion and, second, to prepare for an assault to dislodge the Iraqis from Kuwait. As U.S. troops continued to pour into Saudi Arabia in the fall of 1990, high U.S. government officials had Vietnam uppermost in their minds. Secretary of Defense Dick Cheney warned, "the military is finished in U.S. society if we screw this up."[24] President Bush assured congressional leaders that the war with Iraq would not be fought by the United States alone or half-heartedly. "We don't need another Vietnam War," Bush said. "World unity is there. No hands are going to be tied behind backs. This is not a Vietnam."[25]

Chairman of the Joint Chiefs of Staff Colin L. Powell, the officer who had helped draft Defense Secretary Weinberger's 1984 speech, took the lead in applying the doctrine during the buildup to war with Iraq. "If we don't have to fight it will be better," Powell told the Saudi ambassador to the United States. "If we have to, I'll do it, but we're going to do it with every thing we have."[26] Mindful of the military's requirement of popular support before undertaking any commitment of American troops, Powell insisted that the Bush administration obtain an explicit congressional resolution authorizing the use of force before sending men and women into battle.[27]

Congress provided the authority, and the United States bombed Iraqi targets on January 16, 1991, hours after the expiration of a United Nations ultimatum, demanding that Iraq leave Kuwait. The United States continued bombing for another five weeks, and then sent over five hundred thousand ground troops across the Iraq and Kuwait borders from Saudi Arabia to dislodge the Iraqi forces. In barely five days, Iraq left Kuwait. Hundreds of thousands of Iraqis surrendered to U.S. and other coalition forces. Throughout the bombing and the ground campaign the Bush administration sought to apply the Weinberger-Powell Doctrine of using overwhelming force. Secretary of Defense Dick Cheney also applied another lesson the military had learned from Vietnam. The military, not civilian authorities, should determine targets, troop levels, and tactics. Bush felt comfortable giving the military the latitude it sought. Three days after the lightning victory, Bush proclaimed, "by God, we've kicked the Vietnam syndrome!"[28]

Bush was partially right. Millions of Americans turned out for victory parades honoring troops who returned from the Gulf War. The enthusiastic welcomes for the winners stood in contrast to the indifference or hostility directed at Vietnam War veterans. But the foreign and military policymakers drew different lessons from the victory in the Persian Gulf War from the conclusions drawn by members of the general public. The foreign policy and military community believed that the quick defeat of Iraq's armed forces vindicated the muscular military policy the United States had pursued since 1980. American voters did not disagree that the triumph in the Gulf War and the collapse of the Soviet Union demonstrated American might. Yet the very unchallenged supremacy of American power made the threat or the use of force seem less important to many ordinary Americans. The devaluation of the military seemed borne out when Bill Clinton defeated George H.W. Bush for the presidency in 1992. Clinton's opposition to the Vietnam War and his draft record became an issue during the campaign, but he ultimately overcame them, mainly because voters believed that foreign affairs mattered less in the post–Cold War era. [29]

As president, however, Clinton soon learned how strong the memory of the Vietnam War remained. The new administration inherited from its predecessor a humanitarian intervention to save the residents of the East African country of Somalia from starvation. Bush had dispatched several thousand soldiers and marines to distribute food aid in November 1992 after his electoral defeat. The American presence soon provided a modicum of stability, and the United States began to turn over security to a United Nations force in May 1993. The UN, with U.S. backing, tried to foster an effective Somalia government out of the chaos of warlords. In October UN forces sought to arrest Mohammed Farid Adeed, a militia commander who refused to accept UN control and repelled its troops. The UN forces asked for military help from the Americans. When the American Army Rangers arrived in the capital city of Mogadishu, they faced a force of several thousand Somalis armed with automatic weapons. Adeed's men shot down a Blackhawk helicopter. In the ensuing firefight Americans killed over one thousand Somalis. Somali gunmen killed eighteen Americans and dragged the body of one through the streets to show off their accomplishment.

The TV coverage of the defilement of the dead ranger shocked American viewers. The public, which had applauded the humanitarian mission in December 1992, demanded the withdrawal of American forces. Secretary of Defense Les Aspin resigned amidst criticism that he had declined to provide heavy armor for the U.S. forces. Within weeks the Clinton administration removed the Americans troops from Somalia. The Defense Department revisited the Weinberger-Powell Doctrine in the aftermath of the disaster in Mogadishu. Clinton issued Presidential Directive (PD)-25, which called for the definition of an explicit "endpoint for U.S. participation" in humanitarian operations abroad.[30] Soon commentators translated this phrase into demands that the United States develop a clearly articulated "exit strategy" before undertaking any overseas military operation. The bitter public memories of the military humiliation in Somalia prevented the Clinton administration from intervening to halt the genocide in Rwanda in 1994. Vietnam and Somalia became twin disasters, linked together as "Vietnalia." [31]

The requirement that military operations receive overwhelming public support, to promote vital U.S. interests, be achievable, and have a clearly defined exit strategy, haunted the Clinton administration as it developed a policy toward ethnic cleansing and other atrocities committed by Serbs against Muslims in the Balkans. The United States delayed intervention in the Bosnian civil war in the last year of the Bush administration and the first two years of the Clinton administration. Lawrence Eagleburger, Secretary of State in the last months of the Bush administration, said he always worried "about the shadow of Vietnam" when thinking about Western intervention to stop Serb atrocities in the Balkans. He likened the Serbs to the Viet Cong and doubted whether the United States would have the stamina to overcome their aggression.[32]

General Powell, continuing as chairman of the Joint Chiefs of Staff in the first year of Clinton's presidency, objected to sending American troops into harm's way in the Balkans. He considered humanitarian assistance there to be a matter more of European than American concern. "American GI's were not toy soldiers to be moved around on a game board," he recalled.[33] Madeleine Albright, the U.S. ambassador to the UN, disagreed, considering the Serb atrocities in the Balkans a moral challenge to the United States. Earlier in her career Albright had been an adviser to Senator Edmund Muskie and Zbigniew Brzezinski, both of whom had served in the Carter administration, and, like these two mentors, she believed that the proper lesson to draw from Vietnam was that the United States should use military force cautiously but not foreswear it entirely. After listening to Powell repeat that Bosnia could turn into a Vietnam-style quagmire, an exasperated Albright asked, "What are you saving this superb military for, Colin, if we can't use it?" Powell said he nearly had a stroke when he heard what he considered to be Albright's cavalier disregard for the dangers posed to U.S. forces should they be deployed to the Balkans. Albright, in turn, believed that Powell had learned the "lessons of Vietnam . . . too well." Richard Holbrooke, a veteran of the Carter administration's unsuccessful efforts to restore diplomatic relations with Vietnam, who was then serving as Clinton's special ambassador to the Balkans saw "fundamental differences between Bosnia and 'Vietnalia.' Our goals and stakes were different. The Bosnia Serbs were neither the disciplined ruthless revolutionaries of North Vietnam, nor the drunken ragtag 'technicals' who raced around Mogadishu shooting people." [34]

Only after Serb forces massacred seven thousand to eight thousand Muslim men and boys in Srebrenicia in July 1995 did the United States and other NATO countries bomb Serb forces. These attacks forced Serb leader Slobodan Milosevic to agree to Bosnian independence in lengthy negotiations that resulted in the Dayton Agreements in November 1995.[35] This proved only a temporary interruption to the atrocities in the Balkans. Three years later a new crisis erupted in the Serbian province of Kosovo, where over 90 percent of the inhabitants were Muslims of Albanian origins who suffered severe discrimination in jobs, education, housing, and politics. The Western European countries joined the United States in demanding the removal of Serb troops from Kosovo.

Negotiations in early 1999 between Richard Holbrooke, the U.S. ambassador to the UN, and Milosevic failed to dislodge Serbian forces from Kosovo. In March Clinton ordered the bombing of Serbia to force Milosevic to yield autonomy to the Kosovars. Clinton and members of Congress saw the struggle for Kosovo through the prism of their memories of the Vietnam War. The president sought to avoid a quagmire of casualties and prisoners arising from a ground war. Even as Clinton sent warplanes against targets in Serbia proper and Kosovo, he stated that the United States would not send in ground forces. When Congress debated the war for Kosovo, opponents of Clinton's action repeatedly made comparisons to America's bad experience with Vietnam. Republican Representative Sue Myrick of North Carolina urged Congress to "remember Dien Bien Phu, when many of his key advisers pressured President Eisenhower to send our armed forces to help bail out the French." Clinton's fellow Democrats, who were more supportive of the war, likened Milosevic to Hitler and the Serbs' policies of ethnic cleansing to the Holocaust. The Republican-controlled Congress declined to endorse the war.[36]

The initial results of the bombing dashed Americans' hopes that Milosevic would capitulate after a brief show of NATO firepower. The war dragged on for more than two months. Critics of the Clinton administration's strategy complained that he ignored the Weinberger-Powell Doctrine by not employing overwhelming force. Republican Senator John McCain accused Clinton of conducting the war in "willful ignorance of every lesson we learned in Vietnam. . . . I never thought we would again witness . . . the specter of politicians picking targets and ruling out offensive measures in the absurd hope that the enemy would respond to our restraint by yielding to our demands."[37] Democrats, supportive of the war in the beginning, also became restless as the bombing continued and reports of civilian causalities brought other reminders of Vietnam. Some opponents of the war called for a halt to the bombing and renewed attempts to negotiate with Milosevic. Then, suddenly, the war ended in mid-June when Russian President Vladimir Putin, a long-time supporter of the Serbs, forced Milosevic to agree to terms proposed by the United States.[38]

The legacy of Vietnam and the Weinberger-Powell Doctrine also set the terms of many discussions of the U.S. war against terrorism in Afghanistan and Iraq following the World Trade Center and the Pentagon attacks on September 11, 2001. In October 2001 the United States launched an air and ground campaign against the Taliban government of Afghanistan, which had given sanctuary to Osama bin Laden and his Al Qaeda network that carried out the September 11 atrocities. The U.S. bombed extensively throughout Afghanistan but used few ground troops, instead dispatching Special Forces and covert operatives to work with local warlords opposed to the Taliban.

Once more some critics complained that the United States was escalating gradually rather than employing overwhelming force. Almost immediately, Americans saw the war in Afghanistan through the lens of the Vietnam War. The Taliban did not collapse within days as some advocates of war had predicted. *New York Times* correspondent R. W. Apple, who had reported extensively from Vietnam in the mid-1960s, heard ominous echoes. He was hardly alone in asking, "Could Afghanistan become another Vietnam? Is the United States facing another stalemate on the other side of the world?" President George W. Bush denied that the Afghan campaign would be another Vietnam.[39] In December the Taliban abandoned the capital of Kabul, and the strategy of working with local warlords seemed vindicated, at least for a time.

In 2003 the United States began a far larger and far more controversial war to remove Saddam Hussein from power in Iraq. Opposition to war with Iraq mounted in the fall and winter of 2002–2003. Opponents doubted the Bush administration's linking of Saddam Hussein to Al Qaeda. The administration's claim that Saddam had developed weapons of mass destruction also provoked skepticism. Secretary of State Powell persuaded Bush to seek support from the United Nations before embarking on a war with Iraq. Powell succeeded in securing a resolution from the UN Security Council demanding that Iraq comply fully with UN weapons inspectors or face "serious consequences," diplomatic code words for war.

Yet the United States could not assemble the same kind of broad coalition it had led against Iraq in the first Gulf War of 1991. Some of the largest antiwar demonstrations since the Vietnam era took place in Europe, Asia, Australia, and the United States in early 2003. In February and March 2003 the UN Security Council declined to adopt another resolution explicitly authorizing military action against Iraq. Echoes of Vietnam resounded during the debates over the potential for fighting in Iraq. Bush eagerly pointed out differences between Vietnam and Iraq. The United States failed in Vietnam, he said, because "we could not explain the mission, had no exit strategy, and did not seem to be fighting to win." In early March 2003 he explained how things would be different in Iraq. "Should we have to go in" to Iraq, he predicted, "our mission is very clear: disarmament. And in order to disarm, it would mean regime change. . . . It's very clear what we intend to do and our mission won't change."[40]

Confident of victory, the United States went to war on March 20, 2003. Britain, Spain, Australia, and some Eastern European NATO allies joined the war. But France, Germany, Russia, and China opposed attacking Iraq. This time the United States employed both massive air and land assault on Iraq. Iraqi military forces melted away rather than confront the oncoming American and British forces. On April 9 the United States forces took control of Baghdad, and less than a month later on May 1 Bush announced the end of major combat operations in Iraq.

What seemed like a swift, brilliant, and relatively bloodless victory in the spring of 2003 turned into a far deadlier and more costly occupation. Remnants of Saddam's deposed regime, al Qaeda fighters, and other Iraqis opposed to the American military presence in their country began guerrilla attacks against American and British forces. By the fall about six American soldiers or civilian employees of the occupation died each week in shootings, roadside bombings, and suicide bombings. Over twenty-one hundred U.S. servicemen and women had lost their lives and another fifteen thousand were wounded in Iraq by the end of 2005. The financial costs mounted to over two hundred billion dollars alongside the human toll.

When Bush requested an additional eighty-seven billion dollars in September 2003 to keep American forces in Iraq and Afghanistan for another year, the echoes of Vietnam resounded in the Congressional debate over the money. Iowa Democratic Senator Tom Harkin, a Vietnam-era veteran, warned, "This may not be Vietnam, but it sure smells like it."[41] Democratic Representative David Obey objected to the request for eighty-seven billion dollars by recalling the rosy scenarios and misjudgments of earlier administrations. "I haven't seen such a spectacular or breathtaking set of miscalculations since LBJ was bringing us into Vietnam deeper and deeper."[42]

Massachusetts Senator John Kerry, then making a bid for the Democratic presidential nomination, also detected echoes of Vietnam in the president's justifications of his Iraq policy. "At the rate that they're going, it reminds me of the 'light at the end of the tunnel' language during Vietnam," Kerry said in October 2003.[43] Kerry's Vietnam War service figured prominently in his campaign for the Democratic nomination for president in 2004. He won the Iowa caucuses in January after he held a dramatic reunion with fellow veteran, Retired Army Lieutenant James Rassman. Thirty-five years earlier in 1969 Kerry, a Navy lieutenant in command of a Swift boat patrolling the Mekong River, had saved Rassman's life by hauling him out of the river under intense fire from Viet Cong fighters along the shore. The two had not been close in the intervening years, but Rassman, a registered Republican, validated Kerry's reputation for courage under fire.[44] As a candidate, Kerry explicitly contrasted his battlefield experiences with Bush's spotty service record in the Texas Air National Guard from 1969 to 1973, implying that his Vietnam record made him a more prudent steward of the nation's foreign policy than Bush. Kerry criticized Bush for conducting a reckless war in Iraq with limited foreign support— exactly the same mistake the United States had made in Vietnam.[45]

When Kerry accepted the Democratic Party's presidential nomination, he drew comparisons between the Vietnam and Iraq wars. Before Kerry rose to speak, thirteen crewmates from his Navy Swift boat that had patrolled the Mekong River in 1969 filled the platform. Then Kerry recalled his experience fighting in Vietnam, and he criticized the deceptions of the Bush administration in conducting the war in Iraq. "I will be a commander-in-chief who will never mislead us into war," he promised.[46] Kerry's invocation of his heroic military service in Vietnam did not carry him to victory against Bush in the November elections. In August 2004 his political opponents organized Swift Boat Veterans for Truth, a group richly funded by longtime contributors to Bush's electoral campaigns, which ran TV attack ads denying that Kerry deserved his medals for valor and assailing his antiwar activities after he returned home from the fighting. Kerry responded slowly to the slurs. The facts supported his claims to valor, and independent observers concluded that the charges that Kerry did not earn his medals were false. Yet the TV ads proved to be highly damaging to his candidacy when the TV networks repeated the charges even as they broadcast the refutations. Kerry also let the attacks sink into voters' minds by declining to repeat during the campaign the criticism he had made of U.S. policies in Vietnam. This avoidance of his earlier antiwar stance contributed to a public perception that Kerry's position on the current war in Iraq was unclear. Voters who chose Bush in 2004 concluded that whatever each man had done decades earlier during the Vietnam War was less important to them than their ability to wage war against terrorism in the present. For these voters, Bush seemed tougher in the current fight.[47]

Supporters of the war in Iraq consistently denied the analogy to Vietnam. *New York Times* columnist Thomas Friedman criticized opponents of Bush's policies in Iraq for likening the resistance to the American occupation to the Vietnamese revolutionaries. "The people who mounted the attacks [on foreign relief workers or American troops] are not the Iraqi Viet Cong," he wrote. "They are the Iraqi Khmer Rouge—a murderous band of Saddam loyalists and al Qaeda nihilists, who are not killing us so Iraqis can rule themselves. They are killing us so they can rule Iraqis."[48]

Conservative *Wall Street Journal* columnist Robert Bartley agreed. He derided Democratic presidential contender Howard Dean for saying "We sent troops to Vietnam, without understanding why we were there. And the American people weren't told the truth and it was a disaster. And Iraq is gonna' be a disaster under this presidency." For Bartley the disaster in Vietnam was not fighting harder. Bartley wrote derisively of those who thought Iraqi fighters might actually push the United States out. He found a "dishonorable strain of American neurosis," among opponents of American policies in the Vietnam War. Therefore, he wrote, "by all means, don't do it again in Iraq."[49]

New York Times reporter Craig Whitney surveyed the growing American dissatisfaction with the occupation of Iraq in November 2003. "A listener to the debate over the situation in Iraq might think that it is truly Vietnam all over again," he wrote. Yet Whitney found as many differences as similarities. "Iraq is not Vietnam," he maintained. "There is no independent sanctuary named 'North Iraq' . . . no equivalent of Laos or Cambodia in the Middle East for whole divisions of [Saddam Hussein's] loyalists to hide in, no Ho Chi Minh trail that suicide bombers can use to drive to Baghdad." Americans processed what they saw in the war in and occupation of Iraq through their memories of Vietnam, because their understanding of the Vietnam War remained so poignant and divisive. The Vietnamese Communists "won the war in 1975," Whitney noted, "but nobody won the battle about it here at home."[50]

The comparisons between Vietnam and the war in Iraq only intensified as U.S. casualties mounted and the financial cost surpassed two hundred billion dollars in 2004 and 2005. The original justifications for going to war given by the Bush administration came under withering criticism, and skeptics recalled the Johnson administration's exaggerations at the time of the Tonkin Gulf incident of 1964. U.S. inspectors found neither stockpiles of chemical or biological weapons nor evidence that Iraq was developing nuclear weapons. The Senate Committee on Intelligence concluded that in the months before the Iraq war that "most of the key judgments" made by U.S. intelligence regarding Iraq's possession of weapons of mass destruction were "either overstated or were not supported by the underlying intelligence reporting."[51] The commission established to study the September 11, 2001, attacks on the World Trade Center and the Pentagon found no links between Saddam Hussein's Iraq and al Qaeda.[52]

Critics of the Bush administration charged that the president and his principal foreign policy advisers, like those in the Johnson administration during Vietnam, had misled the country into supporting an unnecessary and dangerous preemptive war. In April 2004 Massachusetts Democratic Senator Edward M. Kennedy leveled accusations that administration advocates of the Iraq war "repeatedly invent 'facts' to support their preconceived agenda— facts which Administration officials knew or should have known were not true. This pattern has prevailed since President Bush's earliest days in office. As a result, this President has now created the largest credibility gap since

Richard Nixon." Kennedy charged that Bush administration officials "misled Congress and the American people because the Administration knew that it could not obtain the consent of Congress for the war if all the facts were known." In his fiery speech he concluded that "Iraq is George Bush's Vietnam, and this country needs a new President." Kennedy said, "Vietnam ended up in a quagmire. Iraq is as well." [53]

As the war continued to go badly for the United States in Iraq, analysts tried another analogy—the French war in Algeria. Andrew Bacevich, a professor of international relations at Boston University, responded to Senator Kennedy's characterization of Iraq as Vietnam with the grim assertion, "The news is actually much worse. Iraq may be shaping up to be America's Algeria. . . . French authorities found that conventional tactics did not work. To abide by the traditional law of war was to concede to the other side an enormous advantage. So, in their frustration, the French opted to fight a 'dirty war,' employing systematic torture, extrajudicial killings and their own brand of terrorism."[54] Comparisons between the wars in Vietnam and Iraq were made not just at home but around the world. Derek Woolner, the director of the Foreign Affairs, Defense, and Trade Group in the Australian Parliamentary Research Service, told the Australian Broadcasting Service, "I see the current circumstances in Iraq having the potential to develop into a Vietnam-like situation" because "the Americans do not seem to have entered there with any clear perceptions of what they wanted to achieve. Those that they had now must be recognized as impossibly rosy eyed and they don't appear to have an operational strategy which will enable them to achieve results without the situation having a great danger of worsening."[55]

Other uncomfortable reminders of the gravest American offenses of the Vietnam War continued to emerge in 2004. Journalist Seymour Hersh, who broke the story of the March 1968 My Lai massacre in November 1969, published an in-depth report about U.S. military personnel and civilian contractor abuse of prisoners in Iraq and Afghanistan.[56] Photographs and eyewitness testimony of sexual humiliations, intimidations with dogs, fake executions, and beatings shocked Americans, and they brought back unwelcome memories of the atrocities committed during the Vietnam War. After the public revelations of the abuses of prisoners, for the first time more Americans thought it had been a mistake for the United States to have gone to war in Iraq than supported Bush's decision to attack.[57]

Former officials from the Vietnam War era joined the debate. Melvin Laird, who served as secretary of defense during the time Richard Nixon began the draw down of American troops, argued that the American experience in Vietnam actually provided valuable positive lessons for the potential for success in Iraq. Laird wrote, "The shame of Vietnam is not that we were there in the first place, but that we betrayed our ally in the end." He proposed the policy of

Vietnamization as a model for how the United States could prevail in Iraq, because, he said, "the United States had not lost when we withdrew in 1973." If the public, the Congress, and the administration had the fortitude to stay the course in Iraq, as they did not in Vietnam, Laird expressed confidence that the result would be the creation of a successful, modern, peaceful, and Democratic Iraq.[58]

The public's patience with the inconclusive struggle in Iraq was tested in 2005, and the uneasiness about it dragged down Bush's popularity. By mid-2005 only 37 percent of the public believed that Bush had a clear plan for the two-year-old war in Iraq and a slim majority wanted him to set a deadline for the removal of U.S. troops from the country. By July 2005, 57 percent of Americans did not believe it had been worth it for the United States to have gone to war in Iraq. [59] In August 2005 Republican Senator Chuck Hagel of Nebraska, a decorated Vietnam veteran, said "we should start figuring out how we get out of there. . . . [B]y any standard, when you analyze 2 1/2 years in Iraq . . . we're not winning."[60] The political scientist John Mueller, who had written extensively about public opinion in wartime, tracked the fluctuations in public support for military operations in Korea, Vietnam, and Iraq and concluded that "as casualties mount, support decreases. . . . The only thing remarkable about the current war in Iraq is how precipitously American public support has dropped off." Mueller speculated about the development of an "Iraq syndrome" replacing the Vietnam syndrome and leading to public aversion to the "unilateralism, preemption, preventive war, and indispensable nationhood" that characterized American foreign and military policy at the beginning of the twenty-first century.[61] The historian David Anderson noted the parallels between American policymakers' expectations of reshaping the political life of Vietnam in the 1960s and Iraq in the twenty-first century. He cautioned that the United States is a nation "with limits to its power, with national objectives that have to compete with or be reconciled with the national objectives of others, and which has to identify reasonably attainable goals that can be achieved by reasonably available means."[62]

Historical analogies always are imperfect. Angola, Central America, the Gulf War, Somalia, Rwanda, Bosnia, Kosovo, Afghanistan, and Iraq are not exactly Vietnam, and each contained unique perils. Even while the Vietnam War was being fought, many U.S. critics of the war chastised officials of the Lyndon Johnson administration for their misapplication of the apparent lessons of history by referencing of the appeasement of Nazi Germany and the Munich conference of 1938. But personal memories and analogies exercise a powerful hold.

The perceived lessons of the past are most compelling when the memories are troubling, and there is a nearly irresistible urge to avoid repeating mistakes. Americans have tended to see every contentious or dangerous foreign policy issue through the prism of Vietnam for more than a quarter century, and there is no reason to think this will abate since memory of the Vietnam War singed the consciousness of several generations of Americans. These included the officials who directed the war in the 1960s and 1970s; the younger men and women who fought the war, were subject to the draft, or who protested against it; and the generations too young to have personal experience of the war. Each of these generations has assimilated their own conflicted and troubled memories of Vietnam and has tried to apply them to the present. The divisions over Vietnam were so wide and the lessons learned so contested that the Vietnam War endures as the emblematic episode of contemporary United States foreign policy.

Notes

INTRODUCTION

1. James T. Patterson, *Restless Giant: The United States from Watergate to* Bush v. Gore (New York: Oxford University Press, 2005), 84–85.
2. Robert D. Schulzinger, *A Time for War: The United States and Vietnam, 1941–1975* (New York: Oxford University Press, 1997), 326.
3. Robert. D. Schulzinger, *Henry Kissinger: Doctor of Diplomacy* (New York: Columbia University Press, 1989), 205, and Walter Isaacson, *Kissinger: A Biography* (New York: Simon and Schuster, 1992), 647–48.
4. Library of Congress, "Country Study: Vietnam, Vietnam after 1975" http://lcweb2.loc.gov/frd/cs/vntoc.html.
5. Ibid.
6. Ibid., and Gabriel Kolko, *Anatomy of a War: Vietnam, the United States, and the Modern Historical Experience* (New York: New Press, revised edition 1994), 568.
7. G. Kurt Piehler, *Remembering War the American Way* (Washington, D.C.: Smithsonian Institution Press, 1995), 3, and Arthur G. Neal, *National Trauma and Collective Memory: Major Events in the American Century* (Armonk, N.Y.: M. E. Sharpe, 1998), 5.
8. Jay Winter, "The Generation of Memory: Reflections on the 'Memory Boom'" in "Contemporary German Historical Studies," *Bulletin of the German Historical Institute* 27, 3 (fall 2000): 69–92, and Emily S. Rosenberg, *A Date Which Will Live: Pearl Harbor in American Memory* (Durham: Duke University Press, 2003), 116–17.
9. Paul Connerton, *How Societies Remember* (Cambridge: Cambridge University Press, 1989). See chapter 1, "Social Memory," 6–40, and chapter 2, "Commemorative Ceremonies," 41–71.
10. Michael G. Kammen, *Mystic Chords of Memory: The Transformation of Tradition in American Life* (New York: Knopf, 1991), 535.
11. Paul Fussell, *Wartime: Understanding and Behavior in the Second World War* (New York: Oxford University Press, 1989), 167.
12. Neal, *National Trauma and Collective Memory*, 3.

CHAPTER 1

1. For good general discussions of the state of U.S.-Vietnamese relations at the immediate end of the war see Robert J. McMahon, *The Limits of Empire: The United States and Southeast Asia Since World War II* (New York: Columbia University Press, 1999), 182–94; Evelyn Colbert, "U.S. Policy Toward Vietnam Since the Fall of Saigon," in Joseph J. Zasloff, ed., *Postwar Indochina: Old Enemies and New Allies* (Washington, D.C.: Foreign Service Institute of the U.S. Department of State 1988), 225–31; Richard T. Childress and Stephen J. Solarz, "Vietnam: The Road to Normalization," in C. Richard Nelson and Kenneth Weisbrode, eds., *Reversing Relations with Former Adversaries: U.S. Foreign Policy after the Cold War* (Gainesville: University Press of Florida, 1998), 88–91.
2. Gerard R. Ford, *A Time to Heal: The Autobiography of Gerald R. Ford* (New York: Harper and Row, 1979), 142.
3. Lawrence M. Baskir and William A. Strauss, *Reconciliation after Vietnam: A Program of Relief for Vietnam Era Draft and Military Offenders* (Notre Dame, Ind.: University of Notre Dame Press, 1977), 25.
4. Ibid., 28, 37, 45.
5. Oliver Babson, "Diplomacy of Isolation: United States Unilateral Sanctions Policy and 1975–1995," WWS Case Study 4/02, Woodrow Wilson School of Public and International Affairs, Princeton University, January 16, 2002.
6. Ford, *A Time to Heal*, 257.
7. James G Gimpel and James R. Edwards, *The Congressional Politics of Immigration Reform* (Needham Heights, Mass.: Allyn and Bacon, 1999), 119–20.
8. T. Christopher Jespersen, "The Bitter End and the Lost Chance in Vietnam: Congress, the Ford Administration and the Battle Over Vietnam, 1975–76," *Diplomatic History* 24, 2 (spring 2000): 272.
9. Ibid., 274.
10. Ibid., 277.
11. Ibid., 279.
12. Quoted in Gaddis Smith, *Morality, Reason, and Power: American Diplomacy in the Carter Years* (New York: Hill and Wang, 1986), 29.
13. http://www.pbs.org/newshour/bb/asia/vietnam/vietnam_1-21-77.html
14. Childress and Solarz, "Vietnam: The Road to Normalization," 92.
15. Steven Hurst, *The Carter Administration and Vietnam* (New York: St. Martin's Press, 1996), 27.
16. Memorandum for the Record. White House Meeting, January 31, 1977. MIA in Asia, 1–2, 1977. Box 39–49. National Security Affairs. Brzezinski Files. Jimmy Carter Library (JCL). Atlanta, Georgia.
17. Cambodian Foreign Ministry Press Communiqué on U.S. Request for Talks. March 18, 1977. MIA, March 1977. Box 39–49. National Security Affairs. Brzezinski Files. JCL. Also see, Childress and Solarz, "Vietnam: The Road to Normalization," 93.
18. Aide memoire, position of the SRV. Attached to Brzezinski to president, N.D. [March 22, 1977]. MIA, March 1977. Box 39–49. National Security Affairs. Brzezinski Files. JCL.
19. Hurst, *The Carter Administration and Vietnam*, 33.
20. Issue Paper, Establishment of Diplomatic Relations. Attached to Brzezinski to president, April 28, 1977. Box 85. National Security Affairs. Brzezinski Files. JCL.

21. Ibid., and Hurst, *The Carter Administration and Vietnam*, 35.
22. Hurst, *The Carter Administration and Vietnam*, 36.
23. Brzezinski to president, December 1, 1977. Brzezinski to secretary of state, December 1, 1977. Box 85. National Security Affairs. Brzezinski Files. JCL.
24. Oksenberg to Brzezinski, January 30, 1978. Box 85. National Security Affairs. Brzezinski Files. JCL.
25. Oksenberg to Brzezinski, January 8, 1978. Box 85. National Security Affairs. Brzezinski Files. JCL.
26. Zbigniew Brzezinski, *Power and Principle: Memoirs of the National Security Adviser, 1977–1981* (New York: Farrar, Strauss, and Giroux, 1983), 552.
27. Quoted in Hurst, *The Carter Administration and Vietnam*, 65.
28. Ibid., 88.
29. Ibid., 94.
30. Quoted in Nayan Chanda, *Brother Enemy: The War after the War* (San Diego: Harcourt, Brace, Jovanovich, 1986), 271.
31. Brzezinski, *Power and Principle*, 228.
32. Quoted in Chanda, *Brother Enemy*, 264.
33. Oksenberg to Brzezinski, September 28, 1977. Box 85. National Security Affairs. Brzezinski Files. JCL.
34. Quoted in Chanda, *Brother Enemy*, 266.
35. Ibid., 285.
36. Colbert, "U.S. Policy Toward Vietnam," 235–37.
37. Quoted in Hurst, *The Carter Administration and Vietnam*, 98.
38. Quoted in Chanda, *Brother Enemy*, 290.
39. Quoted in Hurst, *The Carter Administration and Vietnam*, 98–99.
40. Franklin B. Weinstein, "U.S.–Vietnam Relations and the Security of Southeast Asia," *Foreign Affairs* (July 1978): 843.
41. Quoted in Douglas Pike, *Vietnam and the Soviet Union: Anatomy of an Alliance* (Boulder, Colo.: Westview Press, 1987), 185.
42. Chanda, *Brother Enemy*, 341–46.
43. Brzezinski, *Power and Principle*, 409,
44. Quoted in David W. P. Elliott, "The Third Indochina Conflict: Introduction," in David W. P. Elliott, ed., *The Third Indochina Conflict* (Boulder, Colo.: Westview, 1982), 14.
45. Brzezinski, *Power and Principle*, 411–12.
46. Chanda, *Brother Enemy*, 357, and Pike, *Vietnam and the Soviet Union*, 203.
47. Pike, *Vietnam and the Soviet Union*, 204.
48. Vance to president, with Oksenberg comments. May 16, 1979. Box 86. National Security Affairs. Brzezinski Files. JCL.
49. Nayan Chanda, "Vietnam and Cambodia: Domination and Security," in Joseph J. Zasloff, ed., *Postwar Indochina: Old Enemies and New Allies* (Washington, D.C.: Foreign Service Institute of the U.S. Department of State, 1988), 73–75.
50. McMahon, *The Limits of Empire*, 191–94.

CHAPTER 2

1. *New York Times*, August 19, 1980.
2. Beth A. Fischer, *The Reagan Reversal: Foreign Policy and the End of the Cold War* (Columbia: University of Missouri Press, 1997), 1–23, and Raymond L.

Garthoff, *The Great Transition: American-Soviet Relations and the End of the Cold War* (Washington, D.C.: Brookings Institution, 1994), 15–32.

3. Theodore Draper, *A Very Thin Line: The Iran-Contra Affairs* (New York: Hill and Wang, 1991), passim.

4. Richard Childress to John M. Poindexter, April 3, 1985. Box 92402, Richard Childress Files, Ronald Reagan Library (RRL), Simi Valley, California. Also see, Richard T. Childress and Stephen J. Solarz , "Vietnam: Detours on the Road to Normalization," in C. Richard Nelson and Kenneth Weisbrode, eds. *Reversing Relations with Former Adversaries: U.S. Foreign Policy after the Cold War* (Gainesville: University of Florida Press, 1998), 201.

5. Vietnam: US–SRV Relations, January 13, 1982. Box OA9076. Morton Blackwell Files. RRL.

6. John Gunther Dean, U.S. ambassador, Bangkok to secretary of state, July 7 and 8, 1982. Box 92402. Richard Childress Files. RRL.

7. Vietnam: US–SRV Relations, January 13, 1982. Box OA9076. Morton Blackwell Files. RRL.

8. POW/MIA Interagency Group meeting, January 19, 1982. Box OA9076. Morton Blackwell Files. RRL.

9. Ibid.

10. POW/MIA Meetings, March 4 and 8, 1982. Handwritten Notes. Box OA9026. Morton Blackwell Files. RRL.

11. Chronology of US/SRV POW/MIA Activities, February 1982–January 1986. Box 90647. Ron Sable Files. RRL.

12. Richard Childress to Steve Sestanovich, April 1, 1985. Box 92396. Childress Files. RRL.

13. Frederick Z. Brown, "The U.S. Perspective on an 'Emerging' Indochina," in Joseph J. Zasloff, ed., *Postwar Indochina: Old Enemies and New Allies* (Washington, D.C.: Center for the Study of Foreign Affairs, Foreign Service Institute of the U.S. Department of State, 1988), 255

14. Richard Childress to Robert McFarlane, April 10, 1985. Childress to John Poindexter, April 3, 1985. Box 92402. Childress Files. RRL.

15. Paul D. Mather, *M.I.A.: Accounting for the Missing in Southeast Asia* (Washington, D.C.: National Defense University Press, 1994), 101–3.

16. Childress and Solarz, "Vietnam: The Road to Normalization," 108.

17. Mather, *M.I.A.*, xxi. Also, Arnold R. Isaacs, *Vietnam Shadows: The War, Its Ghosts, and Its Legacy* (Baltimore: Johns Hopkins University Press, 1997), 103–39. H. Bruce Franklin, *M.I.A.: Or Mythmaking in America* (New York: Lawrence Hill Books, 1992), 137–38.

18. Mather, *M.I.A.*, 106–7.

19. Grant S. Green to Ronald K. Peterson, July 7, 1987. Melvyn Levitsky to Frank C. Carlucci, September 4, 1987. Richard Childress to Grant S. Green, September 8, 1987. Tom Henney, Memcon typed from handwritten notes, December 4, 1986. Box OA92014. Alison Fortier Files. RRL. Also see, Bill Paul, "Vietnam Legacy," *Wall Street Journal*, January 21, 1987, 1.

20. Mather, *M.I.A.*, 114–15.

21. POW/MIA Commission Requested. August 2, 1985. Box 92596. Richard Childress Files. RRL.; General Tighe's Personal Opinion on Live Prisoners in Southeast Asia, [N.D. 1986]. Box OA90647. Ron Sable Files. RRL.; and M.B.

Ogelsby, Jr., "Meeting with Congressmen Bill Hendon and Congressman Robert Smith, January 9, 1986. Box OA90647. Ron Sable Files. RRL.

22. Chapman P. Cox to Dante Fascell, September 12, 1985. Ball to Fascell, [N.D., October 1985]. Richard Childress to John Poindexter, February 3, 1986. Poindexter to president, [N.D., February 1986]. Box OA90647. Ron Sable Files. RRL.

23. M.B. Oglesby, Jr., "Meeting with Congressmen Bill Hendon and Robert Smith," January 9, 1986. Box OA90647. Ron Sable Files. RRL.

24. Talking points for use with Perot's representatives, [N.D. fall 1985]. Box 90647. Ron Sable Files. RRL.

25. Bush to Robert McFarlane, October 9, 1985. Talking points for use with Representative Montgomery [attached]. Box OA90647. Ron Sable Files. RRL.

26. List of Supporters of John LeBoutillier's appointment, December 1986. Box OA92014. Alison Fortier Files. RRL.

27. "The Vessey Mission to Hanoi," Hearing before the Subcommittee on Asian and Pacific Affairs of the Committee on Foreign Affairs. House of Representatives. 100th Congress, 1st sess., September 30, 1987, 28–29.

28. George P. Shultz, "The Meaning of Vietnam," address at the State Department, April 25, 1985. *Department of State Bulletin*, June 1985, 15–16.

29. "China-Vietnam: Fighting Likely to Escalate," Intelligence Estimate, May 4, 1984. Box OA92402. Richard Childress Files. RRL.

30. U.S. Embassy, Moscow to Secretary of State, October 30, 1984. Box OA92402. Richard Childress Files. RRL. Also see, Memo for the Record. Phone Communication with VN Mission. June 19, 1985. U.S.-Vietnamese Negotiations [1 of 3]. OA/ID CF 00319. George Bush Library (GBL). College Station, Texas.

31. Fischer, *The Reagan Reversal*, 69–76, and Michael Beschloss and Strobe Talbott, *At the Highest Levels: The Inside Story of the End of the Cold War* (Boston: Little, Brown, 1993).

32. Gabriel Kolko, *Anatomy of a War: Vietnam, the United States and the Modern Historical Experience* (New York: The New Press, revised edition 1994), 578.

33. Morton Abromwitz to George P. Shultz, "Vietnam: Succession Process Begins in Adversity," April 1986. Carl W. Ford to Director of Central Intelligence, May 28, 1986. Special Analysis, Party Congress to Set Reform Agenda. November 20, 1986. Box OA92402. Childress Papers. RRL.

34. Richard Armitage to Nguyen Co Thach, June 24, 1986. Attached "U.S. Support for the Socialist Republic's of Vietnam's Operational Plan to Resolve the Issue of Americans Missing in Action." Box OA92014. Alison Fortier Files. RRL. Also see, Richard Armitage, Memo for the Record: Meeting with Ambassador (Acting) Bui Xuan Nhat. January 17, 1986. U.S.-Vietnamese Negotiations [2 of 3]. OA/ID CF 00319. GBL.

35. Mather, *M.I.A.*, 155.

36. "The Vessey Mission to Hanoi," 4, 6.

37. Ronald Reagan to Vo Chi Cong, July 27, 1987. U.S. Vietnamese Negotiations [3 of 3]. OA/ID CF 00319. GBL. Also see, Childress and Solarz, "Vietnam: The Road to Normalization," 98–99.

38. "The Vessey Mission to Hanoi," 12–13.

39. Ibid., 14–17. Vessey Agreements-87. Classified Record. Ann Mills Griffith to Nguyen Co Thach, August 7, 1987. Bangkok, Message to Hanoi, August 27, 1987. U.S. Vietnamese Negotiations [3 of 3]. OA/ID CF 00319. GBL.

40. U.S. Department of State, *The Problem of the Disabled in Vietnam: A Report to Non-Governmental Organizations Stemming from the Mission to Hanoi by Presidential Emissary General John W. Vessey (retired)*, October 13, 1987. Foreign Minister Nien. September 25, 1987. U.S. Vietnamese Negotiations [3 of 3]. OA/ID CF 00319. GBL.

41. "The Vessey Mission to Hanoi," 81.

42. Ibid., 20

43. Ibid., 83.

44. Ibid., 76.

45. Ibid., 110–11. Richard H. Solomon, *Exiting Indochina: U.S. Leadership of the Cambodia Settlement and Normalization with Vietnam* (Washington, D.C.: U.S. Institute of Peace, 2000), 85–86.

46. Childress to Colin L. Powell, March 7, 1988. Alison Fortier Files, OA 92014. RRL.

47. "The Vessey Mission to Hanoi," 27.

48. Ibid., 29–30.

49. Ibid., 102–3.

50. Childress to Colin L. Powell, March 7, 1988. Box OA92014. RRL.

51. Talking Points for Use with Congressman Dornan. N.D. [March 1988]. Box OA92014. Alison Fortier Files. RRL.

52. Childress to Powell, March 14, 1988. Box OA92014. Alison Fortier Files. GIST, "Amerasians in Vietnam," August 1988. Box 72397. Richard Childress Files. RRL.

53. Talking Points for Use with Congressman Dornan, [N.D., March 1988]. Childress to Powell. March 14, 1988. Box OA92014. Alison Fortier Files.

54. James Kelly to Colin L. Powell, May 13, 1988. Kelly to Powell, June 6, 1988. Thomas C. Griscom to Powell, June 8, 1988. Box OA92406. Childress Files. RRL.

55. Remarks at the Annual Meeting of the National League of Families, July 29, 1988. *Public Papers of the Presidents: Ronald Reagan, 1988–89* (Washington, D.C.: Government Printing Office, 1991), 998.

CHAPTER 3

1. George Bush, "Inaugural Address," January 20, 1989, *Public Papers of the Presidents: George Bush, 1989* (Washington, D.C.: Government Printing Office, 1989), 3.

2. Raymond Garthoff, *The Great Transition: American-Soviet Relations and the End of the Cold War* (Washington, D.C.: Brookings Institution, 1994), 374–89; John R. Greene, *The Presidency of George Bush* (Lawrence: University Press of Kansas, 2000), 90; George Bush and Brent Scowcroft, *A World Transformed* (New York: Knopf, 1998), 16–21; and James A. Baker, III, and Thomas M. DeFrank, *The Politics of Diplomacy: Revolution, War, and Peace, 1989–1992* (New York: G.P. Putnam's Sons, 1995), 37–46.

3. Keith Richburg, "Back to Vietnam," *Foreign Affairs* 70 (fall 1991):111.

4. Bush and Scowcroft, *A World Transformed*, 16–21, 86–99, 106–111; Baker and DeFrank, *The Politics of Diplomacy*, 84–96; Michael R. Beschloss and Strobe Talbott, *At the Highest Levels: The Inside Story of the End of the Cold War* (Boston: Little, Brown, 1993), 126–51; and Don Oberdorfer, *The Turn: From the*

Cold War to a New Era: The United States and the Soviet Union, 1983–1990 (New York: Poseidon Books, 1991), 328–45.

5. Bush and Scowcroft, *A World Transformed*, 86–99, 106–11. Baker and DeFrank, *The Politics of Diplomacy*, 97–114.

6. Richard T. Childress and Stephen J. Solarz, "Vietnam: The Road to Normalization," in C. Richard Nelson and Kenneth Weisbrode, eds., *Reversing Relations with Former Adversaries: U.S. Foreign Policy After the Cold War* (University Press of Florida: Gainesville, 1998), 99.

7. U.S. Senate, "POW/MIAs Report of the Select Committee on POW/MIA Affairs," 103rd Congress, 1st Session, January 13, 1993, 378.

8. Frederick Z. Brown, "Taking a Fresh Look at Indochina," *Foreign Service Journal* 67 (July 1990): 27.

9. Senate, "POW/MIAs Report," 379.

10. Ibid.

11. Ibid., 379–80; Oliver Babson, "Diplomacy of Isolation: United States Unilateral Sanctions Policy and 1975–1995," WWS Case Study 4/02. January 16, 2002. Woodrow Wilson School of Public and International Affairs. Princeton University; Richard H. Solomon, *Exiting Indochina: U.S. Leadership of the Cambodian Settlement and Normalization With Vietnam* (Washington, D.C.: United States Institute of Peace, 2000),86–87.

12. Senate, "POW/MIAs Report," 380–81.

13. Ibid., 381–82; and "U.S. Discussions with Vietnam and Laos," *Foreign Policy Bulletin* 2 (January–February 1992): 109.

14. Carroll J. Doherty, "Administration Moves Slowly Toward Normal Relations," *Congressional Quarterly* (April 13, 1991): 924.

15. Senate, "POW/MIAs Report" 384–85.

16. Author interview with Tommy Le Van, November 16, 1995, Boulder, Colo.

17. Peter Goldman et al., *Quest for the Presidency, 1992* (College Station: Texas A&M Press, 1994).

18. Senate, "POW/MIAs Report," 386; "Remarks on Developments in the POW/MIA Situation," October 23, 1992. *Public Papers of the President, George Bush, 1992* (Washington, D.C.: Government Printing Office, 1993), 2059.

19. David Maraniss, *First in His Class: A Biography of Bill Clinton* (New York: Simon and Schuster, 1995), 165, 179–80; Goldman et al., *Quest for the Presidency,* 112–14; and William C. Berman, *From the Center to the Edge: The Politics and Policies of the Clinton Administration* (Lanham, Md.: Rowman and Littlefield, 2001), 12.

20. Nick J. Freeman, "International Economic Responses to Reform in Vietnam: An Overview of Obstacles and Progress," *Studies in Comparative Communism* 25 (September 1992): 291–93.

21. Quoted in Childress and Solarz, "Vietnam: The Road to Normalization," 102.

22. Senate, "POW/MIAs Report," 388–89.

23. Ibid., 388–89.

24. Ibid., 390–91.

25. U.S. Senate, "U.S. Policy Toward Vietnam," Hearing Before the Subcommittee on East Asian and Pacific Affairs, Committee on Foreign Relations, 103rd Congress, 1st session, July 21, 1993, 2–3.

26. Ibid., 4–5.

27. Ibid., 7.
28. Ibid., 12–13.
29. Ibid., 12–13.
30. Childress and Solarz, "Vietnam: The Road to Normalization," 104.
31. U.S. Senate, "U.S. Policy Toward Vietnam," 31.
32. Ibid., 32.
33. Ibid., 32.
34. John Bresnan, *From Dominoes to Dynamos: The Transformation of Southeast Asia* (New York: Council on Foreign Relations, 1994), 17–21; and Nick J. Freeman, "International Economic Responses to Reform in Vietnam," 293.
35. U.S. Senate, "U.S. Policy Toward Vietnam," 48.
36. Ibid., 41.
37. Ibid., 43.
38. Ibid., 48.
39. Ibid., 49.
40. Ibid., 51.
41. Ibid., 60.
42. Ibid., 62.
43. Ibid., 89.
44. Ibid., 70.
45. Ibid., 71.
46. The American Chamber of Commerce in Hong Kong, "Position paper, Lifting the Embargo on Vietnam," in "U.S. Policy Toward Vietnam," 113–14.
47. "U.S. Policy Toward Vietnam," 113.
48. Elizabeth Drew, *On the Edge: The Clinton Presidency* (New York: Simon and Schuster, 1994), 46–48; and Berman, *From the Center to the Edge,* 22–23.
49. "Remarks at a Memorial Day Ceremony at the Vietnam Veterans Memorial, May 31, 1993." *Public Papers of the Presidents, William J. Clinton, 1993,* (Washington, D.C.: Government Printing Office, 1994), 786.
50. Murray Hiebert and Susumu Awanohara, "Good Morning, Vietnam," *Far Eastern Economic Review* 157 (February 17, 1994): 15.
51. Asfaw Kumsaw, "Economic Reform Policies and Viet Nam's Transition to a Market-Oriented Economy," *Regional Development Dialogue* 18, 1 (spring 1997): 76–80.
52. Hiebert and Awanohara, "Good Morning, Vietnam," 16.
53. "Remarks Announcing the Normalization of Relations with Vietnam, July 11, 1995." *Public Papers of the Presidents, William Jefferson Clinton, 1993,* 1073.
54. Quoted in Allan E. Goodman, "The Political Consequences of Normalization of U.S.-Vietnam Relations," *Contemporary Southeast Asia* 17, 4 (March 1996): 421.
55. Adam Schwartz, "Vietnam: Trade and Investment: The Problems of Progress," *Far Eastern Economic Review* 158 (October 25, 1995): 51.
56. Ibid., 51.
57. Ibid., 50.
58. Gabriel Kolko, *Anatomy of a War: Vietnam, the United States and the Modern Historical Experience* (New York: The New Press, revised edition 1994), 579.
59. Schwartz, "Vietnam: Trade and Investment: The Problems of Progress," 56.
60. "Vietnam Survey," *Economist,* July 8, 1995, 13.

61. Ibid.
62. Author's visit to Vietnam, March 2001.
63. Raphael Cung, "Vietnam in the Nineties," *SAIS Review* 11, 17 (summer–fall 1991): 181–83; and "Vietnam Survey," *Economist,* 13.
64. Adam Schwartz, "Culture Shock," *Far Eastern Economic Review* 159, August 22, 1996, 63.
65. M. Dutta, "Vietnam: Marketization and Internationalization of Its Economy, *Journal of Asian Economics* 6 (fall 1995): 315, 317.
66. Author's visit to Vietnam, March 2001.
67. "Vietnam Survey," *Economist,* 14–15.
68. Ibid.
69. U.S. Senate, "Chronology of Normalization of Relations Between the U.S. and Vietnam," Hearing Before the Subcommittee on International Trade of the Committee on Finance. 105th Congress, 2nd session. July 7, 1998, 182.
70. Ibid., 32–33.
71. Ibid., 37.
72. Ibid., 38–39.
73. Ibid., 165.
74. U.S. House of Representatives Committee on Ways and Means. "United States–Vietnam Trade Relations." Hearing Before the Subcommittee on Trade. 106th Congress, 1st session. June 17, 1999, 33.
75. U.S. House of Representatives. "An Agreement Between the United States and the Socialist Republic of Vietnam on Trade Relations." Message from the President of the United States. House Document 107–85. 107th Congress, 1st session. June 12, 2001.
76. U.S. House of Representatives Committee on International Relations. "Prelude to New Directions in United States–Vietnam Relations: The 2000 Bilateral Trade Agreement. Joint Hearing. 106th Congress. 2nd session. September 19, 2000, 6; Andrew Wells-Dong, "Establishing Normal Trade Relations with Vietnam and Laos," *Foreign Policy in Focus* 6, 30 (July 30, 2001):1.
77. "Clinton trip aimed at cementing relationship with old U.S. foe," http://transcripts.cnn.com/2000/US/11/13/clinton.asia.ap/index.html, November 14, 2000.
78. Seth Mydans, "America Today: Through Vietnamese Eyes," *New York Times,* November 15, 2000, A 1.

CHAPTER 4

1. Lewis B. Puller, Jr., *Fortunate Son: The Autobiography of Lewis B. Puller, Jr.* (New York: Grove Weidenfeld, 1991), 234.
2. Lawrence M. Baskir and William A. Strauss, *Chance and Circumstance: The Draft, the War, and the Vietnam Generation* (New York: Knopf, 1978), 5. The number of American combat soldiers is especially difficult to state with certainty. At most four hundred thousand soldiers took part in search and destroy operations. These men stayed in the field for days and weeks at a time and participated in the bloodiest firefights. But a larger number heard gunfire and artillery barrages and was vulnerable to attack. The fighting took place intermittently. There were no clear front lines, and the Viet Cong sometimes ambushed American soldiers stationed in seemingly secure areas.

3. Paul Starr, *The Discarded Army: Veterans After Vietnam, The Nader Report on Vietnam Veterans and the Veterans Administration* (New York: Charterhouse, 1973), 31.

4. House of Representatives, Committee on Veterans Affairs, *Legacies of Vietnam: Comparative Adjustment of Veterans and Their Peers: A Study Prepared for the Veterans' Administration*, March 9, 1981 (Washington, D.C.: Government Printing Office, 1981), 325.

5. Todd S. Purdum, "Idealistic Man on Campus to Realistic Sailor at War," *New York Times*, July 6, 2004, A 4.

6. Douglas Brinkley, *Tour of Duty, John Kerry and the Vietnam War* (New York: William Morrow, 2004), 351.

7. Ibid., 11–12.

8. House of Representatives, Committee on Veterans Affairs, *Legacies of Vietnam*, 345.

9. Ibid., 351.

10. Ibid.

11. Ibid., 345.

12. Ibid., 357.

13. Ibid., 359.

14. Ibid., 349.

15. Ibid., 344.

16. Ibid., 358.

17. Robert J. Lifton, *Home from the War: Vietnam Veterans: Neither Victims nor Executioners* (New York: Simon and Schuster, 1973), 351–54.

18. V. Wallen, "Background Characteristics, Attitudes and Self-Concepts of Air Force Psychiatric Casualties from Southeast Asia," in Peter Bourne, ed., *The Psychology and Physiology of Stress* (New York: Academic Press, 1969), 188.

19. Sarah Haley, "When the Patient Reports Atrocities: Specific Treatment Considerations of the Vietnam Veteran," *Archives of General Psychiatry* 30 (February 1974): 192–93; and Gerald Nicosia, *Home to War: A History of the Vietnam Veterans' Movement* (New York: Crown Publishers, 2001), 184.

20. Chaim Shatan, "The Grief of Soldiers in Mourning: Vietnam Veterans Self-Help Movement," *American Journal of Orthopsychiatry* 45 (1973): 648.

21. Wilbur J. Scott, *The Politics of Readjustment Vietnam Veterans Since the War* (New York: Aldine De Gruyter, 1993), 43.

22. Nicosia, *Home to War*, 160–67.

23. Scott, *The Politics of Readjustment*, 17.

24. Ibid., 34.

25. Ibid., 52.

26. House of Representatives, Committee on Veterans Affairs, *Readjustment Counseling*, Hearings, 97th Congress, 1st session, April 8, 1981, 43.

27. House of Representatives, Committee on Veterans Affairs, *Concerns of Vietnam War Veterans*, Hearing, 101st Congress, 1st session, May 3, 1989, 52–53.

28. Veterans Administration, *Vet Center Program Guide*, January 6, 1988, 2–3.

29. Scott, *The Politics of Readjustment*, 68.

30. Max Cleland, *Strong at the Broken Places* (Atlanta: Cherokee, 1986), 97–98.

31. Scott, *The Politics of Readjustment*, 64.

32. Ibid., 61–63; and Allan Young, *The Harmony of Illusions: Inventing Post-Traumatic Stress Disorder* (Princeton: Princeton University Press, 1995), 101–17.

33. Veterans Administration, *Vet Center Program Guide*, I–1.
34. House of Representatives, *Readjustment Counseling*, 253.
35. Ibid., 21.
36. Ibid., 251–53.
37. Eric T. Dean, Jr., *Shook Over Hell, Post-Traumatic Stress, Vietnam, and the Civil War* (Cambridge: Harvard University Press, 1997), 17; and Daniel L. Pollack et al., "Estimating the Number of Suicides Among Vietnam Veterans," *American Journal of Psychiatry* 147, 6 (June 1990): 772–76.
38. Dean, *Shook Over Hell*, 251.
39. House of Representatives, *Readjustment Counseling*, 244.
40. Ibid., 56, 206–9.
41. House of Representatives, *Concerns of Vietnam Era Veterans*, 17.
42. Young, *The Harmony of Illusions*, 136–37.
43. Ibid., 253.
44. Christine A. Courtois, *Recollections of Sexual Abuse: Treatment Principles and Guidelines* (New York: Norton, 1999); Kenneth S. Pope and Laura S. Brown, eds., *Recovered Memories of Abuse: Assessment, Therapies, Forensics* (Washington, D.C.: American Psychological Association, 1996); and Susan L. Riviere, *Memory of Childhood Trauma: A Clinician's Guide to the Literature* (New York: Guilford Press, 1996).
45. Young, *The Harmony of Illusions*, 216.
46. Ibid., 215.
47. Ibid., 166
48. Ibid., 204.
49. Ibid., 206.
50. Joe Sharkey, "Ideas and Trends: Memories of a War Never Fought," *New York Times,* June 28, 1998, E-6; and Jerry Lembcke, *CNN's Tailwind Tail: Inside Vietnam's Last Great Myth* (Lanham, Md.: Rowman and Littlefield, 2003), 1–11, 111–18, 138–42.
51. Graham Davies and Tim Dalgleish, *Recovered Memories: Seeking Middle Ground* (New York: Wiley, 2001); Robert A. Baker, ed., *Child Sexual Abuse and False Memory Syndrome* (Amherst, N.Y.: Prometheus Books, 1998); Martin A. Conway, ed., *Recovered Memories and False Memories* (New York: Oxford University Press, 1997); Steven J. Lynn and Kevin M. McConkey, eds., *Truth in Memory* (New York: Guilford Press, 1998); Kathy S. Pedzek and William Banks, eds., *The Recovered Memory/False Memory Debate* (San Diego: Academy Press, 1996); and William Rogers, *"Recovered Memory" and Other Assaults Upon the Mysteries of Consciousness: Hypnosis, Psychotherapy, Fraud and the Mass Media* (Jefferson, N.C.: McFarland Publishers, 1995).
52. Jerry Lembcke, *The Spitting Image Myth, Memory and the Legacy of Vietnam* (New York: New York University Press, 1998), 81.
53. B. G. Burkett and Glenna Whitley, *Stolen Valor: How the Vietnam Generation Was Robbed of Its Heroes and Its History* (Dallas: Verity Press, 1998), 36–73.
54. Robin Pogrebin and Felicity Barringer, "CNN Retracts Report That U.S. Used Nerve Gas," *New York Times*, July 3, 1998, A1. Also see, www.cnn.com/tailwind.
55. Institute of Medicine Committee to Review the Health Effects in Vietnam Veterans of Exposure to Herbicides, *Veterans and Agent Orange: Health Effects of Herbicides Used in Vietnam* (Washington, D.C.: National Academy Press, 1994), 24–27; Fred Wilcox, *Waiting for an Army to Die: The Tragedy of Agent Orange* (New York: Random House, 1983), 31–43; and Nicosia, *Home to War,* 387.

56. Wilbur J. Scott, *The Politics of Readjustment*, 75–79.
57. Wilcox, *Waiting for an Army to Die*, 80; and Scott, *Vietnam Veterans Since the War*, 88.
58. Peter H. Schuck, *Agent Orange on Trial: Mass Toxic Disasters in the Courts* (Cambridge: Harvard University Press, 1986), 165.
59. Ibid.
60. Nicosia, *Home to War*, 573–75.
61. Scott, *The Politics of Readjustment*, 118.
62. Richard Severo and Lewis Milford, *The Wages of War: When American Soldiers Come Home—From Valley Forge to Vietnam* (New York: Simon and Schuster, 1989), 400.
63. David E. Bonior, Steven M. Champion, and Timothy S. Kelly, *The Vietnam Veteran: A History of Neglect* (New York: Praeger, 1984), 148–49.
64. Nicosia, *Home to War*, 592–93.
65. Ibid., 602.
66. Institute of Medicine, *Veterans and Agent Orange*, 6.
67. Institute of Medicine Committee to Review the Health Effects in Vietnam Veterans of Exposure to Herbicides, *Veterans and Agent Orange: Update 2002* (Washington, D.C.: National Academy Press, 2003), 8.
68. Nicosia, *Home to War*, 617.

CHAPTER 5

1. Jan C. Scruggs and Joel L. Swerdlow, *To Heal a Nation: The Vietnam Veterans Memorial* (New York: Harper and Row, 1985), 7.
2. Patrick Hagopian, "The Social Memory of the Vietnam War," Ph.D. dissertation, Johns Hopkins University, 1994, 288.
3. Scruggs and Swerdlow, *To Heal a Nation*, 16.
4. Ibid., 289.
5. "Remarks on Signing S. J. Res. 119 [Vietnam Veterans Memorial Bill]," July 1, 1980. *Public Papers of the President of the United States, Jimmy Carter, May 24–September 26, 1980* (Washington, D.C.: Government Printing Office, 1981), 1270–71.
6. Ibid., 1268–69.
7. Philip Caputo, *A Rumor of War* (New York: Ballantine, 1977), 212–13; and John Wheeler, *Touched with Fire: The Future of the Vietnam Generation* (New York: Avon Books, 1984), 65.
8. James M. Mayo, *War Memorials as Political Landscape: The American Experience and Beyond* (New York: Praeger, 1988), 201.
9. Maya Ying Lin, "Design Competition: Winning Designer's Statement," (Washington, D.C.: Vietnam Veterans Memorial Fund, 1982); and Hagopian, "The Social Memory of the Vietnam War," 302–4.
10. Fred Turner, *Echoes of Combat: The Vietnam War and American Memory* (New York: Anchor, Doubleday, 1998), 178–79; Arnold R. Isaacs, *Vietnam Shadows: The War, Its Ghosts, and Its Legacy* (Baltimore: Johns Hopkins University Press, 1997), 2–3; and Keith Beattie, *The Scar That Binds: American Culture and the Vietnam War* (New York: New York University Press, 1998), 45–46.

11. Hagopian, "The Social Memory of the Vietnam War," 302–4; Christopher Buckley, "The Wall," *Esquire*, September 1985, 67; and Kristin Ann Hess, *Carried to the Wall: American Memory and the Vietnam Veterans Memorial* (Berkeley: University of California Press, 1998), 16.

12. Ibid., 17–18; and Marita Sturken, *Tangled Memories: The Vietnam War, the AIDS Epidemic, and the Politics of Remembering* (Berkeley: University of California Press, 1997), 52, 56.

13. Piehler, *Remembering War the American Way*, 177.

14. Sturken, *Tangled Memories*, 17.

15. Ibid.

16. Mayo, *War Memorials as Political Landscape*, 15.

17. Ibid., 22; Laura Palmer, *Shrapnel in the Heart: Letters and Remembrances from the Vietnam Veterans Memorial* (New York: Random House, 1987), 108, 116–17, 133, 149; Sal Lopes, ed., *The Wall: Images and Offerings from the Vietnam Veterans Memorial* (New York: Collins, 1987); and Michael Katakis, *The Vietnam Veterans Memorial* (New York: Crown, 1988), 6, 19, 58, 63, 69.

18. Kristin Ann Hass, *Carried to the Wall: American Memory and the Vietnam Veterans Memorial* (Berkeley: University of California Press, 1998), 26–30.

19. Ibid., and Patrick Hagopian, review of "Personal Legacy: The Healing of a Nation," *Journal of American History* 82, 1 (June 1995), 159–60.

20. Hagopian, "The Social Memory of the Vietnam War," 316–20.

21. Ibid.

22. "Remarks at a Memorial Day Ceremony at the Vietnam Veterans Memorial, May 31, 1993." *Public Papers of the Presidents, William J. Clinton, 1993* (Washington, D.C.: Government Printing Office, 1994), 786.

23. Linda Wheeler, "Sale of T-Shirts on Mall to End," *Washington Post*, August 19, 1997.

24. Hagopian, "The Social Memory of the Vietnam War," 335, 446; and Hess, *Carried to the Wall*, 19.

25. Quoted in Mayo, *War Memorials as Political Landscape*, 200.

26. Hagopian, "The Social Memory of the Vietnam War," 220–25, 338–43; and Jerry L. Strait and Sandra S. Strait, *Vietnam War Memorials: An Illustrated Reference Guide to Veterans Tributes Throughout the United States* (Jefferson, N.C.: McFarland Publishers, 1988), 8–10.

27. James Fallows, "What Did You Do in the Class War, Daddy?" *Washington Monthly*, October 1975, 5–19. James Fallows, *More Like Us: Making America Great Again* (Boston: Houghton Mifflin, 1989), 126–28.

28. "Congressional Chickenhawks," in www.liberalslikechrist.org/about/chickenhawks/html

29. Lewis B. Puller, Jr., *Fortunate Son: The Autobiography of Lewis B. Puller, Jr.* (New York: Grove Weidenfeld, 1991), 295.

30. Jane Mayer, "Vietnam Service Isn't on the Resumes of Some Vocal, Middle-Aged Hawks," *Wall Street Journal*, February 11, 1985, 10.

31. Marc Jason Gilbert, "Broadening the Horizons of a Course on the American War in Vietnam," in Marc Jason Gilbert, ed., *The Vietnam War: Teaching Approaches and Resources* (New York: Greenwood Press, 1991), 79.

32. Quoted in Joe P. Dunn, "The State of the Field: How Vietnam is Being Taught," www.vietnam.ttu.edu/vetanmcenter/events/1996. See also Walter Capps, "On

Teaching Today's Students about the Vietnam War," *Federation Review* 8 (May–June 1985): 10–13 and Capps, *The Unfinished War: Vietnam and the American Conscience* (Boston: Beacon Press, 1982).

33. "Speakers' Toolkit," www.wcpss./netcommunity-in-the-classroom/vietnam.
34. J. Russell McGoodwin's lectures and slides, History 4166, The War in Vietnam and Its Legacy, University of Colorado, Boulder, March 11, 13, 2001.
35. Peter Steinhauer, Sr.'s lectures and slides, History 4166, The War in Vietnam and Its Legacy, University of Colorado, Boulder, October 25, December 7, 2001.
36. Kali Tal, "When History Talks Back: The Voice of the Veteran," in Gilbert, ed., *The Vietnam War: Teaching Approaches and Resources*, 162, 165.
37. Steve Potts, "Using Primary Sources," in Gilbert, ed., *The Vietnam War: Teaching Approaches and Resources*, 192.
38. Author interviews with Peter Steinhauer, Sr., in Boulder, Colorado, October 18, 1994; October 17, 1998; and December 3, 2000.
39. Author's visits to Vietnam with groups of University of Colorado alumni, March 1999 and March 2001.
40. Seth Mydans, "Cu Chi Journal; Visit the Vietcong's World: Americans Welcome," *New York Times*, July 7, 1999, A4.

CHAPTER 6

1. Jeremy Hein, *From Vietnam, Laos and Cambodia: A Refugee Experience in the United States* (New York: Twayne, 1995), 11–15; and Jeremy Hein, *States and International Migration: The Incorporation of Indochinese Refugees in the United States and France* (Boulder, Colo.: Westview Press, 1993), 123.
2. Keith William Nolan, *Battle for Hue: Tet, 1968* (Novato, Calif.: Presidio Press, 1983); Stanley Karnow, *Vietnam: A History* (New York: Penguin Books, 1991), 543–44; and Lansdale to Bunker, February 27, 1968. *Foreign Relations of the United States, 1964–1968 Vol. VI, Vietnam, January–August 1968* (Washington, D.C.: Government Printing Office, 2002), 256–57.
3. Larry Berman, *No Peace, No Honor: Nixon, Kissinger, and Betrayal in Vietnam* (New York: Free Press, 2001), 271; and Robert D. Schulzinger, *A Time for War: The United States and Vietnam, 1941–1975* (New York: Oxford University Press, 1997), 326–27.
4. W. Courtland Robinson, *Terms of Refuge: The Indochinese Exodus and the International Response* (New York: Zed Books, 1998), 18.
5. James G. Gimpel and James F. Edward, Jr., *The Congressional Politics of Immigration Reform* (Boston: Allyn and Bacon, 1999), 119–20; Hein, *From Vietnam, Laos and Cambodia*, 15–25; and Hein, *States and International Migration*, 23–24.
6. Gimpel and Edwards, *The Congressional Politics of Immigration Reform*, 120.
7. Robinson, *Terms of Refuge*, 19.
8. Hein, *States and International Migration*, 24–29.
9. Robinson, *Terms of Refuge*, 22.
10. Ibid., 46.
11. Ibid., 47.

12. Bruce Grant, *The Boat People: An Age Investigation with Bruce Grant* (New York: Penguin, 1978), 72.
13. Robinson, *Terms of Refuge*, 61.
14. Ibid., 50.
15. Ibid., 51.
16. Grant, *The Boat People*, 76.
17. Keith St. Cartmail, *Exodus Indochina* (Exeter, N.H.: Heineman, 1983), 123.
18. Robinson, *Terms of Refuge*, 52–53.
19. Ibid.
20. Paul James Rutledge, *The Vietnamese Experience in America* (Bloomington: Indiana University Press, 1992), 18.
21. Ibid., 20
22. Ibid., 21–22.
23. Hein, *From Vietnam, Laos and Cambodia*, 51–52.
24. Grant, *The Boat People*, 161–62.
25. Rutledge, *The Vietnamese Experience in America*, 40–41.
26. Ibid.
27. Hein, *From Vietnam, Laos and Cambodia*, 52.
28. Grant, *The Boat People*, 163.
29. Rutledge, *The Vietnamese Experience in America*, 41.
30. Hein, *From Vietnam, Laos and Cambodia*, 75–76.
31. Ibid., 78.
32. Rutledge, *The Vietnamese Experience in America*, 42.
33. Hein, *From Vietnam, Laos and Cambodia*, 79; and Rutledge, *The Vietnamese Experience in America,* 43.
34. Hein, *From Vietnam, Laos and Cambodia*, 80.
35. Rutledge, *The Vietnamese Experience in America*, 44.
36. Ibid., 43.
37. Ibid., 120.
38. Ibid.
39. Bruce R. Dunning, "Vietnamese in America: The Adaptation of the 1975–1979 Arrivals," in David W. Haines, ed., *Refugees as Immigrants: Cambodians, Laotians and Vietnamese in America* (Totowa, N.J.: Roman and Littlefield, 1989), 77.
40. Ibid., 78.
41. Ibid., 85.
42. Rutledge, *The Vietnamese Experience in America*, 122–23.
43. Hein, *From Vietnam, Laos and Cambodia*, 127.
44. Ibid., 121.
45. Ibid., 123.
46. Rutledge, *The Vietnamese Experience in America*, 132.
47. Ibid., 125.
48. Ibid., 127.
49. John K. Whitmore, Marcella Trautmann, and Nathan Caplan, "The Social Cultural Bases for the Economic and Educational Success of Southeast Asian Refugees (1978–1982 Arrivals)," in Haines, ed, *Refugees as Immigrants: Cambodians, Laotians and Vietnamese in America*, 131.
50. Rutledge, *The Vietnamese Experience in America*, 127.

51. Whitmore, Trautmann, and Caplan, "The Social Cultural Bases for the Economic and Educational Success of Southeast Asian Refugees (1978–1982 Arrivals)," in David W. Haines, ed., *Refugees as Immigrants: Cambodians. Laotians and Vietnamese in America* (Totowa, N.J.: Roman and Littlefield, 1989), 130.
52. Rutledge, *The Vietnamese Experience in America*, 128.
53. Hein, *From Vietnam, Laos and Cambodia*, 123.
54. Rutledge, *The Vietnamese Experience in America*, 131.
55. Ibid., 137–138.
56. Hein, *From Vietnam, Laos and Cambodia*, 104.
57. Rutledge, *The Vietnamese Experience in America*, 142.
58. Hein, *From Vietnam, Laos and Cambodia*, 102–3.
59. Andrew Lam "Vietnamese Diaspora and California," in Marcia Eymann and Charles Wollenberg, eds., *What's Going On: California and the Vietnam Era* (Berkeley: Oakland Museum of California and University of California Press, 2004), 189.
60. Hein, *From Vietnam, Laos and Cambodia*, 103, 106.
61. Ibid., 103.
62. Ibid., 104.
63. "Vietnamese Activists Push for Old Flag," May 23, 2003, http://cnn.usnews.printthis.clickability.com/pt/cpt?action.
64. David Reyes, "Vietnam War Memorial Stirs Memories," http:/ntuan.8m.com/memorial/inaug_e.htm.

CHAPTER 7

1. John Newman, ed., *Vietnam War Literature: An Annotated Bibliography of Imaginative Works About Americans Fighting in Vietnam*, 3d ed. (Lanham, Md.: Scarecrow Press, 1996), ix.
2. Philip Beidler, *Rewriting America: Vietnam Authors in Their Generation* (Athens: University of Georgia Press, 1991), 3; and Thomas Myers, *Walking Point: American Narratives of Vietnam* (New York: Oxford University Press, 1988), 26.
3. Graham Greene, *The Quiet American* (New York: Penguin, 1977), 140.
4. Ibid., 32.
5. Ibid., 95.
6. Ibid., 75.
7. Ibid., 36.
8. Myers, *Walking Point*, 39.
9. Norman Mailer, *Why Are We in Vietnam: A Novel* (New York: Putman, 1967).
10. Ibid., 31.
11. Ibid., 203.
12. Ibid., 208.
13. Philip Melling, *Vietnam in American Literature* (Boston: Twayne Publishers, 1990), 117.
14. Michiko Kakutani, "Novelists and Vietnam: The War Goes On," *New York Times Book Review*, April 15,1984, 1.
15. Samuel Hynes, *The Soldiers' Tale: Bearing Witness to Modern War* (New York: Penguin, 1997), 206–7.

16. Tim O'Brien, *If I Die in a Combat Zone, Box Me Up and Ship Me Home* (New York: Delacorte Press, 1973), 26.
17. Ibid., 73.
18. Tim O'Brien, *Going After Caccioto* (New York: Delacorte Press, 1978), 28.
19. Ibid., 82.
20. Ibid., 304.
21. Tim O'Brien, *The Nuclear Age* (New York: Knopf, 1985), 8.
22. Tim O'Brien, *The Things They Carried: A Work of Fiction* (Boston: Houghton Mifflin, 1990), 14.
23. Ibid., 38.
24. Ibid., 15.
25. Ibid., 178.
26. Tim O'Brien, *In the Lake of the Woods* (Boston: Houghton Mifflin, 1994), 38–39.
27. Ibid., 27.
28. Ibid., 64.
29. Ibid., 68.
30. Robert Stone, *Dog Soldiers: A Novel* (Boston: Houghton Mifflin, 1974), 57.
31. Ibid., 42.
32. Ibid., 57.
33. Ibid.
34. Robert Stone, *A Flag for Sunrise: A Novel* (New York: Knopf, 1981), 119.
35. Ibid., 109.
36. Ibid., 206.
37. Gustav Hasford, *The Short-Timers* (New York: Bantam Books, 1979), 74.
38. Ibid., 73.
39. Ibid., 74.
40. Ibid., 59.
41. Ibid., 60.
42. John M. Del Vecchio, *The 13th Valley* (New York: Ballantine Books, 1982).
43. Ibid., 506.
44. Ibid., 579.
45. Ibid., 228.
46. Ibid., 589.
47. John Hellmann, *American Myth and the Legacy of Vietnam* (New York: Columbia University Press, 1986), 134.
48. Myers, *Walking Point*, 61.
49. Larry Heinemann, *Paco's Story* (New York: Penguim, 1987, 1989), 3.
50. Ibid., foreword.
51. Ibid., 126.
52. Larry Heinemann, *Close Quarters* (New York: Farrar, Straus, and Giroux, 1977).
53. Heinemann, *Paco's Story*, 202.
54. Ibid., 205.
55. Ibid., 207.
56. Ibid., 208–9.
57. Ibid., 156.
58. Ibid.
59. Ibid., 159.

60. Bao Ninh, *The Sorrow of War: A Novel of North Vietnam* (New York: Riverhead Books, 1996). The Vietnamese original was published in 1991; the English translation first appeared in 1993.
61. Robert Brigham, "Revolutionary Heroism in Postwar Vietnam," In Charles E. Neu, ed., *After Vietnam: Legacies of a Lost War* (Baltimore: Johns Hopkins University Press, 2000), 101.
62. Ninh, *The Sorrow of War*, 50.
63. Ibid., 75.
64. Duong Thu Huong, *Novel Without a Name* (New York: Morrow, 1995), 31; and Brigham, "Revolutionary Heroism," 101.
65. Robert Olen Butler authored the following books: *The Alleys of Eden* (New York: Holt, 1981); *Sun Dogs* (New York: Holt, 1994); and *On Distant Ground* (New York: Knopf, 1985).
66. Robert Olen Butler, *The Deuce* (New York: Simon and Schuster, 1989), 7.
67. Ibid., 22.
68. Robert Olen Butler, *A Good Scent from a Strange Mountain* (New York: H. Holt, 1992), 66.
69. Ibid.
70. Ibid., 72.
71. C.D.B. Bryan, "Barely Suppressed Screams: Getting a Bead on Vietnam Literature," *Harper's*, June 1984, 68.
72. Philip Caputo, *A Rumor of War* (New York: Holt, Rinehart, and Winston, 1977), xii–xiii.
73. Winston Groom, *Better Times Than These: A Novel* (New York : Summit Books, 1978), 221.
74. Ibid., 261.
75. Ibid., 75.
76. Ibid., 228.
77. James Webb, *Fields of Fire: A Novel* (Englewood Cliffs: Prentice Hall, 1978), 33.
78. Ibid., 233–34.
79. Ibid., 283.
80. Ibid., 175.
81. Ibid., 1.
82. Ibid., 338.
83. James Webb, *A Country Such as This: A Novel* (Garden City: Doubleday, 1983), 337.
84. Ibid., 273.
85. Ibid., 359.
86. Ibid., 88–89.
87. Ibid., 360–61.
88. David A. Willson, "Novels," in John A. Newman, ed., *Vietnam War Literature: An Annotated Bibliography of Imaginative Works About Americans Fighting in Vietnam*, 3d ed. (Lanham, Md.: Scarecrow Press, 1996), 212.
89. Other titles published by Star with similar sexual and sadistic content include *Vietnamese Pleasure Girls* (1983), *Viet Cong Slave Camp* (1983), *Abused Vietnamese Virgins* (1984), and *Teen Sex Slaves of Saigon* (1984).

CHAPTER 8

1. Jeremy M. Devine, *Vietnam at 24 Frames a Second: A Critical and Thematic Analysis of Over 400 Films About the Vietnam War* (Jefferson, N.C.: McFarland Publishers, 1995), 8.
2. Albert Auster and Leonard Quart, *How the War Was Remembered: Hollywood and Vietnam* (New York: Praeger, 1988), 31; Linda Dittmar and Gene Michaud, "America's Vietnam War Films: Marching Toward Denial," in Dittmar and Michaud, eds., *From Hanoi to Hollywood: The Vietnam War in American Film* (New Brunswick: Rutgers University Press, 1990), 1–19; and Leo Crawley, "The War about the War: Vietnam Films and American Myth," in Dittmar and Michaud, eds., *From Hanoi to Hollywood*, 69–80.
3. Randy Roberts and James Olson, *John Wayne: American* (New York: The Free Press, 1995), vii, 537; and Michael Anderegg, "Hollywood and Vietnam: John Wayne and Jane Fonda as Discourse," in Anderegg, ed., *Inventing Vietnam: The War in Film and Television* (Philadelphia: Temple University Press, 1991), 19.
4. Roberts and Olson, *John Wayne*, 547–48.
5. Devine, *Vietnam at 24 Frames a Second*, 104–5.
6. Ibid., 140; and John Carlos Rowe, "Eyewitness: Documentary Stakes in the American Representations of Vietnam," in John Carlos Rowe and Rick Berg, eds., *The Vietnam War and American Culture* (New York: Columbia University Press, 1991), 155–56.
7. Devine, *Vietnam at 24 Frames a Second*, 145; and Leonard Quart, "The Deer Hunter: The Superman in Vietnam," in Dittmar and Michaud, eds., *From Hanoi to Hollywood*, 159–70.
8. Devine, *Vietnam at 24 Frames a Second*, 170.
9. Anderegg, "Hollywood and Vietnam," 22–23. As late as 2002 a book appeared demanding that she be tried for treason. Henry Mark Holzer and Erika Holzer, *"Aid and Comfort": Jane Fonda in North Vietnam* (Jefferson, N.C.: McFarland Publishers, 2002).
10. Devine, *Vietnam at 24 Frames a Second*, 154.
11. Ibid., 156.
12. Susan Jeffords, *The Remasculinization of America: Gender and the Vietnam War* (Bloomington: Indiana University Press, 1989), 146.
13. Roberts and Olson, *John Wayne*, 554; Anderegg, "Hollywood and Vietnam," 29, and Michael Selig, "Boys Will Be Men: Oedipal Drama in *Coming Home*," in Dittmar and Michaud, eds., *From Hanoi to Hollywood*, 189–203.
14. Devine, *Vietnam at 24 Frames a Second*, 189.
15. Dialogue from Scene 1, *Apocalypse Now Redux*. DVD. Los Angeles: Paramount, 2001.
16. Harry W. Haines, "The Pride is Back: *Rambo, Magnum PI*, and the Return Trip to Vietnam," in Richard Morris and Peter Ehrenhaus, eds., *Cultural Legacies of Vietnam: Uses of the Past in the Present* (Norwood, N.J.: Ablex Publishing Corp., 1990), 99–123; Harry Haines, "'They Were Called and They Went': The Political Rehabilitation of the Vietnam Veteran," in Dittmar and Michaud, eds., *From Hanoi to Hollywood*, 81–100; and Rick Berg and John Carlos Rowe, "The Vietnam War and American Memory," in John Carlos Rowe and Rick Berg, eds., *The Vietnam War and American Culture* (New York: Columbia University Press, 1991), 9–10.

17. Jeffords, *The Remasculinization of America,* 151–53. These pages contain an astute reading of the POW rescue movies. The entire book is a subtle study of the way in which Americans refought the war during the Reagan years. See also Susan Jeffords, "Reproducing Fathers: Gender and the Vietnam War in American Culture," in Richard Morris and Peter Ehrenhaus, eds., *Cultural Legacies of Vietnam: Uses of the Past in the Present* (Norwood, N.J.: Ablex Publishing Corp., 1990), 124; Jeffords, "Tattoos, Scars, Diaries, and Writing Masculinity," in John Carlos Rowe and Rick Berg, eds., *The Vietnam War and American Culture* (New York: Columbia University Press, 1991), 208–25; George Dionisopoulos, "Images of Warriors Returned: Vietnam Veterans in Popular American Films," in Rowe and Berg, eds., *The Vietnam War and American Culture*, 80–98; and Keith Beattie, *The Scar That Binds: American Culture and Vietnam War* (New York: New York University Press, 1998), 22–23.
18. Fred Turner, *Echoes of Combat, The Vietnam War in American Memory* (New York: Anchor Books, Doubleday, 1998), 90.
19. Devine, *Vietnam at 24 Frames a Second*, 233.
20. Ibid., 234.
21. Ibid., 257.
22. Ibid.
23. Ibid., 259.
24. Ibid., 251; and Clyde Taylor, "The Colonialist Subtext in Platoon," in Linda Dittmar and Michaud, eds., *From Hanoi to Hollywood*, 170–74.
25. Devine, *Vietnam at 24 Frames a Second*, 251.
26. Turner, *Echoes of Combat*, 139.
27. Devine, *Vietnam at 24 Frames a Second*, 260.
28. Auster and Quart, *How the War Was Remembered*, 144.
29. Devine, *Vietnam at 24 Frames a Second,* 269; and Barry Dornfeld, "Dear America: Transparency, Authority and Interpretation in a Vietnam War Documentary," in Linda Dittmar and Michaud, eds., *From Hanoi to Hollywood,* 283–98.
30. Daniel Miller, "Primetime Television's Tour of Duty," in Anderegg, ed., *Inventing Vietnam: The War in Film and Television* (Philadelphia: Temple University Press, 1991), 170.
31. Carolyn Reed Vartainian, "Women Next Door: China Beach," in Anderegg, ed., *Inventing Vietnam: The War in Film and Television* (Philadelphia: Temple University Press, 1991), 190.
32. See Daniel Hallin, "Vietnam on Television" and Michael Saenz, "China Beach" at www.museumtv/archives/ev/C/html/chinabeach; and Leah R. Vande Berg, "China Beach, Prime Time War in the Post Feminist Age: An Example of Patriarchy in a Different Voice," *Western Journal of Communication* 57, 3 (Summer 1993), 349–53.
33. Devine, *Vietnam at 24 Frames a Second*, 303.
34. Ibid., 313.
35. Ibid., 314.
36. Rita Kemley, review of *Forrest Gump, Washington Post*, July 6, 1994.
37. Richard Alleva, review of *Forrest Gump, Commonweal* (September 23, 1994): 18.
38. Hal Hanson, "Forrest Gump, Our National Folk Zero," *Washington Post*, August 14, 1994.

39. Dialogue for *We Were Soldiers*, quoted at http://www.weweresoldiers.com/splash.html.

40. Andrew Lam, "Quiet American Irony," Pacific News Service, February 20, 2003, www.altenet.org.

41. Noy Thrupkaew, "Paved with Good Intentions," *The American Prospect*, April 2003, 45.

42. Neil McDonald, "Vietnamese Shadows, American Reflections," *Quadrant* 47, 3 (March 2003): 68.

43. Kenneth Turan, "An Elegant Story of Corruptibility," *Los Angles Times*, November 22, 2002.

44. Review of *The Quiet American*, mrcranky.com/movies/quietamerican/html.

CHAPTER 9

1. Robert J. McMahon, "SHAFR Presidential Address: Contested Memory: The Vietnam War and American Society, 1975–2001," *Diplomatic History* 26, 2 (spring 2002):171; and Fred Turner, *Echoes of Combat: The Vietnam War in American Memory* (New York: Anchor Books, Doubleday, 1998), 63–64.

2. Raymond L. Garthoff, *Détente and Confrontation: American-Soviet Relations from Nixon to Reagan* (Washington, D.C.: Brookings Institution Press, revised edition 1994), 505–9.

3. Jussi Hanhimaki, *The Flawed Architect: Henry Kissinger and American Foreign Policy* (New York: Oxford University Press, 2004), 412.

4. H. W. Brands, *Since Vietnam: The United States in World Affairs, 1973–1995* (New York: McGraw Hill, 1996), 18–19.

5. Quoted in Gaddis Smith, *Morality, Reason, and Power: American Diplomacy in the Carter Years* (New York: Hill and Wang, 1986), 29–30.

6. Robert J. McMahon, "Rationalizing Defeat: The Vietnam War in American Presidential Discourse, 1975–1995," *Rhetoric and Public Affairs* 2, 4 (1999): 533–35.

7. Ibid., 535; and *Public Papers of the Presidents, Administration of James E. Carter, 1977* (Washington, D.C.: Government Printing Office, 1978), 954–62.

8. John Ehrman, *The Rise of Neoconservatism* (New Haven: Yale University Press, 1995), 61–62, 97.

9. *Public Papers of the Presidents, Ronald Reagan, 1985* (Washington, D.C.: Government Printing Office, 1986), 454.

10. Raymond Bonner, *Weakness and Deceit: U.S. Policy and El Salvador* (New York: Times Books, 1984), 230, 244–51.

11. Theodore Draper, *A Very Thin Line: The Iran-Contra Affairs* (New York: Hill and Wang, 1991), passim; and Robert Timberg, *The Nightingale's Song* (New York: Touchstone Books, 1996), 411–16.

12. Kenneth E. Sharpe, "The Post-Vietnam Formula Under Siege: The Imperial Presidency and Central America," *Political Science Quarterly* 102, 4 (1987): 567.

13. Norman Podhoretz, *Why We Were in Vietnam* (New York: Simon and Schuster, 1983).

14. Timothy Lomparis, *From People's War to People's Rule: Insurgency, Intervention, and the Lessons of Vietnam* (Chapel Hill: University of North Carolina Press, 1996).

15. Michael Lind, *Vietnam: The Necessary War* (New York: The Free Press, 1999).
16. George C. Herring, "The Impact of the Vietnam War on the U.S. Military," in Charles E. Neu, ed., *After Vietnam: Legacies of a Lost War* (Baltimore: Johns Hopkins University Press, 2000), 66.
17. Harry G. Summers, Jr., *On Strategy: A Critical Analysis of the Vietnam War* (Navato, Calif.: Presidio Press, 1982), 94; James Kitfield, *Prodigal Soldiers: How the Generation of Officers Born of Vietnam Revolutionized the American Style of War* (New York: Simon and Schuster, 1995), 203; and Arnold R. Isaacs, *Vietnam Shadows: The War, Its Ghosts and Its Legacy* (Baltimore: Johns Hopkins University Press, 1997), 68–69.
18. Harry Summers, *On Strategy: A Critical Analysis of the Vietnam War* (Novato, Calif.: Presidio Press, 1982).
19. Herring, "The Impact of the Vietnam War on the U.S. Military," 59.
20. Philip Davidson, *Vietnam at War: The History, 1946–1975* (Novato, Calif.: Presidio Press, 1988); and Ulysses S. Grant Sharp, *Strategy for Defeat* (San Rafael, Calif.: Presidio Press, 1978).
21. George P. Shultz, *Turmoil and Triumph: My Years as Secretary of State* (New York: Scribner's, 1993), 654; and Shultz, "Terrorism and the Modern World," *Department of State Bulletin* 84, 2093 (December 1984): 14–17.
22. Colin L. Powell and Joseph E. Persico, *My American Journey* (New York: Random House, 1995), 303
23. Inaugural Address, January 20, 1989. *Public Papers of the Presidents, George Bush, 1989* (Washington, D.C.: Government Printing Office, 1990), 1–4.
24. Bob Woodward, *The Commanders* (New York: Simon and Schuster, 1991), 324.
25. Ibid., 339.
26. Ibid., 324.
27. Powell and Persico, *My American Journey*, 489–90.
28. "Excerpts from Bush News Conference," *New York Times*, March 2, 1991, 5; and Isaacs, *Vietnam Shadows*, 82–84.
29. David Halberstam, *War in a Time of Peace: Bush, Clinton, and the Generals* (New York: Touchstone Books, 2002), 10–23.
30. Mark T. Clark, "End Games: Reconsidering What it Means to Make War," November 2, 2002, www.claremont.org/writings/precents/20021119clark.html.
31. Samantha Power, *"A Problem from Hell": America in the Age of Genocide* (New York: Basic Books, 2002), 283–85, 316–17, 373; and Madeleine Albright, *Madame Secretary: A Memoir* (New York: Hyperion, 2003), 177–81.
32. Halberstam, *War in a Time of Peace*, 136.
33. Powell and Persico, *My American Life*, 576.
34. Albright, *Madame Secretary*, 181; and Richard Holbrooke, *To End a War* (New York: Random House, 1998), 217.
35. Holbrooke, *To End a War*, 262–87.
36. Roland Paris, "Kosovo and the Metaphor War," *Political Science Quarterly* 117, 3 (fall 2002): 423–50.
37. Address by Senator John McCain at the Georgia Public Policy Institute, Atlanta, Georgia, April 19, 1999, http://mccain.senate.gov/index.cfm?fuseaction=Newscenter.ViewPressRelease&Content_id=962.
38. Ivo H. Daalder and Michael E. O'Hanlon, *Winning Ugly: NATO's War to Save Kosovo* (Washington, D.C.: Brookings Institution Press, 2000), 170–75.

39. R.W. Apple, Jr., "Quagmire Recalled: Afghanistan as Vietnam," *New York Times,* October 31, 2001, B1.
40. "Another Vietnam? Critics Say Iraq War Is Dredging Up Memories of '60s Quagmire," *Detroit Free Press*, September 20, 2003, 1.
41. David Firestone, "Bush Likely to Get Money He Sought," *New York Times*, September 9, 2003, A1.
42. "Another Vietnam?" *Detroit Free Press*, September 20, 2003, 1.
43. "U.S. Sen. Kerry Bush 'Sidestepping the Truth' on Iraq," *Wall Street Journal*, October 29, 2003, wsj.com.
44. Douglas Brinkley, *Tour of Duty: John Kerry and the Vietnam War* (New York: William Murrow, 2004), 315.
45. "Could Vietnam Win the White House?," *The Guardian*, February 3, 2004.
46. "'We Have It in Our Power to Change the World Again,' Kerry's Acceptance," *New York Times*, July 30, 2004.
47. "Responses to Swift Boat Veterans for Truth Ads," http://www.gwu.edu~action/2004/ads04/response.html/; "Records Counter a Critic of Kerry," *Washington Post*, August 19, 2004, A1; Center for the Study of Elections and Democracy, Brigham Young University, "527s Had a Substantial Impact on the Ground and Air Wars in 2004," December 12, 2004, http://www.public-org/docs/527s/pvfc.pnf;Jodi Wilgoren, "Truth Be Told: The Vietnam Crossfire Hurt Kerry More," *New York Times*, September 24, 2004, A24; Errol Morris, "Where's the Rest of Him," *New York Times*, January 18, 2005, A21; Susan Meadows, "Target Kerry," Review of John E. O'Neill and Jerome E. Corsi, *Unfit for Command: Swift Boat Veterans Speak Out*, *New York Times Book Review*, October 10, 2004, 6.
48. Thomas Friedman, "It's No Vietnam," *New York Times*, October 30, 2003, A-29.
49. Robert Bartley, "Iraq: Another Vietnam?" *Wall Street Journal*, November 3, 2003, http://online.wsj.com.
50. Craig R. Whitney, "Watching Iraq, Seeing Vietnam," *New York Times*, November 9, 2003, Section 4, 1.
51. U.S. Senate, Select Committee on Intelligence, *Report on the U.S. Intelligence Community's Pre-war Intelligence Assessments on Iraq*, July 7, 2004. http://intelligence.Senate.gov.
52. National Commission on Terrorist Attacks Upon the United States, *The 9/11 Commission Report* (New York: W. W. Norton, 2004), 334–36.
53. Senator Edward M. Kennedy Speech at the Brookings Institution, Washington, D.C., April 5, 2004.
54. Andrew J. Bacevich, "Algeria, not Vietnam, Is Apt Analogy for Iraq War," *Los Angeles Times*, April 9, 2004.
55. "The World Today," Australian Broadcasting Corporation, Defense experts Debate Iraq-Vietnam Comparison, April 8, 2004, http://www.abc.net.au/worldtoday/content/2004/s1084174.html.
56. Seymour M. Hersh, "Torture at Abu Ghraib," *The New Yorker*, May 10, 2004. Posted April 30, 2004, http//:www.TheNewYorker.com; and Hersh, "The Gray Zone," *The New Yorker*, May 24, 2004. Posted May 15, 2004, http://www.TheNewYorker.com.
57. "Power Transfer in Iraq Doesn't Alter Perceptions of Iraq War," The Gallup Poll, July 19, 2004, http://www.gallup.con/content.
58. Melvin R. Laird, "Iraq: Learning the Lessons of Vietnam, *Foreign Affairs* 84, 6 (November/December 2005), 26, 25.

59. "Gallop Poll on Iraq War," at http://www.cnn.com/2005/POLITICS/06/27/iraq.poll/index.html, and http://www.cnn.com/2005/US/05/03/iraq.poll/.
60. Douglas K. Daniel, "Sen. Hagel Says Iraq Looking Like Vietnam," AP Story, August 22, 2005. http://ABCnewsgo.com.Politics/wireStory?id-1058034.
61. John Mueller, "The Iraq Syndrome," *Foreign Affairs* 84, 6 (November/December 2005), 44, 53.
62. David L. Anderson, "SHAFR Presidential Address: One Vietnam War Should Be Enough and Other Reflections on Diplomatic History and the Making of Foreign Policy," *Diplomatic History* 30, 1 (January 2006): 21.

Bibliography

MANUSCRIPT SOURCES

Morton Blackwell Files. Ronald Reagan Library (RRL). Simi Valley, California.
Zbigniew Brzezinski Files. Jimmy Carter Library (JCL). Atlanta, Georgia.
Richard Childress Files. RRL.
Alison Fortier Files. RRL.
Richard Russell conversation. May 27, 1964, 10:55A.M. Lyndon B. Johnson Library (LBJL). Austin, Texas.
Ron Sable Files. RRL.
Adlai Stevenson conversations. May 27, 1964, 10:50A.M. LBJL.
U.S.-Vietnamese Negotiations. George Bush Library (GBL). College Station, Texas.

NEWSPAPERS/PERIODICALS

Detroit Free Press
The Economist
Far Eastern Economic Review
The Guardian (London)
Los Angeles Times
New York Times
Wall Street Journal

GOVERNMENT DOCUMENTS

Institute of Medicine. Committee to Review the Health Effects in Vietnam Veterans of Exposure to Herbicides. *Veterans and Agent Orange: Health Effects of Herbicides Used in Vietnam.* Washington, D.C.: National Academy Press, 1994.
———. *Veterans and Agent Orange: Update 2002.* Washington, D.C.: National Academy Press, 2003.
National Commission on Terrorist Attacks Upon the United States. *The 9/11 Commission Report.* New York: W. W. Norton, 2004.

Public Papers of the Presidents, James E. Carter, 1977. Washington D.C.: Government Printing Office, 1978.

Public Papers of the Presidents, George Bush, 1989. Washington, D.C.: Government Printing Office, 1990.

Public Papers of the Presidents, William J. Clinton, 1993. Washington, D.C.: Government Printing Office, 1994.

Public Papers of the Presidents, William J. Clinton, 1995. Washington, D.C.: Government Printing Office, 1996.

Public Papers of the Presidents, Ronald Reagan, 1985. Washington, D.C.: Government Printing Office, 1986.

Public Papers of the Presidents, Ronald Reagan, 1988–89. Washington, D.C.: Government Printing Office, 1991.

Senator Edward M. Kennedy Speech at the Brookings Institution, Washington, D.C., April 5, 2004.

Shultz, George P. "The Meaning of Vietnam." Address at the State Department, April 25, 1985. *Department of State Bulletin*, June 1985, 13–16.

———. "Terrorism and the Modern World." *Department of State Bulletin* 84, 2093 (December 1984): 14–17.

U.S. Department of State. *Foreign Relations of the United States, 1964–1968 Vol. VI, Vietnam, January–August 1968.* Washington, D.C.: Government Printing Office, 2002.

———. *The Problem of the Disabled in Vietnam: A Report to Non-Governmental Organizations Stemming from the Mission to Hanoi by Presidential Emissary General John W. Vessey (retired).* October 13, 1987.

U.S. House of Representatives. "An Agreement Between the United States and the Socialist Republic of Vietnam on Trade Relations." Message from the President of the United States. House Document 107–85. 107th Congress, 1st session. June 12, 2001.

———. Committee on International Relations. "Prelude to New Directions in United States-Vietnam Relations: The 2000 Bilateral Trade Agreement." Joint Hearing. 106th Congress, 2nd session. September 19, 2000.

———. Committee on Ways and Means. "United States-Vietnam Trade Relations." 106th Congress, 1st session. June 17, 1999.

———. Committee on Veterans Affairs. "Concerns of Vietnam War Veterans," Hearing. 101st Congress, 1st. session. May 3, 1989,

———. Committee on Veterans Affairs. *Readjustment Counseling.* 97th Congress, 1st session. April 8, 1981.

———. Committee on Veterans Affairs. *Legacies of Vietnam: Comparative Adjustment of Veterans and Their Peers: A Study Prepared for the Veterans' Administration.* March 9, 1981

———. Subcommittee on Asian and Pacific Affairs of the Committee on Foreign Affairs. "The Vessey Mission to Hanoi." 100th Congress, 1st session. September 30, 1987.

U.S. Senate. Select Committee on Intelligence. *Report on the U.S. Intelligence Community's Pre-war Intelligence Assessments on Iraq.*" July 7, 2004. Available from http://intelligence.Senate.gov.

———. Subcommittee on International Trade of the Committee on Finance. "Chronology of Normalization of Relations between the U.S. and Vietnam." 105th Congress, 2nd session. July 7, 1998.

————. Subcommittee on East Asian and Pacific Affairs. Committee on Foreign Relations. "U.S. Policy Toward Vietnam." 103rd Congress, 1st session. July 21, 1993.

————. "POW/MIAs Report of the Select Committee on POW/MIA Affairs." 103rd Congress, 1st session. January 13, 1993.

Veterans Administration. *Vet Center Program Guide*. January 6, 1988.

SECONDARY SOURCES

Albright, Madeleine. *Madame Secretary: A Memoir*. New York: Hyperion, 2003.

Alleva, Richard. "Review of 'Forrest Gump.'" *Commonweal*, 121, i16 (September 23, 1994): 17–18. www.altenet.org

Anderegg, Michael A. "Hollywood and Vietnam: John Wayne and Jane Fonda as Discourse." In *Inventing Vietnam: The War in Film and Television*, edited by Michael A. Anderegg. Philadelphia: Temple University Press, 1991.

Anderson, David L. "SHAFR Presidential Address: One Vietnam War Should Be Enough and Other Reflections on Diplomatic History and the Making of Foreign Policy," *Diplomatic History* 30, 1 (January 2006): 1–21.

————. "The Vietnam War." In *A Companion to American Foreign Relations*, edited by Robert D. Schulzinger. Malden, Mass.: Blackwell Publishing, 2003.

Auster, Albert, and Leonard Quart. *How the War Was Remembered: Hollywood and Vietnam*. New York: Praeger, 1988.

Babson, Oliver. "Diplomacy of Isolation: United States Unilateral Sanctions Policy and 1975–1995." WWS Case Study 4/02. Woodrow Wilson School of Public and International Affairs, Princeton University. January 16, 2002.

Baker, James A., III, and Thomas M. DeFrank. *The Politics of Diplomacy: Revolution, War, and Peace, 1989–1992*. New York: G.P. Putnam's Sons, 1995.

Baker, Robert A., ed. *Child Sexual Abuse and False Memory Syndrome*. Amherst, N.Y.: Prometheus Books, 1998.

Baldwin, Neil. "Going After the War." *Publishers Weekly*, February 11, 1983, 34–38.

Baskir, Lawrence M., and William A. Strauss. *Chance and Circumstance: The Draft, The War, and the Vietnam Generation*. New York: Knopf, 1978.

————. *Reconciliation after Vietnam: A Program of Relief for Vietnam Era Draft and Military Offenders*. Notre Dame, Ind.: University of Notre Dame Press, 1977.

Beattie, Keith. *The Scar that Binds: American Culture and the Vietnam War*. New York: New York University Press, 1998.

Beidler, Philip D. *American Literature and the Experience of Vietnam*. Athens: University of Georgia Press, 1982.

————. *Re-Writing America: Vietnam Authors in Their Generation*. Athens: University of Georgia Press, 1991.

Berg, Rick, and John Carlos Rowe. "The Vietnam War and American Memory." In *The Vietnam War and American Culture*, edited by John Carlos Rowe and Rick Berg. New York: Columbia University Press, 1991.

Berman, D. M. "Perspectives on the Teaching of Vietnam," *Social Studies* 77 (July–August 1986): 165–68.

Berman, Larry. *No Peace, No Honor: Nixon, Kissinger, and Betrayal in Vietnam*. New York: Free Press, 2001.

Berman, William C. *From the Center to the Edge: The Politics and Policies of the Clinton Administration.* Lanham, Md.: Rowman and Littlefield, 2001.

Beschloss, Michael, and Strobe Talbott. *At the Highest Levels: The Inside Story of the End of the Cold War.* Boston: Little, Brown, 1993.

Blair, Clay. *The Forgotten War: America in Korea, 1950–1953.* New York: Times Books, 1987.

Bonior, David E., Steven M. Champion, and Timothy S. Kelly. *The Vietnam Veteran: A History of Neglect.* New York: Praeger, 1984.

Bonner, Raymond. *Weakness and Deceit: U.S. Policy and El Salvador.* New York: Times Books, 1984.

Boyer, Paul. "Exotic Resonances: Hiroshima in American Memory." In *Hiroshima in History and Memory,* edited by Michael J. Hogan. New York: Cambridge University Press, 1996.

Bradley, Christie, N. "Teaching Our Longest War: Constructive Lessons from Vietnam." *English Journal* 75 (February 1986): 55–56.

Bradley, James, and Ron Powers. *Flags of our Fathers.* New York: Bantam Books, 2000.

Brands, H. W. *Since Vietnam: The United States in World Affairs, 1973–1995.* New York: McGraw Hill, 1996.

Bresnan, John. *From Dominoes to Dynamos: The Transformation of Southeast Asia.* New York: Council on Foreign Relations, 1994.

Brigham, Robert. "Revolutionary Heroism in Postwar Vietnam." In *After Vietnam: Legacies of a Lost War,* edited by Charles E. Neu. Baltimore: Johns Hopkins University Press, 2000.

Brinkley, Douglas. *Tour of Duty: John Kerry and the Vietnam War.* New York: William Morrow, 2004.

Brokaw, Tom. *The Greatest Generation.* New York: Random House, 1998.

Brown, Frederick Z. "Taking a Fresh Look at Indochina." *Foreign Service Journal* 67 (July 1990): 26–32.

———. "The U.S. Perspective on an 'Emerging' Indochina." In *Postwar Indochina: Old Enemies and New Allies,* edited by Joseph J. Zasloff. Washington, D.C.: Center for the Study of Foreign Affairs, Foreign Service Institute of the U.S. Department of State, 1988.

Bryan, C. D. B. "Barely Suppressed Screams: Getting a Bead on Vietnam Literature." *Harpers,* June 1984, 67–72.

Buckley, Christopher. "The Wall." *Esquire,* September 1985, 65–68.

Burkett, B. G., and Glenna Whitley. *Stolen Valor: How the Vietnam Generation was Robbed of Its Heroes and Its History.* Dallas: Verity Press, 1998.

Bush, George, and Brent Scowcroft. *A World Transformed.* New York: Knopf, 1998.

Butler, Robert Olen. *Sun Dogs.* New York: Holt, 1994.

———. *A Good Scent from a Strange Mountain.* New York: Holt, 1992.

———. *The Deuce.* New York: Simon and Schuster, 1989.

———. *On Distant Ground.* New York: Knopf, 1985.

———. *The Alleys of Eden.* New York: Holt, 1981.

Calloway, Catherine. "American Literature and Film of the Vietnam War: Classroom Strategies and Critical Sources." In *The Vietnam War: Teaching Approaches and Resources,* edited by Marc Jason Gilbert. New York: Greenwood Press, 1991.

Capps, Walter. "On Teaching Today's Students about the Vietnam War." *Federation Review* 8 (May–June 1985): 10–13.

———. *The Unfinished War: Vietnam and the American Conscience.* Boston: Beacon Press, 1982.

Caputo, Philip. *A Rumor of War.* New York: Ballantine, 1977.

Casciato, Arthur D. "Teaching the Literature of the Vietnam War." *Virginia Quarterly Review* 9 (1987): 125–47.

Chace, James. *Solvency, the Price of Survival: An Essay on American Foreign Policy.* New York: Random House, 1982.

Chanda, Nayan. "Vietnam and Cambodia: Domination and Security." In *Postwar Indochina: Old Enemies and New Allies*, edited by Joseph J. Zasloff. Washington, D.C.: Center for the Study of Foreign Affairs, Foreign Service Institute of the U.S. Department of State, 1988.

———. *Brother Enemy: The War after the War.* San Diego: Harcourt, Brace, Jovanovich, 1986.

"The Chickenhawks." In *Liberals like Christ.* Available from http://liberalslike christ.org/about/chickenhawks.html.

Childress, Richard T., and Stephen J. Solarz. "Vietnam: The Road to Normalization." In *Reversing Relations with Former Adversaries: U.S. Foreign Policy after the Cold War,* edited by C. Richard Nelson and Kenneth Weisbrode. Gainesville: University Press of Florida, 1998.

Clark, Mark T. "End Games: Reconsidering What it Means to Make War." In *Claremont Institute*, November 2, 2002. Available from http://www.clarement.org/writings/precents/20021119clark.html.

Cleland, Max. *Strong at the Broken Places.* Atlanta: Cherokee, 1986.

Clodfelter, Mark. *The Limits of Air Power: The American Bombing of North Vietnam.* New York: Free Press, 1989.

Colbert, Evelyn. "U.S. Policy Toward Vietnam Since the Fall of Saigon." In *Postwar Indochina: Old Enemies and New Allies,* edited by Joseph J. Zasloff. Washington, D.C.: Center for the Study of Foreign Affairs, Foreign Service Institute of the U.S. Department of State, 1988.

Connerton, Paul. *How Societies Remember.* New York: Cambridge University Press, 1989.

Conway, Martin A., ed. *Recovered Memories and False Memories.* New York: Oxford University Press, 1997.

Courtois, Christine A. *Recollections of Sexual Abuse: Treatment Principles and Guidelines.* New York: Norton, 1999.

Crawley, Leo. "The War About the War: Vietnam Films and American Myth." In *From Hanoi to Hollywood*, edited by Linda Dittmar and Gene Michaud. New Brunswick: Rutgers University Press, 1990.

Cung, Raphael. "Vietnam in the Nineties." *SAIS Review* 11 (summer–fall 1991): 179–97.

Daalder, Ivo H., and Michael E. O'Hanlon. *Winning Ugly: NATO's War to Save Kosovo.* Washington, D.C.: Brookings Institution Press, 2000.

Davidson, Philip. *Vietnam at War: The History, 1946–1975.* Novato, Calif.: Presidio Press, 1988.

Davies, Graham, and Tim Dalgleish. *Recovered Memories: Seeking Middle Ground.* New York: Wiley, 2001.

Dean, Eric T., Jr. *Shook Over Hell, Post-Traumatic Stress, Vietnam, and the Civil War.* Cambridge: Harvard University Press, 1997.

Del Vecchio, John M. *The 13th Valley.* New York: Ballantine Books, 1982.

Devine, Jeremy M. *Vietnam at 24 Frames a Second: A Critical and Thematic Analysis of Over 400 Films About the Vietnam War.* Jefferson, N.C.: McFarland Publishers, 1995.

Dittmar, Linda, and Gene Michaud. "America's Vietnam War Films: Marching Toward Denial." In *From Hanoi to Hollywood*, edited by Linda Dittmar and Gene Michaud. New Brunswick: Rutgers University Press, 1990.

Divine, Robert. "Vietnam Reconsidered." *Diplomatic History* 12 (1988): 79–93.

Doherty, Carroll J. "Administration Moves Slowly Toward Normal Relations." *Congressional Quarterly* 49, 15 (April 13, 1991): 924–29.

Dornfeld, Barry. "'Dear America': Transparency, Authority, and Interpretation in a Vietnam War Documentary." In *From Hanoi to Hollywood*, edited by Linda Dittmar and Gene Michaud. New Brunswick: Rutgers University Press, 1990.

Draper, Theodore. *A Very Thin Line: The Iran-Contra Affairs.* New York: Hill and Wang, 1991.

Drew, Elizabeth. *On the Edge: The Clinton Presidency.* New York: Simon and Schuster, 1994.

Duiker, William J. *Vietnam Since the Fall of Saigon.* Athens: Ohio University Center for Southeast Asian Studies, 1985.

Duong Thu Huong. *Novel Without a Name.* New York: Morrow, 1995.

Dunn, Joe P. "The State of the Field: How Vietnam Is Being Taught." In Texas Tech University, the Vietnam Center, 1996. Available from http://www.vietnam.ttu.edu/vietnamcenter/events/1996_Symposium/96papers/dunn-vn.htm.

———. "Texts and Auxiliary Resources." In *The Vietnam War: Teaching Approaches and Resources*, edited by Marc Jason Gilbert. New York: Greenwood Press, 1991.

Dunning, Bruce R. "Vietnamese in America: The Adaptation of the 1975–1979 Arrivals." In *Refugees as Immigrants: Cambodians, Laotians and Vietnamese in America,* edited by David W. Haines. Totowa, N.J.: Roman and Littlefield, 1989.

Dutta, M. "Vietnam: Marketization and Internationalization of Its Economy." *Journal of Asian Economics* 6 (fall 1995): 311–26.

Eckert, Edward, and William J. Searle. "Creative Literature of the Vietnam War: A Selective Bibliography." *Choice* 24 (January 1987): 725–35.

Elliott, David W. P. "The Third Indochina Conflict: Introduction." In *The Third Indochina Conflict*, edited by David W. P. Elliot. Boulder: Westview, 1982.

Fallows, James. *More Like Us: Making America Great Again.* Boston: Houghton Mifflin, 1989.

———. "What Did You Do in the Class War, Daddy?" *Washington Monthly*, October 1975, 5–19.

Fischer, Beth A. *The Reagan Reversal: Foreign Policy and the End of the Cold War.* Columbia: University of Missouri Press, 1997.

Franklin, H. Bruce. *The Vietnam War in American Stories, Songs and Poems.* Boston: Bedford Books, 1996.

———. *M.I.A.: Or Mythmaking in America.* New York: Lawrence Hill Books, 1992.

Freeman, Nick J. "International Economic Responses to Reform in Vietnam: An Overview of Obstacles and Progress." *Studies in Comparative Communism* 25, 3 (September 1992): 287–302.

Fussell, Paul. "Thank God for the Atomic Bomb." In *Hiroshima's Shadow*, edited by Kai Bird and Lawrence Lifschultz. Stony Creek, Conn.: Pamphleteer's Press, 1998.

————. *Wartime: Understanding and Behavior in the Second World War.* New York: Oxford University Press, 1989.

Gallup, George H. *The Gallup Poll: Public Opinion, 1935–1971.* New York: Random House, 1972.

Garthoff, Raymond L. *Détente and Confrontation: American-Soviet Relations from Nixon to Reagan.* Washington: Brookings Institution Press, revised edition 1994.

————. *The Great Transition: American-Soviet Relations and the End of the Cold War.* Washington: Brookings Institution, 1994.

Gettleman, Marvin E., et al., eds. *Vietnam and America: A Documentary History.* New York: Grove, 1985.

Gilbert, Marc Jason. "Broadening the Horizons of a Course on the American War in Vietnam." In *The Vietnam War: Teaching Approaches and Resources*, edited by Marc Jason Gilbert. New York: Greenwood Press, 1991.

Gimpel, James G., and James R. Edwards. *The Congressional Politics of Immigration Reform.* Needham Heights, Mass.: Allyn and Bacon, 1999.

Goldman, Peter, et al. *Quest for the Presidency, 1992.* College Station: Texas A&M Press, 1994.

Goodman, Allan E. "The Political Consequences of Normalization of U.S.-Vietnam Relations." *Contemporary Southeast Asia* 17, 4 (March 1996), 421.

Grant, Bruce. *The Boat People: An Age Investigation with Bruce Grant.* New York: Penguin, 1978.

Greene, Bob. *Duty: A Father, His Son, and the Man Who Won the War.* New York: Harper Collins Publishers, 2000.

Greene, Graham. *The Quiet America.* New York: Penguin, 1977.

Greene, John R. *The Presidency of George Bush.* Lawrence: University Press of Kansas, 2000.

Groom, Winston. *Better Times Than These: A Novel.* New York: Summit Books, 1978.

————. *Forrest Gump.* Garden City: Doubleday, 1986.

Hagopian, Patrick. Review of "Personal Legacy: The Healing of a Nation." *Journal of American History*, 82, 1 (June 1995): 158–64.

————. "The Social Memory of the Vietnam War." Ph.D. diss., Johns Hopkins University, 1994.

Haines, Harry W. "The Pride Is Back: *Rambo, Magnum PI*, and the Return Trip to Vietnam." In *Cultural Legacies of Vietnam: Uses of the Past in the Present*, edited by Richard Morris and Peter Ehrenhaus. Norwood, N.J.: Ablex Publishing Corp., 1990.

————. "'They Were Called and They Went': The Political Rehabilitation of the Vietnam Veteran." In *From Hanoi to Hollywood*, edited by Linda Dittmar and Gene Michaud. New Brunswick: Rutgers University Press, 1990.

Halberstam, David. *War in a Time of Peace: Bush, Clinton, and the Generals.* New York: Touchstone Books, 2002.

Halbwachs, Maurice. *On Collective Memory.* Translated by Lewis Coser. Chicago: University of Chicago Press, 1992.

————. *The Collective Memory.* Translated by Francis Ditter, Jr., and Vida Yazda Ditter. New York: Harper and Row, 1980.

Haley, Sarah. "When the Patient Reports Atrocities: Specific Treatment Consider-
    ations of the Vietnam Veteran." *Archives of General Psychiatry* 30 (February
    1974): 192–93.
Hallin, Daniel. Review of "Vietnam on Television." Available from http://
    www.museum.tv/archives/etv/V/htmlV/vietnamonte/vietnamonte.htm.
Hasford, Gustav. *The Short-Timers.* New York: Bantam Books, 1979.
Hass, Kristin Ann. *Carried to the Wall: American Memory and the Vietnam Veterans
    Memorial.* Berkeley: University of California Press, 1998.
Hein, Jeremy. *From Vietnam, Laos and Cambodia: A Refugee Experience in the United
    States.* New York: Twayne, 1995.
————. *States and International Migration: The Incorporation of Indochinese Refu-
    gees in the United States and France.* Boulder, Colo.: Westview Press, 1993.
Heinemann, Larry. *Paco's Story.* New York: Penguin, 1989.
————. *Close Quarters.* New York: Farrar, Straus, and Giroux, 1977.
Hellmann, John. *American Myth and the Legacy of Vietnam.* New York: Columbia
    University Press, 1986.
Herring, George C. "The Impact of the Vietnam War on the U.S. Military." In *After
    Vietnam: Legacies of a Lost War,* edited by Charles E. Neu. Baltimore: Johns
    Hopkins University Press, 2000.
Hersh, Seymour M. "The Gray Zone." *The New Yorker,* May 24, 2004. Available
    from http//:www.TheNewYorker.com.
————. "Torture At Abu Ghraib." *The New Yorker,* May 10, 2004. Available from
    http//:www.TheNewYorker.com.
Hess, Gary R. "Historians and the Vietnam War." *Diplomatic History* 18 (1994): 239–
    64.
Holbrooke, Richard. *To End a War.* New York: Random House, 1998.
Holzer, Henry Mark, and Erika Holzer. *"Aid and Comfort": Jane Fonda in North
    Vietnam.* Jefferson, N.C.: McFarland Publishers, 2002.
Hurst, Steven. *The Carter Administration and Vietnam.* New York: St. Martin's Press,
    1996.
Hynes, Samuel. *The Soldiers' Tale: Bearing Witness to Modern War.* New York: Pen-
    guin, 1997.
Isaacs, Arnold R. *Vietnam Shadows: The War, Its Ghosts and Its Legacy.* Baltimore:
    Johns Hopkins University Press, 1997.
Isaacson, Walter. *Kissinger: A Biography.* New York: Simon and Schuster, 1992.
Jeffords, Susan. "Tattoos, Scars, Diaries, and Writing Masculinity." In *The Vietnam
    War and American Culture,* edited by John Carlos Rowe and Rick Berg. New
    York: Columbia University Press, 1991.
————. "Reproducing Fathers: Gender and the Vietnam War in American Culture."
    In *Cultural Legacies of Vietnam*, edited by Richard Morris and Peter Ehrenhaus.
    Norwood, N.J.: Ablex Publishing Corp., 1990.
————. *The Remasculinization of America: Gender and the Vietnam War.* Bloom-
    ington: Indiana University Press, 1989.
Jespersen, T. Christopher. "The Bitter End and the Lost Chance in Vietnam: Con-
    gress, the Ford Administration and the Battle Over Vietnam, 1975–76." *Diplo-
    matic History,* 24, 2 (spring 2000): 265–93.
Kakutani, Michiko. "Novelists and Vietnam: The War Goes On." *New York Times
    Book Review*, April 15, 1984, 1, 39–41.

Kammen, Michael G. *Mystic Chords of Memory: The Transformation of Tradition in American Life.* New York: Knopf, 1991.

Karnow, Stanley. *Vietnam: A History.* New York: Penguin Books, 1991.

Katakis, Michael. *The Vietnam Veterans Memorial.* New York: Crown, 1988.

Kerrey, Robert. *When I Was a Young Man: A Memoir.* New York: Harcourt Inc., 2002.

Kissinger, Henry. *Ending the Vietnam War: A History of America's Involvement in and Extrication from the Vietnam War.* New York: Simon and Schuster, 2003.

Kitfield, James. *Prodigal Soldiers: How the Generation of Officers Born of Vietnam Revolutionized the American Style of War.* New York: Simon and Schuster, 1995.

Kolko, Gabriel. *Anatomy of a War: Vietnam, the United States and the Modern Historical Experience.* New York: The New Press, revised edition 1994.

Kumssa, Asfaw. "Economic Reform Policies and Viet Nam's Transition to a Market-Oriented Economy." Regional Development Dialogue, 18, 1 (spring 1997): 72–85.

Laird, Melvin R. "Iraq: Learning the Lessons of Vietnam." *Foreign Affairs* 84, 6 (November/December 2005): 22–43.

Lam, Andrew. "Vietnamese Diaspora and California." In *What's Going On: California and the Vietnam Era*, edited by Marcia Eymann and Charles Wollenberg. Berkeley: Oakland Museum of California and University of California Press, 2004.

———. "Quiet American Irony." Pacific News Service, February 20, 2003.

Lembcke, Jerry. *CNN's Tailwind Tale: Inside Vietnam's Last Great Myth.* Lanham, Md: Rowman and Littlefield, 2003.

———. *The Spitting Image: Myth, Memory and the Legacy of Vietnam.* New York: New York University Press, 1998.

Lifton, Robert J. *Home from the War: Vietnam Veterans: Neither Victims nor Executioners.* New York: Simon and Schuster, 1973.

Lin, Ying. "Design Competition: Winning Designer's Statement." Washington, D.C.: Vietnam Veterans Memorial Fund, 1982.

Lind, Michael. *Vietnam: The Necessary War.* New York: The Free Press, 1999.

Lomparis, Timothy. *From People's War to People's Rule: Insurgency, Intervention, and the Lessons of Vietnam.* Chapel Hill: University of North Carolina Press, 1996.

Lopes, Sal, ed. *The Wall: Images and Offerings from the Vietnam Veterans Memorial.* New York: Collins, 1987.

Lowenthal, David. *The Past Is Another Country.* New York: Cambridge University Press, 1985.

Lynn, Steven J., and Kevin M. McConkey, eds. *Truth in Memory.* New York: Guilford Press, 1998.

MacDougall, John James. "A Decision-making Approach to Understand American Policy Makers." In *The Vietnam War: Teaching Approaches and Resources,* edited by Marc Jason Gilbert. New York: Greenwood Press, 1991.

Mailer, Norman. *Why Are We in Vietnam: A Novel.* New York: Putman, 1967.

Mann, James. *Rise of the Vulcans: The History of Bush's War Cabinet.* New York: Viking, 2004.

Maraniss, David. *First in His Class: A Biography of Bill Clinton.* New York: Simon and Schuster, 1995.

Mather, Paul D. *M.I.A.: Accounting for the Missing in Southeast Asia.* Washington, D.C.: National Defense University Press, 1994.

Mayo, James M. *War Memorials as Political Landscape: The American Experience and Beyond.* New York: Praeger, 1988.

McDonald, Neil. "Vietnamese Shadows, American Reflections." *Quadrant* 47, 3 (March 2003): 66–69.

McMahon, Robert J. *The Limits of Empire: The United States and Southeast Asia Since World War II.* New York: Columbia University Press, 1999.

———. "Rationalizing Defeat: The Vietnam War in American Presidential Discourse, 1975–1995." *Rhetoric and Public Affairs*, 2, 4 (winter 1999): 529–49.

———. "SHAFR Presidential Address: Contested Memory: The Vietnam War and American Society, 1975–2001." *Diplomatic History*, 26, 2 (spring 2002): 159–84.

Melling, Philip. *Vietnam in American Literature.* Boston: Twayne Publishers, 1990.

Miller, Daniel. "Primetime Television's Tour of Duty." In *Inventing Vietnam: The War in Film and Television,* edited by Michael A. Anderegg. Philadelphia: Temple University Press, 1991.

Mills, Nicolaus. *Their Last Battle: The Fight for the National World War II Memorial.* New York: Basic Books, 2004.

Molaskey, Michael S. *The American Occupation of Japan and Okinawa: Literature and Memory.* New York: Routledge, 1999.

Mueller, John. "The Iraq Syndrome," *Foreign Affairs* 84, 6 (November/December 2005): 44–54.

Myers, Thomas. *Walking Point: American Narratives of Vietnam.* New York: Oxford University Press, 1988.

Neal, Arthur G. *National Trauma and Collective Memory: Major Events in the American Century.* Armonk, N.Y.: M. E. Sharpe, 1998.

Neu, Charles, ed. *After Vietnam: Legacies of a Lost War.* Baltimore: Johns Hopkins University Press, 2000.

Newman, John, ed. *Vietnam War Literature: An Annotated Bibliography of Imaginative Works about Americans Fighting in Vietnam.* 3d ed. Lanham, Md.: Scarecrow Press, 1996.

Nicosia, Gerald. *Home to War: A History of the Vietnam Veterans' Movement.* New York: Crown Publishers, 2001.

Ninh, Bao. *The Sorrow of War: A Novel of North Vietnam.* New York: Riverhead Books, 1996.

Nixon, Richard M. *No More Vietnams.* New York: Arden House, 1985.

Nolan, Keith William. *Battle for Hue: Tet, 1968.* Novato, Calif.: Presidio Press, 1983.

Oberdorfer, Don. *The Turn: From the Cold War to a New Era: The United States and the Soviet Union, 1983–1990.* New York: Poseidon Books, 1991.

O'Brien, Tim. *In the Lake of the Woods.* Boston: Houghton Mifflin, 1994.

———. *The Things They Carried: A Work of Fiction.* Boston: Houghton Mifflin, 1990.

———. *The Nuclear Age.* New York: Knopf, 1985.

———. *Going After Cacciato.* New York: Delacorte Press, 1978.

———. *If I Die in a Combat Zone, Box Me Up and Ship Me Home.* New York: Delacorte Press, 1973.

Olson, James, and Randy Roberts. *Where the Domino Fell: America and Vietnam, 1945–1995.* St James, N.Y.: Brandywine Press, 1996.

Palmer, Laura. *Shrapnel in the Heart: Letters and Remembrances from the Vietnam Veterans Memorial.* New York: Random House, 1987.

Paris, Roland. "Kosovo and the Metaphor War." *Political Science Quarterly* 117, 3 (fall 2002): 423–50.

Patterson, James T. *Restless Giant: The United States from Watergate to* Bush v. Gore. New York: Oxford University Press, 2005.

Pedzek, Kathy S., and William Banks, eds. *The Recovered Memory/False Memory Debate.* San Diego, Calif.: Academy Press, 1996.

Piehler, G. Kurt. *Remembering War the American Way.* Washington, D.C.: Smithsonian Institution Press, 1995.

Pike, Douglas. *Vietnam and the Soviet Union: Anatomy of an Alliance.* Boulder, Colo.: Westview Press, 1987.

Podhoretz, Norman. *Why We Were in Vietnam.* New York: Simon and Schuster, 1983.

Pollack, Daniel L., et al. "Estimating the Number of Suicides among Vietnam Veterans." *American Journal of Psychiatry* 147, 6 (June 1990): 772–76.

Pope, Kenneth S., and Laura S. Brown, eds. *Recovered Memories of Abuse: Assessment, Therapies, Forensics.* Washington, D.C.: American Psychological Association, 1996.

Potts, Steve. "Using Primary Sources." In *The Vietnam War: Teaching Approaches and Resources,* edited by Marc Jason Gilbert. New York: Greenwood Press, 1991.

Powell, Colin L., and Joseph E. Persico. *My American Journey.* New York: Random House, 1995.

Power, Samantha. *"A Problem from Hell": America in the Age of Genocide.* New York: Basic Books, 2002.

Pratt, John Clark, comp. *Vietnam Voices: Perspectives on the War.* New York: Viking, 1984.

Puller, Lewis B., Jr. *Fortunate Son: The Autobiography of Lewis B. Puller, Jr.* New York: Grove Weidenfeld, 1991.

Review of *The Quiet American.* In MrCranky.com. Available from http://www.mrcranky.com/movies/quietamerican/html.

Reyes, David. "Vietnam War Memorial Stirs Memories," *Los Angeles Times,* April 28, 2003. Available from http://vietpage.com/archive_news/politics/2003/Apr/28/0013.html.

Richburg, Keith. "Back to Vietnam." *Foreign Affairs* 70 (fall 1991): 111–31.

Riviere, Susan L. *Memory of Childhood Trauma: A Clinician's Guide to the Literature.* New York: Guilford Press, 1996.

Roark, James L., et al. *The American Promise: A History of the United States.* Boston: Bedford Books, 1998.

Roberts, Randy, and James Olson. *My Lai: A Brief History With Documents.* New York: Bedford Books, 1998.

———. *John Wayne: American.* New York: The Free Press, 1995.

Robinson, W. Courtland. *Terms of Refuge: The Indochinese Exodus and the International Response.* New York: Zed Books, 1998.

Rogers, William. *"Recovered Memory" and Other Assaults Upon the Mysteries of Consciousness: Hypnosis, Psychotherapy, Fraud and the Mass Media.* Jefferson, N.C.: McFarland Publishers, 1995.

Rosenberg, Emily S. *A Date Which Will Live: Pearl Harbor in American Memory.* Durham: Duke University Press, 2003.

Rowe, John Carlos. "Eyewitness: Documentary Styles in the American Representations of Vietnam." In *The Vietnam War and American Culture,* edited John Carlos Rowe and Rick Berg. New York: Columbia University Press, 1991.

Rutledge, Paul James. *The Vietnamese Experience in America*. Bloomington: Indiana University Press, 1992.

Saenz, Michael. Review of *China Beach*. 1995. Available from http://www.museum.tv/archives/etv/C/htmlC/chinabeach/chinabeach.htm.

Sanders, Jerry W. *Peddlers of Crisis: The Committee on the Present Danger and the Politics of Containment*. Boston: South End Press, 1983.

Sato, Tadao. "Japanese Films about the Pacific War." In *America's Wars in Asia: A Cultural Approach to History and Memory,* edited by Philip West, Steven I. Levine, and Jackie Hiltz. Armonk, N.Y.: M. E. Sharpe, 1998.

Schlene, Vicki J. "Teaching About the Vietnam War." ERIC Clearinghouse for Social Studies, September 1996. Available from http://www.ericdigests.org/1998-1/vietnam.htm.

Schuck, Peter H. *Agent Orange on Trial: Mass Toxic Disasters in the Courts*. Cambridge: Harvard University Press, 1986.

Schulzinger, Robert D. *A Time for War: The United States and Vietnam, 1941–1975*. New York: Oxford University Press, 1997.

———. *Henry Kissinger: Doctor of Diplomacy*. New York: Columbia University Press, 1989.

Scott, Wilbur J. *The Politics of Readjustment: Vietnam Veterans Since the War.* New York: Aldine De Gruyter, 1996.

Scruggs, Jan C., and Joel L. Swerdlow. *To Heal a Nation: The Vietnam Veterans Memorial*. New York: Harper and Row, 1985.

Selig, Michael. "Boys Will Be Men: Oedipal Drama in *Coming Home*." In *From Hanoi to Hollywood*, edited by Linda Dittmar and Gene Michaud. New Brunswick: Rutgers University Press, 1990.

Severo, Richard, and Lewis Milford. *The Wages of War: When American Soldiers Come Home—From Valley Forge to Vietnam*. New York: Simon and Schuster, 1989.

Sharp, Ulysses S. Grant. *Strategy for Defeat*. San Rafael, Calif.: Presidio Press, 1978.

Sharpe, Kenneth E. "The Post-Vietnam Formula Under Siege: The Imperial Presidency and Central America." *Political Science Quarterly*, 102, 4 (1987): 549–69.

Shatan, Chaim. "The Grief of Soldiers in Mourning: Vietnam Veterans Self-Help Movement." *American Journal of Orthopsychiatry* 45 (1973): 648.

Sherwin, Martin. "Hiroshima and Modern Memory." *Nation* 10, 1 (October 1981): 349–53.

Shultz, George P. *Turmoil and Triumph: My Years as Secretary of State*. New York: Scribner's, 1993.

Solomon, Richard H. *Exiting Indochina: U.S. Leadership of the Cambodia Settlement and Normalization with Vietnam*. Washington, D.C.: United States Institute of Peace Press, 2000.

St. Cartmail, Robert Keith. *Exodus Indochina*. Exeter, N.H.: Heineman, 1983.

Starr, Paul. *The Discarded Army: Veterans after Vietnam, The Nader Report on Vietnam Veterans and the Veterans Administration*. New York: Charterhouse, 1973.

Stewart, Margaret E. "Vietnam War Novels in the Classroom." *Teaching History: A Journal of Methods* 6 (fall 1981): 60–66.

Stone, Robert. *A Flag for Sunrise: A Novel*. New York: Knopf, 1981.

———. *Dog Soldiers: A Novel*. Boston: Houghton Mifflin, 1974.

Strait, Jerry L., and Sandra S. Strait. *Vietnam War Memorials: An Illustrated Reference Guide to Veterans Tributes Throughout the United States.* Jefferson, N.C.: McFarland Publishers, 1988.

Sturken, Marita. *Tangled Memories: The Vietnam War, the AIDS Epidemic, and the Politics of Remembering.* Berkeley: University of California Press, 1997.

Summers, Harry G., Jr. *On Strategy: A Critical Analysis of the Vietnam War.* Navato, Calif.: Presidio Press, 1982.

Tal, Kali. "When History Talks Back: The Voice of the Veteran." In *The Vietnam War: Teaching Approaches and Resources,* edited by Marc Jason Gilbert. New York: Greenwood Press, 1991.

Taylor, Clyde. "The Colonialist Subtext in Platoon." In *From Hanoi to Hollywood,* edited by Linda Dittmar and Gene Michaud. New Brunswick: Rutgers University Press, 1990.

"Teacher Guidelines for linking Students to the Vietnam Era." In Wake County Public School System. Available from www.wcpss.net/community_in_the_classroom/vietnam.

Thrupkaew, Noy. "Paved with Good Intentions." *The American Prospect,* April 2003, 45–47.

Turan, Kenneth. "An Elegant Story of Corruptibility." *Los Angles Times,* November 22, 2002.

Turley, William. *The Second Indochina War: A Short Political and Military History, 1954–1975.* Boulder, Colo.: Westview Press, 1986.

Turner, Fred. *Echoes of Combat: The Vietnam War in American Memory.* New York: Anchor Books, Doubleday, 1998.

Vertainian, Carolyn Reed. "Women Next Door: China Beach." In *Inventing Vietnam: The War in Film and Television,* edited by Michael A. Anderegg. Philadelphia: Temple University Press, 1991.

"Vietnamese Activists Push for Old Flag." Available from http://www.cnn.com/2003/US/West/05/23/vietnamese.flags.ap/Vietnam War Memorial in Westminster.

"The Volokh Conspiracy," April 7, 2004. Available from http//lists/ucla.edu/cgi-bin/mailman/info/volokh.

Wallen, V. "Background Characteristics, Attitudes and Self-Concepts of Air Force Psychiatric Casualties from Southeast Asia." In *The Psychology and Physiology of Stress,* edited by Peter Bourne. New York: Academic Press, 1969.

Webb, James. *A Country Such as This: A Novel.* Garden City: Doubleday, 1983.

———. *Fields of Fire: A Novel.* Englewood Cliffs: Prentice Hall, 1978.

Wells-Dang, Andrew. "Establishing Normal Trade Relations with Vietnam and Laos." *Foreign Policy in Focus* 6, 30 (July 30, 2001): 1–2.

Weinstein, Franklin B. "U.S.–Vietnam Relations and the Security of Southeast Asia." *Foreign Affairs* 56 (July 1978): 842–56.

Wheeler, John. *Touched with Fire: The Future of the Vietnam Generation.* New York: Avon Books, 1984.

Whitmore, John K., Marcella Trautmann, and Nathan Caplan. "The Social Cultural Bases for the Economic and Educational Success of Southeast Asian Refugees (1978–1982 Arrivals)." In *Refugees as Immigrants: Cambodians, Laotians and Vietnamese in America,* edited by David W. Haines. Totowa, N.J.: Rowman and Littlefield, 1989.

Wilcox, Fred. *Waiting for an Army to Die: The Tragedy of Agent Orange.* New York: Random House, 1983.

Williams, William A., et al., eds. *America in Vietnam: A Documentary History.* New York: Anchor/Doubleday, 1985.

Willson, David A. "Novels." In *Vietnam War Literature: An Annotated Bibliography of Imaginative Works about Americans Fighting in Vietnam,* 3d ed., edited by John A. Newman. Lanham, Md: Scarecrow Press, 1996.

Winter, Jay. "The Generation of Memory: Reflections on the 'Memory Boom.'" In "Contemporary German Historical Studies," *Bulletin of the German Historical Institute,*27, 3 (fall 2000): 69–92.

Woodward, Bob. *The Commanders.* New York: Simon and Schuster, 1991.

"The World Today." In Australian Broadcasting Corporation, Defence Experts Debate Iraq-Vietnam Comparison, April 8, 2004. Available from http://www.abc.net.au/worldtoday/content/2004/s1084174.htm.

Young, Allan. *The Harmony of Illusions: Inventing Post-Traumatic Stress Disorder.* Princeton: Princeton University Press, 1995.

Young, Marilyn B. *The Vietnam Wars, 1945–1950.* New York: Harper Collins, 1991.

Index